RIEMENSCHNEIDER · WEST- UND OSTAFRIKA

GRUNDLAGEN ZUR
LITERATUR IN ENGLISCHER SPRACHE

Herausgeber:
Werner Arens
Dieter Riemenschneider
Gerhard Stilz

Band 1: Kanada
Band 2: Australien
Band 3: Neuseeland
Band 4: Indien
Band 5: West- und Ostafrika
Band 6: Südafrika
Band 7: Westindien

WILHELM FINK VERLAG MÜNCHEN

DIETER RIEMENSCHNEIDER

GRUNDLAGEN ZUR
LITERATUR IN ENGLISCHER SPRACHE

WEST- UND OSTAFRIKA

1983

WILHELM FINK VERLAG MÜNCHEN

ISBN 3-7705-2057-2

© 1983 Wilhelm Fink Verlag, München
Gesamtherstellung: Ferdinand Schöningh, Paderborn

VORWORT DER HERAUSGEBER

Die weltweite Verbreitung der englischen Sprache und Kultur schafft Einheit und Vielfalt in ungelöstem Konflikt. In der Literatur der sogenannten "Commonwealth-Länder" wird daher eine Fülle von politischen, ökonomischen und sozialen Problemen ausgetragen, deren gemeinsamer Nenner offenbar im Zwiespalt zwischen regionaler Eigenständigkeit und zentraler Rückbindung zu suchen ist.

Ziel der Reihe „Grundlagen zur Literatur in englischer Sprache" ist es, sowohl die integrativen Faktoren als auch die differenzierte Entwicklung in den englischsprachigen Literaturen der Welt anschaulich zu machen. Das Vorhaben versteht sich als Orientierungshilfe; es soll Zusammenhänge aufzeigen, Vergleiche ermöglichen und Detailstudien erleichtern. Angesprochen sind deshalb nicht nur die Fachleute und Studenten einer längst über die Grenzen Großbritanniens hinausblickenden Anglistik, sondern auch alle diejenigen, die sich im Rahmen einer fachübergreifenden Kulturwissenschaft mit der besonderen politischen, gesellschaftlichen und literarischen Situation in der englischsprachigen Welt beschäftigen.

Die kulturelle Sonderentwicklung der U.S.A. ist, aus guten Gründen und in einer namhaften akademischen Tradition, ausführlich dargestellt und umfangreich dokumentiert worden. Dies gilt nicht in gleichem Maße für andere Regionen der englischsprachigen Welt, die aufgrund verwandter Voraussetzungen und Entwicklungen als kulturelle Einheiten angesehen werden können: für (1) Kanada, (2) Australien und (3) Neuseeland als verschiedenen Gebieten intensiver britischer Besiedlung, für (4) Indien (einschließlich der heutigen Staaten Pakistan, Bangla Desh und Sri Lanka) als britisch überformter Hochkultur, für die kulturell unterschiedlich geprägten anglophonen Regionen des (5) westlichen und östlichen sowie des (6) südlichen Afrika, und schließlich für (7) Westindien, dessen komplexe kulturelle Position zwischen Afrika, Amerika und Europa besonderer Betrachtung bedarf.

In den sieben *Einzelbänden* dieser Reihe widmen sich daher die Verfasser auf der Basis jahrelanger einschlägiger Forschungsarbeit je einer der genannten Regionen, wobei der spezifische Befund transparent bleiben soll für die Entdeckung überregionaler Gemeinsamkeiten und Unterschiede.

Vergleiche werden vor allem durch ein einheitliches *Aufbaumuster* gewährleistet. Jeder Band soll als Einführung, Dokumentation und Nachschlagewerk dienen. In der *Einleitung* wird die geschichtliche und gesellschaftliche Situation der englischen Literatur in der betreffenden Region umrissen und eine Perspektive für die nachfolgende *Textsammlung* eröffnet. In zwei Teilen soll die Auswahl kompakter, informativer, sowohl programmatischer als auch kritischer Texte grundlegende regionale Probleme der englischen Literatur in Geschichte und Gegenwart sichtbar machen: Im *geschichtlichen Rückblick* gilt es zunächst, die Probleme der Identität und Abgrenzung einer regionalen Literatur, die Entwicklung der kolonialen Sprach- und Bildungspolitik sowie die Rolle der englischen Literatur bei der nationalen Selbstfindung zu dokumentieren. Sodann wird die *heutige Situation* der regionalen englischen Literatur umrissen. Dabei gilt es, die sprachliche und die literatursoziologische Problematik sowie das Spannungsverhältnis zwischen Regionalität und internationalem Anspruch herauszustellen. *Kommentare* und *Anmerkungen* zu den ausgewählten Texten vermitteln wichtige Zusammenhänge und ergänzende Informationen. Im *Nachschlageteil* verweist ein Literaturverzeichnis auf ausgewählte Autoren und ihre Werke. Eine *Bibliographie* grundlegender Sekundärliteratur soll ebenso wie eine Übersicht über einschlägige Forschungs- und Hilfseinrichtungen weiterführende Untersuchungen erleichtern. Ein detailliertes *Sach-* und *Namenregister* erschließt die Einführung, die Literaturverzeichnisse und die Textsammlung.

Werner Arens (Regensburg)
Dieter Riemenschneider (Frankfurt)
Gerhard Stilz (Tübingen)

INHALTSVERZEICHNIS

EINLEITUNG 7

TEXTE UND DOKUMENTE 33

A. *Englische Sprache und Literatur im geschichtlichen Rückblick* 33

1. Probleme der Entstehung und Abgrenzung: „afrikanische", „neoafrikanische" und „afro-europäische" Literatur 33
   1. Davidson Nicol, *The Soft Pink Palms: On British West African Writers* (1956) 33
   2. Wilfred Howell Whiteley, *The Concept of an African Prose Literature* (1962) 34
   3. Cyprian Ekwensi, *African Literature* (1964) 38
   4. T. R. M. Creighton, *An Attempt to Define African Literature* (1965) 38
   5. Janheinz Jahn, *The Literatures of Africa* (1968) 43
   6. E. N. Obiechina, *Transition from Oral to Literary Tradition* (1967) 46
   7. David Rubadiri, *The Development of Writing in East Africa* (1971) 49
   8. Lalage Bown, *The Development of African Prose-Writing in English: A Perspective* (1971) 53
   9. E. N. Obiechina, *Literature for the Masses* (1971) 56
   10. Bernth Lindfors, *Popular Literature for an African Elite* (1974) . . 59
   11. F. Lumwamu, *Black Civilization and Literature* (1977) 63

2. Ziele und Wege der kolonialen Sprach- und Bildungspolitik 68
   12. Hannah Kilham, *The Claims of West Africa to Christian Instruction through the Native Languages* (1830) 68
   13. Education Committee of the Privy Council, *Brief Practical Suggestions on the Mode of Organizing and Conducting Day Schools of Industry, Model Farm Schools, and Normal Schools, as Part of Education for the Coloured Races of the British Colonies* (1847) . . 71
   14. James Africanus B. Horton, *West African Countries and Peoples* (1868) 74
   15. Edward Wilmot Blyden, *The Aims and Methods of a Liberal Education for Africans* (1881) 76
   16. J. R. Orr, *Education of Natives* (1912) 80
   17. *C. M. S. and Education in Africa* (1922) 82
   18. Phelps-Stokes Commission, *Educational Objectives and Adaptations* (1925) 84
   19. Ben N. Azikiwe, *How Shall We Educate the African?* (1934) . . . 89
   20. Kwame Nkrumah, *The Intellectual Vanguard* (1963) 92

	21.	Pierre van den Berghe, *European Languages and Black Mandarins* (1968)	96
	22.	A. Babs Fafunwa, *The Curriculum, National Needs and the Problem of Adaptation* (1971)	103
3.	Afrikanische Literaturen und nationale Unabhängigkeit		107
	23.	Joseph E. Casely Hayford, *Presidential Addresses to the National Congress of British West Africa* (1923/1925)	107
	24.	*Resolution on Literature* (1959)	109
	25.	Eldred D. Jones, *Nationalism and the Writer* (1965)	114
	26.	Chinua Achebe, *The African Writer and the Biafran Cause* (1968)	118
	27.	E. N. Obiechina, *Cultural Nationalism in Modern African Literature* (1968)	120
	28.	David Rubadiri, *The Theme of National Identity in East African Writing* (1968)	125

B. *Englische Sprache und Literatur heute* 130

4. Die Landessprachen und das Englische 130
    29. Obiajunwa Wali, *The Dead End of African Literature?* (1963) . . 130
    30. Ezekiel Mphahlele, *Are We Going to Fold Our Arms and Wait for that Kingdom to Come?* (1963) 134
    31. Gabriel Okara, *African Speech... English Words* (1963) 136
    32. Chinua Achebe, *English and the African Writer* (1964) 138
    33. J. O. Ekpenyong, *The Use of English in Nigeria* (1965) 142
    34. John Pepper Clark, *The Legacy of Caliban* (1970) 145
    35. Solomon Adebaye Q. Babalola, *The Role of Nigerian Languages and Literatures in Fostering National Cultural Identity* (1975) . . 148
    36. Ngugi wa Thiong'o, *Afro-European Literature and African Literature* (1980) 151

5. Autoren, Leser und die afrikanische Literaturszene 154
    37. Chinua Achebe, *The Role of the Writer in a New Nation* (1964) . 154
    38. James Ngugi, Henry Owuor-Anyumba, Taban Lo Liyong, *On the Abolition of the English Department* (1968) 157
    39. Ngugi wa Thiong'o, *The Writer in a Changing Society* (1969) . . 162
    40. E. S. Atieno-Odhiambo, *Historical Sense and Creative Literature* (1971) 165
    41. S. I. A. Kotei, *Some Cultural and Social Factors of Book Reading and Publishing in Africa* (1973) 169
    42. Angus Calder, *Some Practical Questions* (1974) 173
    43. Kole Omotoso, *The Indigenous Publisher and the Future of Culture in Nigeria* (1976) 177

6. Afrikanische Literatur im Spannungsverhältnis zwischen nationaler Verpflichtung und internationaler Anerkennung 181
    44. Martin Tucker, *The Headline Novels of Africa* (1962) 181

45.	Joseph Ohiomogben Okpaku, *African Critical Standards for African Literature and the Arts* (1967)	183
46.	Eldred D. Jones, *The Decolonization of African Literature* (1968)	188
47.	Ernest Emenyonu, *African Literature: What Does It Take to Be Its Critic?* (1971)	191
48.	Solomon O. Iyasere, *Cultural Formalism and the Criticism of Modern African Literature* (1976)	194
49.	Bruce King, *Thoughts on African Literature* (1976)	198
50.	Femi Ojo-Ade, *Subjectivity and Objectivity in the Criticism of Neo-African Literature* (1977)	203

ANMERKUNGEN zur Einleitung	207
zu Kapitel 1	208
zu Kapitel 2	210
zu Kapitel 3	211
zu Kapitel 4	213
zu Kapitel 5	213
zu Kapitel 6	215

BIBLIOGRAPHIE		218
1	*Hintergrund*	218
2	*Literatur*	226
3	*Einrichtungen zur Pflege und Forschung der englischen Literatur Afrikas*	247
REGISTER		250
1	Personen und Titel	250
2	Sachen	258

EINLEITUNG

Die Literatur, bzw. die Literaturen Afrikas in englischer Sprache sind bislang nur von wenigen Kritikern in umfassender Weise dargestellt worden. Ein Blick auf die vorliegenden Publikationen[1] läßt die Gründe hierfür leicht erkennen. Zum einen handelt es sich, sofern von der geschriebenen Literatur die Rede ist, um Werke, deren Entstehung fast ausschließlich auf die durch den Kolonialismus bewirkten grundlegenden ökonomischen, sozialen und kulturellen Veränderungsprozesse in Afrika zurückzuführen sind. Im Gegensatz zu anderen englischsprachigen Literaturen der Welt innerhalb des inzwischen geographisch weit gesteckten Spektrums der Commonwealth-Literatur stellt die afrikanische Literatur somit eine ihrer jüngeren Varianten dar. Die zeitliche Nähe[2] zur überwiegenden Zahl afrikanischer Romane, Kurzgeschichten, Dramen und Gedichte, Autobiographien und nicht-fiktiver Prosa erklärt also, wenigstens zum Teil, die Scheu der Literaturhistoriker, eine umfassende Geschichte afrikanischer Literatur in Angriff zu nehmen.

Zum anderen – und hierin ist ein wesentlich schwerwiegenderer Grund für die geringe Zahl an Literaturgeschichten zu sehen – stellt sich dem Literaturhistoriker eine Fülle von Abgrenzungs- und Definitionsschwierigkeiten entgegen, denn der Anspruch auf eine totale Erfassung der Literaturen Afrikas ist nicht mehr einzulösen angesichts des Nebeneinanders ideologisch unterschiedlicher oder auf unterschiedlicher historischer Entwicklungsstufe stehender politischer, ökonomischer und gesellschaftlicher Systeme, aufgrund der ethnischen, kulturellen und sprachlichen Vielfalt und Überlagerungen, der verschiedenartigen Erfahrungen afrikanischer und karibischer Länder mit Sklaverei und Kolonialismus, sowie angesichts des unterschiedlichen Abhängigkeitsgrades von den Industrienationen. Diese nicht kohärente, sondern widersprüchliche Wirklichkeit als Raum des geistig-kulturellen und literarischen Lebens, besonders im gegenwärtigen Afrika, läßt es eigentlich nicht mehr zu, literarische Verarbeitungen dieser Realität unter dem Sammelbegriff *afrikanische Literatur* zu subsumieren, es sei denn, er ist bloß geographisch gemeint. Im konkreten Falle des jeweiligen literarischen Werkes bedarf seine Verwendung reflektierter Begründung, soll er mit über seine geographische Bedeutung hinausgehendem Sinn versehen werden. Dies gilt auch dann, wenn „afrikanisch" die „eigene Art" des afrikanischen Menschen, seine rassisch-kulturanthropologisch begründete Besonderheit meint, die ebenfalls in seinen kulturellen und literarischen Produktionen gesucht und gesehen wird. Solange der wissenschaftliche Nachweis einer so gemeinten Eigenart nicht erfolgt, haftet dieser Bedeutungsverwendung von „afrikanisch" ein ideologisches Moment an, wie dies ja weitgehend die Négritude-Bewegung unter Beweis stellte.

Die Einsicht in die immer stärkere Diversität des afrikanischen Kontinents und seiner „Diaspora" scheint sich nun allerdings auch in der Literaturgeschichtsschreibung durchzusetzen, für die eine zunehmende Zahl von auf Einzelregionen oder -länder bezogenen Untersuchungen zu konstatieren ist. Ob hierin bereits eine Tendenz zum Ausdruck kommt, afrikanische Literaturen in

Zukunft nun als Regional-bzw. sogar Nationalliteraturen zu begreifen, bleibt abzuwarten. Moore scheint eine solche Entwicklung zu erwarten, wenn er auf das Beispiel der amerikanischen, bzw. australischen Literatur verweist, deren autonomer Charakter sich zu dem Zeitpunkt herstellte, "when an acceptance, a deep and intimate awareness, of his present world begins to infuse the writer's work."[3] Er scheint es nicht auszuschließen, daß dies eines Tages auch für andere englischsprachige Literaturen verzeichnet werden kann.

Die hier nur angerissene Problematik einer *afrikanischen Literaturgeschichtsschreibung* kann nicht ohne Belang für die Abgrenzung der vorzulegenden knappen Übersicht über die *englischsprachigen Literaturen West- und Ostafrikas* bleiben. Die vorangegangenen Bemerkungen schließen vielmehr eine erschöpfende und umfassende Darstellung aus. Andererseits bewirken die in den vorliegenden Literaturgeschichten gewählten Abgrenzungs- und Klassifikationskriterien – etwa geographisch-politischer, biographischer oder gattungsgeschichtlicher Art – eine häufig zu schematische, gelegentlich aber auch von außen den Gegenständen aufgesetzte methodische Verfahrensweise. Der Blick auf den traditionell engen Zusammenhang von Kunst und Gesellschaft in Afrika wird hierdurch eher verstellt als geöffnet. Dies ist dagegen vermeidbar, wenn literarische Texte in englischer Sprache als sprachlich-ästhetische Verarbeitungen gesellschaftlicher Erfahrungen afrikanischer Menschen in einen Bezugs- und Funktionszusammenhang mit den historischen Epochen seit ihrer Entstehung, also seit dem Eingriff Europas in die geschichtliche Entwicklung des Kontinents, gestellt werden: den Abschnitten der Sklaverei, des Kolonialismus, des Unabhängigkeitskampfes und der politischen Unabhängigkeit. Die Frage nach der gesellschaftlichen Funktion der Kunst bzw. Literatur beinhaltet damit zugleich auch die nach der Entwicklung emanzipatorischer Prozesse eines über Jahrhunderte von Europa abhängigen Kontinents. Anhand notwendigerweise knapp zu haltender Ausführungen zu ausgewählten, wiewohl als repräsentativ eingeschätzten Werken soll im folgenden eine Beantwortung dieser Fragen versucht werden.

Während der Beginn *schriftlicher Literaturen in Afrika* lange vor die im 15. Jahrhundert erstmalig hergestellten Kontakte von europäischen Seeleuten und Händlern mit Westafrikanern zurückreicht, datieren die frühesten *englischsprachigen Texte afrikanischer Autoren* aus der zweiten Hälfte des 18. Jahrhunderts. Fast ausnahmslos läßt sich hier von einer ersten Phase afrikanischer Exilliteratur sprechen, der im 20. Jahrhundert weitere folgen sollten, denn die Verfasser waren im jungen Alter aus Afrika entführte Sklaven. Einige verließen England nie wieder, so zum Beispiel Ignatius Sancho (1729–1780), Ottobah Cuguano (1757–ca. 1790), Olaudah Equiano (1745–1797) oder James Albert Ukawsaw Gronniosaw (1740–?); andere verbrachten den größten Teil ihres Lebens in den USA, etwa Phyllis Wheatley (1754–1784), die als erste Autorin Gedichte in der englischen Sprache verfaßte, Briton Hammon, John Marvant (1755–1791) oder Jupiter Hammon (ca. 1710–ca. 1790).

Fast allen Veröffentlichungen dieser Autoren ist ein starkes autobiographisches Moment, einigen von ihnen darüberhinaus ein deutliches Engagement für die abolitionistische Bewegung gemeinsam, das deutlich in den nach 1780 veröffentlichten Schriften zutagetritt, nachdem gesetzgeberische Maßnahmen den Bemühungen um die weltweite Abschaffung der Sklaverei starken Auftrieb gegeben hatten. 1782 erschienen posthum die *Letters of the Late Ignatius Sancho,* einem Afrikaner, der bereits in frühester Kindheit nach England gebracht worden war und hier die Möglichkeit zur weitgehenden Integration in die gebildete Gesellschaft erhielt. Doch klingt in vielen seiner Briefe das Unverständnis an über den Widerspruch zwischen der von ihm selbst geteilten christlichen Lehre der Gleichheit aller Menschen und der Praxis der Versklavung von Afrikanern durch europäische und amerikanische Christen. Eine gewisse Ambiguität Sanchos gegenüber der britischen Gesellschaft ist in seinen Briefen nicht zu übersehen, denn einerseits übt er Kritik an unchristlichen Verhaltensweisen, andererseits teilt er den Glauben an die Überlegenheit der christlichen Religion und der kulturellen Errungenschaften Europas. Diese Haltung ist charakteristisch für die ersten englischen Texte von Afrikanern, so auch für Cuguanos *Thoughts and Sentiments of the Evil and Wicked Traffic of Slavery and Commerce of the Human Species,* die 1787 in London erschienen. Cuguano geht im Anspruch schon über die *Letters* hinaus, denn er artikuliert nicht nur Empfindungen, sondern fügt einem autobiographischen Bericht über seine ersten Lebensjahre in Westafrika, dem heutigen Ghana, scharfe Kritik an der Institution der Sklaverei sowie deren Apologeten bei. Es ginge allerdings zu weit, hier schon von einem Bewußtsein zu sprechen, das unter der Identitätsproblematik leidet. Dies trifft erst, wenn auch nur in Ansätzen, für das seinerzeit populärste Werk eines Afrikaners zu, Olaudah Equianos *The Interesting Narrative of the Life of Olaudah Equiano or Gustavus Vassa, the African* (London, 1789). Der Autor, im Alter von elf Jahren von Sklavenjägern aus dem Gebiet des heutigen Ostnigeria nach Westindien verschleppt, stellt die glückliche Zeit seiner Kindheit den erniedrigenden Erfahrungen als Sklave, aber auch den von ihm voll Selbstwertgefühl und Stolz vorgetragenen Ausführungen über sein Leben als freier Mann in England gegenüber. Harte Arbeit erlaubte es ihm, sich 1766 freizukaufen, eine Engländerin zu heiraten und sich in England niederzulassen. Beeindruckend sind die Schilderungen des Lebens in Afrika und der ersten schmerzlichen Begegnungen und Erfahrungen mit einer für ihn unverständlichen Welt. Deutlich sieht er die eigene afrikanische als friedlichere und glücklichere an, obwohl er sich auch als inzwischen überzeugter Christ nicht mit afrikanisch-religiösen Vorstellungen identifizieren möchte. Als christlicher Humanist, der gelegentlich pathetisches Predigen nicht vermeidet, setzt sich Equiano bis zum Lebensende in Schriften, Reden und Taten für die Abschaffung der Sklaverei sowie die Gründung der Siedlung Sierra Leone als Heimat befreiter Sklaven ein.

Alle drei Autoren stehen einer humanistisch-aufklärerischen europäischen Tradition näher als ihrem oft kaum noch erinnerbaren afrikanischen Erbe; doch die Konsequenz ihres Denkens läßt sie radikale Forderungen nach deren Umsetzung in die Wirklichkeit aufstellen, weil sie als Afrikaner die rassische

Diskriminierung und Versklavung als konkrete Erfahrung erlitten hatten. Sancho, Cuguano und Equiano begründen eine literarische Tradition, die bis in Werke der Gegenwart hinein aufzuspüren ist.

So wie die Prosaformen des Briefes, des politischen Traktats und der Autobiographie afrikanischer Autoren Ende des 18. Jahrhunderts auf ihrer Suche nach Selbstdarstellung entgegenkamen – wobei eine didaktische Intention in den aufklärerischen Schriften nicht zu übersehen ist –, bestimmten ganz ähnliche Ziele die Verwendung dieser, aber auch noch anderer, im engeren Sinne nicht-literarischer Gestaltungsweisen die weitere Entwicklung der englischsprachigen Literatur im 19. und teilweise auch noch im 20. Jahrhundert. Nun allerdings zogen nicht mehr ehemalige Sklaven in England und Amerika schriftliche Formen der Selbstdarstellung heran, die sie in den dortigen Schriftkulturen vorgefunden hatten, sondern es waren die Mitglieder einer kleinen, freien afrikanischen Elite, die fast ausschließlich den Küstenstädten Westafrikas entstammten und durch europäische Missionare, im Verlauf des 19. Jahrhunderts auch durch Studienaufenthalte an britischen Universitäten, ausgebildet worden waren. Die Bevorzugung nicht-poetischer Darstellungsformen hing wesentlich mit der „praktischen" Ausbildung dieser Menschen als Juristen, Ärzte oder Priester zusammen, sicher aber auch mit der ihnen durch missionarische Vorbilder eingeflößten Abneigung gegen die „Frivolität" der Schönen Literatur. Auch daß der Beschäftigung mit der eigenen afrikanischen Kultur, vor allem der oralen Literatur, in den Missionsschulen so gut wie kein Raum gegeben wurde, bedingte, daß im 19. Jahrhundert ausschließlich Sach- und Fachliteratur verfaßt wurde. So tritt neben die bereits erwähnten Äußerungsformen ab Mitte des Jahrhunderts die schriftlich niedergelegte Rede, der Bericht – einschließlich des Reiseberichts –, der journalistische Beitrag in Zeitungen und Zeitschriften, die geschichtliche und kulturgeschichtliche Darstellung.

Mehr als ein halbes Jahrhundert war seit den Veröffentlichungen Sanchos, Cuguanos und Equianos vergangen, doch die nun ab etwa 1850 einsetzende schriftstellerische und publizistische Tätigkeit von Westafrikanern knüpfte unmittelbar an die Vorgänger nicht nur in formaler Hinsicht sondern auch thematisch an. Als repräsentatives Beispiel soll an dieser Stelle nur von dem in Westindien geborenen Edward Wilmot Blyden (1832–1912) die Sprache sein, der über die Vereinigten Staaten 1851 nach Liberia emigrierte, das vier Jahre zuvor die Unabhängigkeit von den USA erhalten hatte. Blyden lebte vor allem in Liberia, verbrachte aber auch einige Jahre in der 1808 von der englischen Krone übernommenen Kolonie Sierra Leone, die auf die 1787 von englischen Abolitionisten und ehemaligen Sklaven gegründete Ansiedlung in Freetown zurückging.

Im Mittelpunkt von Blydens Tätigkeit als Schriftsteller, die sich über einen Zeitraum von 1856 bis 1910 erstreckte, steht zunächst die Kritik an der Mitte des 19. Jahrhunderts immer noch nicht gänzlich abgeschafften Sklaverei, wobei er sich insbesondere gegen die Vereinigten Staaten richtete. In "A Voice from Bleeding Africa on Behalf of Her Exiled Children" (Monrovia, 1856) attackiert er die Profitsucht der Sklavenhalter, weist anhand von Beispielen den Vorwurf der intellektuellen Unterlegenheit der schwarzen Rasse zurück und fordert "immediate emancipation . . . as an act of justice to the despoiled African . . . ." Während das Thema der Sklaverei Blyden mit Cuguanos und Equianos Anliegen verbindet, spiegelt sich in der Forderung nach der Möglichkeit afrikanischer Emanzipation von Europa die gänzlich andere Situation wider, in der Blyden und seine Generation sich Mitte des 19. Jahrhunderts in Afrika im Gegensatz zu den in England achtbar und frei lebenden Sancho, Cuguano, Equiano und anderen befinden. Dies veranschaulichen noch deutlicher die folgenden Veröffentlichungen, in denen er Vorstellungen von politisch freien und sich ihres kulturellen afrikanischen Erbes besinnenden Ländern entwickelt. So erwartet er eine führende politische Rolle seines Wahllandes und glaubt, im Islam Westafrikas das religiöse und kulturelle Zentrum afrikanischen Lebens entdeckt zu haben, während er in *African Life and Customs* (London, 1908) noch einmal eine zusammenfassende Darstellung des afrikanischen Gesellschaftssystems gibt, dessen positive Werte wie Gemeinbesitz, Kooperation, Familie und Erziehung dem europäischen Profit-, Eigentums-, Wettbewerbs- und Überlegenheitsdenken gegenübergestellt werden.

Von besonderem Interesse sind in diesem Zusammenhang Blydens Gedanken zur Errichtung einer afrikanischen Universität, an der nicht "Europeanized Africans" ausgebildet werden sollen, sondern neben einem Studium der klassischen Sprachen das Schwergewicht auf die Geschichte, Kultur und Sprachen Afrikas gelegt werden soll.[4] Angesichts der Mitte des 19. Jahrhunderts in Afrika existierenden Ausbildungssituation waren Blydens Vorschläge seiner Zeit um fast einhundert Jahre voraus. Doch ist es sicher seinem und dem Drängen Hortons zuzuschreiben, daß 1876 an der einzigen seinerzeit vorhandenen universitätsähnlichen Institution, am 1827 gegründeten *Fourah Bay College* in Freetown, neben Theologie geisteswissenschaftliche Fächer aufgenommen wurden. Die hier zu erwerbenden Abschlußgrade wurden ab 1876 von der Universität Durham erteilt. Den Status einer Universität jedoch erhielt das Fourah Bay College nicht und auch nicht zwei weitere einhundert Jahre später gegründete westafrikanische Institutionen, das *Achimota College* (1924) in der Nähe von Accra und das *Higher College in Yaba* (1934) bei Lagos. Ein Grund hierfür lag wohl darin, daß bis zum Ausbruch des 2. Weltkrieges Nigeria zum Beispiel nur über zwölf "secondary schools" verfügte; trotz der Empfehlungen von Kommissionen erschien der Kolonialregierung ein Ausbau des höheren Schulwesens bzw. die Einrichtung von Colleges nicht wichtig und politisch opportun. Erst nach dem Krieg, 1948, wurden vier Universitätscolleges gegründet: in Ibadan, Achimota, Makerere (Uganda) und Khartoum; 1960 erhielt dann das traditionsreiche Fourah Bay College schließlich auch Universitätsstatus.

Blydens Schriften tragen entscheidend zum intellektuellen Protest gegen den Kolonialismus bei, der im Verlaufe seines Lebens immer tiefgreifender in die Entwicklung Afrikas eingriff. Als Ausdruck eines sich zugleich um Emanzipation vom Kolonialismus bemühenden Bewußtseins kommt ihnen jedoch eine noch wichtigere Funktion zu, die sie den geistigen wie praktischen Bemühungen der auf Blyden folgenden Generationen um politische und kulturelle Befreiung und Selbständigkeit zur Seite stellt und näherrückt, als der doch recht ambivalenten Suche afrikanischer "expatriates" des 18. Jahrhunderts nach der eigenen Identität. Eine gewisse Ambivalenz kann jedoch auch ihm nicht abgesprochen werden. Vor allem in seiner Rolle als Erzieher sieht Blyden sich der Masse der Bevölkerung, insbesondere der im Inneren Afrikas lebenden Menschen gegenübergestellt, denn "the people generally are not yet prepared to understand their own interest in the great work to be done for themselves and their children..."[5] Eine solche Einschätzung von gegenwärtiger Situation und zukünftiger Aufgabe macht deutlich, daß er prinzipielle pädagogische Vorstellungen von Europa übernommen hatte. Sein Elitedenken weist auf Konflikte voraus, die nach der Erlangung der Unabhängigkeit vieler afrikanischer Staaten in den fünfziger und sechziger Jahren unseres Jahrhunderts zu einem ganz zentralen Thema der englischsprachigen kreativen Literaturen Afrikas werden sollten.

Die von Blyden und anderen westafrikanischen Intellektuellen wie Dr. James Africanus B. Horton (1835–1883), Carl Christian Reindorf (1834–1917), Samuel Johnson (1846–1901) und einer ganzen Reihe zumeist kreolischer Intellektueller etablierte englischsprachige Schriftkultur in Westafrika erlitt mit der seit Ende des 19. Jahrhunderts verfolgten repressiveren Kolonialpolitik der Engländer, die zur Diskriminierung der kreolischen Minderheit führte, einen Rückschlag, von dem sie sich nicht mehr erholte. Doch die von dieser kleinen Elite erfolgten Anstöße wurden im 20. Jahrhundert von einer neuen Generation westafrikanischer Intellektueller aufgegriffen und zunehmend mehr in ihrem Kampf um die Beteiligung an der politischen Macht und schließlich um die Unabhängigkeit neuen Zielvorstellungen zugeführt. In dieser zweiten Phase gewann das Bewußtsein für die Notwendigkeit politischer Organisation an Boden, das sich in der Gründung einer Reihe politischer Gruppierungen als Vorläufer von Parteien niederschlug. So folgte der *Gold Coast Aborigines Rights Protection Society*, 1897, die *People's Union* von Lagos, 1908, und eine der ersten überregionalen Vereinigungen, der *National Congress of British West Africa*, 1920.

In engem Zusammenhang mit dieser Entwicklung muß die publizistische und journalistische Tätigkeit führender Intellektueller gesehen werden, die sich meist, wie zum Beispiel der Ghanaer Joseph E. Casely Hayford (1866–1930), existierender oder auch neugegründeter Zeitungen als Mittel der Verbreitung ihrer Vorstellungen bedienten. Hayford trat aber nicht nur als Herausgeber der Zeitung *Gold Coast Leader* oder als Mitbegründer des *National Congress of British West Africa*[6], sondern auch als Verfasser des Werkes *Gold Coast Native Institutions* (London, 1903) und des ersten, teilweise fiktiven westafrikanischen Werkes in englischer Sprache, *Ethiopia Unbound* (London, 1911), hervor. Die literarische, emanzipatorisch-kritische Tradition setzte er in seinen Schriften ebenso fort wie John Mensah Sarbah (1864–1910) mit *The Fanti National Constitution* (London, 1906), J. B. Danquah (1895–1965) mit *Gold Coast: Akan Laws and Customs* (London, 1928) und, später, Nnamdi Azikiwe (geb. 1904) mit *Renascent Africa* (Lagos, 1937); sie greift schließlich mit Jomo Kenyattas

(1889–1978) *Facing Mount Kenya* (London, 1938) auf Ostafrika über und reicht, um nur zwei Werke zu nennen, mit Kwame Nkrumahs (1909–1972) *Towards Colonial Freedom* (London, 1947) und Chief Obafemi Awolowos (geb. 1909) *Path to Nigerian Freedom* (London, 1948) bis in die Gegenwart hinein.

Vor diesem Hintergrund der realpolitischen wie intellektuellen Entwicklung West- und – später – Ostafrikas seit den zwanziger Jahren ist die Entstehung der ersten, teilweise fiktiven Darstellungen wie des bereits erwähnten *Ethiopia Unbound* oder auch von *Africa Answers Back* (London, 1935) des aus Uganda stammenden Akiki Nyabongo (geb. 1904) zu verstehen. In ihnen stehen Ausführungen zu politischen und kulturellen Fragen und Problemen neben autobiographischen Einschüben und fiktiven Passagen. Die Verknüpfung dieser Elemente läßt ein spezifisches Genre in der Literatur Afrikas entstehen, eine Mischung dokumentarischer und fiktiver Elemente, die sich bis in die Gegenwart hinein findet und die Grundlage der fiktiven Erzählliteratur bildet, die sich, zunächst in Westafrika, seit Ende der vierziger Jahre zu entwickeln beginnt.

Die nun verfaßten erzählerischen Werke lassen sich zwar den von Europa übernommenen Formen des Romans und der Kurzgeschichte zuordnen – von einigen, wenn auch bedeutenden Ausnahmen wie Amos Tutuolas (geb. 1920) *The Palm-Wine Drinkard* (London, 1952) einmal abgesehen –, doch viele Romane besitzen deutlich dokumentarische Passagen, ein Charakteristikum, das in einer Reihe von Publikationen der ersten Phase nachweisbar ist, die bis in die sechziger Jahre hineinreicht. Diese Eigentümlichkeit des afrikanischen Romans ist aber nicht nur entstehungsgeschichtlich zu erklären, insofern die „Suche" nach neuen ästhetisch-literarischen Ausdrucksformen jene nach einer eigenen gesellschaftlichen Identität als Widerstand gegen den Kolonialismus widerspiegelt, sondern sie muß, im Zusammenhang mit der eigenen künstlerischen Tradition – und dem Bewußtsein hiervon – gesehen werden, die sich nie als eine besondere, sondern als gesellschaftlich funktionale begriffen hatte: was in der modernen europäischen Literaturkritik die Trennung von Kunst und Gesellschaft im Begriff der didaktischen oder gar propagandistischen Kunst meint, war der traditionellen afrikanischen Gesellschaft fremd, in der ästhetisches Produzieren zugleich immer ein gesamtgesellschaftlich funktionales war und nicht Ausdruck eines individualistisch zu fassenden Schaffensprozesses.

Als eine besonders historisch bedingte Ausprägung dieses Charakteristikums afrikanischer Literatur gilt die seit Ende des 2. Weltkriegs entstehende sogenannte Pamphlet- oder Massenliteratur, die von der Stadt Onitsha, dem Handels- und Ausbildungszentrum Ostnigerias, ihren Ausgang nahm, in anderen Kolonien Westafrikas aufgenommen wurde und seit den späten sechziger Jahren auch in Ostafrika, insbesondere in Kenia, aufzufinden ist. Ein großer Teil dieser Literatur erhebt den Anspruch auf Aufklärung und Belehrung, der auf das traditionelle Verständnis von Literatur als einer gesellschaftlich-funktionalen Kommunikationsweise rekurriert, aber auch auf die ökonomischen, gesellschaftlichen und kulturellen Entstehungs-, Distributions- und Rezeptionsbedingungen, die der *Onitsha Market Literature* zweifellos ihr spezifisches Gepräge gaben, zurückzuführen ist. Hierzu zählen der Ausbau des Schulwesens in den englischen Kolonien, der besonders in den vierziger und fünfziger Jahren rascher als vorher erfolgte, zu einer größeren Verbreitung des Alphabetismus führte wie auch zu dem verstärkten Wunsch vieler Afrikaner nach "education"; weiterhin sind zu nennen die Entwicklung von Industrie, Technik und Handel, zunehmende Mobilität und Verstädterung, schließlich die Einführung indischer, in englischer Sprache verfaßter Pamphlete – Musterbriefe, Ratgeber, sentimentale Liebesgeschichten – durch die aus dem Krieg in Südostasien zurückkehrenden Soldaten. Die Einrichtung privat betriebener Druckereien in Onitsha bildet eine letzte wichtige Voraussetzung für den von Jahr zu Jahr wachsenden literarischen Markt in dieser Handelsstadt.

Welches waren nun die Erwartungen eines interessierten und immer größeren Lesepublikums, die offenbar von der "market literature" erfüllt wurden? Prinzipiell erhofften die Leser von den meist im Umfang knapp gehaltenen und außerordentlich preiswerten Heftchen Belehrung und Beratung, Erbauung, Information und Unterhaltung. Die zum Teil hohen Auflagen einzelner Hefte illustrieren, daß dem seitens der Autoren und Verleger – die oft identisch waren – durchaus entsprochen wurde. Die Titel deuten an, wie weitgespannt das Spektrum der Pamphletliteratur war: Neben praktischen Ratgebern wie *How to Write and Reply Letters for Marriage, Engagement-Letters and How to Know a Girl to Marry* oder *From Fear to Confidence* stehen Aufklärungs- und Erbauungsschriften, etwa *Man Know Thyself* oder *Beware of Women*; Beiträge zur Information und Weiterbildung sollen das eigene National- und Rassenbewußtsein stärken, so die Lektüre von *Suffers of Africans: A Complete History of White Imperialism Towards African Nationalism.*[7]

Den größten Teil der Veröffentlichungen stellen jedoch die oft als moralische Warnungen fungierenden Liebesgeschichten, in denen melodramatisch gestaltete Konflikte zwischen den Geschlechtern oder den Generationen geschildert werden. Hier dient das didaktische Moment nicht selten als Alibi für den Unterhaltungswert, aber auch den eskapistischen und gelegentlich pornographischen Charakter der Geschichten. Zu den populärsten und auflagestärksten Titeln zählen viele der von O. A. Ogali (geb. 1931) veröffentlichten Erzählungen oder das Drama *Veronica, My Daughter*, oder auch Speedy Erics *Mabel the Sweet Honey that Poured Away*.

Das Interesse von Lesern und Autoren an Themen wie dem Verhältnis von Mann und Frau oder den Generationen zueinander, dem Erwerb von Reichtum und sozialem Ansehen, die ein luxuriöses, dem westlichen Standard angepaßtes Leben zu ermöglichen scheinen, schließlich den politischen Konflikten der Zeit – dem Kampf um die politische Unabhängigkeit, oder den innenpolitischen Auseinandersetzungen im Kongo – läßt sich nur von den Auswirkungen des Kolonialismus auf die Psyche der Kolonialisierten erklären. Die ökonomischen, sozialen und kulturellen Veränderungen hatten die Entstehung neuer gesellschaftlicher Gruppen bewirkt, deren Wertvorstellungen, vermittelt durch das britische Erziehungssystem, bürgerlich-europäischer Art waren. Das neue Lesepublikum der kleinen Angestellten, Facharbeiter, Lehrer, Geschäftsleute, Händler, Schüler und Akademiker richtete seine Wünsche auf Besitz- und

Gelderwerb; seine ethischen Vorstellungen waren oft puritanisch-christlich geprägt; gesellschaftlichen Überlegungen lag zumeist ein der afrikanischen Tradition und in dieser Weise unbekannter Individualitätsbegriff zugrunde.

Die *Onitsha Market Literature* als Abschnitt der Entwicklung englischsprachiger Literaturen in Afrika ist zum einen Fortsetzung der auf Emanzipation gerichteten Bemühungen afrikanischer Schriftsteller, die allerdings in eine Richtung zielt, die den fast totalen Bruch mit der eigenen Kultur bedeutet. Zum anderen stellt sie eine Übergangsstufe zur Herausbildung der anspruchsvollen imaginativen Literatur dar und verkörpert – und hierin liegt ihre wichtigste Bedeutung – den Beginn der nun einsetzenden kulturellen wie gesellschaftlichen Trennung zwischen Masse und intellektueller Elite: In dem Maße, wie sich die sprachlich-literarischen Bemühungen der gebildeten Minderheit von der für unzulänglich erachteten Massenliteratur zu unterscheiden beginnen, verliert sie als soziale Gruppe zunehmend den Kontakt zur Masse der Bevölkerung. Diese Entwicklung spiegelt sich in der nun schnell anwachsenden anspruchsvollen Literatur – die von einer nur kleinen afrikanischen Leserschaft rezipiert wird – und in der einsetzenden Diskussion über die gesellschaftliche Funktion des Schriftstellers wider.

Wenn der bekannteste englischschreibende Prosaautor Westafrikas, der Nigerianer Chinua Achebe (geb. 1930), es für die Aufgabe des afrikanischen Schriftstellers hält, dazu beizutragen, daß die afrikanischen Menschen nach den Erfahrungen von Kolonialismus und Sklaverei ihre Selbstachtung wiederfinden,[8] so spricht er zweifellos eine Problematik an, die jeden von ihnen in der einen oder anderen Weise trifft, ganz gleich welcher sozialen Gruppe er zuzurechnen ist. Verwendet er selbst und andere Autoren aber neben einer nichtafrikanischen Sprache auch noch unbekannte literarische Formen, wie den Roman oder die Kurzgeschichte, oder bedient sich der schriftlichen Mitteilungsform nicht nur hier, sondern auch bei der Produktion von Theatertexten oder Gedichten, so versucht er die gestellte Aufgabe zu lösen, indem er Mittel einsetzt, die allenfalls von einer kleinen elitären Gruppe von Afrikanern rezipiert und verstanden werden können. Dies bedeutet, daß die vorgelegten literarischen Bewältigungsversuche notwendigerweise vieles, wenn nicht Einseitiges über die spezifische Betroffenheit einer besonderen Gruppe von Afrikanern zum Ausdruck bringen. In der Beurteilung der Leistung der imaginativen englischsprachigen Literaturen Afrikas wird dies oft übersehen und veranlaßte unter anderem den nigerianischen Dramatiker, Prosaautor und Dichter Wole Soyinka (geb. 1934) zu der boshaft klingenden Bemerkung, der afrikanische Schriftsteller "even tried to give society something that the society has never lost – its identity", denn, so ergänzt er an anderer Stelle, "the African writer-intellectual chooses often to dramatize his dilemma and the hollowness of his anguish indicates only too clearly that he first of all created it."[9]

Die überspitzte, in der Tendenz aber sicher zutreffende Einschätzung einer allzu leicht von der eigenen Situation auf die ganze Gesellschaft projizierten Problematik soll jedoch keinesfalls den Blick darauf verstellen, daß die bevorzugte Gestaltung bestimmter Themen Indiz der Betroffenheit von der kolonilen Situation in Afrika ist. Übersehen werden darf aber nicht, daß ein Großteil der nun in englischer Sprache schreibenden Autoren dem intellektuellen und akademischen Klima der Universitätscolleges entstammt, die nach dem 2. Weltkrieg gegründet wurden.[10] Darüberhinaus war der Anstoß, den die nigerianische Literatur aus *Black Orpheus* erhielt, der dem University College Ibadan nahestehenden, 1957 gegründeten ersten Kultur- und Literaturzeitschrift Westafrikas, oder aus dem 1961 entstandenen Mbari Club, der viele Schriftsteller zum ersten Male in den *Mbari Publications* veröffentlichte, von prägender Bedeutung, denn zu dieser Zeit studierten in Ibadan so bekannte Autoren wie Achebe, Soyinka, Christopher Okigbo (1932–1967) und John Pepper Clark (geb. 1935). Die Massenmedien bildeten schließlich einen weiteren wichtigen Faktor, der zu der besonders günstigen Konstellation in Nigeria beitrug, waren doch einige Schriftsteller in Presse und Rundfunk tätig – etwa Achebe, Cyprian Ekwensi (geb. 1921), Gabriel Okara (geb. 1921), Onuora Nzekwu (geb. 1928) oder Nkem Nwankwo (geb. 1936). Weder in Ghana, Sierra Leone noch in den ostafrikanischen Ländern waren die Ausgangsbedingungen für die anspruchsvolle Literatur ähnlich günstig, und erst Mitte der sechziger Jahre sollte das *Literature Department der University of Nairobi* ähnlich wegweisende Bedeutung erlangen wie Ibadan.[11]

Achebes programmatische Forderung nach einer zur Emanzipation Afrikas beitragenden Tätigkeit des Schriftstellers steht in engstem Zusammenhang mit seiner eigenen literarischen Produktion. Sein erster Roman, *Things Fall Apart* (London, 1958), dessen Titel W. B. Yeats' "The Second Coming" entstammt, stellt die unübertroffen gebliebene literarische Gestaltung dieser Aufgabe dar, begründet zugleich eine Tradition innerhalb der englischsprachigen Literaturen Afrikas, die bis heute fortwirkt und ist schließlich zum millionenfach verkauften „Lehrbuch" an afrikanischen Schulen und Universitäten geworden. *Things Fall Apart,* die Schilderung der traditionellen Ibo-Gesellschaft im Osten Nigerias, ihrer Berührung mit christlichen Missionaren und britischen Administratoren gegen Ende des 19. Jahrhunderts sowie der hieraus folgenden Zerstörung durch die kolonialistischen Agenturen, besitzt inzwischen den Status eines Klassikers, denn in geradezu paradigmatischer Weise wird hier vorkoloniale wie koloniale Erfahrung afrikanischer Menschen dargestellt. Die Rekonstruktion der Vergangenheit wird mit diesem Roman zum zentralen Thema der ersten Phase innerhalb der englischsprachigen Literaturen Afrikas, die etwa die Jahre von 1958 bis 1965 umspannt. In den herausragenden literarischen Werken dieser Zeit geschieht die Darstellung und Auseinandersetzung mit der vorkolonialen und kolonialen Epoche allerdings stets selbstkritisch. Die Autoren beabsichtigen weder ein beschönigendes Bild afrikanischer Gesellschaften zu malen, noch die Vergangenheit um ihrer selbst willen lebendig werden zu lassen, sondern den Blick zurück als Ausgangspunkt für den Blick in die Zukunft zu verstehen. Achebes Kritik in *Things Fall Apart* richtet sich zweifellos gegen europäische Überheblichkeit und Borniertheit, wenn er die Absicht des "District Commissioner" satirisch bloßstellt, der nach kurzem Aufenthalt im Iboland ein Handbuch schreiben will, das er "Pacification of the Primitive Tribes of the

Lower Niger" nennen wird; andererseits übersieht er auch nicht Schwächen und Widersprüche in der Ibo-Gesellschaft, die sich an der Figur Okonkwos, des Protagonisten der Handlung, manifestieren.

Auch die beiden folgenden Romane, *No Longer at Ease* (London, 1960) und *Arrow of God* (London, 1964) stehen unter dem Zentralthema dieser Zeit, wie sie auch von einem ebenso kritischen Geschichtsbewußtsein geprägt sind wie *Things Fall Apart*. In *No Longer at Ease* variiert der Autor sein Thema jedoch, denn im Zwiespalt zwischen afrikanischer Herkunft und westlicher Erziehung wird Obi, die Hauptfigur, zum Repräsentanten der neuen Mittelklasse, die der eigenen Kultur entfremdet wurde, ohne sich mit der europäischen identifizieren zu können. Damit gestaltet Achebe einen Konflikt, der wie kein zweiter immer wieder aufgegriffen worden ist, da er die persönliche Erfahrung gerade auch afrikanischer Autoren unmittelbar betraf.

Eine spezifisch ostafrikanische, bzw. kenianische Variante stellen die in den sechziger und siebziger Jahren publizierten Werke Ngugi wa Thiong'os (geb. 1938) dar, der mit seinem Theaterstück, *The Black Hermit* (Kampala, 1963) an die Öffentlichkeit trat, das anläßlich der Unabhängigkeit Ugandas im gleichen Jahr aufgeführt wurde. Während die Darstellung des Kulturkonfliktes hier jedoch dramatisch-literarisch kaum überzeugt, gelingt Ngugi dies in *Weep Not, Child* (London, 1964) und *A Grain of Wheat* (London, 1967). Der Schauplatz der Handlung – das Kenia der Mau-Mau-Revolte in den fünfziger Jahren, bzw. das Land am Abend der Unabhängigkeit 1963 – bedingt aber eine Akzentuierung des Themas, die Ngugis Romane von den westafrikanischen unterscheidet, denn die unmittelbar erlebte Erfahrung der Mau-Mau-Aufstände stellt nicht nur politisch denkende und handelnde Intellektuelle vor die Frage ihrer kulturellen Loyalität, sondern gerade auch unpolitische Menschen. Der Kulturkonflikt als Folge der Kolonialisation betrifft bei diesem Autor also nicht nur die europäisch gebildete Elite Afrikas, sondern die gesamte Gesellschaft. – Wie konsequent im übrigen Ngugi den Begriff des Kulturkonfliktes in den siebziger Jahren erweitert, verdeutlicht sein vorletzter, außerordentlich populärer Roman *Petals of Blood* (London, 1977). Am Schicksal eines kenianischen Dorfes wird die fundamentale und unaufhaltsam scheinende sozio-ökonomische und kulturelle Umgestaltung Kenias zu einem kapitalistischen Land geschildert, in dem die afrikanische Kultur zur Ware degradiert wird; der Kulturkonflikt ist zum fundamentalen Konflikt zwischen einer ihre Humanität verlierenden Welt und inhumanen Kräften geworden.

Die Suche nach der Identität, die letztlich hinter der Beschäftigung mit der eigenen Geschichtlichkeit steht, beherrscht als Thema nicht nur die erzählende Literatur, sondern auch das Drama und die dramatische Dichtung. 1963 erschien *A Dance of the Forests* (London/New York), eins der ersten und auch der schwierigsten Theaterstücke Wole Soyinkas, des aus dem westlichen Nigeria stammenden bedeutendsten Dramatikers Afrikas. Das für die Unabhängigkeitsfeier des Landes geschriebene und im Oktober 1960 aufgeführte Stück problematisiert die "celebration of the past" als Credo vieler afrikanischer Politiker und will zu einer realistischen Einschätzung der auf Nigeria zukommenden Aufgaben beitragen. Im Gegensatz zu Achebes objektivistischer und scheinbar einfacher Gestaltungsweise bevorzugt Soyinka eine komplexe Oberflächenstruktur, indem er mythologisch-religiöse Vorstellungen und Figuren neben realistische, "ancestral spirits" und Naturgeister neben Menschen von heute stellt.

Ganz ähnlich wie Achebe variiert auch Soyinka das zentrale literarische Thema seiner Zeit in dem ebenfalls 1963 veröffentlichten Drama *The Lion and the Jewel* (London/New York). An der Figur des Dorflehrers Lakunle zeigt er die Dekulturation eines europäisierten Afrikaners auf, der sich vergeblich um die Hand der Dorfschönen, "the Jewel", bemüht, denn Europäisierung, so meint sie erkannt zu haben, bedeutet den Verlust der Männlichkeit. Im Gegensatz zu der an das Tragische grenzenden Figur Obis in *No Longer at Ease* wird Lakunle Zielscheibe satirischen Spottes. Soyinkas Witz und seine Beherrschung unterschiedlicher Sprachebenen, die funktional und wirkungsvoll eingesetzt werden, haben The *Lion and the Jewel* nicht nur zu einem wirkungsvollen und populären Theaterstück werden lassen, sondern zu dem bisher einzigen mit leichter Hand gestalteten Drama Soyinkas.

In den an ironisch-satirischen Gestaltungen nicht reichen Literaturen Afrikas ist dieses Stück neben *Song of Lawino* (Nairobi, 1966) zu stellen, einem lyrisch-dramatischen Monolog, der von dem aus Uganda stammenden Okot p'Bitek (1931–1982) zunächst in dessen Muttersprache Luo und dann, als Übersetzung, in Englisch abgefaßt wurde. Die der eigenen Tradition noch eng verbundene junge Afrikanerin Lawino beklagt ihr Los als Frau eines völlig europäisierten Mannes, für dessen Wertvorstellungen und Lebensgewohnheiten sie kein Verständnis aufbringen kann und will. Auch Ocol, ihr Mann, dient als Zielscheibe des Spottes. Doch Lawinos Lob des afrikanischen Lebens relativiert den satirischen Charakter der kritischen Passagen. Diese Mischung satirisch-kritischer und eulogischer Abschnitte läßt ein neuartiges Genre entstehen, den "song", der an traditionelle orale Formen anknüpft. Seine Popularität, insbesondere in der englischsprachigen Literatur Kenias, ist wesentlich auf das Weiterwirken der oralen Tradition zurückzuführen, auch wenn der unmittelbare Erfolg von *Song of Lawino* nicht nur p'Bitek, sondern eine Reihe anderer Autoren veranlaßte, ihrerseits diese Form zu verwenden. Doch weder p'Biteks *Song of Ocol* (Nairobi, 1970) oder *Song of Malaya* (= Prostituierte) (Nairobi, 1971) noch Okello Oculis (geb. 1942) *Orphan* (Nairobi, 1968) besitzen die literarische Qualität ihres Vorbilds, und an Popularität steht dies *Things Fall Apart* kaum nach.

Besinnung auf die eigene Geschichtlichkeit, und dies bedeutet auch Auseinandersetzung mit der fremden Kultur, bestimmt als zentrales Thema der Frühphase auch die englischsprachige Dichtung Afrikas. Ihre Entwicklung verläuft ganz ähnlich wie die der Prosaliteratur. Die ersten Gedichte sind deutlich didaktischer Art und betonen auf emphatische, oft beschwörende Weise die Eigenständigkeit des Kontinents, der schwarzen Rasse oder der Idee Afrikas. Allmählich tritt dieser Ton gegenüber dem Ausdruck subjektiven Empfindens, insbesondere der Erfahrung kultureller Entfremdung zurück. Die Verse des

Ghanaers R. E. G. Armattoe (1913–1953) in dessen erstem Gedichtband *Between the Forest und the Sea* (Londonderry, 1950), oder die des Nigerianers Dennis Osadebay (geb. 1911) in *Africa Sings* (Ilfracombe, 1952) veranschaulichen den Ausgangspunkt der englischsprachigen Lyrik Westafrikas; die Gedichte Christopher Okigbos in *Heavensgate* (Ibadan, 1962) oder *Limits* (Ibadan, 1964), auch die Wole Soyinkas in *Idanre and Other Poems* (London, 1967), dagegen stellen repräsentative Beispiele subjektiver Äußerungen dar, die sich wegen ihres persönlichen Charakters oft einem Verständnis entziehen. An die Stelle des noch öffentlich wirksam werden wollenden Barden und Sängers der vierziger und frühen fünfziger Jahre, der sich als "communal voice" verstand, ist die "private voice" des sich persönlich mitteilenden Individuums getreten. In keiner anderen literarischen Gattung ist die Veränderung der Rolle des Schriftstellers so deutlich wahrzunehmen wie in der Lyrik.

Diese Entwicklung schließt allerdings keineswegs aus, daß ein traditionelles Dichtungs- und Rollenverständnis des Dichters nicht mehr anzutreffen wäre, wie auch die orale Tradition nun nicht einfach abreißt. An einer ganzen Reihe von Beispielen wird deren Fortwirken bzw. Nutzbarmachung in der Schriftliteratur erkennbar; das zeigt ein Blick auf die umfangreiche von Soyinka edierte Lyrikanthologie, *Poems of Black Africa* (London, 1975), insbesondere auf Gedichte der Abschnitte "Ancestors and Gods" oder "Animistic Phases". Doch erst gegen Ende der sechziger Jahre ist davon zu sprechen, daß afrikanische Dichter sich bewußter mit traditionellen Formen und deren Verwendungsmöglichkeiten in der modernen Lyrik beschäftigen und mit ihnen experimentieren: vorher gilt, so zeigen es u. a. Okigbos und Soyinkas Gedichte, der Blick eher der europäischen Dichtungsentwicklung im 20. Jahrhundert.

Eine solche, oft zum Vorwurf erhobene Feststellung läßt sich nun keineswegs zum Prosaschaffen des Nigerianers Amos Tutuola treffen, dessen Werke ein weiterer Aspekt des Zentralthemas, der Rekonstruktion der Geschichte Afrikas, kennzeichnet. Daß er vor allem seitens seiner afrikanischen Kritiker abgelehnt wurde, ist auf das bereits erwähnte Rollenverständnis des Autors als Lehrer zurückzuführen, dem Tutuola überhaupt nicht zu entsprechen schien. Außerdem waren sie nicht geneigt, dessen sprachliche wie literarische „Inkompetenz" von weißen Kritikern als „typisch afrikanisch" loben und sich selbst damit als Imitatoren europäischer Vorbilder abstempeln zu lassen. Die vorwiegend negative Kritik, die Tutuolas erstes Prosawerk, *The Palm-Wine Drinkard and His Dead Palm-Wine Tapster in the Deads' Town*, vor allem von afrikanischer Seite erhielt,[12] verweist aber auf die Ambivalenz der in einer fremden Sprache schreibenden, sich teilweise auch fremder literarischer Formen bedienender Autoren, die ihrem eigenen Anspruch nach als Lehrer ihren Landsleuten ja gerade den Wert der eigenen Geschichte und Kultur zu vermitteln versuchten. Die Empfindlichkeit, mit der auf Tutuolas "bush stories" reagiert wurde, konnte kaum weniger wirksam durch eine aus Europa stammende Kritik an den eigenen Werken getroffen werden.

In *The Palm-Wine Drinkard* wie auch in einer Reihe ganz ähnlich strukturierter Werke, die Tutuola seinem ersten literarischen Erfolg nachschickte, greift der Autor auf Elemente der oralen Tradition seines Volkes, der Yoruba im Westen Nigerias, zurück, verwendet überlieferte Erzählungen und Episoden, Mythen und Fabeln und verknüpft sie durch das Motiv der Suche des Helden, des Palmweintrinkers, nach seinem toten Weinzapfer zu einer kaum realistisch zu nennenden Handlung. Dabei geht Tutuola als Autor völlig unbefangen vor: weder berührt ihn die Frage des Plagiats noch richtet er sich nach den Regeln der englischen Grammatik; die Konventionen des europäischen Romans scheinen ihm völlig fremd. Daß die im Entstehen begriffene englischsprachige Prosaliteratur mit ihrer Suche nach einem eigenen Standort dem *Palm-Wine Drinkard* nicht unbedingt zur Seite gestellt werden wollte, erklärt sich aus der Ablehnung all dessen, was diese Erzählung zur Ausnahme macht: sprachliche und literarische „Inkompetenz" und die Gestaltung afrikanischer Erfahrungen, die in Mythen, Fabeln und Erzählungen geschichtlich geworden sind – kurz, eine Welt Afrikas, mit deren Geistern, Dämonen und Zaubern die jungen Intellektuellen und Schriftsteller nichts mehr im Sinn haben.

Die Weiterentwicklung der afrikanischen Prosaliteratur nicht nur in Westafrika hat nun aber gezeigt, daß die Reaktion auf Tutuola eher als psychologisches denn literarkritisches Phänomen eingestuft werden muß. So ist die Rezeption insbesondere des *Palm-Wine Drinkard* zunehmend positiver geworden,[13] und auch in der Prosaliteratur selbst sind die von Tutuola erfolgten Anstöße bald – wenn auch in modifizierter Weise – aufgegriffen worden. Dies gilt allerdings nicht für dessen ungewolltes Sprachexperiment, sondern für das Verständnis der Geschichtlichkeit Afrikas. Es scheint, daß in dem Maße, in dem afrikanische Autoren sich ihrer eigenen Geschichte als selbstverständlicher Tatsache zuzuwenden beginnen, sie diese als Geschichte oder Geschichten des alltäglichen Lebens auffassen und zur Vorlage ihrer literarischen Werke machen. Zwar erweisen sich die Romane der Nigerianer Elechi Amadi (geb. 1934) oder Flora Nwapa (geb. 1931), aber auch des aus Malawi stammenden Legson Kayira (geb. 1940) als weitaus realistischere Erzählungen als *The Palm-Wine Drinkard,* doch das Fortwirken des Glaubens an übernatürliche Kräfte wie auch deren glaubhaft gemachtes Wirken in den Erzählungen knüpfen an Tutuolas Welt an. Sie sind Bestandteil des Lebens traditioneller Gesellschaften mit ihren persönlichen und sozialen Spannungen und Konflikten, etwa in Amadis *The Concubine* (London, 1966) und *The Great Ponds* (London, 1969), oder in Nwapas *Efuru* (London, 1966) und *Idu* (London, 1969), den beiden ersten von einer Nigerianerin veröffentlichten englischsprachigen Romanen. Auch Kayiras *The Looming Shadow* (London, 1968) sowie Theaterstücke des in Yoruba schreibenden Duro Ladipo (geb. 1931) zählen hierzu.[14] Gerade an diesem Beispiel zeigt sich aber nun, daß solche Art Rückbesinnung auf die afrikanische Geschichte nicht auf die englischsprachigen Literaturen begrenzt geblieben ist. Daß hier nunmehr Kolonialismus und Kulturkonflikt keine Rolle spielen, ist als ein weiterer Schritt der Emanzipation der Literaturen Afrikas zu sehen.

Die Rekonstruktion der eigenen Geschichte als beherrschendes Thema der englischsprachigen Literaturen in den fünfziger und frühen sechziger Jahren tritt nach der Unabhängigkeit afrikanischer Länder gegen Ende des Jahrzehnts zurück, ohne daß sie jedoch bis heute gänzlich ihre Bedeutung verloren hat. Die Mitte der sechziger Jahre läßt sich andererseits sehr genau als Beginn eines neuen Abschnitts in der literaturgeschichtlichen Entwicklung Afrikas lokalisieren, für den sich seither die Bezeichnung "period of disillusionment"[15] durchgesetzt hat. Sie bezieht sich allerdings nicht allein auf den thematischen Richtungswechsel, der mit Romanen Achebes, Soyinkas und anderer west- und ostafrikanischer Schriftsteller einsetzt, sondern verweist ganz generell auf die politische Situation ihrer Länder. Die immer stärker auftretenden wirtschaftlichen und sozialen Spannungen und Konflikte, die Ohnmacht und das Versagen der politischen Parteien und der Regierungen, die fortbestehenden Abhängigkeiten von den Industrienationen, die ständig größer werdende Kluft zwischen Arm und Reich, der kleinen politischen und intellektuellen Elite, der es relativ gut geht, und der Masse der Bevölkerung, veranlaßt viele Schriftsteller, die Relevanz ihres Tuns zu bezweifeln. Ihr bisheriges Selbstverständnis erscheint ihnen als überholt und den Problemen der Gegenwart nicht mehr angemessen. Soyinkas bereits zitierten Worte entstammen diesem Gefühl der Ernüchterung, des Selbstzweifels, der Einsicht in die Notwendigkeit, sich neu besinnen zu müssen. Aus keiner Phase der erst kurzen Geschichte afrikanischer Literaturen liegen uns so viele selbstkritische Zeugnisse vor, wie aus der zweiten Hälfte der sechziger Jahre.[16] Der bisher so oft beschworene Begriff "commitment" muß neu gefüllt werden, denn wenn der Autor sich weiterhin als gesellschaftlich funktional begreifen will, gilt es für ihn, sich zu entscheiden, ob er sich mit der eigenen elitären Gruppe oder der Masse der Bevölkerung identifizieren soll. Erneut gerät der afrikanische Schriftsteller in einen Identitätskonflikt, der nun aber radikal gesellschaftlicher Art ist: Afrika als sozio-politische und sozio-kulturelle Alternative zu Europa hat sich angesichts der postkolonialen Wirklichkeit als Illusion erwiesen, die es aufzudecken, aber auch zu überwinden gilt.

Gabriel Okaras *The Voice* (London, 1964), Soyinkas *The Interpreters* (London, 1965) und Achebes *A Man of the People* (London, 1966) als Romane sowie Soyinkas *Kongi's Harvest* (London, 1965) als Theaterstück markieren die thematische Wende. Doch alle drei nigerianische Autoren rekonstruieren in ihren Werken nur die unzulängliche Wirklichkeit. Weder sie noch Autoren anderer Länder – etwa David Rubadiri (geb. 1930) in *No Bride Price* (Nairobi, 1967), Robert Serumaga (1932–1980) in *The Return to the Shadows* (Nairobi, 1969), Leonard Kibera (geb. ca. 1940) in *Voices in the Dark* (Nairobi, 1970), Ayi Kwei Armah (geb. 1939) in *The Beautyful Ones Are Not Yet Born* (New York, 1968) und Ngugi wa Thiong'o in *A Grain of Wheat* – antizipieren literarisch eine hoffnungsvollere Zukunft. Allzusehr, so scheint es, beschäftigt die Schriftsteller zunächst einmal die Verarbeitung der Ursachen und Gründe, die zu den gegenwärtigen gesellschaftlichen und politischen Problemen geführt haben.

Romanciers, Dramatiker und Dichter aus Ghana und Nigeria, Kenia, Uganda und Malawi verbindet das Gefühl der Desillusionierung, aber auch der Hilflosigkeit angesichts der Entfremdung und Wurzellosigkeit des Einzelnen, von dem sie selbst betroffen sind. Gemeinsam ist ihnen die Abscheu vor Korruption, Machtmißbrauch und Gewalt, die sie allenthalben vor Augen haben und teilweise selbst erfahren. Viele von ihnen versuchen, ihre Einsichten und Erfahrungen literarisch angemessen zu verarbeiten. Da ihnen selbst aber oft nur ein Abschnitt der komplexen Wirklichkeit erhellbar zu sein scheint, bedienen sie sich gestalterischer Mittel, die dies leisten sollen: der Einzelne ist nicht mehr in der Lage, die Wirklichkeit zu durchschauen, den Zusammenhang von in der Vergangenheit liegenden Ursachen und deren Folgen in der Gegenwart herzustellen. So tritt der Protagonist eines Romans identitäts- und namenlos auf, nur noch motiviert von einem Rest moralischer Integrität – etwa Okolo (= die Stimme) in *The Voice*, oder The Man in *The Beautyful Ones Are Not Yet Born*. Ngugi und Soyinka vermeiden zwar eine so bewußte Allegorisierung oder Symbolisierung wie Okara und Armah, doch ihre Charaktere bleiben sich selbst und den Lesern nicht weniger fremd, wenn ihren Handlungsmotiven, ihrem widersprüchlichen Verhalten und ihrer Unabgeschlossenheit in Rückblenden, Rückgriffen, Erinnerungen und innerem Monolog nachgegangen wird.

Bei aller Gemeinsamkeit der moralischen Betroffenheit und technischen Gestaltungsweise in vielen Werken der "period of disillusionment" soll allerdings nicht übersehen werden, daß die nach der Unabhängigkeit einsetzenden unterschiedlichen politisch-sozialen Entwicklungsprozesse in den verschiedenen ehemaligen britischen Kolonien sich auch in deren Literaturen widerspiegeln. Okigbos Gedichte "Path of Thunder, Poems prophesying War" (*Black Orpheus*, February 1968), die nach seinem Tod 1967 im nigerianischen Bürgerkrieg in einem Sammelband posthum erschienen,[17] sind ebensowenig von der politischen Entwicklung in Nigeria zu trennen wie Achebes *A Man of the People*. Gedichte und Romane sehen visionär Militärputsch und kriegerische Auseinandersetzung voraus, die das politische Geschehen des Landes von 1966 bis Anfang 1970 bestimmten. Andererseits nahm Armahs resignierender Schluß in seinem ersten Roman *The Beautyful Ones Are Not Yet Born* die Einsicht vorweg, daß ein Machtwechsel in Ghana, der Sturz Nkrumahs, wohl kaum der Beginn einer neuen, hoffnungsvolleren Zeit bedeuten werde. Schließlich verweisen Rubadiris, Ngugis und Serumagas Romane der späten sechziger Jahre auf die in Kenia im folgenden Jahrzehnt deutlich zutage tretenden politischen und sozialen Probleme: Entwicklung zu einem kapitalistisch orientierten Wirtschaftssystem, Verfilzung von ökonomischen und politischen Interessen der kleinen, machtausübenden Elite, Urbanisierung und Vernachlässigung des bäuerlichen Hinterlandes, Arbeitslosigkeit, Prostitution und Kriminalität sowie Verfall der Städte.

Der bis zur Mitte der sechziger Jahre zurückzuverfolgende Differenzierungsprozeß in den englischsprachigen Literaturen Afrikas tritt, durch die politische Entwicklung seit 1966 bedingt, insbesondere in der nigerianischen Literatur seit Anfang der siebziger Jahre deutlich zutage. In keinem anderen englischsprachigen Land hat sich bisher innenpolitisches Geschehen so nachhaltig, in solcher Vielfalt und Vielzahl literarisch niedergeschlagen. Die Bürgerkriegsliteratur, repräsentiert vor allem durch Roman, Kurzgeschichte und Lyrik, stellt in der Tat eine in sich geschlossene Gruppe von Werken dar, die gesonderter Aufmerksamkeit bedarf. Dabei gilt es zu bedenken, daß *Biafra* für viele Schriftsteller persönliche Erfahrung hieß, für andere dagegen als Metapher für die politische Situation des Landes in den späten sechziger Jahren diente. Darstellungen aus der Sicht Biafras, bzw. durch Autoren, die dem Ibovolk angehören, überwiegen bisher, ohne daß ihnen aber der Vorwurf der Einseitigkeit der propagandistischen Färbung gemacht werden kann; die in jüngster Zeit erschienenen Romane sind eher selbstkritisch, wie etwa Eddie Irohs *Toads of War* (London, 1979).

Neben sehr vordergründigen, teils langatmig und weit ausholenden, teils reißerischen Erzählungen, z. B. John Munonyes (geb. 1929) *A Wreath for the Maidens* (London, 1973), bzw. Eddie Irohs *Forty-Eight Guns for the General* (London, 1976), stehen autobiographische Gestaltungen, so Elechi Amadis *Sunset in Biafra* (London, 1973) oder Wole Soyinkas Gefängnisaufzeichnungen, die er während seiner über zweijährigen Einkerkerung von 1967 bis 1969 verfaßte und in *The Man Died* (London, 1972) veröffentlichte. Weniger direkt auf das Kriegsgeschehen bezogen sind Kole Omotosos (geb. 1943) *The Combat* (London, 1972), eine knappe, allegorische Satire des Bruderkrieges, und Soyinkas, Roman *Season of Anomy* (London, 1973). Mit seiner bisher letzten Prosaveröffentlichung legt einer der vielseitigsten und produktivsten Schriftsteller Afrikas die bisher anspruchsvollste literarische Verarbeitung der letzten Jahre vor, in der die Zeit unmittelbar vor Ausbruch des Bürgerkrieges geschildert wird. Aus einer Fülle von Gedankengängen, die Soyinka in einer dicht gewebten Handlung immer wieder aufgreift, sei nur auf zwei verwiesen. Angesichts der Pogrome, die der Protagonist der Handlung miterleben muß, stellt sich ihm als Intellektuellen immer wieder die Frage nach der Legitimität der Gegengewalt. Als Repräsentant einer friedlichen und solidarischen bäuerlichen Kommune versucht er darüberhinaus, die Konzeption dieser Gesellschaft im Land zu verbreiten; er hofft, daß es eines Tages gelingen wird, die Macht des korrupten, die Menschen unterdrückenden und ausbeutenden Kakao-Kartells zu brechen und an die Stelle eines inhumanen Systems das humane seiner bäuerlichen Gesellschaft treten zu lassen.

Mit *Season of Anomy* setzt der nigerianische Autor zwei Akzente, die die zukünftige Entwicklung der englischsprachigen Literaturen Afrikas ganz wesentlich beeinflussen dürften. Zum einen überwindet er die "period of disillusionment", indem er nicht nur die unzulängliche Gegenwart abbildet, sondern einen realistischen und realisierbaren Weg zu ihrer Überwindung aufzeigt. Zum anderen greift er hierbei auf geschichtliche Erfahrungen in Afrika zurück: Europa als Wegweiser in die Zukunft hat seine Rolle ausgespielt, wie es eine der Romanfiguren formuliert. In *Season of Anomy* besinnt sich der afrikanische Schriftsteller in ganz konkreter Weise auf die eigene Geschichte, auf das Beispiel Aiyetoros, einer bäuerlichen Kommune im Süden des Landes, die eine alternative Gesellschafts- und Wirtschaftsform praktiziert hatte, um an diesem Modell die Möglichkeit zur Bekämpfung der gegenwärtigen Übelstände zu überprüfen.[18]

Soyinka funktionalisiert also geschichtliche Erfahrungen in *Season of Anomy* und dürfte hierin als Modell und Wegbereiter einer Entwicklung in den englischsprachigen Literaturen der siebziger Jahre angesehen werden, die zunehmend bedeutungsvoller zu werden scheint. Etwa zur gleichen Zeit wie *Season of Anomy* erscheinen nämlich zwei Theaterstücke des neben Soyinka und Clark dritten bedeutenden nigerianischen Dramatikers, Ola Rotimi (geb. 1940): *Kurunmi* (Ibadan, 1971) und *Ovonramwen Nogbaisi* (Ibadan, 1974). Ayi Kwei Armahs inzwischen vierter Roman, *Two Thousand Seasons* (Nairobi, 1973), das Theaterstück des Ghanaers Joe de Graft (ca. 1932–1977), *Muntu* (Nairobi, 1977), und der Roman *The Return* (London, 1977) des ebenfalls aus Ghana stammenden Schriftstellers Yaw M. Boateng (geb. 1950) werden wenige Jahre später veröffentlicht. Alle diese Werke schildern Geschehnisse aus der Zeit vor dem Kolonialismus bzw. aus dessen frühester Phase in Afrika. Dies traf zwar auch für Achebes *Things Fall Apart* zu, doch nun ist es nicht länger Ziel der Autoren, die traumatische Dimension der Erfahrungen des Kolonialismus aufzubrechen, sondern diese geschichtliche Phase als nur einen Abschnitt innerhalb einer umfassend gesehenen Entwicklung des Kontinents zu begreifen. Besonders anschaulich geschieht dies in zwei deutlich vom Formwillen ihrer Verfasser bestimmten Werken, Armahs *Two Thousand Seasons* und de Grafts *Muntu*. Hier treten keine individualisierten Einzelne auf, sondern Typen, an denen die Autoren das kollektive Schicksal afrikanischer Menschen aufzeigen wollen, deren Leiden, aber auch ihren Widerstand und ihre Selbstbehauptung. Sowohl der Erzählduktus Armahs – ein im Hintergrund verharrender Erzähler, der als Griot aus der Perspektive seines Volkes dessen Schicksal an einer repräsentativen Gruppe von Menschen schildert –, wie auch die dramatische Gestaltung in *Muntu*, die durch eine Reduktion der dramatischen Charaktere auf Typen und der dramatischen Handlung auf typische Verhaltensweisen charakterisiert ist –, um so die Geschichte des Kontinents in einem kurzen Theaterstück einzufangen –, stellen neue experimentelle Formen literarischer Gestaltung dar, deren Verwendung im Zusammenhang mit der Intention der Schriftsteller verstanden werden muß, afrikanische Geschichte als kollektive Geschichte zu sehen. Die hierdurch zum Ausdruck kommende Zurückweisung einer europäisch gefärbten Geschichtsbetrachtung, die von herausragenden Individuen ausgeht, ist nicht zu übersehen.

Daß Ereignisse aus der vor- und frühkolonialen Zeit besonders häufig in der dramatischen Literatur als Vorlage herangezogen werden, ist sicher nicht zufällig. Gerade dieses Genre bietet sich mit seinen traditionellen Gestaltungselementen an, *die* Bedeutung geschichtlicher Ereignisse zu vermitteln, die der Dramatiker ins Bewußtsein heben will. Das Auftreten eines Erzählers, allegorische und pantomimische Darstellung, die Verwendung von Masken, Musik und Tanz kommen dieser Absicht der Autoren geradezu entgegen. Damit verkörpert das afrikanische Drama die Gattung, durch die Fragen des Zusammenhangs von Tradition und Moderne sowie von der Funktion der Literatur als Mittlerin eines Zusammengehörigkeitsgefühls am deutlichsten thematisiert werden können. Autoren wie Soyinka, Clark und Rotimi aus Nigeria, de Graft, Efua Sutherland (geb. 1924) und Ama Ata Aidoo (geb. 1942) aus Ghana, Robert Serumaga und John Ruganda (geb. 1941) aus Uganda/Kenia stellen dies als

Dramatiker, Dramaturgen, Leiter von Theatergruppen und Kritiker immer wieder unter Beweis. Praktische Ergänzung erfahren sie durch die Drama- und Theaterinstitute der Universitäten, etwa in Ibadan, Ife und Legon/Accra, aber auch durch meist dem universitären Bereich entstammenden Theatergruppen, die als Wandertheater fungieren und bei einem theaterfreudigen Publikum auch mit englischsprachigen Stücken Erfolg haben.

Die siebziger Jahre kennzeichnet schließlich neben dieser vor allem das Drama berührenden Thematik ein weiteres neues Sujet, das bisher allerdings weitgehend auf Roman und Kurzgeschichte beschränkt geblieben ist: die Schilderung des modernen städtischen Lebens, das sich aufgrund zunehmender Urbanisierung und Zentralisierung, technischer Entwicklung und Industrialisierung immer rasanter entwickelt und tiefgreifende gesellschaftliche Veränderungen bewirkt hat. Einer der ersten nigerianischen Romane, Cyprian Ekwensis *People of the City* (London, 1954) widmete sich bereits dem großstädtischen Leben als Schauplatz. Doch Ekwensis episodisch gestaltete Erzählung, in der er die dunklen Seiten des Stadtlebens – Kriminalität, Prostitution, Arbeitslosigkeit, mangelhafte Wohnverhältnisse und Entfremdung – schildert, stellt einen frühen Vorläufer der urbanen Literatur der siebziger Jahre dar, der die Realität einer afrikanischen Großstadt wiedergibt, die wenige Jahre nach Ende des Weltkrieges noch eine Ausnahme darstellte.

Ein zweiter, ganz wesentlicher Aspekt trennt *People of the City*, aber auch jene Romane der "period of disillusionment", die in afrikanischen Städten spielen, z. B. *The Beautyful Ones Art Not Yet Born*, *The Interpreters* oder Kofi Awoonors (geb. 1935) *This Earth, My Brother* (New York, 1971), vom urbanen Roman der siebziger Jahre. Den vorwiegend einer jüngeren Generation entstammenden Autoren geht es nicht mehr um jene Probleme, die Ekwensi, Soyinka oder Armah beschäftigte, um die Suche nach den Gründen für die Entfremdung des Einzelnen oder den Ursachen der sozialen Konflikte und des politischen Niedergangs ihrer Länder. Meja Mwangi (geb. 1948), Mwangi Ruheni, Nkem Nwankwo, I. N. C. Aniebo (geb. 1939) und eine Reihe anderer Schriftsteller konstatieren vielmehr eine Wirklichkeit, in der nicht herausragende Einzelne, sondern Durchschnittsmenschen mit ihren psychologischen, wirtschaftlichen und sozialen Schwierigkeiten dargestellt werden. Selten besteht bei ihnen das Verlangen, sich aus ihrer gesellschaftlichen Existenz heraus zu verstehen. Arbeitslosigkeit und Arbeitssuche, oft nur flüchtige Beziehungen zu anderen Menschen, Entfremdung von Familie oder dörflicher Gemeinschaft bestimmen in Romanen wie *The Future Leaders* (London, 1973), *Kill Me Quick* (London, 1973), *Going Down River Road* (London, 1976), *My Mercedes is Bigger than Yours* (London, 1975) oder *The Journey Within* (London, 1978) Leben und Schicksal der Menschen; das noch ihrer Vätergeneration eigene Bemühen um Identitätsfindung ist ihnen unbekannt. Erst die weitere Entwicklung dieses Themas kann Antwort auf die Frage geben, ob die jungen Autoren angesichts einer undurchschaubar gewordenen Wirklichkeit nur als Chronisten fungieren wollen, oder ob sich in der von ihnen gewählten Darstellungsweise niederschlägt, daß ihnen sogar die Frage nach ihrer Funktion als Schriftsteller unwichtig geworden ist.

Umfang und Qualität der englischsprachigen Literaturen Afrikas stellen unter Beweis, daß ihre Vitalität trotz politischer und wirtschaftlicher Krisen in nahezu allen seit Anfang der sechziger Jahre unabhängigen ehemaligen englischen Kolonien ungebrochen ist. Ja, sie ist seit Ende der sechziger Jahre auch für ostafrikanische Länder wie Sambia, Malawi, Tanzania und Simbabwe zu konstatieren, die zunächst vergleichsweise weniger produktiv waren.[19] So sollte auch der Einschnitt, den die Diktatur Amins für die literarische Entwicklung Ugandas bedeutet hat, nach der Erfahrung in Nigeria bald überwunden werden, wo die Jahre des Bürgerkrieges zu einem fast völligen Erliegen der literarischen Produktion geführt hatte, die dann nach 1970 aber umso stärker wieder einsetzte.[20]

Dramen, Romane und Gedichte gerade der gegenwärtigen Epoche veranschaulichen den Zuwachs an Selbstbewußtsein afrikanischer Schriftsteller von der geschichtlichen Aufgabe Afrikas, sich nicht nur wiederzuentdecken nach Jahrhunderten der Sklaverei und des Kolonialismus, sondern einen eigenen Weg in die Zukunft zu finden – eine Aufgabe, die als bisher letzte Stufe eines Emanzipationsprozesses anzusehen ist, der seit den Schriften freigewordener Sklaven im 18. Jahrhundert in stets dialektischem Spannungsverhältnis zur Unterdrückung der eigenen Geschichtlichkeit gestanden hatte, und aus dem heraus die Literaturen Afrikas bis in die Gegenwart hinein ihr Leben bezogen hatten. Soyinkas *Season of Anomy*, Ngugis *Petals of Blood* oder Armahs *Two Thousand Seasons* – um nur die bedeutendsten Werke der letzten Jahre zu nennen –, verkörpern einen neuen Abschnitt in der afrikanischen Literaturgeschichte, der als Beginn ihrer endgültigen Ablösung von Europa verstanden werden muß und den Literaturhistoriker der Zukunft erneut mit der Frage nach Abgrenzungs- und Bewertungskategorien konfrontieren wird.

Die vorliegende Auswahl von Texten orientiert sich an sechs Problemfeldern, die allerdings wegen ihrer engen Verknüpfung miteinander eine klare und eindeutige Textzuordnung nicht in jedem einzelnen Fall ermöglichen. So mag es gerade dort gelegentlich zu Überschneidungen kommen, wo mehrere Aspekte zugleich angesprochen werden. Die Zusammenstellung der Texte bedurfte darüberhinaus einiger grundsätzlicher Überlegungen, die kurz angeführt werden sollen.

Trotz der nur wenige Jahrzehnte umfassenden Entwicklung der afrikanischen Literatur in englischer Sprache liegt bereits eine Fülle von kritischen Äußerungen vor, die zur Auswahl zwang. Auch die unterschiedliche Entwicklung in West- und Ostafrika bedurfte einer angemessenen Berücksichtigung, insofern Literatur und Literaturkritik Westafrikas nicht nur einen längeren Zeitraum umspannen als die Ostafrikas, sondern auch bis in die jüngste Gegenwart wesentlich produktiver waren.

In den Texten sollen vor allem Afrikaner zu Wort kommen. Die besonderen Entstehungsbedingungen von Literatur und Literaturkritik ließen es jedoch als erforderlich erscheinen, ihnen europäische Stimmen zur Seite zu stellen, denn es waren zunächst vor allem britische, gelegentlich auch amerikanische Kritiker, die sich, bedingt durch ihre Tätigkeit in Afrika, mit dem Phänomen der neu entstehenden Literatur auseinandersetzten.

Bei der Zusammenstellung der Texte zur kolonialen Sprach- und Bildungspolitik, deren Diskussion bis weit ins 19. Jahrhundert zurückreicht, wurden Äußerungen und Stellungnahmen britischer Kolonialbeamter und Missionare mit solchen afrikanischer Intellektueller konfrontiert, um den schon frühzeitigen Widerstand gegen die britische Politik zu dokumentieren, ohne den die Unabhängigkeitsbewegung gar nicht denkbar ist. Die Frage nach einer eigenen Literatur spielte dabei zunächst gar keine Rolle; vielmehr galt die Aufmerksamkeit dem Bestreben der Kolonialherren, die englische Sprache aus rein praktischen Gründen Afrikanern zu lehren. Erst mit der Forderung nach nationaler – und damit auch nach kultureller – Unabhängikeit beginnt sich hier die Akzentuierung der Problematik zu verschieben und die Sprachenfrage zugleich die nach einer angemessenen afrikanischen Literatur zu werden.

Für die vielfältigen Anregungen und die Unterstützung bei der Abfassung des Buches gilt mein Dank Kollegen und Mitarbeitern, insbesondere Prof. Dr. Gerhard Stilz (Universität Tübingen), Dr. D. Wolcke (Stadt- und Universitätsbibliothek Frankfurt) sowie Brigitte Rathert, Martina Rassmann und Frank Schulze (Institut für England- und Amerikastudien, Universität Frankfurt). Für die freundliche Überlassung der Druckrechte danke ich dem August Bagel Verlag (Einleitung), Ibadan University Press (Text 4), Eugen Diederichs Verlag (5), Heinemann Educational Books (7, 8, 25, 26–28, 33, 37–39, 47), Nwamife Publishers (9), Centre for Black and African Arts and Civilization (11), Edinburgh University Press (15), East African Publishing House (16), Church Missionary Society (17), Oxford University Press (18), Royal African Society (19), Panaf (20), Allen und Unwin (22), Frank Cass (23), Présence Africaine (24), Longman (34), Kenya Literature Bureau (40, 42), University of Ife Press (41), Onibonoje Press and Book Industries (43), Crowell (45) sowie Almqvist and Wiksell (46). Für den Abdruck von Zeitschriftenaufsätzen danke ich den Verfassern. Das Abdrucksrecht für zwei Aufsätze Wole Soyinkas wurde vom Autor leider nicht gewährt.

The texts assembled here are grouped under six headings although quite a few cannot easily be classified since they touch upon several aspects and thus could be placed under different headings. In spite of these obvious difficulties I have tried to structurize each chapter logically and coherently.

To begin with, *chapter one* deals with problems of origin and definition including various attempts at a proper and adequate nomenclature. Since the time critics have started tackling this problem, i.e. the 1950s, two approaches have characterized their endeavours, an aesthetically-oriented and an historically-oriented method. Texts 1, 3, 5 and 11 clearly belong to the former in focussing on the thematic concerns of African literature in English (text 1), in defining their Africanness by looking at characterization (text 3), style (text 5) or a specific interdependence of content and form (text 11). Text 4 though dealing with several of these aspects advocates a redefinition of "English literature": the term should, in future, be applicable to any creative work in the English language irrespective of its ethnical, geographical or national origin as long as it deserves being called "good" literature.

Choosing an historical – or socio-literary – method, quite a number of critics have attempted to define African literature in English by examining historical factors which influenced or shaped its emergence and development. First and foremost, the relationship between the oral tradition and the newly emerging written literature has been probed into (texts 2, 6, 7 and 8). Besides, critics have looked at historical, cultural, political and social factors in general (texts 6 and 7). – Finally, specific aspects were scrutinized by researchers to explain characteristic features of African literature. Thus text 8 discusses stylistic features of discursive writing in Africa which preceded creative literature in the 19th and early 20th century. Text 9 examines popular and mass literature in Nigeria which formed one of the foundation stones of intellectually more exacting literature. Text 10 probes into the influences school and university magazines had on the young African elite from which the majority of writers sprang in the late 1950s and early 1960s.

Chapter two outlines British educational policy from the early 19th century to independence and African reaction to missionaries, educators and administrators during this period. British educational ideas rested on the belief that a superior race was morally bound to lift up their inferior brethren by Christianizing (text 12) and generally civilizing them (texts 13, 16 and 17). Their attempts gave rise to Africans suspecting their motives (text 14), advocating their own ideals (text 15) or straightforwardly repudiating British arrogance (text 19). – Though seemingly more enlightened white pedagogues and educators were careful in their arguments (texts 16, 17 and 18), Nkrumah's cool analysis of the conditions prevailing in Africa at the time of independence (text 20) proves the deplorable neglect of educational programmes and suggestions put forward by well-meaning reformers. – Analysing post-independence developments, texts 21 and 22 express harsh criticism of the new African elite who obviously continued to widen the gulf between the ruling minority and the majority of the people by refusing to implement their own cultural, educational and/or language policies as had been promised at the time of independence.

The relationship between African literature and the struggle for independence as illustrated by the texts in *chapter three* was, for a long time, confined to African intellectuals expressing their views discursively and in an abstract manner rather than against the background of works of creative literature, since the latter did not really emerge before the 1950s (text 23). However, since its publication, one of the earliest documents (text 24) has hardly been surpassed for its programmatic character, succinctness of arguments and analytical precision. A few of its main ideas and concepts were taken up and discussed in detail, e. g. the importance of Africa's cultural revival in her struggle for independence (text 25), the need to relate the cultural and political development (text 27), or to develop a concept of national identity – or an equivalent notion – through literature (text 28). – Finally, the depressing experiences of post-independent Africa, in particular the Nigerian civil war in the late 1960s, forced writers and intellectuals anew to define their own duties and the function of literature (text 26).

One of the most important issues ever since the emergence of African literature in English has been the use of a foreign language as the medium of creative expression – a topic often discussed impassionedly as some of the texts in *chapter four* demonstrate. They represent both views, those urging the adoption, or the rejection of English. The latter position is held by a minority who argues that choosing a foreign language will be detrimental for the development of African literature (text 29) and/or impede the growth of a national language as well as a national consciousness (text 35). Text 36 turns our attention towards the alienating effects foreign-language literatures of Africa have on its elite and, consequently, on the widening of the gulf between the elite and the masses. – The majority of writers, however, defend their choice of English although they warn of pitfalls (texts 31, 32 and 34). Besides, there are no good reasons to reject English as long as it cannot easily be substituted by African languages as media of communication (text 30). – An extreme position, though one often championed, is illustrated by text 33 which looks at the complex linguistic, ethnic and political situation in Nigeria from a purely pragmatic point of view.

The literary scene as regards English-language literature in West- and East Africa is discussed from different perspectives in *chapter five*. Some of the leading writers express their role in society (texts 37 and 39), while an historian critically assesses the achievement of African literature in English and blames many authors for lacking "historical sense" (text 40). – Reception and distribution problems of an elite literature are being dealt with in texts 41, 42 and 43. Attention is being paid to different factors influencing book-reading habits in West Africa (text 41), the extremely important role played by publishers in shaping the literary scene (text 42), and the need for building up an indigenous publishing and distribution network to check against European publishing policies (text 43). Text 38 occupies a special place in this chapter because the claims it makes on giving African literature its due credit at the university have been put into practice meanwhile.

The *last chapter* outlines the development of the reception of African literature in English. Texts 44 and 45 represent extreme positions in that they argue one-sidedly in favour of a purely Eurocentric approach to the manifold problems (text 44), and of an Afrocentric approach which rejects any critical interference of European critics (text 45). While both of them could be called ideological in outlook the following texts are more realistic and pragmatic. Text 46 holds the opinion that African literature in English should extend its treatment of themes and overcome its local and regional limitation. Text 47 and 48 focus on problems of reception and discuss methodological implications. Both agree that critics, especially those from outside Africa, need as their starting point a sound knowledge of the African background with which to temper their aesthetic considerations. – The last two texts attempt to place the achievement of African literature in English into an international context. While text 49, in conclusion, doubts whether African writers have been in a position to genuinely reflect and express creatively the predicaments of modern Africa since they belong to the minority of the elite, text 50 is more optimistic in outlook stressing the achievements of African literature and pointing out the positive factors of its reception.

TEXTE UND DOKUMENTE

A. Englische Sprache und Literatur im geschichtlichen Rückblick

1. Probleme der Entstehung und Abgrenzung: „afrikanische", „neo-afrikanische" und „afro-europäische" Literatur

1. DAVIDSON NICOL, *The Soft Pink Palms: On British West African Writers – an Essay* (1956)

Aus: *Présence Africaine: Special Issue: The 1st International Conference of Negro Writers and Artists 19th – 22nd September 1956,* 8–10 (1956), 107–121. – D. Nicol (geb. 1924) nahm in seiner Eigenschaft als Rektor der Universität von Sierra Leone an der Konferenz in Paris 1956 teil. Er zählt zur ersten Schriftstellergeneration Westafrikas und veröffentlichte neben Gedichten und Kurzgeschichten Essays zur Kultur und Literatur. Der vorliegende Textauszug beschließt den frühesten Überblick über die englischsprachige Literatur Westafrikas und stellt bereits zwei wichtige Merkmale heraus, die die folgende Entwicklung kennzeichnen sollten: eine eher nuancierte als radikale Auseinandersetzung mit der Rassenfrage und die intellektuelle Autorschaft der neu entstehenden Literatur.

This survey is meant not only to outline the trends which modern writing in English from West Africa is taking, but chiefly to give representative figures of the past and present in this field. It is doubtful whether any account of this sort will be written or published soon except under African patronage as in this Congress. This is because the appeal and to be courageous, the standards of West African writing, especially of the creative sort, are as yet limited. There may be several reasons for this. An obvious one, which may escape the notice of West Africans, is that they learn English relatively late, and do not use it frequently and familiarly as the Coloured South African, the West Indian, the American Negro, and for that matter the Sierra Leone Creole do. These coloured writers may speak a dialect form of English but its construction approximates to English more than an indigenous language. West Africans can sidetrack this difficulty neatly by not writing proper English at all, as Tutuola has triumphantly done. But the language difficulty need not weigh too heavily, remembering Joseph Conrad the Pole, Mulk Raj Anand[1] the Indian, Lin Yu Tang[2] the Chinese, who all wrote in English, not as an English writer would, but in a way which is exotic although pure, and which is liked and admired by all who use or read English.

Another reason is that in West African writing there is a lack of the motive power of burning racial injustice which carries through in the writing of other peoples of African descent. This driving force will be noticed in most of the literature by modern Negro writers. The nineteenth century attitude of easy social inter-racial mixing and the current British post-war colonial policy of rapid advance towards self-government has outstripped extreme nationalism, Communism, and racial bitterness in British West Africa. The distressing but stimulating convenience of a setting of Afro-European conflict is thus fortunately or unfortunately denied them. They have to seek other verities and tensions. Like Tutuola again (he has unconsciously conquered all the dilemmas of the West African writer), they may transfer their setting to the spirit world. Like the English writer, Galsworthy, they may write of the new society, the new leaders; like Flaubert, they may write of the frustrated individual trying to break through to a wider life. After all, that is what Ekwensi and Iyatemi[3] are respectively trying to write.

Over the past twenty years and more, the author of this paper has tried at his leisure, but with urgency to read everything written in English by West Africans and about West Africans. Of the latter he has written briefly ("On Not being a West African" – Ibadan University College Press). Of the former he now writes. It is like trying to catch an accelerating train. It is to be hoped that the sheer amateurishness and lack of depth and skill displayed in these two reviews will inspire or goad someone, coloured in skin, or understanding at heart, to undertake these tasks with the professional thoroughness they deserve.

At the end now, it is permissible to explain the beginning. Nearly all West African writers are intellectuals, not manual workers; and so their palms are soft. This characteristic and the colour of these palms are two of the things they share with most writers of every nation and race. (120–121)

2. WILFRIED HOWELL WHITELEY, *The Concept of an African Prose Literature* (1962)

Aus: *Diogenes*, 37 (1962), 28–49. – Der Linguist W. H. Whiteley (1924–1972) studierte an der London School of Economics und lehrte afrikanische Sprachen in Tanzania, Uganda, England und den USA. Unter seinen zahlreichen Veröffentlichungen nimmt *Swahili: the Rise of a National Language* (London, 1969) einen zentralen Platz ein. Der vorliegende Text geht den Faktoren nach, die zur Verschriftlichung der Literatur in Afrika führten und damit das Verhältnis von „reciter" und Publikum grundlegend veränderten.

An immediate and profound result of missionary endeavour for African society was the introduction of a western-type education: earlier in the south and west of the continent than in the east and centers. Oral traditions could now be written down by Africans and thus acquire permanent form with specific authorship.[4] New forms could be created from traditional patterns, but it would be realized that one wrote for a different audience: the written word can be enjoyed in solitude and in silence. The mere writing down of what could be listened to with enjoyment cannot – as we have seen already – lead to enjoyable reading unless adaptation is made to the requirements of the written word. One cannot, for example, expect the reader to be familiar with the outline of the story, as before, and the form of the "short story", "novel" or "play" does not lend itself to the kind of discursive treatment characteristic of many folk tales. The written word, moreover, depends for its production in book form upon economic factors relating to the number of readers anticipated, and the price they are willing to pay, together with educational and religious factors relating to its fitness for publication.[5]

As an oral literature differs in its attributes from those of a written literature, so does the status of the reciter differ from that of a writer. Except in areas where there were semi-professional reciters, such as the "griots" in parts of West Africa, the reciter was likely to be a local person, practising an art with which all were familiar before a highly critical audience. The writer, on the other hand, belonged to an *élite;* with his art, the majority of his elders would certainly be quite unfamiliar, and he would have little contact with his readers. If the reciter tended to look to members of an older generation for his standards of excellence, the writer had to work out for himself a written style in his own language or submit to world standards if he chose to write in a metropolitan language. Whatever the writer might think about the desirability of writing down his oral literature, the rapid expansion of education created an immediate demand for textbooks of all kinds and the first, indeed the only reading public for early writers was the school population and the church congregation. It was natural, therefore, that much traditional lore should find its way – suitably expurgated – into school books of one kind or another. These were supplemented by what might be termed "romances", some with a historical setting, others with a biographical basis, both often strongly moral in tone. With the expansion of literacy, newspapers and periodicals were quickly established and they have remained for the great majority of literate Africans, the most regular and accessible form of secular "literature", though the level of journalism only exceptionally rose to a literary level. Finally, in recent times there have begun to appear short stories, novels, plays and essays, at differing levels of sophistication and addressed to different reading publics.

The question of a reading public is a crucial one: it has been suggested that "... it is the people who can afford to buy books who really determine what shall be written and how it shall be written ..." *but* this would seem to be true only under certain conditions; where, for example, there exists, already, a reading population who exercise a choice with regard to what they read. It seems probable that in Africa it was educational policy which determined what books should be read, and the circumscribed goal of education which has determined what books people have bought. Where African languages were used in education, and where the majority of the literate population was literate only in these languages – that is to say over the greater part of the regions administered by the British, and including South Africa – a great deal of effort was spent in producing books in such languages, as can be seen from the productions of the Mission Presses in South Africa, the S.P.C.K.[6] in England, and, in recent years, the Literature and Publications Bureaux in East and Central Africa. The great bulk of African writing from these areas has, consequently, been in local languages, and directed towards educational or religious ends. Several factors, however, combine to make African languages unpopular for the younger generation of African writers. Firstly, only among the largest groups can one hope to command a reasonable reading public, and for this reason alone, writers from the smaller groups must write either in a *lingua franca* or a European language if they are to achieve publication. Secondly, the use of African languages is generally restricted to the lower levels of education and this encourages the view that they have no part to play beyond this level. Thirdly, the use of English at the higher levels of education with its aura of prestige and sophistication, together with its offer of a vast potential reading public, all contribute to its popularity for the aspiring prose writer. The body of African writing in English is, as yet, too small to make any really useful observations but one does notice tendencies towards a documentary rather than an imaginative treatment of events, and an interest in the impact of situation rather than in the individual personality. (39–41)

. . .

It is interesting to recall that perhaps the first prose work to be written in English by an African was written in England for an English reading public, and provided substance for the early campaigns against slavery: *The Interesting Narrative of the Life of Olaudah Equiano, or Gustavus Vassa the African* was published in 1789 in London, and proved so popular that it ran into several editions during the next few years. Equiano's recollections of life in West Africa in the middle of the eighteenth century are interesting but fragmentary and one has to wait for more than a century for the picture to be filled in by C. Reindorf in his *The History of the Gold Coast and Asante* (1911?). Reindorf makes extensive use of oral traditions in his history, and if his techniques of analysis leave something to be desired by modern standards, the richness of these traditions is never in doubt. Indirect evidence for another aspect of the oral tradition, that of oratory, is provided by the speeches of the early politicians, and those of J. E. Casely-Heyford (*West African Leadership,* Ed. Magnus Sampson, Stockwell, 1951) recall the skill of the Ashanti "linguists" which he had himself elsewhere described.

Fiction, however, developed slowly during the early years of the present century, first in the local language and then, during the last fifteen years, in English. Virtually all of this has come from Southern Nigeria: first, D. O. Fagunwa and A. Tutuola, then writers like C. O. D. Ekwensi and C. Achebe.[7] When Amos Tutuola's first book, *The Palm-Wine Drinkard* appeared in 1952, it was immediately hailed both for its content and its style; "the first work of literature to be written in English by a West African and published in London" averred one critic, whilst a fellow African writer referred to it as ". . . an exciting story told with characteristic brevity . . . an anthropological study." The content of Tutuola's work is clearly derivative from Yoruba tradition, with a liberal sprinkling of modern concepts to bring it up to date. His style – described by one writer as "loose talking-prose" – is a curious mixture of spontaneity and contrivance; the language is simple but disjointed; the choice of words vivid but careless. There is often the feeling that the language is being distorted to match the events described, and as a literary device, this does not always succeed. By contrast, his fellow Yoruba, D. O. Fagunwa has chosen to cast his traditional material wholly in Yoruba, and while this makes for inaccessibility to English readers he appears to command a considerable following in Nigeria. Both Cyprian Ekwensi and Chinua Achebe are concerned with change, and with the situations that change produces, rather than with the development of individual characters: both Okonkwo in Achebe's first novel, and Jagua in Ekwensi's latest novel are victims, and typical victims, of circumstances. This doesn't make the works any less interesting but it does give them a flavour which is possibly peculiarly African. It is worth noting that while Tutuola, Ekwensi and Achebe have primarily been writing for a non-African reading public, there are signs that some of their contemporaries are finding a local market for fiction written in English. (43–45)

...

East and Central Africa represent *par excellence* the area of the vernacular: there has, up till now, been virtually no writing at all in English. For economic reasons most of the books are short – rarely more than 75 pages – and, in East Africa in particular, there is a high proportion of translations and adaptations of folk-material. The establishment of Literature and Publications Bureaux in Nairobi and Lusaka after 1945 gave an impetus to the production of books in many local languages and several authors owe their introduction to print to these sources. To Lusaka belongs the credit of having sponsored at least one novelist of distinction, Stephen Mpashi, who has managed to combine some of the characteristics of oral Bemba with the subject matter of twentieth-century life in Northern Rhodesia. From Nairobi, in recent months, has come the first Swahili detective story to swell the small body of reading material for an adult reading public. (46–47)

...

At the present time both oral and written traditions exist side by side, with the amount written in African languages varying from country to country according to a wide range of circumstances. It seems certain that the written word will gradually supersede the oral tradition, but for many years this latter will probably continue to flourish in many parts of Africa. At this stage it is important that literary interest – and academic interest, too – should be focussed on this oral tradition, so that, with the refined techniques now available, some assessment of its status as literature may now be made. Whether it is desirable or profitable to estimate how much modern African writing is, or can be, derivative in structure and content from African or European traditions I shall not here consider. What is certain, is that no such attempt can be made without a proper awareness of the literary status of the oral tradition and of the contribution of the individual artist to the prose tradition as a whole. (49)

3. CYPRIAN EKWENSI, *African Literature* (1964)

Aus: *Nigeria Magazine*, 83 (1964), 294–299.– Cyprian Ekwensi (geb. 1921) ist einer der produktivsten Schriftsteller Afrikas. Er studierte Pharmazie und nahm anschließend verschiedene Tätigkeiten im öffentlichen Dienst wahr. 1947 veröffentlichte er *When Love Whispers*, eines der ersten Beispiele der Onitsha Pamphlet Literatur. *People of the City* (1954) ist der erste nigerianische Roman in englischer Sprache. In regelmäßigen Beiträgen für die Zeitschrift *Nigeria Magazine* besprach Ekwensi Neuerscheinungen und äußerte sich zur Abgrenzung der afrikanischen Literatur. Im folgenden Textauszug stellt er die Begriffe „African character and psychology" in den Mittelpunkt.

What then is African Literature? For it seems to me that we shall be talking at cross purposes if this definition is not made clear from the start. Willie Abrahams, the Ghanaian philosopher and author of *The Mind of Africa* defines African literature as 'not necessarily literature written in an African language nor indeed literature written necessarily by an African; though only Africans can do it with justice and success." Richard Rive[8] described as "the most virile of the non-white writers of South Africa" claims that African literature is literature produced by Africans "regardless of colour, language or distinction", which deals with situations and experiences happening on the continent. At a recent conference on African Literature held at Fourah Bay College in Sierra Leone, African Literature was defined as any work "whose African content is treated with authenticity and whose experiences undergone in Africa are reported in their entirety".

I do not agree with the stress which has been laid on experiences confined to the African continent, especially in these modern times when the most travelled man in the world is the educated African. My own definition of African Literature is literature based on African character and psychology. This means that the main theme may be anthropological, traditional or modern, but the traits, temperaments and reactions of the characters will be peculiarly African due to influences of tribe, culture and history. Thus the presence in the United Nations of an African does not make literature based on him non-African because it is set on foreign soil. The African's position has been entirely conditioned by a long chain of events traceable even to the folk tale under the village palms or the political meeting held in the market place.

African writing is writing based on the living heritage of the African people. It reflects African history as a background to today's events and tomorrow's crises. It is a critique of present-day society and a projection into the future. (294–295)

4. T. R. M. CREIGHTON, *An Attempt to Define African Literature* (1965)

Aus: Gerald Moore (ed.), *African Literature and the Universities* (Ibadan, 1965), 84–88. – Der folgende Textauszug stellt die Zusammenfassung einer Diskussion dar, die während der „Freetown Conference on African Literature and the University Curriculum" vom 3.–8. April 1963 zwischen afrikanischen und europäischen Literaturkritikern,

Pädagogen und Autoren stattfand. Die hier erarbeitete Definition der afrikanischen Literatur diente in den folgenden Jahren immer wieder als Ausgangspunkt literaturtheoretischer Bemühungen um eine Abgrenzung des Gegenstandes.

Whether this conference will consider it its duty to provide a general definition of what we mean by African literature, I do not know. I think it will probably be useful if we think about this. And in order to start the ball rolling, I would like to quote a possible definition. I proposed this formulation to the literature section of the Congress of Africanists in Accra before Christmas, and it was in fact accepted by that Congress – I don't know whether this has very much meaning, because the Congress was very large and was mainly concerned with questions other than literature. It did, however, adopt a resolution urging all universities in Africa to encourage the reading and study of African literature in African universities, and indeed in universities all over the world. It accepted a definition of African literature as "any work in which an African setting is authentically handled, or to which experiences which originate in Africa are integral."

It is probably no clearer than any other definition made inexpertly on the spur of the moment. But supposing that you want to include, should we say, both *Heart of Darkness* and Wole Soyinka's poems about being an African in London; well, somebody might say on the one hand, *Heart of Darkness* is written by a white man and therefore isn't African, and somebody else might say that Wole Soyinka's poems are written about London and therefore they are not African. I myself would regard these as irrelevant criticisms, but the definition was phrased in order to include works as far apart as that, and to exclude *The Heart of the Matter*[9], for instance, or shall we say the works of Robert Ruark or quite a number of other people who use Africa as a background which is not always authentically handled. *The Heart of the Matter* might as well have taken place in Singapore or in Tooting as in Freetown. This is the reason for this rather clumsy formulation.

Discussion

NWOGA:[10] It has been suggested that what we call African writing is really primarily English or French or Portuguese or Italian or Spanish literature, and only secondarily African. It is possible that I am splitting hairs, but I disapprove of this suggestion. I would prefer to consider that what we call African literature is *primarily African* and *secondarily English* or *French* etc. It has also been said that writing in any of the indigenous languages of Africa is unequivocally African. This would appear to imply that if you wrote a novel, say, in Ijaw, it would be unequivocally primarily African literature, and if you wrote this same novel, or translated it, into English, it would then become primarily English literature, and secondarily African. I think the emphasis on the language used is misplaced.

MPHAHLELE: You in fact feel that African writing is African writing whether it is written in a vernacular language, or in English?

NWOGA: Yes, but coming nearer to the definition, there are two elements pointed out which should, if they are present, give us the confidence to speak of African literature, elements of, let us call it, nationality and experience. If an African writes about an African situation, that is clearly African literature. If he goes to France for five years, and writes of his experience in France, then he is still writing African literature. And on the other hand, I would want to leave out Joyce Cary's novels,[11] which are very good in their setting of Africa, but I would still prefer to call it English literature in an African setting, just as Wole Soyinka's poems based on his experience in London are African literature in an English setting.

MPHAHLELE: You would like Africans to refer to the man who writes it rather than to what is written?

NWOGA: Yes.

MPHAHLELE: I see. Yes, I never thought of that angle. It is quite interesting.

CREIGHTON: Could I just ask, would you say the writer of African literature must be black?

NWOGA: No, Joyce Cary is English. The man himself is the important thing.

CREIGHTON: What non-black writer would you accept as an African writer?

NWOGA: The native South Africa white.

CREIGHTON: So it is birth that counts?

MOORE: Surely, we should start from the point of view that all this is English literature. This is in fact one of the things which we are trying to sell to the universities – English literature is not just what is written in England by Englishmen, English has become a world language, a native language for millions of other people who are also writing. So shouldn't we start without any barriers at all, and start with the proposition that this is English literature? If we have got to put barriers around one section of it, for the purposes of getting it into the university curriculum, we should regard these barriers as purely expedient and not significant in themselves. They are an expedient device for extending the boundaries of English literature. West Indian writing is equally neglected, it is very rich. American writing is neglected in English universities. It is not a problem unique to Africa. The problem is to make people in England realise, and in France for that matter, that their languages are no longer their sole property, because they have almost defeated themselves by their own success in propagating their languages. They have now got to accept, and it is a very glorious fact, that their literature is being enriched and enlarged in other parts of the world.

AKAR: I think I pointed out that African literature is first and foremost literature, with curious historical experiences. We should not limit it to black or white Africans. I think it should fall under the discipline of English literature in universities, it should be taught as English literature, as such, but with its peculiar African background.

RAVENSCROFT:[12] The pigeon-hole, as it were, into which African literature should be placed in the teaching in universities, will inevitably be the English Department. This is, in fact the point that Dr. Moore[13] has made – that it is a practical consideration, it is one way of getting it into the curriculum.

DUNN: We are talking as if we contemplate some difficulty in getting it into the syllabus. Surely, this is not the case? I am confronted with the problem – I have this book by Doris Lessing.[14] I have a course on recent English literature, and I have as from next year a special paper on African writing: into which category do I put it? I think that every book has to be approached differently.

STUART: Well, does it matter? Whether one puts it in one paper or another?

DUNN: I merely raised this because Doris Lessing has been specifically quoted as an example of an African writer. But here is a book that I myself would not consider putting in a course of African writing.

CREIGHTON: Of course, this raises the question of whether one wants in one's syllabuses and courses to isolate African writing, or to take Gerald Moore's point, to consider it all part of English literature.

MPHAHLELE: I think we are complicating matters if we specify African literature and make it a special paper. What we are actually trying to do in this conference, is to try to correct an outmoded attitude, an old-fashioned attitude, which was that students must be taught literature written by Englishmen.

CREIGHTON: Preferably dead Englishmen.

MPHAHLELE: Yes, preferably dead. That is what we are trying to correct, to bring African literature into the syllabus. But this is only part of it, as Gerald Moore says. There are other literatures written in English, West Indian literature, for instance, and Indian literature written by Indians is just as valid. But we should bring this into the syllabus not as this literature or that, but as literature within the English syllabus. I insist that we don't want to have a special paper on African literature. I think that English should here be considered not a nationality.

MOORE: I think we seem to be in danger of setting up boundaries in our discussions. If you draw a boundary in this way, inevitably, every novel which is written in Africa achieves a false importance. But if you bring African literature into the picture by extension of the boundaries of English literature, by recognition that worthwhile things are being written in English in Africa, and in the West Indies, you make a much more discriminating extension. I don't think that literature need be arranged in a catalogue for anybody who has read it. Anybody who has read Achebe and Ekwensi doesn't have them in his mind as a catalogue. One should be aware that one is a good writer and the other isn't.

JONES: Because our students start by reading a literature that arises out of a completely different environment, English literature becomes something detached, something not connected with life. And the connection between literature and life is writing. This is really why we are talking about Africa. And I may go on to another point – and this might offend some of our scholars here,

I hope it does – we must remember that we are dealing with a young literature which in a way has got to be nursed. Now, when we talk about English literature, we are talking about a live body of work which is established, over which critical minds have played for centuries, and we can talk about good and bad novels, and that sort of thing, and we can vary the number of authors without very much loss. Now, when you say that every novel that is written in Africa has a false importance, I disagree, because it is of very great importance, not a false importance at all. Anything that is written and published has got great importance, because out of all this ferment of ideas you are going to get your good literature, and I think we have to be very tolerant without lowering our critical standards. To start categorising things too soon – this is good and this is bad, this must be taught, this must not be taught – is very wrong indeed.

MOORE: I am a bit worried about Dr. Jones's point. I would like to come back to it. I don't see how you can suppress your judgement when you read. When you read, you read with all your senses and your intelligence alive, and you are not only experiencing, you are judging. And when you have finished reading a book, you decide whether it is good, not bad, or whether it is lousy. And I think that this is the only thing that matters. If you then say it is lousy, but it is written by an African, therefore it has a great sociological force or a great political force, then you are transferring the whole operation into the field of sociology or politics. I think that what we are concerned with here is the field of literature. If you are going to be an African writer in the field of literature, then the importance must be inherent in the value of the work and not in anything else, not in the colour of the chap who wrote it or anything like that. I don't think that good criticism is inhibiting to good writers and I think that they are entitled to it. I think that people who are good writers are entitled to be singled out and praised specifically for what is good in their work. You can't do that without implying that you are not impressed by the bad writers.

KARIUKI:[15] I agree completely with what Mr. Moore has said. But surely our aim should be to encourage *more* African writing? And I think that what has happened in the past, at any rate in some parts of Africa, has been that African writing, whether good or bad, has not been available. I mean, the students themselves, at any rate in my time at college, hardly ever thought of writing anything, because they had never heard any literature either written by Africans or written about Africa discussed in their classes, and so on. So that they couldn't identify themselves with the possibility of writing. Wherever you want students to be as critical as possible, to be able to judge good literature, you want them to think that they too could write; and by making the literature available in the universities from all parts of Africa and from all sources to do with Africa, you make it possible for a student to say, "Well, I can do it too." I think this has been missing in some parts of Africa, that is, the availability of the kind of literature that we are discussing today.

JONES: I must say something in my own defence; I did not say that every novel written in Africa was good. I said that every novel was important in our present state. I am going to use my opportunity later in this Seminar to give a critical analysis, this is my job. I think we ought to subject everything to critical analysis. But critical analysis cannot be rigid. Somebody said that we should have to use rigid tools; you can't have a rigid kind of analysis. You have got to demonstrate in critical analysis what is good and what is bad. And I think our emphasis should be to show why a novel is good, why it is bad, show what is good in every novel, because I think we are dealing with writers of promise rather than of experience, and if you only want to talk about the good literature of Africa as produced now, it wouldn't take more than a couple of hours. But we are in a critical position – we are dealing with a literature which is just beginning to grow, and I think, unlike other people, that it is possible to kill initiative by unsympathetic criticism. This is all I am saying. Probably my position will be a little clearer when I have presented my paper.

5. JANHEINZ JAHN, *The Literature of Africa* (1968)

Aus: *A History of Neo-African Literature: Writing in Two Continents* (London, 1968), 21–24. – J. Jahn (1918–1973) beschäftigte sich seit 1952 mit afrikanischer Kultur und Literatur. *Muntu: Umrisse der neoafrikanischen Kultur* (Düsseldorf, 1958) folgte mit *Geschichte der neoafrikanischen Literatur: Eine Einführung* (Düsseldorf, 1966) die erste umfassende Darstellung, die von den Anfängen bis in die frühen sechziger Jahre reicht. Jahn lehnte eine definitorische Erfassung aufgrund von rassischen, sprachlichen oder geographischen Gesichtspunkten ab. Zentrale Kategorie stellt für ihn der Stil bzw. die stilistische Haltung literarischer Werke dar, um das Wesen einer neoafrikanischen Literatur bestimmen zu können.

Africa's traditional literature is oral. But since Africans began coming into contact with Arabic and Western cultures, they have produced written literary works; at first only a few did so, but afterwards a great many. Former slaves who somehow ended up in Europe or America were writing in European languages as early as the sixteenth and eighteenth centuries. With the establishment of mission schools in Africa, written literary works have been produced there too, in both European and African languages, since the beginning of this century (for figures see Appendix).

As I said above, literature today can no longer be classified by language, since European languages and Arabic have spread beyond their traditional areas. But literatures cannot be classified geographically either, for geography does not provide literary categories. An African literature which, geographically speaking, would include in one group North Africa, sub-Saharan Africa and the Boers of South Africa, would be bringing together more contrasts than similarities, and would ignore the close relations between Africa and the Caribbean, between North Africa and the Near East. Such a classification pays no regard to culture, history or style, and so has nothing to do with literature.

Nor, finally, can literature be classified by the authors' complexions or birth-places, which are also categories outside literature. For years I have been fighting against phrases like 'Negro literature', *'littérature noire'*, *'littérature des noirs*'; for those who use such terms are expressing a conviction, perhaps unconsciously, that the colour of an author's skin is enough to decide the literary family he belongs to. This would mean that the works of a black-skinned author, who happened to be born in Portugal, who grew up in a purely Portuguese environment, lived there most of his life and wrote Portuguese plays – must belong not to Portuguese but to something called 'Negro' literature. In the works of Alfonso Álvares[16], however, there is nothing to suggest a style or pattern of literary expression different from the Portuguese styles and patterns of his age. Without the quarrel with Chiado nobody would know he came from Africa, nor would anyone think of connecting him with anything but Portuguese literature. He may or may not be the first Negro author in Europe; for the literary works he produced it made no difference.

Literatures can only be classified by style and by attitudes revealed; more precisely, by studying the individual works, analysing their styles and attitudes and grouping them accordingly, then fitting them into a tradition of similar styles and attitudes. You cannot hope to place literary works in their right 'families' without investigating these features; nor, without analysing a particular work, can you find out which literature it belongs to.

Africa's written literature originated in the 'overlap' area of three cultures, the African, the Islamic-Arabic and the Western. The literature from the area where the African and Islamic cultures overlap, I shall call Afro-Arab; the literature from the area where the African and Western cultures overlap, I shall call neo-African.

Neo-African literature, then, is the heir of two traditions: traditional African literature and Western literature. A work which shows no European influences, including not being written down, belongs to traditional African literature, not neo-African. The boundary between the two is easy to draw: it is the boundary between oral and written literature. Conversely, a work which reveals no African stylistic features or patterns of expression belongs to Western, not neo-African literature, even if written by an African. Although theoretically simple, the distinction is hard to make in practice, for it assumes that the styles, patterns of expression and attitudes produced by Africa's traditions are well known. But they are not – for scholars have neglected this field (see Chapter 4).

In my book *Muntu* I sketched some of the stylistic features, patterns and attitudes which spring to the eye in the poetry of 'Négritude'. African authors and poets, for instance, use magical, incantational images, pay more attention to rhythmic than to dramatic structure, and 'speak in imperatives' (see Chapter 15). Some critics have imagined that I regarded such points as the only African stylistic features, etc. that there were, and made them the sole and indispensable criteria for including a work in neo-African literature – as if I were setting myself up as a literary high priest or commissar, who insisted on a particular style from Africa's writers and would excommunicate them from neo-African literature should they be guilty of heretical or 'deviationist' work.

But a writer must always be free to write as his inspiration bids him. Historians of literature cannot hold him to a set of rules, and no one should expect them to do this. They will naturally analyse afterwards the style that authors have used, and describe those writers' work accordingly. In 1957, when I was writing *Muntu,* the Negritude school dominated modern neo-African literature, and those criteria applied to that school. Critics today who accuse me of generalizing, can refer to other works, especially those of the Nigerian school, some of which contain different attitudes and stylistic features; but in 1957 none of those works had appeared. When considering a living literature like the neo-African, historians of literature must expect to be deepening and widening their observations all the time.

They must find out the ingredients of the 'Africanism' which prompts us, when referring to most of Africa's modern works, to talk not of English, French or Portuguese literature in Africa, but of African literature in English, French or Portuguese. So we have to investigate which ideas and stylistic features come from particular African traditions, and which do not. We must examine the work, say, of a Yoruba author writing in English, not only for the modern ideas it contains and the influences of English models, but also for the stylistic features and patterns of expression which come from oral Yoruba literature in the Yoruba language.

It will not do, for instance, to consider Tutuola's *The Palm-Wine Drinkard* as merely a fantastic tale, and trace back its symbolism to psychological and mythological archetypes, through parallels with Dante, Gilgamesh, Orpheus, Yggdrasill, etc. (Moore),[17] which the author himself had certainly not had in mind. Tutuola's source, everyone agrees, is the oral Yoruba tradition, and he is closer to it than the author Fagunwa, who wrote in the Yoruba language and influenced him. So Tutuola's symbolism must be examined also in the light of the Yoruba tradition.

But oral literature has not yet been subjected to literary analysis, which makes such investigations much more difficult. Still, we do not need to ask about *all* the 'bush spirits' and their meaning, but only such a question as: in what connection does Tutuola's bush spirit 'Red Lady' appear in traditional poetry, and what function does it have there? And if we find a particular rhythm, we must ask: does this rhythm occur in the tradition, and what function does it have there? So we do not need to know the whole rhythmic system of oral poetry, desirable as that might be. This method, however, may well be the first step towards understanding the literary forms of the oral tradition.

With an African writer writing in a European language, it would be superficial to assign him to Western literature simply because his works show no 'Africanisms' which can be recognized as such at first sight. To decide where writers should be placed, the investigations referred to above are indispensable – I would gladly have undertaken them myself, but have not had the means at my disposal. Until they are completed, many African and Afro-American authors are only 'under suspicion', as it were, of possibly belonging to neo-African literature. So there are many writers mentioned in this book who are under that 'suspicion'.

An introduction to neo-African literature, in fact, is neither a complete history of this literature nor a conclusive study of its styles; a great deal of further research is needed before works of that sort can he carried out. The purpose of the present book is to point out the problems and classify provisionally the material to be analysed: I shall try to classify this material according to its content and some of its recognizable stylistic features and patterns of literary expression.

6. E. N. OBIECHINA, *Transition from Oral to Literary Tradition* (1967)

Aus: *Présence Africaine*, 63 (1967), 140–161. – E. N. Obiechina (geb. 1933) aus Nigeria schloß seine Ausbildung 1966 in Cambridge mit einer Dissertation über den englischsprachigen Roman Westafrikas ab. Er lehrt als Professor an der University of Nigeria in Nsukka. Aus der Fülle seiner literaturwissenschaftlichen Veröffentlichungen ragen Studien über die Massenliteratur und den Roman Westafrikas heraus. Im vorliegenden Textauszug vertritt er die These, daß die Transposition der oralen Tradition in die westafrikanische Schriftliteratur deren charakteristisches Merkmal darstellt, das sie von europäischer Afrikaliteratur unterscheidet.

The most significant difference which is noticeable between the prose fictional works by native West Africans and those by non-West Africans using the West African setting, is the important position which the representation of oral tradition is accorded in the former, and its almost complete absence in the latter. This is a statement of fact rather than a criticism of non-West African writers few, if any, of whom unterstand West African vernaculars. If, for example, we compare Joyce Cary's Nigerian villagers and Chinua Achebe's villagers (any of the novels by both writers will bear this out), we cannot but notice that Cary's peasants speak in straight-forward English prose – with the exception of Mr. Johnson who speaks and writes what Professor Mahood calls a "Babu" type English, Cary's Nigerian peasants speak like Cary himself – whereas Achebe's Nigerian villagers weave into the fabric of their everyday conversations allusions from folk-tales, legends and myths and punctuate their relevant points of view and attitudes by using appropriately chosen proverbs, traditional maxims and cryptic anecdotes. In other words, whereas the identity of Cary's peasants cannot be guessed at from the way they speak, Achebe's villagers speaking style show them very unmistakably as people who are closer to an oral rather than a literary tradition. The other West-African writers also show unmistakable awareness in their writing of the significance of oral tradition as an integral part of the West African culture. Is is by incorporating the oral tradition of West Africa in their writing that they have largely succeeded in giving an air of authenticity to their writing and established a consciousness which is characteristically West African.

Commentators on West African literature have so far accorded scanty recognition to the significance of oral tradition as one of its major impulses. John

1. Probleme der Entstehung und Abgrenzung 47

Ramsaran of the University of Ibadan is quite right when he makes the following complaint: "No aspect of the developing literature of West Africa is so much neglected as the folk-tale which is still a most vigorous form of expression in the cultural life of the people. Perhaps because of its very popularity and age-old association with a largely non-literature society the folk-tale tends to be forgotten or is deliberately by-passed by sophisticated writers and readers who equate modernity with excellence."[18]

The African writers themselves are not at all deceived into the falsity of striking an exclusively modernist pose and ignoring the surviving elements of the old traditional culture which blend into the post-colonial situation. The essential reality of the contemporary West African culture is that within it oral tradition continues to exist side by side with the encroaching literary tradition. It is sufficiently vigorous to be legitimately portrayed by West African writers in the various literary forms which have been developed there. Whether in the tales of Amos Tutuola, in the novels of Achebe, in the plays of Clark and Soyinka or in the poems by Okigbo, we are aware that the writers are drawing elaborately from West African folklore, traditional symbols and images, and traditional turns of speech, to invest their writing with a truly West African sensibility and flavour.

That West African writers attempt to make much of the West African oral tradition in their writing is no mere literary fad of an attempt to "exoticize" the West African literature. The truth is that oral tradition has survived in West Africa in spite of the introduction of Western writing and the tradition which it bears.

There are many real reasons why West African oral tradition should survive despite the changes induced by the introduction of a literary tradition from Europe. First, by far the largest number of West Africans are still illiterate. If we take Nigeria as an example, the literacy rates in the English language according to the 1952–53 census (about the time of the appearance of Tutuola's *The Palm-Wine Drinkard*) were 33.7% for Lagos, 0.9% for Northern Region, 9.5% for Western Region, 10.6% for Eastern Region and 6% for the country as a whole. Each percentage is higher (especially in Northern Nigeria) when we add the number of those who at this time were literate in the vernaculars only. Yet, it must be clear that from a purely statistical point of view, a preponderating part of the West African populations continue to subsist largely within an oral rather than a literary culture and to express a consciousness which is more typical of the oral than of a literary tradition. Second, at least three out of every four West Africans live in traditional village communities or traditional urban settlements which enjoy relative cultural homogeneity, a common historical outlook and a unified linguistic development all of which contribute to the existence of an oral tradition. Thirdly, even those who are increasingly influenced by the literary culture never lose touch with their oral culture. Literate people in urban areas which are centres of the literate cultural influence very often visit their relations in the villages and are thus also exposed to the influence of the oral culture which predominates in the villages and traditional towns. Thus,

Western-educated West Africans are very often familiar with their folklore, have a fairly comprehensive knowledge of the popular proverbs and other traditional speech forms and can speak their vernaculars with reasonable competence. They also share much of the values, attitudes and structures of feeling (to use Raymond Williams' convenient phrase)[19], which are implicit within their oral culture. We shall see, of course, that the effect of the introduced literacy culture is quite considerable both on the individual and on the general culture. What is being suggested here is that in spite of the effects of the indroduced literary cultural elements, oral tradition still remains a most significant part of the contemporary West African culture.

Moreoever, we ought to recognize a fourth factor which has contributed, not insignificantly, to the continued vitality of oral tradition in West Africa, the fact of cultural inertia. Social anthropologists inform us that certain areas of a changing culture always tend to be more resistant to the pressures of change than others. One such area has to do with the value aspect of a culture. In contrast to the material aspect, the value aspect of a culture tends to persist longest even in the face of factors making for change in a given society. A purely oral culture such as the West African culture obviously was before the introduction of the Roman and Arabic scripts, embodies its values and attitudes in its proverbs and fossilized sayings, its beliefs in its myths and religion and its consciousness of its historical life, collective outlook and ethics, in its legends, folk-tales, and other forms of oral literature. All these have been embedded in the consciousness of the West African peoples as cultural groups; the introduction of certain elements of the Western literary culture has merely affected the traditional oral culture but has not destroyed the consciousness deriving from its oral tradition. So long as the relation between the town and the village in West Africa remains complementary and so long as a large number of people live in the villages and those who live in the towns also live in the villages part of the time, so long will oral tradition continue to inform the consciousness and determine the sensibility of the generality of West Africans.

West African writers who attempt to recreate in fiction the West African cultural life (either in its contemporary or historical setting) have judiciously chosen to do so through the oral tradition of West Africa because it best expresses the West African consciousness and sensibility. Even while they are writing in what may be regarded by the superficial observer as an authentic Queen's English for the benefit of the reader, the sensibility they express is purely West African. In other words, the writers are involved in transposing the oral tradition of West Africa into the literary tradition of Europe. The result is something not only new but also exhilarating in its novelty[20].

No people, of course, are known to have lost completely, the oral quality of their culture. This is even so among those with a highly developed literary culture. Goody and Watt have noted in respect of Europe that in spite of the alphabet script, printing and a universal free education all of which make for a highly developed literary culture, the transmission of values and attitudes in face to face contact remains "the primary mode of cultural orientations"[21].

In West Africa, the fact that literary education is even much less developed than in Europe implies that the importance of oral tradition for cultural transmission and orientation is much so than in Europe. West African writers who represent the oral tradition as a major impulse in their writing are therefore merely being true to the cultural reality. We intend to show by using the works of the Nigerian writer, Amos Tutola, that European-oriented writing has become a major instrument for the recording and transmission of the oral stories and other forms of oral tradition in Africa. He represents for us a successful integration of elements of the West African village oral storytelling tradition and those peculiar to the European-introduced literary tradition. (142–146)

7. DAVID RUBADIRI, *The Development of Writing in East Africa* (1971)

Aus: Christopher Heywood (ed.), *Perspectives on African Literature* (London, 1971), 148–156. – D. Rubadiri (geb. 1930) stammt aus Malawi, der ehemaligen Kolonie Nyassaland. Er studierte an der Makerere Universität in Uganda und in Cambridge. 1964–1965 vertrat er sein Land als Botschafter bei den Vereinten Nationen, bevor er nach Uganda ins Exil flüchtete. Seit 1971 lehrt er an der Universität Nairobi Englisch. Neben Gedichten und einem Roman, *No Bride Price* (1967), veröffentlichte er Essays zur afrikanischen Literatur. In dem 1968 an der Universität Ife, Nigeria, gehaltenen Vortrag, dem die folgenden Textauszüge entnommen sind, gab Rubadiri erstmalig einen Überblick über die ostafrikanische Literatur in englischer Sprache. In der Besinnung auf die traditionell dörflichen Werte ostafrikanischer Gesellschaften erblickt Rubadiri einen entscheidenden Unterschied zur westafrikanischen Literatur.

In this paper I hope to pinpoint some of the main ideas about the development of writing in East and Central Africa. I think I would like to begin in a way of comparison. I think one of the greatest impressions that I have had at this conference has been listening to West African authors being discussed seriously, being discussed almost as if they were commonware which we use from day to day, with a lot of sensitivity and with a lot of understanding. This, to us in East Africa, of course, is something which sometimes makes us feel a little irritated because our own kind of literature has not yet reached the point where the criticism and consideration have come in to their own. We hear that James Ngugi is sometimes mistaken for being a West African novelist – because African novelists all seem to come from West Africa!

A major point which has struck me is the importance of the people's culture in its impact on literature which they produce. This seems to me to be the dominant and major factor in West African writing. The fact that the people have lived through an experience which was half colonial, and yet truly traditional, seems to have produced a literature which is their own and which not only deeply concerns the individual, but also draws out from the communal heritage. (A young lady student once made a point to me which I thought was very revealing: she said that when she first read Okot p'Bitek's poem *Song of Lawino*, she thought that it had been written by a West African because she felt she could hear nuances of Yoruba behind it. I will come back to this later.)

Our writing in East Africa, in English, is truly very recent. Very few things have been published, although Swahili poems, stories and proverbs have enjoyed a long spell of publication in books and in newspapers. English seems to have taken a much longer time to receive the attention not only of publishers but even of school and college magazines. The reason for this is, perhaps, that in East Africa the colonial experience had a different impact than it had in West Africa. For us it was an experience which came to envelop everything totally and which almost stifled any indigenous attempt at expressions through the newly-acquired language, for instance, if one passed through a secondary school in East Africa, the best one came out with was an ability to be able to write a composition or a letter in the best basic English and the best grammar that was demanded of one. If you wanted to publish something there were no publishing facilities and in any case if you didn't write something which would please your teacher, it would never see the light of day. So that as the struggle for independence came, people began to get frustrated and instead of writing creatively as we know ist now, they started to write – mainly using newspapers – letters of protest about the government, about the colonial experience itself and so on. Whichever of the poems saw the light of day during that period either saw it in school magazines or were, with luck, published or discussed outside East Africa itself.

After independence, when writing began to catch on with a number of people encouraging young people to begin writing and publishing newspapers, and themselves publishing pamphlets and magazines, one found that the trends of writing were individualistic – they were personal. If anyone sat down to write a poem, he wrote a poem about himself; no one reached back, as in West Africa, towards the traditional, cultural roots and heritages and so on. A boy wrote a poem because his whole literary tradtion had moulded him to try and emulate the only literature that he had come into contact with. So people wrote like Keats and Wordsworth – on roses and sunsets and moonshine, and this sort of subject all on a very personal and individual sort of basis. They received encouragement from expatriate teachers, and even non-expatriate teachers, because this was the only kind of literary tradition with which all the people had been brought up. The oral tradition in fact is only now beginning to be taken seriously and to be examined with some amount of pride. The folklore tales, some of them collected in books, were even twisted to amuse a different child audience; not an African audience, but rather a European child audience. The folk tales from our own oral tradition read slightly strangely when you look at them now.

It was only obout ten years ago that any amount of serious publishing of writing in East Africa began to take place and one can trace it stage by stage. First there were the neo-European and personal poems which came from schools and colleges and the universities. Then later on the tradition of short story writing slowly developed. Again, these were personal, written from a personal point of view. The stories were trying in a rather vague and rather delicate manner to examine the position of the African and his community but hardly ever digging deeply into the people themselves.

About four years ago something new started to happen and I think the impact of this must have been generated by what was now beginning to come in from West African writing. I remember the first impression I had of reading the novel of Cyprian Ekwensi, *People of the City* (the first West African novel I had read) and how very excited I was about it. It was something new. It seemed to have a new kind of vitality. It was talking about us, as it were, of people in the city and their problems. But it was talking about Africans and their conflicts and problems. I didn't care to try and evaluate it. The sheer fact that this novel was there in itself was sufficient to stimulate a number of us to read more of what was coming out from West Africa. Then slowly more scripts and texts began to come in. People who had come and taught and lectured in West Africa came over to East Africa and started talking about people like Tutuola, Achebe, John Pepper Clark and so on, and we suddenly got into this feverish excitement of trying to explore our literary interests into new fields of expression. So there were no more of those compositions about "My Journey Back to School After the Holiday", or the poems about flowers (not that flowers shouldn't have poems written about them), or the poems about love relationships which were almost copied in innuendo and sometimes in words from love relationships which happened in Jane Austen's situations, and so on. This slowly inspired a number of young people to start writing short stories which tried to come to grips with the basic problem of having to live in a colonial situation and then living out of it, the gaining of independence and what all this means in terms of personal human conflict and communal human conflict.

So basically it is politics which has excited the creative spirit in East Africa. The explosion came with Okot p'Bitek's publication of *Song of Lawino* and was helped on by Gerald Moore. The whole thing came to us like a bombshell. I remember going to a conference in East Africa to discuss what was termed 'The East African Cultural Heritage', and there were a lot of papers being read about Fine Art and other subjects which one talks about at cultural conferences. Then suddenly Okot p'Bitek brought this manuscript, read parts of it and showed it to people and the whole tone of the conference completely changed. The publisher immediately grabbed it and gave an advance to the author and this somehow began the explosion of East African writing of the last five years. As soon as that manuscript was grabbed by this publisher, everybody started bringing things from under their pillowcases because, I think, they suddenly realized that they had been sitting on important literary material and that the inspiration which was there, could now easily be used to express something bigger and something larger than what had traditionally been encouraged either by the East African Literature Bureau,[22] or the other publishing interests. This new trend in East African writing started because it was examining the very kind of conflicts and problems that we had been frightened of trying to examine before. We found we had been brainwashed to think that these were not the kind of things that a fine writer in the English tradition should be concerned with. One should try and emulate the writing of D. H. Lawrence or Charles Dickens and this would receive the nod of the master and get one through.

Now *Song of Lawino* was published in East Africa by the East African Publishing House,[23] itself the first indigenous publishing house, and from its list you begin to see the importance of having local publishing houses. We now have a new publishing house which has had the courage to publish books which have been criticized because they are not always beautifully presented but simply expose some of this fresh material. A battle of the publishing houses has begun and it started with Okot's work being published by the East African Publishing House, this was followed immediately after by a series of novels by Grace Ogot[24] and a host of short stories and two major poems; these, I think, show the new trends in East African writing.

Now, about *Song of Lawino* and *The Orphan* by Ochuli. One may think that we are mowing in the same way as West Africa: or perhaps we are showing a new trend which might be of a different interest and of a different quality. Okot p'Bitek's theme is one of the alienation which occurs when individuals try to emulate the appearance of Western societies. This form is what some people call satire, others call it symbolism; this is achieved by means of a long sustained poem of a 'search'. Lawino is the unwesternized village girl, as the critics would call her (many critics using the word 'village' may think that she's simple). She is actually an extremely complex woman compared with the stock definition of a village girl. One wonders sometimes why Okot deliberately gave her the kind of background of action (that is the village background) which in East African society has often been referred to as 'primitive', whereas in West African society the village community has often received – at least to my impression – a certain kind of praise for being the home of the cultural soul. In the West African situation, it is the town which suffers the accusation of being primitive. It seems to have been the reverse in East Africa: there, if you are in town you are civilized. If you go to the village, that's the end of it. Schoolboys used to refuse to go home for the holidays because they wouldn't like to live in so-called primitive conditions and have to mix with primitive parents. Okot deliberately reversed this value judgement by making everything of importance which happens in the poem happen in the village, which psychologically was regarded as being primitive. (148–151)

...

Now here you find the search for liberation not only of the physical, the emotional and the spiritual, but also the search for an identity which had been lost or glossed over, and this is what this poem keeps on asking you all the time. You find that the poet is in a very subtle way (to us in a truly 'Acoli'[25] way), searching for this lost identity, for a statement, to make a cultural assessment. The strictures are not merely personal. We are beginning to break away from the personal and are becoming concerned now with 'us', as it were, as opposed to simply 'me' – the alienated African graduate from a school, or from a training college, or from a university – face-to-face with a new situation: "What am I going to do on my own, to save myself?" It becomes something larger. (153)

8. LALAGE BOWN, *The Development of African Prose-Writing in English: A Perspective* (1971)

Aus: Christopher Heywood (ed.), *Perspectives on African Literature* (London, 1971), 33–48. – Lalage Bown aus Nigeria ist Professorin für Erwachsenenbildung an der Ahmadu Bello University in Nigeria. Sie studierte Geschichte in Oxford und unterrichtete in Ghana, Uganda und Nigeria. 1973 veröffentlichte sie eine Sammlung afrikanischer Prosatexte, *Two Centuries of African English*. Im vorliegenden Textauszug versucht sie eine Bestimmung der modernen fiktiven Literatur Afrikas durch den Blick auf kennzeichnende Merkmale der diskursiven Literatur der Vergangenheit vorzunehmen, die die Moderne wesentlich beeinflußt habe.

Criticism of African writing has stressed various ideas: the need for a writer's work to be placed in context; and the apparent newness of African literature in English (I use the word 'apparent', because I wish to dispute this view), are principal among these. Juxtaposed with the emphasis on novelty there has also been an emphasis on the traditionalism of African writing. Then there are the questions of style – the problems of writing in English when it is not the author's mothertongue. I want to take up all these themes and look at them from the point of view of my own discipline, history, a discipline which can, I believe, throw some illumination from another angle on the problem of interpreting modern African literature.

First of all, the question of putting African writing in context: African literature in English has an historical as well as a sociological context. The subject-matter, ideas, and style of today spring from those of yesterday and the day before, and I am convinced that our perspective on African literature ought to be a rather longer one than has been assumed by many critics. In order to prove this, it will be necessary to demonstrate something of the range of material written in English in earlier times. In a short paper one can only provide samples, but they are put forward to indicate that there has been interesting African prose-writing in English over at least two centuries. (33)

...

The African English prose available divides into several kinds.

First, there is what might be called *personal prose*. This includes letters and diaries, such as have been quoted, and it also includes autobiography. The latter may be in the form of a complete book, such as *The Interesting Narrative of the Life of Olaudah Equiano or Gustavus Vassa the African*;[26] or it may be part of a work with another purpose, such as Bishop Crowther's *Experiences with Heathens and Mohammedans in West Africa*,[27] or Alex Quaison-Sackey's *Africa Unbound*.[28] It may even appear in a selfjustificatory pamphlet published after, say, a personal attack in a newspaper.

A second type of prose may be put under the heading of *reporting*; and this was quite an important category in the nineteenth century when a number of distinguished Africans were employed either by governments or the churches to do specific new tasks and send back information on them.

...

A third kind of African writing in English is *professional prose* – the kind of thing produced by lawyers or doctors concerning their own work.

...

All this does not amount to an overwhelming mass, but it does add up to a significant body of work, much of it well enough written to be read for literary merit – and out of it, incidentally, one could fashion a worthwhile university course in African prose literature in English, starting off with the eighteenth century and working up to the present. There are of course people who will say: 'Ah but this is not fiction, it's not drama – it's not creative!' The word creative used for classifying has its justification, but is open to mistrust, since there is just as much laborious creation in producing a well-written political pamphlet as there is in making a play or a short story. In other literatures one would not dismiss the three types of prose . . . One would not dismiss from English literature the letters of Lord Chesterfield, the diaries of Pepys or the historical works of Lord Macaulay. By the same token, one should not dismiss these kinds of writing if one is considering the growth of African literature. (37–38)

...

So far we have been concerned with the context of African prose in English and with establishing that it does have a longer past than is often assumed, so that it is not really accurate to characterize African English literature as 'new'. Let us pick up the discussion on traditionalism and trace tradition and development, first within one *form* of African writing, and secondly within one species of *content*.

One form which I would like to discuss is the spoken word. This does not refer to oral tradition (the quarry of both the historian and the student of literature in indigenous languages); it refers to oratory, an art which is the foundation of a number of other literary forms, and an art which has been, and still is, highly praised in Africa. Because of the place of oratory in African tradition, when Africans started writing in English it is arguable that some of the most interesting things they put on paper were those designed to be presented verbally – such things as sermons and political speeches. (40)

...

... it would be worth someone's while to make a study ... of the use of speeches, particularly in West African novels. The kind of speeches which are to be found in Achebe's novels, and the sermons and political addresses in the novels of T. M. Aluko[29], for example. I would contend that these elements in their novels relate back to the fact that there is already a long-standing tradition of people talking like this in English in these forms. They could not have written now the kind of sermons they put in their novels if such sermons weren't customary and if they themselves hadn't sat and listened to them over the years – and such sermons and long speeches are a characteristic feature of many West African novels.

Having sketched some of the lines of development of one literary form, let us look at the evolution in treatment of one kind of subject-matter in African prose in English - Tracts. In many African cultures there is a strong strain of didacticism; one encounters a strong desire for literature to have a message and a moral purpose. It is manifested in the shape of many traditional stories and in the emphasis in many of the speeches which have just been discussed. When Africans began writing in English they carried over the didactic tradition and it is particularly evident in their political writings, for which tracts is the only apposite word. (43–44)

...

This brings us ... to modern African 'creative' literature. Just as the tradition of the spoken word is apparent in many novels, so the tradition of political didacticism can be discerned as a background to them. Plots are often political, politicians feature in them, and they include direct animadversions on political topics.

Further, there exists a peculiar genre in African literature of works which are on the borderline between tract and novel. Three examples may be cited. Casely Hayford's name must be mentioned again, as this versatile writer produced one of the most curious books of this century, *Ethiopia Unbound*, which is part tract, part autobiography, and part fiction. It has a chapter on the influence of Edward Blyden, ..., and then a series of semi-mythological prophecies about the future of Africa. Altogether a jumble of a book, it is held together by its political motivation.

A second half-tract is from East Africa, *Africa Answers Back* by the Ugandan Akiki Nyabongo.[30] The first third of the book is an interpretation of East African history through Nyabongo's eyes. After that it plunges into fiction about a child, a chief's son, uprooted from his culture and taken to the missionaries; in the end he returns home and, to the missionaries' disappointment takes several wives and settles to being a good ruler in traditional style.

Then, in very recent times came out of Rhodesia the quasi-novel *On Trial For My Country* by Stanlake Samkange.[31] It is much more closely organized than the other two, and is not entirely a novel because it is based upon very carefully researched historical material. The author presents two cases, that of Cecil Rhodes and his European followers, and that of Lobengula and his African followers, confronting each other in Rhodesia. He leaves the moral judgement – the verdict – to be made by the reader, although it is quite evident which way the judgements are bound to go after reading the book. It has a definite burning propagandist point behind it. So there are still half-tracts being written today, and a number of so-called novels do have strong didactic and propagandist elements in them right up to the present. (46–47)

...

This then is my case. An historian can point to a long tradition of African prose writing in English, he can point to its range, and demonstrate how certain styles and modes of treatment evolved. He can also demonstrate evidence of one author's influence on another. But this is a field barely tilled as yet. We need to pursue the development of characteristically African stylistic elements; and we need to test the hypothesis that African prose read by Africans reinforces the spoken patterns which they find in it, and which in turn goes back into written prose.

For such tasks, the historian is useful, and the material he produces may serve a number of useful objects. Not least is that African literature may be studied in its historical setting. African literature in the past may have been marginal to English literature, and it is not being suggested that the study of the whole of English literature be displaced by study of a marginal element; but in order to make sense of modern African literature, which is no longer marginal, the background of the past is required.

In providing this background, one also gives some kind of answer to the problem of writing in a second language. The fact that there were Africans writing good English two hundred years ago makes nonsense of the argument that Africans can't really be at home in the English language. They did it under difficult conditions and their example could be a stimulus to emulation today. (48)

9. E. N. OBIECHINA, *Literature for the Masses* (1971)

Aus: *Literature for the Masses: An Analytical Study of Popular Pamphleteering in Nigeria* (Enugu, 1971), 81–84. – Obiechina (cf. Text 6) untersucht in seiner Studie die Entstehungsbedingungen der populären Unterhaltungsliteratur Nigerias, die seit Ende der vierziger Jahre in der im östlichen Landesteil gelegenen Handelsstadt Onitsha ihren Ausgang nahm. In der unreflektierten Darstellung modernen Lebens bildet sie ein Pendant zur intellektuell anspruchsvolleren Literatur und beeinflußte sie auf indirekte Weise.

We have on a number of occasions during this discussion contrasted the attitudes of the intellectual West African authors with those of the pamphlet writers. This is one way of saying that the two types of writers are interested in using their media to provide insights into the contemporary West African life. They see things differently largely because they deal with different areas of the common experiences they are exploring. The pamphlet authors concern themselves with surface appearances while the intellectual authors tend to dig into underlying causes and explanations. A comparison of works by the two groups of authors shows that in terms of their reflection of things as they actually are, we are likely to find the pamphleteers much nearer to the experience of most ordinary people than the sophisticated authors. They reflect the problems and crises of contemporary life in all their rawness. By the time these have undergone intellectual digestion in the quality works of the intellectual authors, a certain amount of blood must have been lost from the life that reappears.

But in the stregth of the pamphlet literature also lies its weakness. Its spontaneity and freshness do not altogether compensate for its lack of intellectual vigour. For, good literature does more than reproduce the problems and crises of life. It should also show evidence of intensive mental activity, evidence that the writer has at least wrestled hard with the problems and crises before consolidating his insight. This is necessary if a literary work is to engage more than the partial consciousness of intelligent readers. Literature should not only reproduce life, it should also point a way to fuller, better and more satisfying life; it should reveal the potentiality of life. Literature that fails to do this demotes itself to mere entertainment and would appeal mainly to the unthinking section of the population. The pamphlet literature has suffered neglect among the more sophisticated readers for this reason.

The matter can be easiliy illustrated. We are confronted in the pamphlets with the agressive assertion of individualism. The claims of the individual are strongly urged in economic matters, in love affairs, in marriage and even in religious identification. All obstacles in the way of individual self expression are impatiently shoed aside. The bearers of old-fashioned ideas which impede individualist fulfilment are quickly knocked on the head and put out of action.

We cannot but applaud the zeal and crusading vigour which the pamphlet authors display in their pursuit of individualism. But then we look for an expression of social awareness, of social responsibility and the values which promote high social goals and we search in vain. Individualism without social responsibility leads inevitably to social parasitism, to a preying on the social resources by individuals who cannot themselves contribute anything substantial towards social progress.

It is in this area of social responsibility that the intellectual authors score over the pamphlet writers. The intellectual authors constantly link the fortunes of individuals to those of society at large. They tend to show that pursuit of individual goals without consideration for its impact on social well-being cannot but undermine even the happiness and well-being of individuals. These authors are therefore critical of individuals who manifest a lack of consideration for the good health and well-being of society.

It would be a mistake of course to quarrel with the pamphlet authors by asking why their view of society has been markedly lacking in positive constructiveness, why the kind of morality they push forward has no root and why their general attitudes do not appear to have depth either of emotional or of intellectual conviction. The pamphlet authors are to a large extent victims of modern commercially-catered media of entertainment which project individualism without social responsibility. We take a look at the commercial films which these popular authors and their audience watch night after night and what do we see? We see a perpetual display of reckless individualism and lack of concern for social morality. For example, the successful armed thief running away with his loot is hero in them. We find the corruption of certain basic emotions and appetites; violence, sex and seduction are played up, crime is glamourized and material "success" is elevated into a kind of fetish. As for the newspapers and magazines directed at the common people, their pages are splashed over with sex and sensuality which are amply reinforced by highly coloured advertisement which debase the taste. All these things together have the effect of undermining social consciousness, of increasing criminal individualism and of luring the victims into shallow pleasures that corrupt the soul and impoverish the emotions. And what is most deplorable about this mass brutalization of taste and attitudes through modern media of entertainment is that it is done by proprietors whose sole interest is to make money.

What chance do the pamphlet authors have to see the problems of contemporary life clearly and constructively when their line of vision is persistently obscured by the haze of inspired amorality engendered by modern commercial films, newspapers and magazines? The intellectual authors are able, by their superior learning and wider experience, to pierce through this haze and reveal the underlying realities as they affect individuals and society.

One further matter remains to be resolved. Seekers after analogy have sought to show that the Nigerian novel must have grown out of the pamphlet literature in the same way that the English novel grew out of the eighteenth century English chapbooks and Grub Street pamphleteering. They have sought, rather ingenuously, to find some connection between the fact that a majority of the Nigerian novelists originate from Onitsha and around and the influence of the Onitsha Pamphlet Literature.

Ingenuity is not always a sure guide to factuality. There are a number of reasons why one must be cautious about this theory. It is true that Igbo novelists constitute more than two-thirds of the whole Nigerian novelists and that most of them have their natal homes in or near Onitsha. But it is also true that many of them have lived away from Onitsha, if not from Igboland altogether. It is not easy to establish in respect of the pamphlet authors and novelists in Nigeria the kind of connection which existed between the eighteenth century English pamphleteering activities by authors like Defoe and Richardson and the emergence of the English novel. Cyprian Ekwensi, of all the Nigerian novelists, has a direct connection with the pamphlet literature. He pioneered the pamphlet literature when he brought out *Ikolo the Wrestler and Other Ibo Tales* and *When Love Whispers* in 1947. He also brought out *People of the City*, the first novel in Nigeria which was also the second in English – speaking West Africa.

It is more likely that the two types of writing developed independently, though under identical stimuli. Ethnopsychologists, will, maybe, find additional reasons why most of the novelists should be Igbo and why the pamphlets should have found their home in Onitsha, the educational and commercial centre of Igboland. The American anthropologist, Herskovits, has spoken of "Igbo receptivity to change." Other commentators like James Coleman and the Ottenbergs have expounded identical views in different contexts. In this kind of situation, literary history stands very much to gain from the insights provided by other branches of scholarship.

Even though we cannot establish directly, in respect of the intellectual authors (with the exception of Ekwensi), the kind of intimate connection with printing and publishing popular journalism and pamphlet-writing which has been established between these and the early English novelists (especially as the

Nigerian intellectual authors have often relied on overseas publishers), it would be wrong to imagine that the Onitsha Pamphlet Literature has in no way influenced the rapid growth of the novel and other sophisticated forms in Nigeria. Its influence is more oblique than direct. The existence of this mass of popular writing is an indication of a general literary awakening of which the novel is the highest achievement. The fact that this mass of home-produced literature is the work of people with relatively meager formal education must have greatly encouraged the better educated and literarily-inclined Nigerians to go a step further than the popular writers and produce literature of a more elevated kind. In other words, the existence of literature for the masses acted as a spur on intellectually sophisticated Nigerians to produce more sophisticated forms of literature fore more sophisticated readers.

10. BERNTH LINDFORS, *Popular Literature for an African Elite* (1974)

Aus: *The Journal of Modern African Studies*, 12, 3 (1974), 471–486. – B. Lindfors (geb. 1938) aus Schweden, studierte in Harvard, an der Northwestern University und in Los Angeles. Seit 1970 ediert er die Zeitschrift *Research in African Literatures* und ist Mitherausgeber einer Reihe von Sammelbänden zu einzelnen afrikanischen Autoren, in der auch sein eigener Band, *Critical Perspectives on Amos Tutuola* (Washington, D. C., 1975), erschien. Im folgenden Beitrag wird die Rolle von Schul- und Universitätszeitschriften zur Herausbildung der afrikanischen Literatur in englischer Sprache untersucht, deren literarischer Anspruch ohne die von ihnen ausgehenden intellektuellen Anregungen kaum verständlich wäre.

One of the first openings for aspiring writers was the secondary school or university magazine. Many of Nigeria's most famous authors began their literary careers by composing stories, poems, and articles for such publications; several served as editors of prestigious campus annuals, short-lived literary and cultural reviews, or mimeographed scandal sheets. Chinua Achebe, for instance, was one of the first student editors of the *Umuahia Government College Magazine* (subsequently renamed the *Umuahian*), and later became editor of *The University Herald*, the official organ of the Ibadan Students' Union, and perhaps the first high-quality journal in English-speaking Africa to be produced entirely by university students. Wole Soyinka, before leaving Ibadan to continue his undergraduate studies at the University of Leeds, edited *The Eagle*, an irregular cyclostyled newssheet of humour and comment put out by the Progressive Party, a campus organisation which regularly lost student elections to its chief rival, the Dynamic Party. John Pepper Clark edited *The Beacon* for the Student's Union at Ibadan, was the founder of a poetry magazine known as *The Horn*, and also served as editor of *Aro*, an Ijaw Students' Association publication which appears to have expired immediately after its maiden issue in 1958. Michael Echeruo was associate editor of the *Catholic Undergraduate* at Ibadan, and later, as a teacher at the Nigerian College of Technology in Enugu, helped to found a student poetry magazine called *Fresh Buds*, which had as its first editor the promising young poet Glory O. Nwanodi (now known as Okogbule Nwanodi).[32]

These and other campus publications did much to stimulate student literary activity, and to keep alive in some of Nigeria's most talented undergraduates a desire and obligation to write. One can study what they wrote as a special kind of popular literature – that is, as a distinctive body of ephemeral writings produced in low-circulation mass media by groups of students for the amusement and instruction of their peers. This was a popular literature of, by, and for an educated African élite.

Secondary School Magazines

The school magazine probably provided many Nigerian writers with their first opportunity for publication. Although annuals were not common in Nigerian secondary schools until the 1950s,[33] there were a few pioneering ventures like *The Mermaid*, which Kings College in Lagos may have started publishing as early as 1925,[34] and *The Interpreter*, which Aggrey Memorial College in Arochuku launched in 1935. Other well-established institutions such as Government College, Ibadan, Ilesha Grammar School, and Hope Waddell Training College were producing their own yearbooks or literary magazines by the end of the 1940s. At first these publications were largely the work of teachers who did the editing, most of the writing, and some soliciting of contributions. Later, student editorial boards working under staff supervision took over responsibility for these chores, and met periodically to pass judgement on manuscripts submitted by their schoolmates. (472–473)

...

The articles published in these annuals covered a wide range of topics, but there were certain perennial favourites. Formal essays defining social rôles were quite common – e.g. the qualities of a gentleman, the characteristics of a good student, and the duties of the school sanitary inspector. Mission schools often featured pious articles on religion and ethics, some of which made a point of condemning traditional superstitions, customs, and beliefs; secular institutions, on the other hand, appear to have encouraged students to describe festivals and ceremonies they had witnessed at home. There were always plenty of old composition exercises on such familiar themes as "My Most Frightening Experience", "A Trip to the City", "Holiday Adventures", and "An Unforgettable Dream". The most creative of these academic set-pieces were usually the 'autobiographies' of rivers, trains, coins, letters, or anything else that moved or changed hands frequently. There were also a few short stories, occasional dialogues or mini-dramas, songs written in honour of the school, poems on subjects sacred and inane, and humorous parodies of well-known pieces from the Bible, Shakespeare, and venerable English classics regularly appearing in School Certificate examinations.

The poems tend to reflect the type of literary education Nigerian secondary-school students received during the colonial and early independence eras. Odes and elegies were favourite forms, especially on the occasion of a famous man's death. One schoolboy bard, in a poem entitled, "Oh, Death! Death!! Death!!!", mourned President Kennedy's assassination in these memorable, memorised words:

> Death be not proud for devouring our
> Noble President Kennedy; though some callest
> Thou mighty and dreadful, thou are not so.[35] (475–476)

...

Although this sounds rather pompous, it was truly with the birth of a literary instinct that these magazines were primarily concerned. Although some may have been started to enhance the reputation of a school, they were all regarded as educational tools designed to provide students with literary satisfactions they could nowhere else experience. In them the "mushroom author" (as he was often called) could see his first words in print. This might encourage him to write again, and further success might lead him to consider seeking the greater gratification of publishing an essay, story, or poem in a magazine of much wider circulation. From there it would be only one short imaginative leap up the ladder of ambition to dreams of his first book. One student, writing on the "specific benefits" of school magazines, put it this way:

"If a student's articles are published, he feels deep self-satisfaction and joy in himself, that his ideas are published. He also feels some pride in himself that he has been able to achieve something – however minute in life. He is also inspired to put a better contribution to subsequent publications and in such a way, he may become another or even a better Shakespeare of our age."[36] In Nigeria the road to a superior Shakespeare was paved with school magazines.

University Publications

Those "mushroom authors" who were fortunate enough to get planted at a university found a much wider range of publications open to them. Besides the students' union magazine, there might be campus newspapers, literary leaflets, departmental periodicals, scholarly journals, church bulletins, and numerous mimeographed circulars serving a variety of societies, clubs, or special interest groups. Here writers could express themselves with much more freedom and frequency than they could in the straight and narrow confines of their school annuals. They also had many opportunities to engage in polemical debates on 'hot' issues. (478–479)

...

Each publication had a unique – and sometimes quite brief – life history of its own, but all contributed to whatever climate of creativity existed on the Ibadan campus while they were alive and functioning. A few actually grew to be quite influential.

To take just one example, *The Beacon* began as a rather conventional repository of student essays on general subjects and on university life in particular. Literary contributions were rare and tended to follow the traditions established in the secondary school magazines. Here, for instance, is a parody of the opening of Shakespeare's *Julius Caesar*, presented as if spoken by a university professor:

> Hence! Sram, you idle creatures, get you to your halls;
> Is this a holiday? What? Know you not
> Being academical, you ought not to walk
> Upon a swotting day without your cap
> And gown? Speak, what faculty art thou?[37]

After J. P. Clark became editor the literary contributions to *The Beacon* improved remarkably, and much more space was devoted to discussion of plays, operas, and exhibitions staged at the University. He began to reprint some of the best poems published in *The Horn*, a mimeographed poetry magazine he had founded. A few of his own poems – "For Granny (Written at Hospital)" and the earliest printed version of "Ivbie" – made their first appearance in *The Beacon* too. Though the literary momentum that Clark was responsible for building up in *The Beacon* was not sustained by some of its later editors, he nevertheless must be credited with having made this journal an important vehicle for literary activity at Ibadan while he was associated with it.

Clark's major contribution to the cultural life of the University was, of course, *The Horn*, a poetry monthly which continued for more than six years after he and Martin Banham[38] launched it in 1958. This tiny 12page leaflet carried poetry, reviews, and criticism by a number of Ibadan's finest literary minds – including Christopher Okigbo, Aig Higo, Frank Aig-Imoukhuede, Abiola Irele, Kalu Uka, Alfred Opubor, Juliet Udezue (now Okonkwo), Omolara Ogundipe (now Leslie), Emmanuel Obiechina, Dapo Adelugba, Oyekan Owomoyela, Daniel Abasiekong, and Okogbule Nwanodi,[39] who have since gone on to distinguish themselves in a variety of literary fields. Wole Soyinka also wrote some poetry and literary criticism for *The Horn* in the early 1960s, after he had returned to Ibadan from England. Several members of staff – notably Martin Banham, Molly Mahood, and Geoffrey Axworthy – actively supported the magazine by contributing brief essays, rebuttals to student drama reviews, and occasional poems. All this activity made *The Horn* one of the most vital publications at Ibadan at a time when African literature in English was just beginning to attract the attention of the outside world. It helped to herald the arrival of a new literary era in Nigeria. (484–485)

. . .

Quantity, of course, is no guarantee of quality, and many of these publications were full of the most sophomoric stuff that university sophomores are capable of producing. Yet quite a few of Nigeria's acknowledged literary masters gained valuable apprentice experience by writing for, or slaving over the galleys of, these frail academic vehicles, and their contributions still make very interesting reading today. It is significant that nearly all those who later became famous as authors did some writing for campus publications while they were university students. They started by attempting to communicate with their peers in a literary idiom they thought educated readers would appreciate. They were writers of a high-brow popular literature.

No one who is interested in the history of Nigerian writing in English can afford to overlook this literature for it reveals a great deal about the intellectual climate in which most Nigerian writers and readers were nurtured. School and university publications were the earliest seedbeds of sustained literary creativity in Nigeria, the first soil in which many mushroom authors could sprout. In them a modern literary movement was started. In them a truly Nigerian literature in English was born. (486)

11. F. LUMWAMU (Rapporteur), *Black Civilization and Literature* (1977)

Aus: A. U. Iwara and E. Mveng (eds.), *Second World Black and African Festival of Arts and Culture: Colloquium on Black Civilization and Education. Colloquium Proceedings,* vol. I (Lagos, 1977), 136–139. – Eine wichtige Veranstaltung von FESTAC 1977 bildete das Kolloquium über Schwarze Zivilisation und Erziehung, das vom 17.–31. Januar 1977 in Lagos stattfand. Eine der fünf Arbeitsgruppen diskutierte das Thema „Black Civilization, African Languages and Literature" und veröffentlichte den folgenden Abschlußbericht, dessen Ergänzung durch die Publikation ausgewählter Vorträge noch aussteht. Die erarbeitete Bestimmung des Begriffs „Afrikanische Literatur" spiegelt die Meinungsvielfalt vorangegangener Debatten wider und versucht im Begriff der „Afrikanität", die afrikanischen Menschen gemeinsamen Kulturmerkmale ebenso wie den ästhetischen Anspruch von Literatur im Kontext einer Weltliteratur aufzuheben.

Africanity and Cultural Identity through African Literature

Several fundamental questions were tackled: What really is modern negro-African literature? What are its characteristics? How does one recognise a black literary work?

Critics have attempted to define modern literature according to the language of expression, the themes treated, the psychology of its authors and that of the characters they create. Added to these characteristics is that of nationality, the only constant apparently, by which any national literature is defined. It is therefore right to consider African literature as being that created by Africans irrespective of the language used or the subject treated.

The writer's nationality is defined in terms of belonging. The black writer belongs organically and physically to the original condition of Africans in the world. He cannot remove himself from his condition nor can he avoid showing it through his language.

But beyond the nationality, five constituent elements of Africanness are proposed:

(a) The writer must be African; he must use
(b) traditional themes from oral literature
(c) African symbols
(d) linguistic expressions taken from negro-African languages.
(e) local imagery, that is, images from the immediate environment.

In other words, the author should make use of traditional negro-African literature (myths, legends, short stories, poetic forms or procedures, proverbs and other forms of expression of negro-African languages). But the presence of these various elements in an African literary piece of work is not enough to lead to the piece of work being considered a success. The author should furthermore endeavour to make use of African oral tradition in an artistic, aesthetic and original manner. In short, from materials furnished by oral tradition, he should create a new piece of work that is really literary.

Opposed to this conception based mainly on the material elements of Africanity is another, more global, conception of Africanity. This conception avoids becoming burdened with discussions on an author's nationality. This particular problem is considered as having been solved already. African literature, it is noted, presents itself under three aspects:
1. Oral literature
2. Literature written in African languages
3. Literature written in foreign languages (English, French, Portuguese, etc . . .)

It is the last category that is called African literature for various reasons: it came into being after the second world war as a reaction against the colonial situation experienced by Africans; it is written by authors who are versed in European and American literatures and who have adopted the forms of these literatures to their writings; it draws on the stylistic traditions and peculiarities of modern European literatures. The greatest criticism against it is that it is expressed in European or foreign languages. But what are the specific characteristics of this modern African literature? The concepts of Pan-Africanism, African Personality or Negritude have essentially political and ideological connotations and have limited the horizon of African literary imagination.

A new definition of Africanity is, therefore, suggested: Africanity is the affirmation of the personality, the identity and the richness of the African way of life in the world literary field. It shows to the world the cultural traits that are common to African peoples; it has domesticated foreign languages and charged them with the specific sensitivity of Africans all through the works of African writers; African artists speak to man and to humanity through a language, images, themes and techniques that belong to Africa. African literature has thus crossed the frontiers of the African universe to become interested in man's condition in general.

One of the fundamental problems evoked during the discussions organised on the theme of Africanity is that of the language in which this concept is expressed. It is easily noted that all African literature referred to as modern is expressed in foreign languages. The black writer, whether he likes it or not, thus chooses for his book in spite of himself, a public from which the large mass of Africans who are uninitiated in European languages are excluded.

The discussions brought out the fact that use of African languages by African writers is not impossible. In countries which have taken to a definite linguistic policy, like Somalia since 1972, a literature in the national language embracing all aspects of the country – political, social, cultural, scientific, etc. – is developing. Encouraging attempts have been started in Ghana, Nigeria, Zaire, Congo, ... Here, the need for a more complete authenticity becomes evident, as does the obligation for every man of culture in general and the African writers in particular to defend African languages and render them famous.

Cultural identity through black literatures

Many papers, especially those of representatives of the Black Communities of the Diaspora (USA, CANADA, BRAZIL, the CARIBBEAN, CUBA) talked of the preservation, through the literatures of these communities, of the characteristics and values that are peculiar to them. These communities have, no doubt, been the object of considerable pressures and cultural onslaughts in the course of history. Their cultures have been strongly marked by these, to the extent that one may wonder whether these literatures are not part of the literatures of the communities within which these blacks of the Diaspora live. But it is noted everywhere today that what is essential is the permanent and continuous effort of black writers of these communities to define (indeed redefine), affirm and enrich a real cultural identity which has survived all the onslaughts of history.

Some participants wondered, however, if the black writers of these communities of the Diaspora do not themselves consider their literature as part of the literature of the larger communities to which they belong. The reply is that there certainly is cultural ambivalence but the black writers show another form of sensitivity which maintains obvious cultural and ethnic differences that have survived history.

In the search for cultural identity, the originality of the black race is exalted, and the acculturated blacks who do not acknowledge the contribution of African culture to the universal civilization are denounced and fustigated.

In the zone of the Caribbeans, there have also been literary trends manifesting and exalting the cultural contribution of blacks. Nevertheless, certain myths, certain social and artistic traditions and certain African religions have survived there. There is, finally, an effort to conserve Black Cultural Identity in a bid to construct a specific West-Indian personality.

The African Literary Criticism

The African literary critics have up till now made use of Western standards in the appreciation of black literary works.

The role of the African critic among others is to educate his readers; to seek and discover, in the works, values which are capable of consolidating the cultural cohesion of the people in order to enable him participate fully in the task of construction both at the national and African levels; to discover artistic values appropriate to black civilisation capable of determining its contributions to universal civilisation.

It is logical that African critics should keep aside standards formulated in the Western countries by and for the West and seek for new ways and new criteria in the appreciation of black literary work.

African literature is, in its double form of written and oral literature, the privileged witness of the history of the social life of Africans, a platform of the awareness of their cultural identity and of their cultural cohesion. It therefore follows that the African literary critic should find for himself new standards of appreciation of the literary work drawn from the very possibilities of our culture. One could for instance think of the traditional didacticism of oral literatures, and the initiating ceremonies which are present in written as well as in oral literature; one could also study the characteristic concept of the black and African mentality capable of providing the new African critic with original theoretical foundations.

Oral African Literature

This is, when situated in the framework of the new perspectives open to the African literary critic, simply an integral part of our literature. It should therefore be taught as such. It is an important part of our cultural heritage, a leaven for our modern literature and a trustee of our history capable of being an indispensable source for the reconstitution of our past.

Oral literature appears as the trustee of an enormous wealth and a way for African people, to conserve their spiritual power. It must not be forgotten that in the history of mankind, the spoken word has preceded writing and that in Africa, oral tradition deteriorated only under the impact of colonisation.

Before colonisation, Africa had her "speakers" as she today has her "men of letters".

Africa owes it to herself to re-instate her oral tradition, an essential element of value in her civilisation. The invasion of Africa by writing must not result in the loss of the oral tradition which, for centuries or even for thousands of years, has transmitted all the values of civilisation with which we all claim kinship today. In Africa, an oral policy is required. *The elimination of illiteracy on the one hand, and oracy on the other hand, must not be viewed as conflicting but must be regarded as complementary.*

The Negro-African Writer

Several problems concerning the negro-African writer were brought to the attention of the working group. The following established facts were arrived at:

1. The African writer is subjected to the caprices of the European editor who accepts or refuses the manuscripts according to the taste of his European readers. Whereas in actual fact the African author writes for the Africans.

2. The distribution is still monopolised by the old metropolis.

A poor distribution can inflict on an otherwise good or even excellent book a very bad fortune.

3. The copyright is the exclusive property of publishers. The transfer of works from one publisher to another is made difficult. It therefore follows that there is a serious limitation in the readership of a book.

4. The status of the black writer is not guaranteed. In many cases, he does not enjoy all the freedom of expression that is desirable.

5. The problem of copyright is linked with the language of the author, and the socio-economic and political system of his country. Europeans don't accept to publish works written in African languages. It is therefore incumbent on Africans to develop publishing in African languages.

6. Literary prizes are awarded in Paris and not in Africa. It is not always the best works that are rewarded.

7. The African writer is poor. It is particularly professors and research scholars who are published. The young talents are often left to themselves.

8. Oral African literature is property of the whole collectivity and not that of authors or publishers. Consequently, the latter should not benefit from any copyright. The following conclusions resulted from the discussions held:

(a) It is urgent to start a publishing policy in Africa.

(b) African states should co-operate in this field. They should work together in organising an effective policy of publishing and of distribution and establish exchanges between publishers.

(c) The African writer must integrate himself in his society and free himself from Europe. He should publish not only in European languages. It is by this means that he will contribute towards the defence and the illustration of African languages.

2. Ziele und Wege der kolonialen Sprach- und Bildungspolitik

12. HANNAH KILHAM, *The Claims of West Africa to Christian Instruction through the Native Languages* (1830)

Aus: *Tracts* (British Museum Library; London, n. d.) [28 pp.] –. Hannah Kilham (gest. 1832) war Mitglied der Society of Friends in England und strebte durch erzieherische Arbeit eine Verbesserung des Loses befreiter Sklaven an. Neben der Abfassung von Schulbüchern und einer Grammatik für die Unterrichtung von Analphabeten schrieb sie Traktate und gründete die erste Schule für Mädchen in Sierra Leone, die sie mehrere Male besuchte. Der folgende Text stellt die erste aus dem englischen Sprachraum stammende Darlegung zur Rolle der Spracherziehung innerhalb des seinerzeit ausschließlich von Missionaren betriebenen Unterrichts von Afrikanern dar und nimmt Gedanken vorweg, die erst einhundert Jahre später in der offiziellen englischen Ausbildungspolitik wieder aufgegriffen wurden.

As with regard to education, from what has been observed of African capacity, when intelligible means of instruction are given, it appears very evident, that were suitable measures adopted to prepare for them the elements of instruction, in clean and simple form, these children would be far from being backward, either in applying to the acquisition of useful knowledge, or in imbibing what they are taught. But in the system hitherto pursued in the schools, of using English lessons only, for children, to whom English is quite a foreign language ... whilst the native languages, for conversation, are of course in general use among themselves, can it be expected that the lessons thus learned should prove any more than mere *sound* to the pupil? (4–5)
. . .
Let the friends of Africa be only willing to meet this difficulty, and provide means for its removal, by opening the doors for intelligible communication with the people, through the native languages, and it will soon be discovered that Africans have powers to cultivate, and dispositions to improve, that would well repay the Christian labours of their European brethren ...

It is not only for the welfare and advancement of the Africans in Sierra Leone, that we are called upon to do what we can for the improvement of the people of that colony, and for the attainment of an intelligible medium of instruction for themselves and for their children; we have also to take into view the prospective, yet deeply interesting object of preparing, through the various languages now spoken in Sierra Leone, the means of Christian instruction to many nations of Africa at a distance from the colony, whose minds we cannot hope to reach but through such a medium ...

The work of translation into a great number of unwritten languages, must indeed be an engagement of close mental labour and anxious responsibility ...

In order to raise a native agency to assist in the important and responsible work of African translations, it would be requisite that the best opportunities be afforded for the natives introduced to this work, to gain a knowledge of the English language, from whence both elementary books and Scripture lessons would have to be translated, previously to the more extensive engagement of their assisting in the translations of the Scriptures at large.

England would, no doubt, afford the best opportunities for the natives of Africa to obtain a knowledge of our language, and England would also afford the means for a strict reviewal and examination of translations attempted, where intelligent natives have to give the required evidence...

But, alas for poor Africa! How little has yet been done for that wide continent, with its thousands of peopled towns and villages; how little is yet known of the great and important work of Scripture translations, or the widely extended labours of the British and Foreign Bible Society. (6–9)

...

Were a few well-chosen Africans to be brought, on their own desire, to this country, from some of the principal tribes, so selected as to retain their languages by conversing with each other, they might, in an Institution prepared here for their reception, rapidly acquire the English language and become valuable assistants in translation; and preserving the general forms and structure of their own languages, these translations, written from their dictation by their English friends appointed to the work, would, if well attended to, be found clear and intelligible when heard or read in the native districts. Europeans engaged in the translation might at the same time acquire sufficient knowledge of these languages, to check or prevent the passing of erroneous translations respecting important truths...

Should encouragement be given for the persecution of this work, it would, in present circumstances, it is hoped, be easy to obtain a good selection of pupils, who would gladly come over for a few years to learn our language, and to assist in translations in some of her principal languages of Africa. Already has the advantage of such translations been experienced in a school on the river Gambia, in which the Jolof elementary and Scripture lessons are now used, which a few years ago were prepared and printed in England under the sanction of a Committee of Friends for promoting African Instruction. These lessons have not only been used in schools for teaching the Jolof children both their own language and the English, but some of the young men have also read the Jolof Scripture lessons contained in them to their families at home. (10–12)

...

At the same time, from the villages of literated Africans in Sierra Leone, we hear perpetually, in the printed statements, the report of discouragement and complaint. The people understand but little of the instructions offered, and the children in the schools are under similar disadvantages. Still there is sounded among some in that colony, the alarm of a supposed impossibility of giving any other instruction than through the English language only; the languages of the natives being so many and so little known. Allowing, that so far as the residence in an English colony is intended, it is indeed desirable that English should be known as a *general* language among the people, and be their common medium of communication; still, in the attainment even of this object, we shall find, that to cultivate, to a certain extent, each of the distinctly ascertained native languages spoken in the colony, would be the most facile and effectual means of teaching the natives English. But if the English language itself be *not understood* by the Africans, how can it be the *medium* of instruction either in their religious assemblies or in their schools? ... Let the friends of African education then avail themselves, in teaching English, of the advantages of the simplest and most effectual system of instruction that of *teaching through the medium of something already known to the pupil,* and acquiring at least the elements of English, through the familiar means of introductory lessons in the native languages, with the English attached to them.

In the attempt te reduce a new language to writing, it is undoubtedly requisite to use great care in every step of a work so responsible, and especially in attempting to convey in such language any religious truth ... From Scripture lessons, if thus gained in each principal language, and read occasionally among the people by whom they were understood, might not we hope that even a few words thus conveyed, would avail more of their real instruction than ten thousand words spoken to them in an unknown tongue? (13–15)

...

Although the wish of translation may not in itself have all the attraction of some other engagements, yet its ultimate object, when directed to the attainment, for a suffering and benighted people, of that divine revelation in the Scriptures of Truth, with which we have ourselves been so mercifully favoured, the prospect of this attainment may well give a deep and lasting interest to long-continued exertions in such a cause ... It should never be forgotten, the Translations are as indispensable requisite to the cause of Christian education in heathen lands, as schools are necessary to the effectual diffusion of the Holy Scriptures ...

With an object in view so important and so delightful to every feeling of Christian love, it is therefore proposed, that a few, to whom the advancement of truth and righteousness on the earth is precious, should, without further delay make arrangements for the introduction of a few native Africans, into this country, selected from some of the most important tribes known in the colony of Sierra Leone, or other parts of West Africa, as Mandingo, Jolof, Bassa, etc. and brought over with their own concurrence and desire, to be taught here the English language, and prepared to give assistance in translating from the English into their own language.

That after appointing a Provisional Committee for carrying their design into effect, arrangements be made for providing the requisite funds, and for directing the means by which Africans shall be selected, and introduced to the proposed means of instruction ...

That the Committee take the charge, as far as may be found expedient, of printing, in different languages, Elementary books and Scripture lessons. (22–24)

13. EDUCATION COMMITTEE OF THE PRIVY COUNCIL, *Brief Practical Suggestions on the Mode of Organizing and Conducting Day Schools of Industry, Model Farm Schools, and Normal Schools, as Part of Education for the Coloured Races of the British Colonies* (1847)

Aus: *Miscellaneous Pamphlets*, I, 1, 1–10, Colonial Office Library, 10985. – Die erste offizielle Verlautbarung der britischen Regierung zur Ausbildung der „coloured races" in den Kolonien legt das Hauptgewicht auf die sogenannte „industrial education". Sprach- und Literaturunterricht stellen nur Mittel zum Zweck der Aneignung der christlichen Religion und westlich geprägter kultureller Verhaltensweisen und Normen dar.

SIR,
Privy Council Office Whitehall, January 6, 1847.

The letter which, by the direction of Earl Grey, was transmitted to this office on the 30th of November, together with the despatches from governors of the West Indian Colonies which accompanied it, have been under the consideration of the Lord President of the Council.

Under his Lordship's directions a short and simple account is now submitted of the mode in which the Committee of Council on Education consider that Industrial Schools for the coloured races may be conducted in the colonies, so as to combine intellectual and industrial education, and to render the labour of the children available towards meeting some part of the expense of their education.

From this account will be purposely excluded any description of *the methods* of intellectual instruction, and all minute details of the organization of schools. Whatever suggestions respecting discipline may be offered will be condensed into brief hints, or confined to those general indications which are universally applicable.

It would be presumptuous to attempt to describe those varieties in discipline which might be suggested by a better knowledge of the peculiarities of a race which readily abandons itself to excitement, and perhaps needs amusements which would seem unsuitable for the peasantry of a civilized community.

While endeavouring to suggest the mode by which the labour of negro children may be mingled with instruction fitted to develope their intelligence, it would be advantageous to know more of the details of colonial culture, and of the peculiarities of household life in this class, and thus to descend from the general description into a closer adaption of the plans of the school to the wants of the coloured races. This, however, cannot now be attempted.

In describing the mode in which the instruction may be interwoven with the labour of the school, so as to render their connection as intimate as possible, it will however be necessary to repeat the illustrations in various forms, which may appear trivial. But this mutual dependence of the moral and physical training; of the intellectual and industrial teaching; and even of the religious education and the instruction of the scholars in the practical duties of life, require a detailed illustration. Christian civilization comprehends this complex development of all the faculties, and the school of a semi-barbarous class should be established on the conviction that these several forms of training and instruction mutually assist each other.

Instead of setting forth this principle more fully, it is considered expedient to furnish numerous though brief practical details of its application, which may with local knowledge be easily expanded into a manual for schools of industry for the coloured races.

Even within the limits which will be assigned to the instruction of the children of these races in this paper, it may be conceived that, bearing in mind the present state of the negro population, and taking into account the means at present at the disposal of the colonial legislatures in the different dependencies, a too sanguine view has been adopted of the amount of instruction which may be hoped to be imparted.

Certainly it is true that some time must elapse before the limits assigned in this paper to such instruction, even in the day-schools, can be reached. But less, that what is described could not be regarded as a transforming agency, by which the negro could be led, within a generation, materially to improve his habits. If we would have him rest satisfied with the meagre subsistence and privation of comfort consequent on his habits of listless contentment with the almost spontaneous gifts of a tropical climate, a less efficient system may be adopted; but if the native labour of the West Indian Colonies is to be made generally available for the cultivation of the soil by a settled and industrious peasantry, no agent can be so surely depended upon as the influence of a system of combined intellectual and industrial instruction, carried to a higher degree of efficiency than any example which now exists in the colonies.

Nor will a wise Colonial Government neglect any means which affords even a remote prospect of gradually creating a native middle class among the negro population, and thus, ultimately, of completing the institutions of freedom, by rearing a body of men interested in the protection of property, and with intelligence enough to take part in that humbler machinery of local affairs which ministers to social order.

With these remarks, I proceed at once to enter on the practical suggestions which I am directed to offer.

The objects of education for the coloured races of the colonial dependencies of Great Britain may be thus described.

To inculcate the principles and promote the influences of Christianity, by such instruction as can be given in elementary schools.

To accustom the children of these races to habits of self-control and moral discipline.

To diffuse a grammatical knowledge of the English language, as the most important agent of civilization, for the coloured population of the colonies.

To make the school the means of improving the condition of the peasantry, by teaching them how health may be preserved by proper diet, cleanliness, ventilation, and clothing, and by the structure of their dwellings.

To give them a practical training in household economy, and in the cultivation of a cottage garden, as well as in those common handicrafts by which a labourer may improve his domestic comfort.

To communicate such a knowledge of writing and arithmetic, and of their application to his wants and duties, as may enable a peasant to economize his means, and give the small farmer the power to enter into calculations and agreements.

An improved agriculture is required in certain of the colonies to replace the system of exhausting the virgin soils, and then leaving to natural influences alone, the work of reparation. The education of the coloured races would not, therefore, be complete, for the children of small farmers, unless it included this object.

The lesson books of colonial schools should also teach the mutual interests of the mother-country and her dependencies; the rational basis of their connection, and the domestic and social duties of the coloured races.

These lesson books should also simply set forth the relation of wages, capital, labour, and the influence of local and general government on personal security, independence, and order. (1–2)

...

The various industrial employment of the scholars would curtail the ordinary hours of school. Certainly, all that has been described might be accomplished, and at least two or three hours daily reserved for religious and other instruction.

The Holy Scripture should be used only as a medium of religious teaching. They should not be employed as a hornbook, associated in the mind of the child with the drudgery of mastering the almost mechanical difficulty of learning to read, at an age when it cannot understand language, too often left unexplained. On the contrary, the Holy Scriptures should only be put into the hands of those children who have learned to read with fluency.

To the younger children a short portion of the Scripture should be daily read, and made the subject of an oral lesson.

Those of riper age should be taught to receive and read the Scriptures with reverence.

The art of reading should be acquired from class books appropriate to an industrial school. Besides the class book for the more advanced scholars on cottage economy, the earlier reading lessons might contribute instruction adapted to the condition of a class emerging from slavery or barbarism.

The lessons on writing and arithmetic, as has been before observed, ought to be brought into daily practical use in the employment of the scholars. Nothing is learned so soon or retained so surely as knowledge the practical relation of which is perceived.

The scholar should *thus* be taught to write from dictation, as an exercise of memory, and of spelling and punctuation, as well as of writing.

They should be gradually trained in the composition of simple letters on the business of the school, the garden, or kitchen; and exercised in writing abstracts of oral lessons from memory. The power of writing on the actual events and business of their future lives would thus be acquired.

Within these limits the instruction of the coloured races, combined with a systematic training in industry, cannot fail to raise the population to a condition of improved comfort; but it will also give such habits of steady industry to a settled and thriving peasantry, as may in time develope the elements of a native middle class. This would probably be a consequence of an education within these limits; but if this were accomplished, and time permitted further instruction, an acquaintance might be sought with the art of drawing plans, and those of land-surveying and levelling. Some instruction in geography also would enable them better to understand the Scriptures, and the connection of the colony with the mother country.

The master and mistress should be assisted by apprentices, whose number should be proportioned to the size of the schools. These apprentices should be chosen from the most proficient and best conducted scholars, who are also likely to have an example set them by their parents in harmony with their education. At the age of thirteen, they should be bound by agreement for six years, and might receive in *lieu* of stipend a quantity of the garden produce, sufficient to induce their parents cheerfully to consent to their employment in the school. Careful separate instruction should be given them by the master, at a period daily set apart for the purpose, and they should be furnished with books, as means of self-education. (5)

14. JAMES AFRICANUS BEALE HORTON, *West African Countries and Peoples* (1868)

Aus: J. A. B. Horton, *West African Countries and Peoples* (London, 1868; rpt. Nendeln, 1969), 201–204. – Horton (1835–1882), einer der führenden Vertreter der kleinen Gruppe hochgebildeter Westafrikaner des 19. Jahrhunderts, wurde in Sierra Leone geboren, an einer Schule der Church Missionary Society und am Fourah Bay College, Freetown, sowie an der University von Edinburgh ausgebildet, wo er 1859 seinen Doktorgrad in Medizin erwarb. Tätig als Mediziner, Journalist und Verfasser zahlreicher Arbeiten legte er 1868 mit *West African Countries and Peoples* eine umfassende Studie zur afrikanischen Kultur vor. Im folgenden Textauszug plädiert er für die Einrichtung einer westafrikanischen Universität, die die Voraussetzungen einer adäquaten „transmission of civilization" böte. Eine kritische Auseinandersetzung mit europäisch geprägten Lehrinhalten und -zielen erfolgte durch Horton noch nicht.

II. – General Improvement in the Educational and Ecclesiastical Department of the Colony.

It cannot be denied that the greatest regenerative influence in this department is the Church Missionary Society. They support at present a college at Fourah Bay, a grammar-school in Freetown, and a large female educational institution, besides several village schools. They have, infinitely more than the Government and than any other religious body, laboured earnestly for the diffusion of useful knowledge in the Colony, and to their untiring exertion is due that degree of improvement which is now to be observed in the Colony of Sierra Leone. It is evident from their yearly report that they could not continue this support for a much longer period, whilst the Colony has grown to be self-supporting, and a large field is open to them elsewhere to do good; and therefore it is necessary that the people and the Local Government should take up the work they have so admirably done.

We want a University for Western Africa, and the Church Missionary Society has long ago taken the initiative and built an expensive college, which should now be made the focus of learning for all Western Africa. The yearly expenses of that Society for education are now 4,700 l.,[1] which falls short of their former expenditure, whilst the total sum expended by the Local Government for this purpose is not far above 400 l. The result is that the educational department of the Colony is greatly on the decline every year, and more support is consequently required; but the local authorities refuse to give this, although they liberally spend 14,000 l. yearly merely for police.

A superficial consideration of the theory of the Local Government for the limitation of its efforts in this important direction –viz., that extensive funds have long been, and still are being, appropriated for that object from other sources, and, consequently, it could not be so until the aid is withdrawn, as reported by Colonel Ord – is so alluring and attractive that it requires a long residence in the Colony to prove that it is most unsound; and should the recommendation of the Chamber of Commerce, that a portion of the revenue be yearly voted for general education, not be adopted, it will be one of the greatest barriers to the general improvement contemplated by the Imperial Government.

Fourah Bay College should henceforth be made the University of Western Africa, and endowed by the Local Government, which should guarantee its privileges, and cherish the interest of literature and science in the Colony. A systematic course of instruction should be given to the students, and Regius professors appointed; for it is high time to abolish that system of Lancastrian schoolboy teaching, and a professor should be appointed to one or two subjects, and should give lectures on the results of extensive reading and research. The subjects will be better mastered by the teachers themselves, and the students would reap largely the benefit. Lectures should be given in the theory and practice of education, classics, mathematics, natural philosophy, mensuration, and bookkeeping; English language and literature; French, German, Hebrew, history in general, mineralogy, physiology, zoology, botany, chemistry, moral and political philosophy, civil and commercial law, drawing and music, besides the various subjects which might be included under the term of theology ...

In fact, the whole Colony should be divided into educational districts. In each there should be a free grammar-school, where scholars should be prepared either for a foundation school, to be established in the city, or for the University. Each district should tax itself according to its capabilities for the support of these free schools; and boys who have shown a good degree of intellectual progress in a parochial school should be sent there.

In every village there should be a parochial establishment, assisted by the Government, and not dependent entirely on the paltry sums collected at the school. The schoolmasters should be better paid, so that a better class of men might be obtained as teachers, and the schools visited yearly by Government agents, to see that the rules and regulations are properly carried out.

The Government should also establish a preparatory school at Freetown for the express purpose of training up teachers, or forming a corps of well-trained teachers, who should give instruction both in the theory and in the practical application of sciences; if very proficient in studies some might be transferred to the University. But before admittance as Government or gratuitous pupils, they must bind themselves to remain in the preparatory school for a stated time and pass a rigid examination. This school could be made to receive paying pupils also, the Government only supporting those who are intended for teachers in the public schools, and who should undertake to devote themselves for ten years at least to public instruction; and thus a set of well-trained and educated teachers would be obtained, which would supply the schools of the whole of Western Africa. It will not be out of place if a minister or officer of public instruction be created, with suitable councils, to regulate and improve the educational branch, not only of the Colony of Sierra Leone, but also of the other Colonies in Western Africa; he should form one system of education for all the public schools, and should see that the instructions for the guidance of teachers are properly carried out. In these schools prizes and certificates of honour should be offered to the most meritorious and deserving students.

The neglect of the West African Colonies as regards the education of the natives by the Government, as the Rev. Henry Venn remarks, "contrasts unfavourably with many of the British Colonies, which have established grammar-schools and colleges for the purpose of securing a high standard of education. The Colony of the Mauritius, in addition to such establishments, has annually granted an exhibition of one thousand pounds, open to competition by all races, to enable the successful candidate to proceed to England, and graduate at one of the Universities. Had this principle been adopted at Sierra Leone, and natives of promising abilities been sent over to complete their education in England, it would only have given the native race their fair chance of achieving a high position in the service of the Crown."

15. EDWARD WILMOT BLYDEN, *The Aims and Methods of a Liberal Education for Africans* (1881)

Aus: E. W. Blyden, *Chistianity, Islam and the Negro Race* (London, 1887), 71–93; repr. Hollis R. Lynch (ed.), *Black Spokesman* (London, 1971), 231–245. – Blyden (1832–1912), der herausragende schwarze Intellektuelle des 19. Jahrhunderts, wurde auf St. Thomas, einer Insel der Virgin Islands in der Karibik geboren, kam über die USA 1851 nach Liberia, dem 1822 gegründeten und seit 1847 unabhängigen westafrikanischen Staat. Als Professor war er am Liberia College von 1862–1871 tätig, vertrat sein Land 1877–1880 als Botschafter in England und wurde 1880 Präsident des Liberia College. Von 1850 bis zum Tod publizierte er eine Fülle von Werken, in denen *Christianity, Islam and the Negro Race* den hervorragenden Platz einnimmt. Blyden befürwortete die Entwicklung der „African Personality" auf der Grundlage der Identifikation mit der eigenen Geschichte, Kultur und Sprache. Im folgenden Textauszug übt er scharfe Kritik an der falschen Erziehung schwarzer Menschen durch Europäer und Amerikaner und befürwortet die Rückbesinnung auf afrikanische Geschichte und Kultur als Aufgabe der Ausbildung am Liberia College.

Negroe's Education "Incorrect"

The object of all education is to secure growth and efficiency, to make a man all that his natural gifts will allow him to become; to produce self-respect, a proper appreciation of our own powers of other people; to beget a fitness for one's sphere of life and action, and ability to discharge the duties it imposes. Now, if we take these qualities as the true outcome of a correct education, then every one who is acquainted with the facts must admit that, as a rule, in the entire civilized world, the Negro, notwithstanding his two hundred years' residence with Christian and civilized races, has nowhere received anything like a correct education. We find him everywhere –in the United States, in the West Indies, in South America – largely unable to cope with the responsibilities which devolve upon him. Not only is he not sought after for any position of influence in the political movements of those countries, but he is even denied admission to ecclesiastical appointments of importance . . .

. . .

To a certain extent –perhaps to a very important extent – Negroes trained on the soil of Africa have the advantage of those trained in foreign countries; but in all, as a rule, the intellectual and moral results, thus far, have been far from satisfactory. There are many men of book-learning, but few, very few, of any *capability* – even few who have that amount, or that sort, of culture, which produces self-respect, confidence in one's self, and efficiency in work. Now, why is this? The evil, it is considered, lies in the system and methods of European training to which Negroes are, everywhere in Christian lands, subjected, and which everywhere affects them unfavourably. Of a different race, different susceptibility, different bent of character from that of Europeans, they have been trained under influences in many respects adapted only to the Caucasian race. Nearly all the books they read, the very instruments of their culture, have been such as to force them from the groove which is natural to them, where they would be strong and effective, without furnishing them with any avenue through which they may move naturally and free from obstruction. Christian and so-called civilized Negroes live, for the most part, in foreign countries, where they are only passive spectators of the deeds of a foreign race; and where, with other impressions which they receive from without, an element of doubt as to their own capacity and their own destiny is fastened upon them, and inheres in their intellectual and social constitution. They deprecate their own individuality, and would escape from it if they could. And in countries like this, where they are free from the hampering surroundings of an alien race, they still read and study the books of foreigners, and form their idea of everything that man may do, or ought to do, according to the standard held up in those teachings. Hence, without the physical or mental aptitude for the enterprises which they are taught to admire and revere, they attempt to copy and imitate them, and share the fate of all copyists and imitators. Bound to move on a lower level, they acquire and retain a practical inferiority, transcribing, very often, the faults rather than the virtues of their models.

Besides the result of involuntary impressions, they often receive direct teachings which are not only incompatible with, but destructive of, their self-respect.

In all English-speaking countries the mind of an intelligent Negro child revolts against the description given in elementary books – geographies, travels, histories – of the Negro; but, though he experiences an instinctive revulsion from these caricatures and misrepresentations, he is obliged to continue, as he grows in years, to study such pernicious teachings. After leaving school he finds the same things in newspapers, in reviews, in novels, in *quasi* scientific works; and after a while ... they begin to seem to him the proper things to say and to feel about his race, and he accepts what, at first, his fresh and unbiased feelings naturally and indignantly repelled. Such is the effect of repetition.

Having embraced, or at least assented, to these errors and falsehoods about himself, he concludes that his only hope of rising in the scale of respectable manhood is to strive after whatever is most unlike himself and most alien to his peculiar tastes. And whatever his literary attainments or acquired ability, he fancies that he must grind at the mill which is provided for him, putting in the material furnished to his hands, bringing no contribution from his own field; and of course nothing comes out but what is put in. Thus he can never bring any real assistance to the European. He can never attain to that essence of progress which Mr. Herbert Spencer describes as *difference;* and therefore, he never acquires the self-respect of an independent contributor. He is not an independent help, only a subordinate help; so that the European feels that he owes him no debt, and moves on in contemptuous indifference of the Negro, teaching him to contemn himself.

Those who have lived in civilized communities, where there are different races, know the disparaging views which are entertained of the blacks by their neighbours – and often, alas! by themselves. The standard of all physical and intellectual excellencies in the present civilization being the white complexion, whatever deviates from that favoured colour is proportionally depreciated, until the black, which is the opposite, becomes not only the most unpopular but the most unprofitable colour. Black men, and especially black women, in such communities, experience the greatest imaginable inconvenience. They never feel at home. In the depth of their being they always feel themselves strangers in the land of their exile, and the only escape from this feeling is to escape from themselves. And this feeling of self-depreciation is not diminished as I have intimated above, by the books they read. Women, especially, are fond of reading novels and light literature; and it is in these writings that flippant and eulogistic reference is constantly made to the superior physical and mental characeristics of the Caucasian race, which, by contrast, suggest the inferiority of other races – especially of that race which is furthest removed from it in appearance.

It is painful in America to see the efforts which are made by Negroes to secure outward conformity to the appearance of the dominant race.

This is by no means surprising; but what is surprising is that, under the circumstances, any Negro has retained a particle of self-respect. Now in Africa, where the colour of the majority is black, the fashion in personal matters is naturally suggested by the personal characteristics of the race, and we are free from the necessity of submitting to the use of "incongruous feathers awkwardly stuck on". Still, we are held in bondage by our indiscriminate and injudicious use of a foreign literature; and we strive to advance by the methods of a foreign race. In this effort we struggle with the odds against us ... The African must advance by methods of his own. He must possess a power distinct from that of the European. It has been proved that he knows how to take advantage of European culture, and that he can be benefited by it. This proof was perhaps necessary, but it is not sufficient. We must show that we are able to go alone, to carve out our own way. We must not be satisfied that, in this nation, European influence shapes our policy, makes our laws, rules in our tribunals, and impregnates our social atmosphere. We must not suppose that the Anglo-Saxon methods are final, that there is nothing for us to find for our own guidance, and that we have nothing to teach the world. There is inspiration for us also. We must study our brethren in the interior, who know better than we do the laws of growth for the race. We see among them the rudiments of that which, with fair play and opportunity, will develop into important and effective agencies for our work. We look too much to foreigners, and are dazzled almost to blindness by their exploits – so as to fancy that they have exhausted the possibilities of humanity ... (233–236)

...

All our traditions and experiences are connected with a foreign race. We have no poetry or philosophy but that of our taskmasters. The songs that live in our ears and are often on our lips are the songs which we heard sung by those who shouted while we groaned and lamented. They sang of their history, which was the history of our degradation. They recited their triumphs, which contained the records of our humiliation. To our great misfortune, we learned their prejudices and their passions, and thought we had their aspirations and their power. Now, if we are to make an independent nation – a strong nation – we must listen to the songs of our unsophisticated brethren as they sing of their history, as they tell of their traditions, of the wonderful and mysterious events of their tribal or national life, of the achievements of what we call their superstitions; we must lend a ready ear to the ditties of the Kroomen who pull our boats, of the Pessah and Golah men, who till our farms; we must read the compositions, rude as we may think them, of the Mandingoes and the Veys. We shall in this way get back the strength of the race ... (244)

16. J. R. ORR, *Education of Natives* (1912)

Aus: J. R. Orr, *The System of Education in the East Africa Protectorate* (Nairobi, 1912); rpt. G. H. Mungeam (comp.), *Kenya Select Historical Documents 1884–1923* (Nairobi, 1979), 237–251. – J. R. Orr, der erste im Protektorat Ostafrika von der Kolonialverwaltung ernannte „Director of Education", legt in seinem 1912 veröffentlichten Bericht wegweisende Überlegungen für eine offizielle Erziehungspolitik der Kolonialmacht vor, in der eine praxisorientierte Ausbildung Vorrang hat. Der schon hier zutagetretende Widerspruch zwischen einer afrikanischen Bedürfnissen angepaßten Erziehung und handfesten Eingriffen in „tribal practices", die als unmoralisch angesehen werden, sollte die offizielle Erziehungspolitik der Kolonialmacht auf Jahrzehnte bestimmen.

Native education in East Africa presents all the difficulties usually attaching to such problems, and is likely to be further complicated by the increasingly heterogeneous nature of the population of the country.

To put the difficulties briefly, it must be realised on the one hand that British East Africa is a Protectorate,[2] and such being the case, the Government has a distinct duty towards the natives in helping them to raise their standard of life in their native villages and to be ruled intelligently by their own councils or chiefs. On the other hand, there is a great tendency for the number of Europeans and Indians in the country to increase at the expense of the native inhabitants. The problem is one of the development of the tribal system versus detribalisation. The question, therefore, "To what definite end are we training the natives?" is one which lies within the province of the administration, and can only be answered in a general way by the educationalist.

So far the tribes of East Africa have kept themselves entirely apart from each other. Until recent years raids were common, and to-day very sharp lines divide them. There is no consciousness whatever of colour; the native takes for granted that the European is far above him, and so great is the native's respect that nothing the European can do astonishes him. The very term "Wa-zungu" means "the clever or wise," and nothing is considered impossible to such people.

But if a policy of detribalisation is pursued, the question of colour will come to the front at once, and there will be a danger of uniting all tribes against the white population. (248).

. . .

At Kitui the late Mr. J. B. Ainsworth, while District Commissioner, persuaded the chiefs to contribute to the building of a small school. To induce the chiefs to send their sons was a difficult task, and pupils came in slowly. There are now about 20 boys in attendance. The teacher is a Giriama native trained at Freretown.[3] He teaches them reading, writing, and arithmetic, using the Swahili language as a medium of instruction. The children are very intelligent, and wrote for me very passable essays in Swahili on their crops and shambas.[4] In addition also they receive instruction in elementary agriculture and tree-planting. When I asked the assembled chiefs if they approved of the little Government school, they replied: "At first we did not like it; we thought the Government meant to take our sons from us; however, we see that this is not so, and

2. Ziele und Wege der kolonialen Sprach- und Bildungspolitik 81

we will continue to send many of our sons. To learn to read and write is good, for then a man may write down all his possessions, and his friends cannot cheat his sons when he is dead. Besides you teach them to grow crops, and that is very good." The boys board at the school and grow their own crops, so that food supplies cost nothing.

The intention is to train the boys to help the District Commissioner. Some have been of use in counting hut tax for the collection. The idea is that the boys shall return to their villages and keep in communication by letter with the District Commissioner, reporting events as they happen from time to time.

Inasmuch as the missionaries have no influence with the Wa-kamba, it has been decided that the Government shall take them in hand. They are probably the most intelligent tribe in East Africa, and are specially inclined towards skilled labour. With a view to training them, a large school is being opened in the Machakos district, three days' march west of Kitui and about 40 miles from Nairobi. The school at present building is under the charge of. Mr. James Manley, who has had considerable experience of natives in Uganda. The school will consist, when developed, of three departments: an elementary school for children, where drawing, handicrafts, simple nature study, geography (chiefly physical), general history, arithmetic, reading, and writing will be taught. The last two subjects will not be ends in themselves, but merely instruments for the conveyance and expression of ideas. No undue emphasis will be laid upon them, and they will be entirely subservient to practical education. Secondly, a number of picked boys will be given a higher form of education to enable them to assist the political officers, to act as headmen or as accountants to settlers or as teachers. This advanced education will include, in all cases, instruction in agriculture diseases and care of stock, and carpentry. Thirdly, the main feature of the establishment will be the industrial department. At the outset, stone-dressing, brick-making, carpentry will be taught, extending later to waggon making, furniture making, tinsmithing, tailoring, agriculture, and care of stock. With industrial training will be closely allied as much drawing, reading, and writing as is deemed necessary. Physical training consists of gymnastics, drill and games will be compulsory for all, and the school will be managed on semi-military lines.

Mr. Manley has instructions to study the Kikamba language, and later instruction will be carried on in the mother-tongue in the lower part of the elementary school. The chief medium of instruction will be Ki-Swahili, English only being taught to a few picked boys where necessary. (248–249)
. . .

Concluding Remarks. – It will be seen from the above that native education has hardly begun. The Government is strongly opposed at present to any save industrial education, which will be carried on extensively by Government schools and grants to Missions. The total expenditure on native training is –

	£
Grants to Missions	1,000
Machakos and Kitui Schools	850
P. W. D. Training depot for apprentices	700
	£ 2,550

The number of boys on the books of the Educational Department as qualifying for grants at the Missions is 194.

The provisional policy, laid down by the Director of Education and supported by the Education Board, is to carry on education in and through the tribe; to prove to the chiefs that there is no desire to take their children from them, or in any way to interfere with their customs.

The natives of East Africa are suspicious of Europeans. For this reason progress must be very slow and cautious and the entire support of the tribal council must be obtained. Heads of schools must work firstly with the District Commissioner, secondly with the native council, and thirdly with the European settlers of the country. The administration will put down with a strong hand such tribal practices as are immoral. Moral instruction will form a leading part in the school curriculum, and by means of mixing with Europeans, by means of definite teaching in schools, objectionable customs will drop away. At the same time the authority of the chiefs and of parents must be strongly upheld and family and tribal ties maintained. It is only thus that the natives will see that no harm is intended to them, and will be won over to support and encourage the uplifting of their race. Lastly, it is believed that scientific teaching and the preeminent usefulness of the black man to society as a whole in the sphere of morals, industry or commerce, can alone contribute to the harmony of races. (250–251)

17. C.M.S. and Education in Africa (1922)

Aus: Church Missionary Society (publ.), *The C.M.S. and Education Abroad* (London, 1922), 10–19. – Die 1792 in London gegründete Church Missionary Society begann ihre Arbeit 1804 in Sierra Leone, 1843 in Ostafrika und 1845 im heutigen Nigeria. In den ehemaligen englischen Kolonien spielte sie unter der großen Zahl von Missionsgesellschaften eine entscheidende Rolle und nahm, insbesondere nach dem 1. Weltkrieg, in einer Fülle von Veröffentlichungen immer wieder zu Erziehungsaufgaben Stellung. Der folgende Text veranschaulicht die Selbsteinschätzung ihrer Leistungen in Afrika.

The Fruits of Education

At this point it is well to pause and inquire what is the net result of the work carried on in the types of schools we have examined. What is education doing for the African? Are we turning out improved Africans or a poor imitation of the European?

To answer the first question, it is essential to realize the changes which education inevitably has brought to the life of the African. Imagine a nation with-

out books, possessing only a slight idea of music, with few pictures and a
scanty knowledge of drawing, often unable to perceive a subject in a photograph, a nation stunted in mental, physical, and spiritual development. Those
among them who have come in contact with missionary education have in their
reading had a new world opened to them; the music of the hymns and canticles
has given their innermost feelings an instrument for expression; pictures, especially copies of the great masters, have supplied food for thought and put in a
simple and intelligible way before them world facts which are quietly acting as
leaven in their child minds. Their whole range of mental outlook has been
widened by education. Their thoughts are new thoughts. And their life and its
content have correspondingly been enlarged. Improved methods of industry
and cultivation have led to the growth of trading, the establishment of small
shop systems, better housing, the introduction of coinage, and the extension of
communication with the outer world.

But more than this, a great spiritual transformation is taking place, the old
fears and fetishes are giving way to the freedom and simplicity of the Gospel.

Among Christians immoral dances have been dropped, horrible ceremonies
have quietly disappeared and are still disappearing, unable to continue in the
light of the Gospel. The blackness of heathenism is retreating before the morning light of the Lord. It will be found that a new and great African nation is being quietly created, a nation of men and women to whom the Sabbath is indeed
a "delight", often far more than to their European masters, and who value the
Word of God more than life. The Christian community is coming to fullness of
stature, through the great C.M.S. ideal of self-support, self-government, and
self-propagation; no longer an irresponsible child, it is becoming a responsible,
reasoning being whose opinion in things that matter will become increasingly
valuable.

The further question is often asked: "Is missionary education producing
good Africans, or a poor imitation of Europeans?" In reply it must first be admitted that often the old ways of life have been exchanged too soon for the
new; in the process something that was indispensable may have been lost. The
recent Phelps-Stokes Commission has shown that in some cases the aim of "life
in the village" has not been kept sufficiently in the forefront. Adaptations to
village life must be the central purpose of the up-country school. English and
its teaching must not wholly displace the unwritten literature or folk-lore of the
African tribe. The garden and the farm must be as worthy a goal to the African
boy as the clerk's desk or the engineer's lathe. But the missionary education
which has produced African leaders like Bishops Crowther, Oluwole, Howells,[5] is the best answer to the criticism just mentioned.

A nation does not reach maturity in a day. Africa has been happy in those
who have helped to rear in their childhood the growing races of that great continent. Now that she lies open to the stream of immigrants who pour in for
commerce, she needs, more than ever, a great-company of elder brothers and
sisters who will guide her through the years of adolescence. So we turn to consider what kind of Europeans are needed in Africa in the days to come. (17–18)

18. *Educational Objectives and Adaptations* (1925)

Aus: Phelps Stokes Commission Report: *Education in East Africa* (New York, 1925), 17–22. – Die philantropische Gesellschaft Phelps-Stokes Fund in den USA betraute 1920 zwei Kommissionen mit der Aufgabe, einen Bericht über das Erziehungswesen in Afrika anzufertigen und Vorschläge zur Verbesserung zu erstellen. Die beiden umfassenden Berichte, *Education in Africa* (1922) und *Education in East Africa*, geben hierüber Auskunft. Im folgenden Text beschäftigt sich die Kommission mit Fragen der Schullektüre und der Unterrichtssprache. Das 1923 von der britischen Regierung eingerichtete „Advisory Committee on Native Education in British Tropical African Dependencies" ließ sich in den folgenden Jahren weitgehend von den Stellungnahmen der Kommissionen lenken.

Reading and Elements of Community Life

Reading and writing probably surpass arithmetic in the possibility of adaptation for the presentation of community needs. Reading lessons may be filled with helpful suggestions as to health needs, such as nutritious food; cleanliness of body and clothing, of home and school. The upper standards may study the achievements in the realm of sanitation and hygiene by such men as Pasteur and other great scientists who have freed humanity from disease and suffering. The Old Testament, and especially the Mosaic laws, and verses from the New Testament may be effectively used to strengthen the interest of the pupil in health.

Agriculture and rural life are receiving increasing recognition in literature. Pupils of primary and advanced grade may profitably be given reading and writing tasks relating to garden and farm, and the life of domestic animals. Where pupils can read a European language the teacher may draw largely on magazines and books describing the remarkable activities of rural Denmark and other parts of the world where agriculture has received proper recognition. The Bulletins of the United States Department of Agriculture and also the Hampton Leaflets[6] describe the influence of farm demonstration and various rural clubs that have increased the food supply and brought prosperity to the people. It is impossible to overstate the pressing urgency of the need for a richer school literature capable of being related to community needs. Few of the existing primers, readers and text-books in the English language lend themselves to this use. In African vernaculars, with a few notable exceptions, such books scarcely exist. There are, however, hopeful indications that this situation is now being realized, at least in part, and that Governments and missions are taking initial steps to meet it. Meantime much might be done by the wise allocation of small additional funds to enable teachers to purchase books and pamphlets on the lines here indicated as a basis for oral instruction. It is worth making inquiry of the Agricultural Department in each colony, as good material for the teacher may be available.

The home and family life have so full a place in literature as to make proper selection difficult. There are descriptions – again only for readers of European languages – of typical European and American homes; biographies of women who have realized the ideals of motherhood and the home in the full meaning of that wonderful place; discussions of fatherhood, with all its responsibilities; and stories of childhood and youth that are filled with inspiration. Both the Old and New Testament have many important references to home life and all that makes it sacred. In the more practical realm there is much material relating to the care of children and of the home, the relation of the sexes, the preparation of food and clothing, and the accommodation for sleep.

Sound ideas of recreation are amply presented in many pamphlets and books. The teacher can obtain – again in European languages – reading material from Europe or from America that describes the healthful games and amusements of civilized peoples. It would be helpful for the teacher to encourage the pupils to describe their own games as compared with those of other lands. Classroom discussion would doubtless result in sifting the desirable from the undesirable elements in the amusements. In the course of time it would be possible for schools in different parts of Africa to exchange compositions describing the games and various forms of recreation of different tribes. Effort should be made to include discussions of recreations that are designed to build up the physique, to quicken the mind and to develop sound ideals of character. (17–18)

...

Languages of Instruction

The languages of instruction rank with the ordinary school subjects as means of acquiring and transferring knowledge. These languages in Africa are usually the Native speech of dialect and the language of the European nation in control. Both these languages have, however, a contribution of far greater significance than that of the mere transfer of knowledge. The European language is not only the agency for acquiring information of the usual character; it is the means of uniting Africa with the great civilizations of the world. With full appreciation of the European language, the value of the Native tongue is immensely more vital, in that it is one of the chief means of preserving whatever is good in Native customs, ideas and ideals, and thereby perserving what is more important than all else, namely, Native self-respect. All peoples have an inherent right to their own language. It is the means of giving expression to their own personality, however primitive they may be. The processes of education must begin with the characteristics of the people as they are and help them to evolve to the higher levels. No greater injustice can be committed against a people than to deprive them of their own language. It is interesting and significant to note that one of the first and most emphatic demands of the nations that are now endeavoring to realize self-determination is to re-establish their own language. Even though it may be a futile attempt because another language is practically in control, the longing for their own language is natural and justifiable.

The use of a European language has been advocated from mixed motives by both Europeans and Natives. In the past practically all controlling nations forced their languages on the Native people and discouraged the use of their Native tongue. This was true centuries ago in Great Britain. Fortunately at the present time the only Powers that still maintain this attitude in some of their possessions are the French and the Portuguese. Whatever the motives, whether pride of language, nationality, or even the generous desire to share their language with those whom they control, the policy is unwise and unjust. The disregard of the Native language is a hindrance even to the acquisition of the European language. Much more does it limit the sympathetic and real exchange of ideas and influences, which are necessary to mutual confidence between Africans and Europeans.

The Native people are as a rule eager to learn an European language. Their desire is based on an intuitive feeling that the language will open new opportunities, and also on experiences where a common language would have avoided many difficulties through the free and natural approach to the government officers. The Native leaders will become increasingly conscious of their dependence on European civilization for much of their progress. They will desire to help Africa to break through the agelong isolation which has kept in a bondage to superstition and suffering. Already they see the great resources, material and human, that may be developed through European agencies. It will not be long before they want to know such great physical sciences as chemistry and biology and to catch the inspiration of the great literatures. They will want through study of history and the social sciences to profit by the failures and the successes of other peoples. It is little wonder, therefore, that some Native leaders in Africa have almost been willing to forget their own language in their enthusiasm for the languages of civilization. It was natural for these leaders to mistake for generosity the narrow nationalism of European colonists in fostering an European language to the neglect of the Native tongue.

This emphatic belief in the value of the Native languages is not to be interpreted to justify the indiscriminate adoption of all African dialects as claiming encouragement and continuous use. While many African languages are rich in words with delicate shades of meaning, others, on the contrary, are merely dialects with only unimportant differentiations from the parent tongue. In many colonies there is a multiplicity of dialects spoken by small groups who are thus estranged from one another to the point of hostility. The process of selecting the Native languages of greatest value to the Native people is often exceedingly difficult. The comparative merits of several dialects in a colony may require years of scientific study. The testimony of Europeans or Natives who speak a particular dialect is likely to be prejudiced favorably by that knowledge. The ability to weigh the value of testimony as to languages must be based on real knowledge of the dialects under consideration. There are also geographical elements that influence the value of a dialect, such as the number of people who speak it, the status and potentiality of the people as compared with others of a different dialect, and territorial proximity.

Missionaries of several nationalities deserve much credit for their study of Native languages. Through their devoted efforts a large number of the dialects have been reduced to writing, and the Bible, either in part or in its entirety, has been translated into them. In this great achievement the British and Foreign Bible Society, whose work in East African languages will presently be noted, has rendered a service of incalculable value. A number of small text-books and pamphlets have also been translated into many vernaculars. Governments have not sufficiently encouraged this important service to the Native people of Africa. With full recognition of what has been done, the task, as has been urged in a preceding section, is only begun. There is now need for the active cooperation of Governments, missions and commercial organizations with scientific students of languages to make a thorough survey of African tongues and dialects, so that the present confusion and uncertainty may be corrected and that vernacular literature may be issued on well-directed and effective lines.

Looked at in the light of community needs, the belief of the teacher in all that has been said concerning the languages of instruction will be strengthened. With such a consciousness the teacher will be eager to know the Native dialects, so that intimate contacts may be established with every phase of community life. Through the Native language the older people will become known as well as the youth in school – their health, their agricultual needs and achievements, their village crafts, their homes, or lack of homes, their play, both good and bad, their music and folk melodies, whether degrading or inspiring, all will gradually unfold through the magic of the Native tongue. What changes will then follow in the teaching and the preaching; in the exchange of shop and field, of home and playground! The more real the insight into Native life through the Native language, the more real and the more intelligent will be the demand for the European language to serve as the medium for the transfer of whatever civilization has to give to primitive Africa in all phases of life.

In view of the great importance of both the Native tongue and the language of the European nation in control, it is significant that universities are giving increased attention to the study of Native languages. In the Union of South Africa, the Universities of Johannesburg, Pretoria and Cape Town are maintaining courses or departments of Native thought and language which are attracting students in increasing numbers. European nations with colonial possessions are beginning to require candidates for colonial service to study Native customs and language. The following statement on language study of missionaries was prepared by members of the staff of the School of Oriental Studies in London, and issued by the Board of Study for the Preparation of Missionaries. It is a comprehensive outline of the language needs of those who would work in colonial Africa, whether they are missionaries, traders, or government officials:

(a) We regard a mastery of the vernacular of the people among whom he works as essential for the missionary. Even though he may be able to do a certain amount of work through the medium of English, a knowledge of the vernacular will add greatly to his effectiveness as a missionary.

(b) As far as our experience and information go, we are of opinion that the average level of proficiency attained by missionaries in the vernacular at the present time is regrettably and even dangerously low.

(c) Candidates should know at least a year before sailing to what country and to what language area they are to be sent, in order that they may undertake special preparatory study. The linguistic side of this special preparation should include a course of lessons in phonetics and some study of modern methods of language learning. But neither the phonetics nor the language methods should be studied merely in the abstract, but side by side with some actual work upon a non-European language – if possible, the vernacular that will be needed on the field.

(d) After reaching the field, it is important that no responsibility should be put upon the new missionary that would hinder his acquiring as rapidly as possible facility in the use of the vernacular.

(e) Where language schools do not exist on the field, steps should be taken to train a sufficient number of whole-time Native teachers in the best modern methods of language teaching.

(f) The language examinations should place far more stress on practical ablity to make use of a language than upon knowledge of systematic grammar.

The observations and experience of the long tour in East Africa support the conclusions and recommendations formulated in the report of the Commission to West and Equatorial Africa and they are presented herewith from *Education in Africa*, pp. 25, 26.

The elements to be considered in determining the languages of instruction are (1) that every people have an inherent right to their Native tongue; (2) that the multiplicity of tongues shall not be such as to develop misunderstandings and distrust among people who should be friendly and cooperative; (3) that every group shall be able to communicate directly with those to whom the government is entrusted; and (4) that an increasing number of Native people shall know at least one of the languages of the civilized nations. In determining the weight of each of these elements, it is of course necessary to ascertain the local conditions. It is clear that there is comparatively little, if any advantage in the continuation of a crude dialect with practically no powers of expression. It is also evident that the need for a *lingua franca* is not essential to a large group of people speaking the same language and living under conditions that do not require much intercommunication. It may even be true that some one of the Native languages may be so highly developed as to make possible the translation of the great works of civilization into that language. With due consideration for all of these elements and the modifying circumstances, the following recommendations are offered as suggestions to guide Governments and educators in determining the usual procedure in most African colonies:

1. The tribal language should be used in the lower elementary standards or grades.

2. A *lingua franca* of African origin should be introduced in the middle classes of the school if the area is occupied by large Native groups speaking diverse languages.

3. The language of the European nation in control should be tought in the upper standards. (19–22)

19. BEN N. AZIKIWE, *How Shall We Educate the African?* (1934)

Aus: *Journal of the African Society*, XXXIII, 131 (1934), 143–150. – Benjamin Nnamdi Azikiwe (geb. 1904) aus Nigeria studierte an der Howard University und der University of Pennsylvania. Politisch engagiert betätigte er sich seit 1937 als Journalist, Herausgeber von Zeitungen und Zeitschriften sowie als Verfasser einer kritischen Kulturstudie, *Renascent Africa* (Lagos, 1937). 1959–1963 war er Governor-General, 1963–1966 der erste Präsident Nigerias. Nach der Rückkehr aus dem Asyl in London 1972 wurde er Chancellor der Lagos University. Azikiwe setzt, schärfer als seine Vorgänger Blyden (cf. Text 13) und Caseley-Hayford (cf. Text 23), die kritische Auseinandersetzung mit der englischen Erziehungspolitik fort.

Education of Africans has been purposely converted into a "problem." In all fairness to the noble work accomplished by Missions and Governments in Africa, frankness demands the conclusion that African education is not a "problem"; the African is a human being, and he could respond to any stimulus in any environment as would any other human being – all hereditary factors being equal. The attempt to transform the education of the African into a "problem" is not only a misdirected effort but an erroneous procedure. It is based on false conceptions of the mentality of the African. Thus African education has become impressionistic, and the European and American educators continue to perpetuate the myth of traditional anthropology on the mental inequality of races.

Modern anthropological scholarship does not subscribe to the notion that one race is mentally at variance with others. Moreover, the accomplishments of Africans in European and American universities during the past five decades, vindicate their mental capacity and also establish the fact that the brain of the average African can function in any environment just as that of the other races. In other words, the African is human, and is intellectually alert just as the average European, Asiatic, or American. What he needs is an opportunity to demonstrate his capabilities. *Education knows no race or colour or creed.* An Efik can win the M. A. from Columbia or Oxford or any university in the world, if given a chance. The same is applicable to a Zulu, Fanti, Ga, Mende, Wangala, Timni, Hausa, Nupe, Jekri, Popo, Ijaw, Ibo, Yoruba, Kru, Vai, Joloff, Mandingo, Bubi, or any other African tribe under God's sun.

Translated into common terms what then do the achievements of Africans intellectually and educationally prove? Just these plain and incontrovertible facts: *The African is not, and never has been, a problem; there is no such thing as an African educational problem; those who believe in such an oddity, are problems in themselves!*

Broadly speaking, the average Liberian or Abyssinian is more educated than the average resident of African colonial possessions. Education implies more than book-learning and a collection of meaningless "degrees" after one's name. It comprises the essentials of life, including a sense of pride in the fundamental rights of man. For this reason, the average resident of these two sovereign states has been better educated, for he lives in an environment of freedom and respectability, relatively speaking. He aspires to the highest offices of the land.

There is no sterotyped "place" for him. His environment is devoid of inferiority complexes. He could achieve his dreams if he would only have the ambition.

Contrasted with the residents of colonial possessions, one discovers that despite their economic progress, the colonial Africans have been so *mis-educated* (to borrow Dr. Carter G. Woodson's term) that their criterion of values is alien to their soil. The universities of Europe and America become the standardisers of their national ideals. A degree from Oxford or London or from the United States, becomes their supreme objective. If a European should assert that a degree from a British university is the quintessence of culture, the African *literati* invariably retort with an "Amen." If an American should claim that a degree from the United States is the only passport to intellectual achievements, the African, in his intellectual docility, accepts the same as final. Consequently, these *mis-educated* Africans imitate the characteristic jealousies and superciliousnesses of alien ideologies. They are so influenced thereby that they return to Africa laden with these sardonic manifestations of bigoted aristocracy and national idiosyncrasies.

True it is, the Liberian and Abyssinian educational systems have not been progressive. But the little they have done has been of *practical* value to their citizenry. While it has not prevented a section of their societies from preying upon the weaker ones, that is nothing singular. It is one of the anomalies of Western education and civilisation. Nevertheless, there is need for educational reform in all Africa. In addition to the subjects taught in elementary, secondary, and collegiate institutions, more emphasis should be placed on African anthropology, ethnology, and ethnography. African educators, be they black or white, should sift the excrescences of African culture and have a scientific attitude in order to delineate the durable and qualitative essentials of African sociology, philosophy, religion, ethics, art, music, law, and government.

Certain friends of the African have advocated industrial and agricultural education to the exclusion of academic and literay ones, as a panacea for the African educational "problem." Whether the industrialisation of Africa will be conducive to the happiness of the aboriginal in view of the unhappy state of affairs in the industrialised West is not for consideration at the moment. No doubt these philanthropists, missionaries, and Government officials are sincere in advocating industrial and agricultural education. But this notion is maliciously false and a retrograde tendency. Just as Hampton and Tuskegee[7] institutes have been unsuccessful in producing any outstanding graduates in the technical or agricultural field, for over five decades of educational endeavours, (see also the editorials in *The Afro-American* 3rd and 10th, 1931) so remarkably does this doctrine fail to pragmatise. It is curious that advocates of this measure should seek to apply to the African conditions which are not only unfavourable with the Afro-American, but are alien to the African mode of living.

Of course, one is not opposed to agricultural or industrial education. There is no need to beg the question for, sooner or later, the West will unconsciously drag Africa into its vicious net of industrialism and capitalism and "rugged" individualism, with their attendant ethics and values. But the basis of the theory for the industrial and agricultural education of the African is fallacious. It conceives the African as better adapted to industrial and agricultural pursuits, which is hardly true. In other words, so long as the African would be content at menial tasks, and would not seek complete social, political, and economic equality with the Western world, he is deemed to be a "good" fellow. But let him question the right to keep him in political and economic servitude, and let him strive to educate himself to the fundamentals of these modern problems, he is immediately branded as an "agitator". He becomes a "bad" fellow for failing to stay in his "place," which, of course, is *the background.*

On the strength of this, one humbly postulates that any educational theory which supports the regimentation of human minds and objectives, is suspicious and ought to be cautiously examined. And then, the fact that the African is merely a "producer" of raw materials, and has no voice in the "fixing of prices" for his produce (and this is generally done for him at the exchanges in London, New York, Paris, Hamburg, or Brussels) renders his attempts at wholesale farming a sentence of economic servitude. If he were encouraged to study economics and banking, instead of farming alone, he might be able to "fix" prices, too; but outside Liberia and Abyssinia, he is not in position so to do. He is a *subject or protégé* (not a citizen or national) of European countries which maintain what has been mistakenly termed an "open door" policy, a policy which actually is a subtle means to lower the price of African produce in the various "spheres of influence," for the consumption of European factories, and also to make the African dependent on what price Europe chooses to pay for African produce. No elaborate knowledge is required to understand this subtlety of colonial economics, yet advocates of agricultural education have failed to warn Africans of the Charybdis awaiting them after the escape from Scylla!

Industrial education may seem plausible, but it has its limitations as well. After industrial training, then what? How can the technically-trained African earn a *decent* livelihood when all avenues of higher appointments are closed to him and he is forced to worship the powers that be ere he could be considered for permanent and respectable appointment? It is nice to have technical ambitions, but as President Arthur Howe, of Hampton Institute, has observed: "There is little use in educating people unless they are to have opportunities to use their abilities." (143–147)

...

How then shall the African be educated? Lest the author be misjudged, there is no ground to conclude that agricultural or industrial education should not be offered the African. Rather, it is the author's conviction that these should be stressed only to the extent that not *all* Africans should become artisans and farmers. Farming is a wholesome vocation, so also are the industries. But the modern state – if the various colonies in Africa ever dream of their capability to develop into sovereign states – is a mosaic of all the professions and vocations. Education in Africa should consist of both literary and technical, and moral subjects in the curriculum of schools. Illiteracy should be diminished by the gradual introduction of compulsory elementary education throughout Africa. Mass education of the adults should be encouraged both by Governments and the African population. In other words, educate the African as a human being and not as a museum specimen or a fossil or preserved animal for scientific experimentation.

Several organisations and individuals who are interested in the "problem" of African education may be shocked at the tone of this modest and frank comment on their pet subject. Some might even consider the author ultra-radical in his pronouncements. But one submits with all deference to their feelings that at the basis of their philosophy of education, concocted as the best suited for the so-called "Native Races," is the conception of mental inequality of the races so vividly and erroneously disseminated by such racialists as Count Gobineau, Benjamin Kidd, Lothrop Stoddard,[8] and other pseudo-scientists who have appropriated the vocabulary of science and have prostituted its methodology and technique in order to prove what they want to prove, namely, the moral right to arrogate to one race a stigma of superiority to the detriment of another. This, of course, is what Professor Miller, of Bryn Mawr College, has termed "the rationalisation of a myth."

Unfortunately these "friends" of African education, despite their paternalism and philanthropism, are humans. They like to be adored and flattered. The fact that they are performing a mission of mercy to "down-trodden and backward children of nature" bolsters their fixations of arrogance and pride, and they unconsciously become evangelists of the myth of racial inferiority. When an educated African challenges such an unnatural relation between his "civilizers" and himself, he is looked upon as a "problem." Should he question the right of his rulers to prevent this *active participation* in the administration of the country, he is dubbed an "agitator." He is thus caricatured as a "Europeanised African" for daring so to live and enjoy his life more abundantly. He is presented to the innocent world as an alienated individual from his indigenous folks. On the other hand, the aboriginals have been prevented by subtle means from imbibing the richness of Western education. Their education has been formalised. They are reduced to the four "R's," namely, *Reading, 'Riting, 'Rithmetic,* and *Religion.* Thus it is impossible to effectuate any social progress in the sense that the Western world knows it, within the next century. Yet the irony of this way of thinking is that African "backwardness" is judged on his failure to measure up to the standards of Western education which has been purposely denied him. (149–150)

20. KWAME NKRUMAH, *The Intellectual Vanguard* (1963)

Aus: Kwame Nkrumah, *Africa Must Unite* (London, 1963), 43–49. – Nkrumah (1901–1972), ausgebildet am Achimota College, in den USA und in England, begann seine politische Karriere nach 1945 und wurde General Secretary der United Gold Coast Convention. 1949 gründete er die Convention People's Party, wurde inhaftiert, nach den Wahlen 1951 entlassen, um seinen Sitz wahrnehmen zu können. 1951 wurde

2. Ziele und Wege der kolonialen Sprach- und Bildungspolitik 93

er Premierminister der Goldküste und 1957, nach der Unabhängigkeit, der erste Premierminister Ghanas. 1960 ließ er sich zum Präsidenten der Republik wählen. Während eines Aufenthalts in China wurde er 1966 gestürzt und verstarb 1972 im Exil in Guinea. Nkrumah verfaßte eine Vielzahl politischer Schriften, in denen er afrikanischen Sozialismus, afrikanische Einheit und die „African personality" als Ziele propagierte. Im folgenden Text werden die praktischen Schwierigkeiten eines unabhängigen afrikanischen Landes im Erziehungswesen sichtbar, die zu beheben Nkrumah – wie andere afrikanische Politiker Anfang der sechziger Jahre – voller Optimismus war.

The History of human achievement illustrates that when an awakened intelligentsia emerges from a subject people it becomes the vanguard of the struggle against alien rule. There is a direct relation between this fact and the neglect of the imperial powers to provide for the proper growth of educational facilities in their colonies. I saw this connection quite soon in my career, and it was one of the main reasons why I became a teacher for a time.

The tremendous enthusiasm for education in Africa never fails to impress visitors. A schoolboy once wrote: "I think the happiest event in my life was the day when my father told me to go to school."[10] Another said: "The most unfortunate thing that could happen to me would be to have had no education, or to be sent away from school now, for then all my life would be wasted."[11] The burning desire for education among both children and adults received little encouragement from the colonial powers, and one of the worst legacies of colonialism has been the absence of a trained body of African technicians and administrators.

A brief glimpse at the educational position in various parts of Africa will illustrate my point. In Northern Rhodesia, in 1960, only 43 per cent of African children of school age were at school; and only 1.1 per cent of those who reached the eligible age for secondary education received it. The 1954 report for Southern Rhodesia showed only 16.5 per cent of the school potential actually at school. In Kenya, the Government provided hardly any schools for Africans until the 1930s, so the Kikuyus created their own. They formed the Kikuyu Independent Schools Association. To provide teachers, Peter Koinange founded the Kenya Teachers' College at Githunguri, where Jomo Kenyatta later became Principal. Not surprisingly, these Kikuyu schools turned out keen nationalists, and they were suppressed by the British after the Mau Mau outbreak in 1952. In 1955 there were only 35 high schools in the entire country for 5½ million Africans.

In the whole of French Equatorial Africa there were about 850 elementary schools, and most of them were badly equipped and staffed. Of the children of school age, only about 18 per cent went to school at all.

As for higher education, until the foundation of the University College at Salisbury incorporated in 1955, Makerere College, founded in 1922, was the only school with university rank in the whole immense distance between Khartoum and Johannesburg. In all the British colonies put together, there were only three other colleges similar to Makerere: Achimota in Ghana, then the Gold Coast, Ibadan in Nigeria, and Fourah Bay in Sierra Leone. In French

Africa, south of the Sahara, there was one: in Portuguese Africa, none. The Sudan had Gordon College, and the Belgians opened a small Roman Catholic University outside Leopoldville, at Lovanium ...

The problem of education was uppermost in my mind and in the minds of my party when we had our first meeting after taking office under the colonial administration. The fact that most of my colleagues had, like me, been trained as teachers reflected their faith, too, in education as the key to our liberation and advance.

Before we could embark on our plans, we made a review of the situation as we found it. It was not heartening. The picture had changed little since a foremost British authority on colonial affairs, Mr Leonard Barnes, writing in the nineteen-thirties, had this to say about education in the Gold Coast:

"In 1913 education there cost £ 25,000: in 1931, the peak year, it cost just over a quarter of a million. This is ten times as much, and there can be no objection to calling it such, or to calling it an increase of 900 per cent, if you prefer. The same fact can be stated, though less impressively, by saying that educational expenditure took eighteen years to rise from 3 per cent to 7 per cent of Government revenue. Both forms of statement omit another fact, which is equally relevant, namely, that even in 1931 four Gold-Coast children out of five were receiving no schooling of any kind, and less than half per cent got past the primary stage ... Authorities have calculated that at our present rate of progress it will be 700 years before the natives of even the Gold Coast can read and write their own language. Note: Or 3,500 years, if the natural increase of population is taken into account."[12]

It is difficult to appreciate from these observations that the educational system in the Gold Coast was considered to be one of the most advanced in tropical Africa. Our primary education, in fact, goes back as far as 1752 and was begun by missionaries and continued by them for a very long time. After a long period, they received grants-in-aid from the local government, but a good part of the money was used for purely religious purposes and in paying for the salaries of European missionaries. Unfortunately, too, they paid the local teachers irregularly and enforced upon them the purely religious duties of lay preachers, catechists and Sunday school teachers. These faults aside, it must be admitted that we owe a considerable debt of gratitude to the missionaries for the contribution they made to such education as the country received. On their side, however, they did not lose, for in addition to the grants received from government, they charged school fees, and some of them set up bookshops for the sale of religious literature and school text-books. A few, like the Basel Mission, even branched out into trading and have developed into not inconsiderable business concerns. Today the mission bookshops more or less control the importation and distribution of school books, and my Government is faced with the task of establishing other means of getting text-books to our school population which will not be subject to the kind of manipulation which now creates a scramble for these books and a too heavy financial burden upon parents.

There did come a time when colonial administrators found that it was too expensive for the local budget to import British officers for the lower grades of the service, and when the European trading communities discovered a need for African workers with some degree of literacy. The colonial administration then took a hand in providing facilities at primary and secondary levels, though they were niggardly, especially in regard to secondary schools. Little attention was given to technical training, and as a result educated Africans have acquired a bias towards clerical work and a contempt for manual labour.

...

When my colleagues and I came into office in 1951, we found some government schools in the principal towns of the country. But they served only a small part of the urban populations and a minute section of the rural areas. The villages, where most of our people live, boasted few schools; such as there were, were operated mainly by the missions. The number of secondary schools was limited, being based mainly in Cape Coast. These, too, were largely the products of missionary endeavour. There was the large semi-governmental institution at Achimota.

When we confronted the colonial administration with this appalling situation on taking office at the beginning of 1951, they told us that the budget was limited and time was needed. Time, they said, was required to train the army of teachers needed for the education of all the children. They did not look very happy when we pointed out that they seemed to have had time enough to allow the traders and shippers and mining companies to amass huge fortunes. As for the budget, we made the point that it did not seem inequitable to use part of those fortunes to educate the children of the land from which they had been drawn. We were determined, we said, to press for increased expenditure on social services.

I cannot say that in the six years in which we formed a token government under British administration, we were able to register unqualified success with our educational plan. We certainly did go some way towards laying the foundations of a country-wide educational system. The plan which we proposed in the Legislative Assembly in August 1951 provided for the abolition of school fees in the primary schools as an initial step towards a more comprehensive policy of free education. The Roman Catholic hierarchy strongly resented our decision to discontinue the subsidizing out of public funds of new schools owned and managed by religious bodies. It was not our aim, as we pointed out, to prevent the establishment and maintenance of new schools by denominational bodies through voluntary contributions, but they could not look to government for financial support.

At the beginning of 1951, primary school enrolments stood at 125,000. At the beginning of 1952, there were 270,000 children enrolled in our primary institutions and we estimated that this number would reach 400,000 by the beginning of 1957. Actually, at the time of independence in March 1957, the figure had expanded far beyond half a million. We had hoped that by that time our educational programme of teacher training and the erection of buildings and equipment would be able to cater for the anticipated increase. But the increase was greater than we had expected and our output of trained teachers and buildings had not, unfortunately, kept pace with it, even though the training college enrolment had more than doubled over the period.

We had established a system of scholarships and had planned for additional secondary schools. We established the College of Arts, Science and Technology at Kumasi, now the Kwame Nkrumah University, which will provide accommodation for 2,000 students and offer courses in building, engineering, accountancy, agriculture, science and commerce, among other subjects. Teacher training institutions in 1951 produced some 700 new teachers annually, a far too inadequate figure. We managed to establish twelve new training colleges and to double the capacity of four. By 1957, we were turning out some 4,000 new teachers each year, but this left us far behind the 70,000 teachers required to serve the national needs of elementary education.

...

Over and beyond this, we needed to plan an educational system that will be more in keeping with the requirements of the economic and social progress for which our new development plans are aiming. Our pattern of education has been aligned hitherto to the demands of British examination councils. Above all, it was formulated and administered by an alien administration desirous of extending its dominant ideas and thought processes to us. We were trained to be inferior copies of Englishmen, caricatures to be laughed at with our pretensions to British bourgeois gentility, our grammatical faultiness and distorted standards betraying us at every turn. We were neither fish nor fowl. We were denied the knowledge of our African past and informed that we had no present. What future could there be for us? We were taught to regard our culture and traditions as barbarous and primitive. Our text-books were English text-books, telling us about English history, English geography, English ways of living, English customs, English ideas, English weather. Many of these manuals had not been altered since 1895.

All this has to be changed. And it is a stupendous task. Even the ordering of text-books is an involved matter that makes the introduction of new ones with a Ghanaian character a prolonged affair. This is something that we are, however, getting on with, as it is vital that we should nurture our own culture and history if we are to develop that African personality which must provide the educational and intellectual foundations of our Pan-African future.

21. PIERRE VAN DEN BERGHE, *European Languages and Black Mandarins* (1968)

Aus: *Transition*, 34 (1968), 19–23. – P. van den Berghe (geb. 1933) studierte Soziologie und lehrte in Kenia, Frankreich und den USA. Im folgenden Text charakterisiert er die neuen Herrschaftsklassen Afrikas und die durch sie vertretenen Interessen der ehemaligen Kolonialmächte als eine Gefährdung für die sprachliche, soziale und kulturelle Einheit afrikanischer Staaten.

One can, of course, easily understand why most countries in black Africa continue officially to recognize and use French and English as administrative and educational languages. Linguistic diversity South of the Sahara, centrifugal forces which arise from this diversity, and practical advantages in the use of French and English are sufficient to account for the survival of these languages and for the relative absence of linguistic nationalism in Africa. Obvious though the advantages of European tongues are, the liabilities arising from their use in Africa are much less evident.

The use of European languages by the new ruling classes of Africa was, in the recent past, an important catalyst for political emancipation, and it continues to present certain advantages in the immediate future, especially in higher education, international relations, and in technical fields. Nevertheless, the use of French and English entails grave dangers for the future of democracy and of social and cultural development in Africa. Specifically, foreign languages accentuate cleavages between the elite and the masses, and between the city and the countryside.

The linguistic field is sensitively related to politics, and the linguistic and cultural policy of a state can profoundly affect reality. In general, African countries, under the influence of both Western and Socialist countries, have stressed the economic aspects of planning. It is high time they devote themselves more to the no less important problems of linguistic and cultural planning.

The first danger inherent to the use of French and English in Africa is that this serves the interests of the United States, the United Kingdom and France. Of all manifestations of neo-colonialism, the cultural and linguistic one is the most insidious, the least visible, and, in the long run, the most effective. Cultural and linguistic links between European nations and their former American colonies are sufficiently important to incite the Western countries to try to repeat this successful cultural assimilation in Africa. In this respect, France and Portugal have been most consistent and systematic in their efforts, because Latin countries have understood that cultural imperialism gives the greatest and longest-lasting returns. Fifty high school teachers are much cheaper and much more effective than a regiment of marines or a hydro-electric dam. (The number of French *lycée* teachers on overseas assignments goes into tens of thousands.) . . .

Conceivably, of course, the use of European languages in Africa can be advantageous both to Africa and to the Western powers. At present, this is probably the case. However, a great internal danger threatens the countries of Black Africa which officially recognize French or English. Here, we must understand the role played by a foreign language and culture in the formation of the ruling classes of African states. Others, especially Frantz Fanon,[13] have already sounded the alarm, but we must try to analyze the problem more closely.

In general, with the exception of the areas such as Northern Nigeria where the colonial administration maintained the traditional aristocracies they found there the new ruling classes in black Africa hold power neither because of their high social or political position in traditional societies, nor because they own the means of production. Marxists make a double mistake when they refer to these ruling classes as "national bourgeoisies". For the most part, members of the ruling classes of black Africa are not bourgeois, nor do they represent nations. (Only by changing the meaning of words can one refer to Ethiopia, Kenya, the Congo or Nigeria as "nations". They are *multi-national* states much like the Soviet Union or Yugoslavia. South of the Sahara, only Somalia, Rwanda, Burundi, Lesotho, Botswana and Swaziland come close to being *nation-states.*) The new elites are cosmopolitan and polyglottal intellectuals who became bureaucrats or army officers. The source of their power is their control of the administrative and military apparatus of their respective multi-national states. This control, in turn, is based on a monopoly of knowledge acquired through a Western school system and in a foreign tongue.

The organization, composition and administration of modern African states have to a large extent been imported and imposed by the colonial powers, and have few roots in indigenous tradition. Consequently, the knowledge and qualifications required to run the state bureaucracy are themselves linked with a Western schooling system. Even though the schools do little to teach specific administrative skills, they impart certain social graces and values (such as deprecation of manual labour and rural life) which are thought to be attributes of high social status. Literacy, the mastery of a European language, and a mixture of humanistic learning and technical skills are the basis of the power of ruling minorities. These minorities were originally and are perhaps still today more widely open to talent than in many other countries with a more solidified class structure. African ruling classes (with the exception of countries like Liberia, Ethiopia and South Africa) are still, to a large extent, an aristocracy of intelligence, a "meritocracy", to use the term of the British sociologist Michael Young.[14]

However, there are numerous signs that the class structure of black Africa is in a process of rapid stabilization, and that the elite is becoming progressively more closed, as all elites tend to do as soon as they come to power. The bureaucratic intelligentsia is becoming a mandarinate. The acquisition of a *licence* or a B. A. is a rite of passage which confers élite status. Knowledge in depth of a European language and culture becomes prestigious in itself as a symbol of class membership. French and English become esoteric languages that separate the elite from the masses; and, of course, members of the ruling class confer this esoteric knowledge to their children. Indications are that this process of crystallization of a manderinate will take no more than a single generation. Already, members of the elite are frantically scrambling to get their progeny into African Etons. Concern for getting one's children into the "proper" schools (which often means formerly all-European ones) even begins at the Kindergarten level. "Senior Staff" or "Senior Service" schools on University campuses insure that children of the elite associate mostly with each other and with the progeny of the cosmopolitan jet-set of "experts".

The new African ruling classes share the following characteristics with the mandarins of Imperial China:

□ Their power as a class derives from their control of key positions in the state bureaucracy, rather than from inherited wealth.

□ Such wealth as they may accumulate is largely the fruit of political or bureaucratic office rather than entrepreneurial activities or land ownership.

□ Access and promotion to bureaucratic or political office is largely determined by one's success in a ranked series of formal examinations in a well established system of higher education.

□ Beyond basic skills such as arithmetic and literacy, the content of what is taught to the future bureaucrats bears little demonstrable relationship to the tasks which they shall be called upon to perform. However, the sheer difficulty of their tasks insures that successful candidates have a relatively high degree of ability and perseverance.

□ The examination system makes it necessary for the prospective bureaucrat to have had the leisure to spend some two decades of his life cluttering his mind with a vast amount of esoteric pedantry. Thus, while the system is in theory open to anybody on the basis of merit, the advantages conferred to children from mandarin families are so great as to result in a considerable measure of élite closure.

The higher and the stricter the criteria of educational achievement which are insisted upon, the more ascriptive the system becomes. At the same time, however, the ruling class retains its vitality by allowing its incompetent members to sink into genteel oblivion, and by accepting into its ranks small numbers of carefully trained and intellectually superior members from the "lower classes". "Meritocracy" has this great superiority over "traditional" types of élites that, although it is nearly as closed in practice as most aristocracies, it is continuously enriched by the intellectual cream of the entire population. This also has the function of skimming the "lower classes" of their potentially revolutionary counter-élite. The Chinese mandarinate and the Catholic clergy are among the most long-lived élites in history.

In one respect, however, the term "mandarinate" is not altogether appropriate in Africa because the Confucian tradition, esoteric, pedantic and sterile though it became, was at least indigenous to China. In Africa, the cultural cleavage between the élite and the masses threatens to become complete. The African intelligentsia is in danger of finding itself in a position analogous to that of the French-speaking bourgeoisie of Flanders or the Russian aristocracy under the czars. History teaches us that class conflicts are much more virulent when they are complicated by ethnic differences. To the extent that African ruling classes remain anglicized or gallicized, they will find themselves in much the same situation as the old colonials whose political power and most of whose economic privileges they already inherited. Supposedly representative institutions, such as national parliaments are not only, for the most part, devoid of effective power; they have become genteel debating societies for the English- or French-speaking élite. Fluency in a European language is frequently a prerequisite for election to Parliament.

Intellectual elitism is perhaps most obvious on the campuses of African universities. Many African academics, rather than to ask themselves how best they can adapt their foreign intellectual baggage to the needs of their country, manifest a concern for "keeping the standards" of their *alma mater*. Their status as scholars seems to depend almost solely on their ability to demonstrate that they can write as pedantically as their European colleagues in esoteric journals, and that they can train students who are as successful as Europeans at taking highly ritualized examinations that bear little practical relationship to European conditions, much less to African ones. The mandarins narcissistically train the youth in their own image. They suffocate in their gowns, say grace in Latin, quote Shakespeare or Racine (or indeed Nkrumah and Castro) while the masses remain illiterate. The pampered undergraduates on generous government bursaries are carefully being groomed for élite status, and expect an upper-level position upon graduation. They remain silent in the face of despotism, but they rise up in protest when they are asked to double up in dormitories in order to make room for more students.

The new African ruling classes have already developed a legitimizing ideology, African Socialists join the liberals of 19th century Europe in denying the existence of class conflicts in their own societies. In fact, they go one step further in denying the very existence of the social classes themselves. The emerging élites try to create the myths that they do not exist and that Africans now rule themselves democratically. If the presence of internal conflicts is recognized, it is ascribed to "tribalism", a vague catch-all term that serves, among other things, to obscure class conflicts. When the country in question has a highly visible racial minority, especially a powerless Asian one, it can always be scapegoated to buttress the myth of commonality of interests among all Africans.[15]

In the absence of sizeable expatriate minorities, neo-colonialism serves much the same functions. If it did not in fact exist, it would have to be invented. Any suggestion that neo-colonialism is also an internal problem, and that the new élite is, in most respects, much like the colonial one is regarded as dangerous heresy. Blinded by their own dramatic accession to power, prestige and affluence, few members of the new élite see that they are virtually the sole beneficiaries (not to say profiteers) of independence.

At present, the wide network of kinship obligations militates to a certain extent against élite closure. Nearly every prominent man finds himself surrounded, in quasi-traditional fashion, by a retinue of clients and courtiers who seek hospitality, political protection, advice, jobs, patronage, or financial help on the basis of common kinship or ethnic origin. But while these obligations certainly retard capital accumulation by the élite, they *enhance* its prestige and power. As in many traditional societies, the big man is not so much the rich man as the "generous" man, i. e. the man who, through his largesse, knows how to convert wealth into "social capital". With increasing urbanization, more and more members of the élite will find ways of emancipating themselves from the economically burdensome demands of poor relatives and fellow ethnics. Class differences will increasingly follow kinship lines.

In recent years, military coups have also made for some "circulation of élites", but they have not fundamentally altered the class structure of the various countries under military rule. For one thing army officers, as technocrats of violence, are themselves an educated élite. While their training is often academically inferior to that of the civilian mandarins, it is better related to their task as specialists in violence. Army officers may displace corrupt politicians, but they are still dependent on the intelligentsia for running the civil service. Besides, Sandhurst and St. Cyr have bred their owen brand of technocratic élitism.

Official and private use of European languages entails the danger of a cleavage not only between the elite and the masses, but also between *town* and *country*. The American anthropologist Robert Redfield spoke of "Great" and "Little Tradition" to distinguish the urban culture of the ruling class from peasant culture. This discontinuity between urban and rural culture which is always very pronounced may become a permanent chasm if the *lingua franca* of the towns is a foreign language. Culturally, this establishes a kind of internal colonialism similar to that found in some of the still predominantly Indian areas of Latin America. Urban culture, which is also that of the ruling class, the professionals, and the clerical occupations becomes identified with the national culture. The Little Tradition is reduced to the status of folklore; indigenous languages become simply peasant dialects.

To the extent that French and English are imposed as national languages, African traditions are condemned to cultural stagnation, indeed to retrogression. There seems to be little likelihood that many African languages will disappear in the near or even distant future. African cultures have shown great vitality and resilience during the colonial period. But if those cultures do not become urban in the modern sense, and if these languages do not develop along technical as well as literary lines, they are condemned to a slow retreat into the backwater of world civilization. The Yoruba, the Swahili, the Hausa and the Zulu of tomorrow may become the Tupi and Trobianders of today.

The recent revival of African cultures and of historical consciousness among the West African, and to a lesser extent, the East African intelligentsia are hopeful signs. But it is not sufficient to proclaim the contribution of African civilizations, to establish museums of African art or to dress in traditional (or pseudotraditional) style. So long as this renaissance is cut off from its linguistic roots, it will lack vitality and remain an artificial flower. Indeed, language is the fundamental vehicle of any culture.

Two principal arguments can be advanced against the point of view presented here. The first is that European languages constitute not only practical and widespread means of communication, but also a cultural enrichment for Africa. There is, of course, no question of eliminating English and French, but simply of not officially favouring them at the detriment of African languages. The very usefulness of French and English will ensure their survival without any need for official encouragement other than their being included as school subjects. Furthermore, the enrichment contributed by English and French is not inherent to these languages. The polyglot is culturally richer than the monolingual person, irrespective of what specific languages he knows. There are no valid criteria which allow one to establish a hierarchy of languages, except their practical utility, i.e., in last analysis, the numerical, social and political importance of their speakers, and the extent of their written literature. To the extent that many Africans already know several indigenous languages, they are culturally richer than the vast majority of Americans, Englishmen or Frenchman who are monolingual.

A second basic objection to the encouragement of African languages is that, except in a few privileged countries like Somalia and Rwanda where a single language is dominant, linguistic fragmentation creates extremely difficult problems, the most serious of which is political balkanization. Undeniably, a policy of ethnic nationalism could have dangerous consequences, and most colonial powers have tried to exacerbate ethnic rivalries under the cover of respect for tradition. The most notorious example of such a policy of divide and rule by means of cultural revivalism is the policy of apartheid in South Africa.

Several important considerations must be mentioned here:
– Reactionary motives can vitiate any policy. All judgments about policy must take into account both the means and the ends.
– The encouragement of local languages does not necessarily imply official polylingualism. Apart from the relatively simple case of the few linguistically homogeneous states, one of the local languages can be elevated to official status as Tanzania did for Swahili. The success of such a policy is still uncertain, and it probably hinges on two main factors which are seldom found together:

(a) How widespread is that language as a *lingua franca*.

(b) How politically and numerically *unimportant* is the ethnic group whose language has become the official one. Indeed, if the ethnic group which speaks the official language is already powerful and numerous, as is the case with the Hindi in India, the exclusive official use of its language gives it an enormous advantage relative to the other groups. Insofar as linguistic policy becomes an instrument of ethnic domination, it will tend to unleash other ethnic nationalisms. Thus, monolingualism in an indigenous tongue can be politically divisive.

– Conversely, official polylingualism does not necessarily entail ethnic separatism. On the contrary, an official recognition of cultural pluralism along Swiss, Yugoslav or Soviet lines may reduce or "defuse" the political character of ethnic sentiments, and thus contribute to the solidity of the multi-national state.

It remains nonetheless true that official polylingualism and the development of little-used languages present numerous practical problems and a certain material cost. The question thus arises whether the investment is worth it. Obviously, the answer depends on a number of ideological, material, ethnic and other factors. Equally clearly, problems vary enormously from one state to another, and, consequently, so must solutions. The linguistic policy of a state is especially delicate because it incorporates technical, ideological and practical elements. The linguist and the sociologist can at most suggest alternatives and forecast their possible consequences; but, in last analysis, the decisions are political. (19–22)

22. A. BABS FAFUNWA, *The Curriculum, National Needs and the Problem of Adaptations* (1971)

Aus: A. Babs Fafunwa, *A History of Nigerian Higher Education* (Lagos, 1971), 271–273, 321–322. – A. Babs Fafunwa studierte Erziehungswissenschaften an der New York University und promovierte 1955 mit einer Arbeit über die Entwicklung des Erziehungswesens in Nigeria. Er lehrt als Professor an der University of Ife. Im folgenden Text setzt Fafunwa sich mit dem Widerstand gegen Veränderungen des Lehrprogramms an nigerianischen Universitäten auseinander. Der 1951 gültige Lehrplan am Department of English des University College Ibadan veranschaulicht die inzwischen wichtige Rolle der englischen Literatur im Lehrprogramm, läßt aber auch die noch völlige Ausrichtung des Lektürekanons am Vorbild des „Mutterlands" erkennen.

Like the curricula in the primary and secondary educational systems, the curriculum in many African universities was initially a carbon copy of the English system. In Nigeria, the first higher education institution, Ibadan, had a special relationship with London University when it was established in 1948. The Ibadan syllabus was a replica of the London one and students at Ibadan were expected to fulfil the degree requirements laid down by London University.[16] By 1952 the Nigerian press was extremely vocal on the question of "relating higher education to the needs of the Nigerian society" and a number of educators were also pressing for a change. However it must be noted that at the initial planning stage of Ibadan University College a number of Nigerians, particularly those trained in Britain, naively believed that any programme that diverged at all from what they themselves had gone through in the United Kingdom would not be good enough – change would be tantamount to lowering standards. As Sir Eric Ashby noted:

"...some African intellectuals, especially those educated in Britain, resist changes in curriculum or in pattern of courses because they confuse such changes with a lowering of standards. They are accordingly suspicious of any divergence from the British pattern. Some of them are particularly allergic to proposals for incorporating African studies into the curriculum. Is this, they say, the first step toward disarming us intellectually; to substitute Arabic and African languages for the classics; to teach English to Africans as Chinese is taught to Englishmen, not as Englishmen learn English at Cambridge; to neglect Tudor history in favour of the history of Africa; to regard oral tradition as legitimate material for scholarship..."[17]

The Nigerian sceptics were quite correct. Adaptation of the curriculum meant everything they said and more. It meant disarming Nigerian and British intellectuals in Nigeria in the sense that, for example, the Tudor experts had to re-orient themselves in the study of African history; those who were experts in nineteenth-century English literature needed to be re-trained in African literature and folklore; and the botanists needed to learn the flora and the fauna of Nigeria.

Whether at the primary or university level the curriculum should reflect the environment in which it operates, with apologies to none. British students study the British constitution, the British government, the British economic system, and this is as it should be. After graduation these students are never faced with the problem of adjustment that was experienced by the Nigerian student who, after completion of his studies in the United Kingdom or at Ibadan at that time, had to return 'home' and try to adjust his thinking to the local situation. It was rightly observed at the UNESCO's Tananarive conference on the development of higher education in Africa in 1962:

"African students are in very many cases ignorant of their own societies and cultures. It is necessary to stress the need for the use of African material in the teaching of all subjects and at all levels of education; and the situation is sufficiently serious to warrant the introduction of organized courses in African studies to be taken by all students. This measure might be purely transitory: it might become superfluous once the adaptation of the secondary school curriculum was completed."[18]

The Ashby Commission[19] recommended that more institutions of higher learning be established in Nigeria, but failed to give adequate attention to the curriculum content although it did make passing reference to African studies and the need to diversify the bachelor's degree structures in the proposed universities. The admission requirements, which naturally have a bearing on the length and depth of a degree course, were glossed over by the Commission's report. The group took the line of the least resistance by recommending not only that the sixth form or G.C.E. 'A' level should continue to be the basis of admission, but also that the Federal Government should intensify sixth form development. The introduction of the sixth form was unfortunate at the time when Nigeria's manpower needs were most acute.[20]

It is interesting, however, to note that the chairman of the Commission, Sir Eric Ashby, six years after the publication of the report, had this to say:

"The answer... is not to go slow on education but ruthlessly to ensure that education is relevant [to the needs of the society], even if it means radical departure from the forms and patterns associated with education in modern industrial societies. With the aid of hindsight it can be said that the Nigerian commission did not emphasize this point forcefully enough; American influence on the commission might with profit have been more powerful. For whether one uses the controversial word "élite" or not for the products of the Asquith [and Ashby] colleges, the assumptions behind the high status of the one-subject honours degree were that a privileged class was being produced. Now the number of posts which can be filled by such products is very limited, and these posts are already within sight of being filled. Therefore not only the numbers going into higher education, but the content of curricula in higher education, need to be austerely adjusted to manpower needs. If, for example, arts graduates are produced in too narrow a range of subjects, or in subjects which are not taught at school, and if (as is already happening in Nigeria) there is no longer much immediate need for arts graduates in the foreign service and the home civil services, then one is confronted with the first symptoms of graduate unemployment. The assertion that Nigeria would need some 30,000 graduates by 1970 is doubtless as good a prediction as anyone could have made from the data available. What the report [Ashby's] might have said more emphatically is that if too much of the national product is spent producing these graduates there will not be enough left over for capital investment to create employment for them; and that if Nigerian commerce, transport, and communications (for example) need economists and statisticians, it will not do in an impoverished developing country to provide these services with honours graduates in history and English."[21] (271–273)

...

Intermediate Examination

1. (a) A paper of two hours on two selected plays of Shakespeare, and (b) A paper of one hour consisting of unseen passages of prose and poetry (including examples of functional English) for comment and criticism.

2. A paper of three hours on the literature of the period 1798 to the present day, with special attention to seven set books.

3. An examination, written and oral, not exceeding two hours, which shall test the candidate's knowledge of phonetics and his command of spoken English.

Text-books for the examination to be held in 1951:
Paper I
Shakespeare, *Macbeth* and *The Tempest.*
Paper II
Wordsworth and Coleridge, *Lyrical Ballads* (1800 ed.) with prefaces; Keats, *Odes*; Tennyson, *Selected Poems*; Mill, *On Liberty*; Conrad, *Lord Jim*; Hardy, *Far from the Madding Crowd*; T. S. Eliot, *Murder in the Cathedral.*
Paper III
No books are prescribed but the following are recommended for study: H. A. Harmann, *The Sounds of English for African Students* (Longmans); H. E. Palmer, *English Intonation with Systematic Exercise* (Heffers); L. Armstrong and I. Ward, *A Handbook of English Intonation* (Heffers); P. A. D. MacCarthy, *English Pronunciation* (Heffers).

B. A. General Examination

A revised syllabus under the Special Relationship Scheme is under consideration. Meanwhile students are being prepared for the External London B. A. General Degree, the syllabus for which is as follows:

1. (a) Old and Middle English set texts.
(b) Old and Middle English Literature and (at the option of the candidate) the history of the English Language.

2. (a) English Literature 1579–1700 with prescribed books.

(b) Shakespeare and either Spenser or Milton (as prescribed by the College): set books.

3. A later period of English Literature, with special reference to set authors.

Text-books for the examination to be held in 1951:

Paper I

Wyatt, *Anglo-Saxon Reader*, extracts: (1) The Chronicle 755–897 A.D.; II (2) and (3) *Ohthere's Voyages and Wulfstan's Voyage*; VII (4) *Caedmon*; XII *Sermo Lupi*; XXIV *The Wanderer*; XXVI *Beowulf*: (1) *Of Soyld*, lines 1–52, (2) *Beowulf's Swimming Match with Breca*, lines 499–606, (3) *The Vengeance of Grendel's Mother*, lines 1251–1309, (4) *Beowulf brings back Grendel's Head*, lines 1572–1676; XXVIII *Dream of the Road*; XXXIV *The Battle of Maldon*.

Chaucer, *The Squire's Tale; Sir Thopas; Havelok the Dane,* lines 1–1390.

Paper II

(a) Beaumont and Fletcher, *The Knight of the Burning Pestle*; Milton, *Shorter Poems* (edited by Wright, Macmillan); Dryden, *All for Love*; Bunyan, *The Pilgrim's Progress*.

(b) Shakespeare, *Antony and Cleopatra* and *The Tempest*; Spenser, *The Faerie Queene*, Book I.

Paper III

Period 1798–1832 with special reference to Scott or Hazlitt, and to Coleridge or Keats. (321–322)

3. Afrikanische Literaturen und nationale Unabhängigkeit

23. JOSEPH EPHRAIM CASELY HAYFORD, *Presidential Addresses to the National Congress of British West Africa* (1923, 1925)

Aus: Magnus J. Sampson (ed.), *West African Leadership* (London, 1969), 67–91. – Casely Hayford (1866–1930) zählte neben Blyden (cf. Text 13) zu den bedeutendsten Intellektuellen Westafrikas im späten 19. und frühen 20. Jahrhundert. Geboren im heutigen Ghana war Casely Hayford als Pädagoge, Jurist und Politiker tätig, begründete und gab eine Reihe von Zeitungen und Zeitschriften heraus und veröffentlichte mit *Ethiopia Unbound. Studies in Race Emancipation* (London, 1911) (cf. Tex 8) das erste, teils fiktiv, teils philosophisch abgefaßte Werk eines Afrikaners in englischer Sprache. Als Präsident des 1919/1920 gegründeten National Congress of British West Africa plädiert er in den Eröffnungsansprachen 1923, 1925 und 1929 immer wieder für eine Liberalisierung der Erziehung. Eine 1921 dem englischen König übergebene Petition, in der Afrikaner ein größeres Mitspracherecht forderten, wurde von der Krone zurückgewiesen.

The matter of education should receive the careful consideration of the present session of the Congress. There is hardly any of the four Colonies in which the matter is not engaging the serious consideration of Government. For our part, I would suggest for your consideration the matter of compulsory education for our youths within certain age limits; the strengthening of the courses in our Elementary schools; the improvement of the curricula in our Secondary schools; leading up to the British West African University; greater attention to female education and training; and industrial and technical training of our youth in all their ramifications. We do not subscribe to the proposition that a peculiar kind of education is desirable for the African *per se*. But we believe in the African being trained by the African with an African outlook, which is a very different thing. Experience has taught that it is oftener than not the half-educated African who is de-africanised rather than the thoroughly educated African. These things being so, we must press upon the attention of Government the early foundation of the British West African University, and it must be respectfully urged that no considerations of finance must retard action. (73)

...

While co-operation between race and race is preached, and it is desirable that it should be preached, surely there can be nothing wrong in suggesting that there should be closer and yet closer co-operation between members of our own race. While there has been a tremendous wave of race consciousness, our coming together for practical purposes is yet uncertain, and our organisations are very loose. In the dominant race while there is rivalry and competition in business and other concerns, yet do you see a general co-operation between banking and shipping and mercantile elements which tends to ensure the prosperity of a progressive society. If the black man hopes to survive, he must assimilate and adopt this sort of intensive co-operation. However great the philanthropist, it is startingly true, that unless he be a Christ, there comes a time when he must choose between his country and another's, between his own people and other people. And you cannot blame him. It is but natural. Therefore there must come a point when we must make up our minds to shoulder our own industrial, educational, political, and religious burdens, expending thought upon them, and resolute in taking action. Hitherto the practice has been for the European to make use of the African to get *there*. We must change that. The African must in future make it a point to get *there* himself. There has been considerable activities in the matter of education in the Colonies since the last Session, and this more particularly in the Gold Coast. At the first Session of Congress a series fo resolutions were passed, urging educational advance on a sound basis by strengthening the courses in the elementary and secondary stages, leading up to the University standard. A sense of African nationality was to be preserved in the students. At the second Session these were more definitely emphasised, and among the recommendations were greater and more systematic attention being paid to the training of the teachers; the raising of the standard of remuneration so as to compare evenly, if not favourably, with other departments of the civil service; the granting of subsidies, where necessary, to missionary and other educational bodies; and the making pensionable the teaching profession in every case. In large towns and cities compulsory education was to be enforced, it being obviously practically impossible to enforce compulsory education throughout. The whole educational system of the several Colonies was to be so co-ordinated, strengthened, and regulated that the highest form in the Elementary branch fitted a pupil for the Secondary School, and the highest form in the Secondary School for the College. Agricultural and industrial training for boys, and domestic training for girls, were not to be delayed for advanced years, but were to be taught in all Schools, and the classics and modern languages were to be taught in the Secondary Schools and Colleges. It was laid down that African outlook being necessary in the training of African youths, there should be no interference with such African customs as were not repugnant to the best feelings of humanity and good conscience. Lastly, attention was called to the previous resolution of Congress as to the founding of a British West African University, Fourah Bay College, Sierra Leone, King's College, Lagos, and the proposed Government College in the Gold Coast forming the nuclei of such University, with a recommendation that Gambian Government may also promote the founding of a College to supplement the efforts of the sister Colonies.

It is satisfactory to note that almost all the recommendations have met with the serious and favourable consideration of almost all the Governments of British West Africa, and nowhere more pronouncedly than in the Gold Coast where some £ 500,000 is earmarked for educational purposes in carrying out the magnificent programme of the Prince of Wales' College, Achimota; and it is to be hoped that, should fulfilment measure up with the intention, Africans everywhere will avail themselves of the opportunities that will be thrown open by this great institution. There is one thing to be said, however, and it is this: It should be the steady aim of the Governments of British West Africa and of the educationists concerned generally to produce African teachers and also to make use of such materials as are at present available. In the Universities of the world it ought to be possible to get select Africans to augment the staffs of Achimota, King's College,[1] and Fourah Bay College. Indeed, with respect to the last named institution, it is hardly necessary to make the suggestion, since from its inception that policy has been kept in view and put into practice with most satisfactory results. In the final analysis the African's true mentality can only be reached by the African, and the only way to inspire complete confidence is by the gradual elimination of huge European staffs in favour of African teachers. (80–82)

24. *Resolution on Literature* (1959)

Aus: *Second Congress of Negro Writers and Artists* (Rome, 26 March – 1 April 1959): *The Unity of Negro African Cultures, Présence Africaine,* 24–25 (February–May 1959), 423–428. – Während der First Congress of Negro Writers and Artists, der 1956 in Paris stattfand, in seiner Resolution zur schwarzen Kultur sehr allgemein blieb, befaßte sich während des folgenden Kongresses in Rom eine Literaturkommission mit den Aufgaben schwarzer Schriftsteller und legte eine detailliertere Resolution vor, die sich mit einer Reihe von Einzelfragen beschäftigt. Sie veranschaulichen das Bemühen um die Suche nach einer spezifisch schwarzen Literatur und Kultur im Kontext der nationalen Befreiung, die die damalige Zeit kennzeichnete.

The Commission on Literature of the Second Congress of Negro Writers and Artists,
after studying the Reports submitted to it, and after a general discussion of these Reports and of their conclusions, at its Sessions of Thursday 26th., Friday 27th., Saturday 28th. and Sunday 29th. March, 1959,
examined:
I) The state of vernacular literature in Negro Africa and the countries of African population, and the need to defend those oral literatures, which constitute the real basis of Negro-African cultures and their ethics, as well as the legitimate expression of national or regional peculiarities in the various countries concerned.
This work of defence and development has already been undertaken, for example, for Ghana, Guinea and Haïti, where the sovereign Governments are encouraging the development of the autochthonous languages, either by financial assistance to existing institutions, or by including these languages in the school curriculum, or by publishing newspapers and reviews etc. and by the creation of Drama Centres.
The Commission also examined:
II) The confrontation of these traditional cultures with the forms of Western culture, in the unhealthy, and most frequently barbarous context of colonization.
This confrontation in most cases resulted in a dead stop and in cultural degeneration. It involved the countries of African population in a long period of silence and loss of personality.

This contact also brought about new structures within the traditional literature, to the extent that, for good or evil, every culture in our time is influenced by other cultures.

There is a need for the study of these new structures and for help in acquiring consciousness of them and thus ensuring the transition from oral literatures to the stage of written literature, without impairing the character and ethics of these literatures.

The Commission examined:

III) The situation of the Negro writer in the modern world.

Such a writer is most frequently cut off from his authentic public by the use of a language which, in its literary form, is inaccessible to the mass of Negro peoples.

Such a writer experiences serious difficulties in getting his work published, in the modern Western conditions in which he finds himself; his public is therefore most frequently a restricted one.

He may also suffer from another cause of disequilibrium in those cases where the use of his autochthonous language is imperative for him and where its creative possibilities are limited by the fact that this language is not in literary use.

Emphasis should nevertheless be laid on the progressive character of the use of the Western languages to the extent that they lead to economy of time in constructing the new Africa.

This observation should in no way lessen the obligation to develop the autochthonous languages.

The Commission studied:

IV) The general literary context in which the Negro writer finds himself. This context can be indicated or defined on the basis of the following points;

a) the influence, consciously or unconsciously felt, of the cultural traditions of Negro Africa.

These traditions are evolving, in the African countries themselves, in relation to the new conditions of the history of Africa.

In the countries of African population, these traditions have been adapted to a new setting and have been integrated with regional or national values.

In both cases, Negro literatures draw their inspiration from these traditions, more or less directly and more or less admittedly.

b) The Commission recognizes the positive character of the reference to these traditions and their new forms, not only in Africa, but also in the countries of African population.

The deported peoples of the Negro continent must restore their dignity by fighting against racism, which manifests itself in the first place by the neglect and stifling of African values.

c) This attachment of the writer to traditions should, nevertheless, not drive local peculiarities and national values into the background. The Commission, on the contrary, asserts that such a reference would be calculated to enrich and sustain the various national cultures.

d) The last point in the full definition of a general literary context is the need to transcend the fixed literary patterns imposed by the literary history of the West. The Negro writer should follow his natural tendency to the full, and invent new patterns which correspond to the history of his people, provided he is ready to transcend these also, once they are established.

The search for such patterns calls for a vast movement, drawing its inspiration from the community. The assertion of the individual, that is to say, the demand for internal freedom, is nowadays linked with the assertion of peoples in the form of the search for national sovereignty and a common progressive outlook.

Negro-African literatures are, therefore, capable of promoting new literary forms, which break with the dominant characteristic of Western literature, in which the individual is too frequently regarded as a necessary and sufficient end, to the exclusion of all others.

A general orientation of this kind is justified in our epoch, when the inscription of the Declaration of the Rights of Man and of the Citizen in the forefront of the Constitution is completed by the Right of Peoples to self-determination.

This observation of the literary facts, however, must not lead to tyrannical obligations. It preserves the fundamental individual liberty of the writer, but it is calculated to aid him in his work and enable him to realize in an entirely original manner the harmonious synthesis between traditions which have been preserved and modern forms of expression.

The Commission then examined:

V) The responsibilities of the Negro writer towards his people. In the present temporary situation of the Negro peoples, these responsibilities cover three urgent and essential points;

a) The contribution of the writer to the development of the autochthonous languages in all countries where this development is essential:

b) The true expression of the reality of his people, long obscured, deformed or denied during the period of colonization.

This expression is so necessary under present conditions that it imposes on the Negro artist or writer a singularly specific concept of commitment. The Negro writer cannot avoid taking a spontaneous and total part in the general movement outlined above. The direction of his struggle is pointed out to him from the outset; how could he turn aside from it?

c) Lastly, and above all, to contribute to the advancement and progress of the Negro peoples, and especially in the countries where the question arises, to the struggle for their independence, since the existence of a National State is calculated to encourage the blossoming of a positive and fertile culture.

The Commission further observed:

VI) That all the above considerations flow from an objective and far reaching study of the present situation and significance of Negro literatures, whatever language they may use.

Being in general universally valid, these considerations are not based on any ethnic or racial grounds. They are the result of common origin and common sufferings.

The Negro peoples have passed through a series of historical avatars,[2] which, in the particular form of total colonization, involving slavery, deportation and racism, has, in the objectively known historical period, been inflicted upon these peoples and upon them alone.

The existence of a Negro-African Civilization transcending national or regional cultural peculiarities, therefore seems historically justified, and reference to that civilization appears both legitimate and rewarding.

This must be the basis of the unity and solidarity of the various Negro peoples, without it being necessary to reduce these peoples, and particularly their men of culture, to the sterile uniformity of a corpus of precepts, doctrines and commandments.

Finally, the Commission turned to

VII) The Theatre, an important form of the literary and cultural expression of the Negro-African peoples.

The traditional African theatre does not obey the same scenic tradition as the theatre of the West. It comprises at the same time, recital, song and dance. But in this form, integrated as it is with oral literature, it is in the process of disappearing under the influence of colonization.

A new theatre will be born when the problem of fixing the African languages has been tackled and dramatic authors find themselves in a national political and social context. Their works will then make it possible to readapt and transcend the traditional theatre by enriching it with the current problems in the life of the Negro peoples.

The attempts at renovation which have been made in the extra-African world, cannot escape the danger of exoticism, since they are almost exclusively addressed to European audiences, nor can they make up for the absence of an African audience.

In the Antilles and the American countries, during the last ten years, some experiments have been tried, which have given birth, in Haïti, for example, to a Creole theatre, and in Brazil to an "experimental Negro theatre"[3]. It is noticeable that this theatre, based on the cultural foundation of the people (for example, the use of voodoo rites in Haïti,[4] or the macumba in Brazil) receives the full support of the masses. With regard to the part played by the Negro theatre in the United States of America, it can be said to have followed the general literary movement of anti-racist and social protest.

Nevertheless, the Negro actor most often finds himself in an equivocal position owing to the fact that there is no work for him in the repertory of the Western countries, and the modern Negro-African repertory does not offer him sufficient opportunities adequate to his powers.

The immediate solution of such a serious problem could only be transitional. In the event of the universal dramatic repertory being adapted to the temperament and needs of the Negro-African public, the choice of plays would be governed by the need to present, among others, examples which might help to inspire the struggle for emancipation and the assertion of the dignity of the human being.

A first step towards a real solution of the problem might be the foundation of African Schools of Dramatic Art, which, at the same time that they were training actors, would carry out research into the creation of an African scenic style. These schools should have a national character, instead of existing as private undertakings, whether subsidized or not. They should also avoid remaining insulated in their local characteristics. A current of exchange would be established between them and the schools in other Negro countries, with a view to constituting the Negro-African theatrical patrimony, which would be constantly enriched and strengthened.

In view of all the reasons and considerations set out above, the Commission on Literature calls the attention of the Delegates of the Second Congress of Negro Writers and Artists to the following projects which should be instituted in the various Negro States;

1) The institution in each independent country of a strict and rigorous plan for the fight against illiteracy, inspired both by the most modern techniques already in use, and the original peculiarities of the country in question.

2) An increase in the number of fundamentally decentralized popular libraries, and the use of films and soundrecordings.

3) The institution of African Cultural Research Centres. These Centres, which would be responsible for working out practical plans, would be in close contact with the International Organizations, and with other nations.

4) The translation into autochthonous languages, wherever possible, of representative works of Negro writers in the French, English, Portuguese, Spanish, etc. languages.

5) The exchange of translations between the various cultural areas (French, English, Spanish, Italian and Portuguese) of Africa and the other countries of African population. Negro writers should not necessarily adopt the contradictions between the various Western cultures emanating from the nations which have dominated the Negro world.

6) The creation of national organizations for aid to writers. Such organizations already exist in various forms in Ghana and Guinea.[5]

7) The Commission proposes the creation of effective aid to young writers within the Society of African Culture itself.

8) The Commission recommends the Society of African Culture to arrange cultural meetings with the writers of all countries.

9) Finally, the Commission hopes that the Congress will call the attention of the Governments of Negro States to the need to support and encourage the creation of theatrical schools along the lines set out above.

The Commission on Literature hopes that Negro-African writers will work to define their common language, their common manner of using words and ideas and of reacting to them. The desire for an ordered language expressing coherent cultures, is embodied, among other things, in work within a national reality from which the flagrant disorder specifically inherent in the colonial situation will be banished. This language, transcending the various languages used, transcending the legitimate forms of national cultures, will thus contribute towards strengthening the unity of the Negro peoples, and will furnish their writers with a working tool.

The Commission also finally recognizes that this contribution to the progress of the Negro-African peoples cannot fail additionally to strengthen the universal brotherhood of mankind. The Commission has endeavoured to carry out its work bearing constantly in mind this brotherhood and the generosity of spirit which it implies.

25. ELDRED DUROSIMI JONES, *Nationalism and the Writer* (1965)

Aus: John Press (ed.), *Commonwealth Literature: Unity and Diversity in a Common Culture* (London, 1965), 151–156. – E. D. Jones (geb. 1925) aus Sierra Leone ist einer der führenden Literaturkritiker Afrikas. Er lehrt als Professor am Fourah Bay College der University of Sierra Leone, deren Rektor er einige Jahre war. Aus der Fülle seiner Veröffentlichungen sind *Othello's Countrymen: The African in English Renaissance Drama* (London, 1965) und die Monographie *The Writing of Wole Soyinka* (London, 1973; rpt. 1975) zu erwähnen. Seit 1968 ediert er die Zeitschrift *African Literature Today*. Der folgende Beitrag entstand als Vortrag, den Jones anläßlich der 1963 an der University of Leeds veranstalteten Konferenz über Commonwealth Literatur hielt.

In this short paper I wish to review some of the possible implications of nationalism as a factor in the work of African writers. Although my particular starting point is Africa, much of what is valid in this paper will be generally applicable.

The force with which African nationalism has burst upon the world in the last fifteen to twenty years tends to obscure the steadiness of its growth particularly since the end of the first world war. Since this earlier time it has been the dominant theme in African writing. The cry of freedom has appeared even in places which would have been thought unlikely. This theme emerges strongly, for instance, in Vilakazi's Zulu poem, "In the Gold Mines", which is now available in an English translation.[6] In that poem, after describing the horror of the mines, Vilakazi strikes a note of revolt:

    Wait just a while, for feeble as I seem,
    From these same little arms one day
    There flew some fierce, long-bladed spears
    Which I hurled till the sun was darkened . . .
    I was robbed
    But still I go on dreaming, son of Iron,
    Dreaming that the land of my fathers' fathers
    Comes back to the hands of the homeless blacks.

There is no need to illustrate this theme from more modern African writing, but only David Diop[7] among the modern Africans seems to exceed in intensity and bitterness this strain in Vilakazi's early poem.

Nationalism, however, has its problems for the writer. The most obvious is connected with language. What language shall he write in: his native language or an acquired but more widely understood tongue? Facility and naturalness may indicate the native language, but the limitations of even the more widely spoken languages of Africa have frequently compelled the choice of an acquired language. The African writer's problem has been compared to that of a writer in mediaeval Europe who had the choice of writing in Latin for an international readership or in his native language for a local one. The language situation in Africa is far more complicated than it ever was in Europe. Of course a writer in Swahili, Yoruba, or Hausa has a potential reading public of several millions, and there is a considerable body of writing in these languages. Swahili and Hausa are considered to have a large enough body of original literature for these languages to form a major part of an honours degree course at the School of Oriental and African Studies in London. But still in terms of a world audience – even in terms of an African audience – these languages are still too regional in character to give the writer full scope.

The African writer therefore has two courses open to him. He can write in his own language for his limited audience or in the hope that translations will make him accessible to a wider audience. The works of Thomas Mofolo, Akiga,[8] Vilakazi whom I quoted earlier, have thus become available in English. We are promised some English translations soon of some of the late D. O. Fagunwa's Yoruba writings.[9] At least one African poet has stated that he writes first in his native language and then translates his works into English.

The second course open to the writer is to write in English or French for an ever-increasing number of his fellow Africans, and a large part of the non-African world besides. Many African writers are choosing the latter. Senghor, Camara Laye, the Diops[10] etc. write in French while Achebe, Ekwensi, Soyinka, Clark, Okigbo, Conton,[11] Nicol, Ngugi, Mphahlele, Abrahams[12] and others have chosen to write principally in English. I do not know how much this decision conflicts with their nationalism. There are no obvious signs of such a conflict in their work. But the choice has its practical difficulties.

In respect of his audience, the writer may be sacrificing that number of his own people who are only literate in their own native language. Different educational policies make the number of these significantly different in different parts of the continent. But the most important problem is the effect of the choice on the writer's own articulateness. He is called upon, if his work is to receive respectful attention, to 'do a Conrad' with the language of his choice. Conrad, of course, adopted England as well as English. The African writer is still in his original environment, and for the bulk of his writing may wish to borrow only the language. (Indeed many writers have voiced their rejection of the values of an alien society in the language of that very society.)

This selective borrowing may be difficult particularly since the new language is generally learnt along with the ideas and beliefs of its native speakers. Full-blooded Africans in French West Africa for several decades of French rule recited passages to the effect that their ancestors were tall, fair-haired Gauls. It would not take too much reflection to reject that particular idea, but there may be others more insidious. The writer therefore, while mastering his new language, has to be wary of what else he borrows with it. He has to be sufficiently aware of himself to avoid being carried away by the tide. But perhaps this is only a particular statement of a more general truth that the artist even when he is writing in his own language must be detached. It may not be redundant, however, to restate this in the particular context of this paper. I have commented elsewhere on Achebe's success with his adopted language in his novel *Things Fall Apart*.[13] I think Soyinka in his essay "Salutations to the Gut" (*Reflections*, ed. Ademola)[14] achieves the same kind of success in a shorter piece of writing.

The writer may out of choice adopt a 'foreign' attitude to his subject in order to create a special effect. As an artist he must possess something of what Keats called 'negative capability', the ability to see a situation through the eyes of someone – or something – else. Achebe achieves his final irony in *Things Fall Apart* by seeing the District Commissioner's task through that character's own half-blinded eyes. This is reflected in the title of the District Commissioner's magnum opus: *The Pacification of the Primitive Tribes of the Lower Niger*.

Having chosen his medium the writer selects themes within his experience and his environment. To the African writer this means, primarily, writing about his tribe, his nation or if he is bold enough, his continent. But the modern African writer like his counterpart elsewhere has become absorbed into the universal environment. To make the fullest use of his emancipation, therefore, he may wish to transcend his immediate environment. To take a West Indian example, Naipaul's early stories were set in the West Indies – his primary environment. His latest novel, *Mr Stone and the Knights Companion*,[15] is set in England. Forster's *Passage to India* is set in India – albeit in Imperial India. Evelyn Waugh exploited his American experience in *The Loved One*, Joyce Cary's Nigeria appears in his African novels and Margaret Laurence's Ghana in *The Tomorrow Tamers* and *This Side Jordan*.[16]

African writers will similarly extend their vision and make full use of their wider experience. Wole Soyinka's twin poems "The Immigrant" and "The Other Immigrant" show the first logical steps away from the primary environment while his "Telephone Conversation"[17] shows the process even further advanced.

The themes of African literature have hitherto been very restricted. Until the era of independence the dominant note was that of protest – protest against foreign domination. Indeed for a long time this theme subsumed every other. With Independence and the disappearance of the standard object of protest the way is open for a breath of fresh air. There will be more introspection and writers will no doubt find themselves protesting not against the doings of foreigners but of their own people. They will have to adapt themselves from the position of being the cheer leaders of the nation to that of sometimes being lone, unpopular voices in the crowd. John Ekwere[18] in one of his poems illustrates this role when he turns his eyes inwards in the following lines:

> Now no more the palefaced strangers
> With unhallowed feet
> The heritage of our fathers profane;
> Now no missioned benevolent despots
> Bull-doze an unwilling race;
> No more now the foreign hawks
> On alien chickens prey –
> But we on us!

The writer must of course be free from national theories of literature. Literature written to a prescription seldom succeeds. There will no doubt be these theories – "A true African must write like this." Indeed this debate has already flared up in writers' conferences within Africa, and blood – or at least red ink – has been drawn. Phrases like 'Négritude' and 'un style négro-Africain' have often been the focus of such controversy. Even more doubtful causes have their defendants – "A young nation cannot afford satire or criticism of its rulers or its institutions", or "writers must defend or glorify this or that nation or policy". Such restrictive positions can only stifle the literature of a country. Adverse criticism of a novel like *Jagua Nana*[19] in Africa is sometimes based not on any artistic failure in the novel, but on the supposition that it shows Nigeria to the outside world in a bad light. I have heard *Room at the Top* condemned on similar grounds as being unsuitable for reading outside England. It is to be hoped that writers in Africa will be undeterred by such narrow nationalistic theories of literature as the best writers elsewhere have been; otherwise our writers will produce not literature but propaganda.

Even without qualifying for the harsh name of propaganda, African writers may indulge in equally infelicitous writing. The writer in a young literary tradition is tempted by a mission. He is tempted to tell a world which is ignorant about his civilization, "all about Africa". This aim can divert him from his true purpose as unfortunately as any establishment prescription can. In this, African writers can benefit from the example of anonymity of the traditional African folk tales which let Anansi (Brer Spider), the tortoise, the wicked step-mother, and the disguised devil do all the work while the narrator shows his artistry by his presentation of the characters and his embellishing of the episodes.

One should add a word of warning to the critics however who may be too quick to condemn a work as being too 'anthropological'. A certain amount of 'anthropology' is inevitable in any novel which has to have a normal human setting. It happens that the 'anthropology' of Europe and America is well known and taken for granted and is seldom now called anthropology. Thus an elaborate description of a cricket match in, say, Ian Hay's *Pip* or a Fellows' winetasting in Snow's *The Masters* eludes criticism, while a description of an initiation in an African novel may needlessly draw fire. Both writers and critics must be aware of this pitfall and observe due proportion. The test of the suitability of any incident or any item of language or character must be the degree of integration it achieves with the writer's chosen theme.

26. CHINUA ACHEBE, *The African Writer and the Biafran Cause* (1968)

Aus: Chinua Achebe, *Morning Yet on Creation Day* (London, 1975), 78–84 [repr. aus *Conch*, I,1 (1969)] – Chinua Achebe (geb. 1930) aus Nigeria ist der wohl bekannteste afrikanische Romancier, der in englischer Sprache schreibt. Sein erster Roman, *Things Fall Apart* (London, 1958), wurde in Millionenhöhe verkauft, in viele Sprachen übersetzt und zählt als moderner Klassiker zum festen Bestand von Schul- und Universitätslektüre in Afrika. Achebe studierte in Ibadan, arbeitet beim Rundfunk, war wiederholt Gast an amerikanischen Universitäten und ediert seit 1971 die Zeitschrift *Okike*. Neben Romanen, Kurzgeschichten und Gedichten veröffentlichte er Kinderbücher. Der vorliegende Text geht zurück auf einen Vortrag, den der Autor 1968 an der Makerere University in Uganda hielt und entstand während des Bürgerkriegs, den Achebe auf der Seite Biafras erlebte.

The third phase of Europe-Africa relationship opened just over ten years ago with the independence of Ghana. "Seek ye first the political kingdom", said Nkrumah, "and all other things will be added unto you."

In Nigeria the national freedom movement created a freedom song:

> Freedom, freedom
> Everywhere there will be freedom!
> Freedom for you and freedom for me
> Everywhere there will be freedom!

And we sang it to a swinging, evangelical hymn-tune from *Sacred Songs and Solos*. And danced it until our feet gained power beating the hard soil. And Europe capitulated. Or so we thought. In the words of Dr Nnamdi Azikiwe Nigeria was given her freedom "on a platter of gold". Like the head of John the Baptist, this gift to Nigeria proved most unlucky. The British who had done precious little to create a spirit of common nationality in Nigeria during the fifty years they were in control, made certain on the eve of their departure that power went to that conservative element in the country which had played no part in the struggle for independence. This would ensure Nigeria's obedience even unto freedom. As a first sign of this, the British High Commissioner took up residence next door to the Prime Minister who was of course a British Knight.

Within six years of independence Nigeria was a cesspool of corruption and misrule. Public servants helped themselves freely to the nation's wealth. A certain professor has recently described the government of many African countries as a kleptocracy. Nigeria could certainly be called that. Elections were blatantly rigged. (One British weekly captioned its story of a Nigerian election NIGERRIMANDERING.) The national census was outrageously stage-managed; judges and magistrates were manipulated by politicians in power. The politicians themselves were manipulated and corrupted by foreign business interests.

This was the situation in which I wrote *A Man of the People*.[20] The irrepressible Wole Soyinka put on the stage a devastating satire *Before the Black-out*[21] which played to packed houses night after night in Ibadan. The popular travelling theatre of Hubert Ogunde[22] and his many wives began to stage a play clearly directed against the crooked premier of Western Nigeria. The theatre group was declared an unlawful society and banned in that region.[23] Things were coming to a head. After an unbelievable election swindle violence erupted as a result of the anger and frustration of Western Nigerians. It was in these circumstances that Wole Soyinka was charged with holding up the Ibadan radio station and removing the Premier's taped speech!

The Prime Minister of Nigeria,[24] who had been built up into a great statesman by the Western press, did nothing to save his country from impending chaos. Yet he found time to call a Commonwealth Conference in Lagos to discuss Rhodesia and to save his good friend Harold Wilson from the consequences of an OAU resolution to which Nigeria had subscribed.[25]

The point I want to make here is that the creative writer in independent Nigeria found himself with a new, terrifying problem on his hands. He found that the independence his country was supposed to have won was totally without content. The old white master was still in power. He had got himself a bunch of black stooges to do his dirty work for a commission. As long as they did what was expected of them they would be praised for their sagacity and their country for its stability.

As everyone knows Nigeria was upset in January 1966 by five young army majors. Nigerians were wild with joy at the fall of the corrupt and hated governments of the federation. Britain writhed in pain. It is said that the British intelligence service in Nigeria was rebuked and completely reorganised.

Meanwhile the story got around that the military coup which had been so well received was in fact a sinister plot by the ambitious Ibos of the East to seize control of Nigeria. In a country in which tribalism was endemic this interpretation did not wait too long to find acceptance. Many people were quickly persuaded that their spontaneous jubilation in January had been a mistake. A little later it became a fact that only the Ibos had rejoiced. A Nigerian poet who had dedicated a new book "to the heroes of January 1966" had second thoughts after the counter-coup of July and sent a frantic cable to his publishers to remove the dedication.

The story of the massacre of thousands of innocent Eastern Nigerians need not be retold here. But a few of its salient features should be recalled. First it was a carefully planned operation. Secondly it has never been condemned by the Nigerian government. In short, thousands of citizens were slaughtered, hundreds of thousands were wounded and maimed and violated, their homes and property looted and burned; and no one asked any questions. A Sierra Leonean living in Northern Nigeria at the time wrote in horror: "The killing of the Ibos has become a state industry in Nigeria."

> The white man killed my father
> My father was strong
> The white man raped my mother
> My mother was beautiful.[26]

David Diop unfortunately died too young. He would have known that the black man can also murder and rape. Wole Soyinka, if he is alive,[27] knows it. Christopher Okigbo, though he too died young, lived long enough to know it.

Biafra[28] stands in opposition to the murder and rape of Africa by whites and blacks alike because she has tasted both and found them equally bitter. No government, black or white, has the right to stigmatise and destroy groups of its own citizens without undermining the basis of its own existence. The government of Nigeria failed to protect the fourteen million people of its former Eastern Nigeria from wanton destruction and rightly lost their allegiance.

Secondly Biafra stands for true independence in Africa, for an end to the 400 years of shame and humiliation which we have suffered in our association with Europe. Britain knows this and is using Nigeria to destroy Biafra.

"We hope to found a single federal Nigeria", said a British Minister in parliament on 13 February 1968. One may ask: what business has Britain to found anything at this late hour in an African country which is sovereign and independent? Only last Wednesday an editorial in the *Financial Times* carried these words:

"It is appropriate that the leader of the Nigerian delegation to the Peace Talks, Chief Anthony Enahoro, should choose this moment to be not in Ethiopia but in London where he has been having talks with the British government. He will have been telling Lord Shepherd, the Minister of State, of the reasons for the failure of his negotiations..."

That is Nigerian independence. Biafran writers are committed to the revolutionary struggle of their people for justice and true independence. Gabriel Okara, Cyprian Ekwensi, Onuora Nzekwu,[29] Nkem Nwankwo,[30] John Munonye,[31] V. C. Ike,[32] Flora Nwapa[33] are all working actively in this cause for which Christopher Okigbo died. I believe our cause is right and just. And this is what literature in Africa should be about today – right and just causes. (81–84)

27. E. N. OBIECHINA, *Cultural Nationalism in Modern African Literature* (1968)

Aus: Eldred D. Jones (ed.), *African Literature Today*, 1 (1968), 24–35. – Obiechina (cf. Text 6) erblickt einen engen Zusammenhang zwischen politischem und literarischem Nationalismus in der modernen Entwicklung des englischsprachigen Westafrika. Hierin liegt für ihn ein fundamentaler Unterschied zur frankophonen Literatur, in der die Bewegung der Négritude als zentrales Element auf die kulturelle Rehabilitation Schwarzafrikas gerichtet war.

The growth of modern creative writing in West Africa by indigenous West African writers is a post-war phenomenon which developed side by side with the nationalist movement for freedom from colonial rule. This literary upsurge has been dominated in French West Africa by the literary vogue known as 'Négritude'. Whereas in the English-speaking West Africa there has been a definite emphasis on the reconstruction and re-evaluation of the autochthonous West African cultures, especially in so far as they still form an essential part of the composite post-colonial culture of West Africa. The close correspondence between political nationalism and literary nationalism is not just an accident; it is a natural result of the nature of colonial relationship.

The direct result of European colonization of Africa was the depreciation of the African image in popular European imagination, for the imposition of political control also involved conscious or unconscious devaluation of the African culture. Loss of political freedom was also inevitably attended by loss of cultural confidence by Africans, induced by the dynamics of domination. Furthermore, African primitivism, essentially a by-product of political domination, received in the second part of the nineteenth century an almost authoritative stamp from evolutionary anthropology which on the evolutionary scheme of cultural hierarchy placed the African culture at the bottom and Western culture at the top. (24)

...

It could be said that the colonial relationship involved the assertion of cultural superiority by the colonizing people and a devaluation of the culture of the colonized people, leading to their loss of cultural confidence and the death of the creative impulse within their indigenous cultural milieu as well as a lack of creative confidence within the introduced culture of the colonizers. Nationalist movements geared towards the ending of colonial domination were therefore attended by cultural nationalism aimed at rehabilitating the autochthonous culture (or such aspects of it that could still be rescued), and restoring the creative impulse of the peoples emerging from colonialism. This cultural phenomenon which sociologists call 'nativism' is of such immense significance in national resurgence that the Irish, just to give one example, in the assertion of their cultural independence of Britain have not only resurrected the ancient and moribund Erse language but have painstakingly revived their antiquarian literature and mythology.

Cultural nativism, or that aspect of it called literary nationalism, is so fundamentally universal a phenomenon in unequal social situations such as that engendered by colonialism that its inevitability hardly deserves an argument. In the West African scene, then, it is not surprising that the artistic creative impulse which had been smothered under the impact of colonialism began to bud once more with the awakening of national consciousness after the Second World War and that it has actually been flowering since the attainment of national independence. Cultural nativism and its expression in literature in English-speaking West Africa cannot be altogether isolated, as is very often imagined, from the main body of cultural revivalism which is sweeping over Africa and in an even larger context, over all those places inhabited by people of African descent – in the Americas as well as in the Caribbean. Whether this nativism or cultural affirmation finds expression in psycho-political terms such as the African Personality or in the literary ideology of Négritude its cultural implications are obvious. There is a fundamental assumption that the African has had a civilization which is distinct from all other civilizations and which distinguishes him from all other human beings. Historical disasters overtook this civilization in the nature of the slave trade and European colonialism; they resulted not only in its partial disintegration but in the distribution of African peoples to new geographical areas. It is the belief that this African civilization and its outpost in the Americas and the Caribbean, even though temporarily submerged under the impact of the technological civilization of Europe, is not completely lost. This has stimulated in varying forms the attempts at reconstruction and the evolution of a new synthesis.

The Négritude movement is the most coherent, because most ideological, of these attempts at African or rather Negro-African cultural rehabilitation. The movement took root among Negro-African intellectuals of French expression perhaps because their French intellectual background with its "ideological orientation, neat intellectual habits and quality of elegance" equipped them to construct an ideological framework to meet a situation which Negro-African intellectuals and writers of English expression, who are less doctrinaire, are content to treat in a more or less pragmatic manner. (25–26)

...

In English-speaking West Africa, unlike in its French-speaking counterpart, the impact of the Négritude movement was insignificant. Apart from a few poets like Francis Parkes,[34] Gabriel Okara, Efua Morgue,[35] Dei Anang[36] and Adebayo Bablola,[37] whose négritudinous poems are slight compared with such French-speaking poets as Senghor and David Diop, there is hardly any recognizable trace of the Négritude ideology in English-speaking West African writing. In fact, the Négritude ideology tends to be treated with scepticism, derision or blatant hostility in this part of West Africa. Wole Soyinka's statement that the tiger does not go around proclaiming 'its tigritude' any more than the Negro should go around proclaiming his Négritude sums up the general attitude of English-speaking West Africans towards Négritude.

An objection to this facile dismissal is that it does not seem to recognize the immense significance of the ideology to the assimilated French African intellectuals in their effort to regain cultural initiative. Dr Davidson Nicol,[38] the versatile West African intellectual and, until recently, Vice-Chancellor of the University of Sierra Leone has made a more balanced review of Négritude than any other English-speaking West African before him. He put these ideas to the Seminar on African Literature and the University Curriculum at Fourah in April 1963. The display of unsympathetic and impatient attitude to Négritude by some West Africans who have never been completely cut off from their cultural roots and made to acclimatize themselves within a foreign culture, as had the French African intellectuals, smacks of complacency.

Ardent exponents of the African Personality in English-speaking West Africa, like former President of Ghana, Kwame Nkrumah, also tend to treat Négritude with considerable suspicion no doubt because its pan-Negroism tends to distract efforts from the bulding up of pan-African solidarity even though on purely cultural grounds, the African personality, which includes the Arab peoples of North Africa as well as the sub-saharan Africans, does not seem to have a more convincing validity than Négritude. It may be supposed, however, that as a result of spatial contiguity, the realization of pan-Africanism, the political objective of the African Personality cultists, is a much more feasible proposition than the pan-Negroid ethno-aesthetic dream of Négritude.

No clear ideological definition of the African Personality and pan-Africanism approaching that of Négritude has yet emerged but it seems that pan-Africanism is an essentially political movement aimed at continental co-operation between independent African states (its most positive achievement to date is the formation of the Organization of African Unity). Whereas the African Personality is a psycho-ethnological concept resembling Négritude but differing from it because it applies to the African continent alone. (28–29)

...

National independence, when it came, liberated the energies of young West Africans with creative talent from preoccupation with nationalist politics and increased their awareness of the individuality of being. But this awareness brings with it cultural frustration. Political independence is meaningless without cultural independence for only the cultural values of a people can inspire them with a national pride, give them a separate identity and something to live and die for. This challenge of culture cannot be met through the cosmopolitan culture of the departed colonial powers; it can only be met through the neo-African culture which is a composite of African and European cultural elements.

The upsurge of creative writing, which is a phenomenon of the fifties and sixties, reveals that the writers are aware of the challenge and are meeting it in their individual ways. The pattern which seems to be emerging is this: in the treatment of the neo-African culture, the traditional aspect (which by and large outweighs the foreign aspects) is restated to emphasize its logic, its dignity and intrinsic beauty; whereas the foreign aspect appears as disintegrative, corruptive and often antithetical. The musico-ethnologist Kwabena Nketia[39] of Ghana records and interprets the funeral dirges of the Akan.[40] The Sierra Leone novelist William Conton invoked the beauty of the country life in Sierra Leone. Achebe reconstructed the Ibo traditional culture in its full dignity and autonomy before the colonial impact undermined it. Tutuola assembled and embellished Yoruba folk-tales. And many other young poets and playwrights draw elaborately not only from traditional themes and motifs but also from the mythology and symbolisms of West African traditional cultures. In the work of all these traditional elements stand out and give the literature a characteristically West African flavour.

We can now speak of the West African literature which has grown and drawn its inspiration from the West African culture. It has no recognizable and overtly formulated ideology as is the case with the literature of Négritude. Rather, it arises out of certain cultural compulsions which are both natural and induced by a recent colonial past. These compulsions are implicit in the contemporary cultural situation of West Africa and the writers instinctively stumble towards them because they synchronise with the national literary expectations of the West African reading public...

The West African writer is not only writing in the way he does in order to reach the largest reading audience (though this surely has something to do with it) but he is also aiming at satisfying the literary expectation of this generation of West Africans. His book will possibly be more widely read by overseas readers but he cannot afford to disappoint the new spirit of national independence. He is expected, as a creative member of his country's literate class, to participate actively in the business of national reconstruction. His contribution is cultural and he is expected to play the important role of rehabilitating the African culture; he is to give the people a new vision of life, to rescue them from the trauma of cultural confusion in which they have been left as a result of European acculturation, to provide them with new values, new outlooks and new spiritual bearings with their base in the African culture and psychology. (31–32)

...

The responsibility on the modern West African writer is immense. He is not only called upon to draw from his imaginative resourcefulness, he is also expected to fulfil other functions which in firmly established cultural communities are fulfilled by sociologists, anthropologists, archaeologists, cultural historians, psychologists or philosophers. Above all, he is expected to be a dedicated nationalist and patriot. There is no room in this particular point in time and place for the artistic philosophy of 'art for art's sake'. All art is committed and directed towards the expression of the integrity and autonomy of the West African culture. There is therefore a didactic streak in contemporary West African writing, a purpose implicit or explicit, to correct the distortions of the West African culture, to recreate the past in the present in order to educate the West African reader and give him confidence in his cultural heritage and also, in order to enlighten the foreign reader and help him get rid of the false impressions about the West African culture acquired from centuries of cultural misrepresentation.

This strong didacticism of the modern West African writing sometimes intrigues and often irritates the English reader who, because literary didacticism has ceased to be a strong element in his literary tradition since Dr Johnson and the neo-classicists, does not take kindly to its recurrence in contemporary literature. (Although one can point to 'the angry young men' as an exception.) (33)

...

It is clear that the West African writers' rejection of the philosophy of art for art's sake and the preoccupation with artistic purism for a definitely utilitarian and didactic literary outlook at this particular point in time and place is to a large extent a necessity imposed by a historical antecedent and the pressures of cultural nationalism. Social change in West Africa is proceeding at a rapid rate. Old values are quickly crumbling and solid new values are not evolving as rapidly with the result that there is confusion in the minds of many. The individual lacking cultural direction tends to constitute himself into a culture-maker. He evolves personal values which would often be determined by self-interest. Altruism as a generating principle of individual action is replaced by egocentricism. The committed writer, as well as the other intellectuals of society, has the duty of explaining his cultural predicament to the individual and, what is more,

of helping him to evolve new values which will accommodate the shock of change. The West African writer is therefore not out only to entertain and please his West African audience but also to instruct it. In this endeavour, the West African writer bases his authority on the traditional culture within which art was functional and utilitarian as well as providing aesthetic pleasure. (34)
...

There is a definite danger in this nationalist pressure on the writer. It is the danger of producing a literature of a new 'Celtic Twilight'. Recreation of the past in the present can easily degenerate into a mere romantic idyllism as false as the European image of a barbaric irrational Africa. One falsehood could easily be replaced by another falsehood. The English-speaking West African writer is fully aware of this pitfall into which the French African writer of the Négritude school has plunged. The French African writer, often the product of the best French intellectual tradition, residing in Paris which has always been a centre of philosophical primitivism and under the shadow of the Rousseauist phantom called *le sauvage noble,* may not easily see the danger of glamorizing his African heritage and thereby calling its authenticity in question. The English-speaking West African with his background of British education and pragmatic outlook, side-steps the pitfall. He regards his cultural heritage as needing no idealization and no apology. All that is required of him is to recreate the traditional culture with fidelity, without flourishes and false colouring. A West African writer whose book fails to satisfy this minimal requirement of fidelity to cultural facts finds it rejected, very often in a cruel and angry manner.

West African writers are in the forefront of this mission to lead Africans from the old to the new Africa. The strong didactic streak in and the pronounced sociological nature of their writings derive from a sense of this cultural mission. Asked by the present writer what the main influence on their writing had been, William Conton replied, "... my growing awareness of the sharp conflicts between African and Western culture, and in particular the frequent triumphing of the materialism of the latter over the spiritualism of the former whenever they do clash." Achebe answered simply, "My greatest inspiration has been Ibo culture and civilization." It could be said therefore that whether glaringly obvious or merely implicit, cultural nationalism is one of the determining factors of contemporary West African fiction by indigenous West Africans. (35)

28. DAVID RUBADIRI, *The Theme of National Identity in East Writing* (1968)

Aus: K. L. Goodwin (ed.), *National Identity* (London, 1970), 51–56. – D. Rubadiri (cf. Text 7) setzte sich in einem Vortrag auf der zweiten "Conference on Writing in English in the Commonwealth", die 1968 an der University of Queensland, Australien, stattfand, mit dem Begriff der nationalen Identität auseinander. Er sieht sich außerstande, diesen europäisch geprägten Begriff einer Wesensbestimmung der ost-afrikanischen Literatur zugrundelegen zu können. Vielmehr bedarf er hier einer neuen definitorischen Abgrenzung.

Writing and political aspirations have gone hand in hand in the development of East African states to the new status of independence. Three phases of this development are discernible: first the colonial phase; second the independence phase; and third the post-independence phase.

The colonial phase produced very little in the way of creative writing. Two reasons were responsible for this. The teaching of language and literature was dogmatic and negative. The main concern of the teachers of language was to produce a product that could with relative ease write tolerable English or vernacular in order to be able to work as a clerk or teacher in the lower grades of the system. Good grammar and spelling were therefore emphasized. The publishing houses thus made their fortunes in selling books with titles like "Basic English" and "How to Write Good Letters". The other was that the colonial power did not wish to encourage the expression of views through the written word in either the press or the creative media. With the rise of political clamour for independence – wrongfully called 'nationalism' – a new kind of written self-expression also emerged. This took the form of pamphlets of assertion, 'national' declaration, and at times romantic idealism of a vague savage and noble past.

Post-independent East Africa has luckily obliterated from the field of creative writing these romantic and rather sentimental assertions of a 'national identity'. I am using the word 'luckily' deliberately – because, however enthusiastic one may feel towards fitting in with the modern, which unfortunately is always equated to the 'civilized', one must continually first ask the question "What is a nation?" and also "What is an identity?"

Western societies find it easy to define a 'nation' and 'identity' because the basic of their society, their human relationships, seem to be based on a kind of hierarchical scheme. Things must have tags on them. They must be identified, or the order becomes impossible to identify or maintain. It is an order of classes, position, and status. That is why it is able to segregate even at the human and national levels. Within this conglomeration of divisions or isolations it can achieve a 'national' umbrella, and therefore an identifying factor.

With the African, 'national identity' could not be described in terms of these particulars, because to us it is a way of life. Within a decade of achieving independence the barriers of statehood have fallen all around us because we tried to emulate the western definition of 'nation' and 'identity'. In other words the concept of 'nation' and 'identity' in Africa does not have physical (i.e. geographical), social or moral boundaries.

This aspect has become a major theme in East African writing. As yet there are very few published works of creative writing in East Africa. I shall refer to a few of these that seem to me to exemplify the point I have been labouring to make.

In *Song of Lawino* (Nairobi: East African Publishing House, 1966) Okot p'Bitek takes the theme of alienation which occurred due to the state and the individual trying to emulate the definition of 'national identity' from western societies in the form of satire, symbolism, and lament. The unwesternized village girl Lawino poses the question, gives the answers, and formulates the transpositions that give us the wives' spiritual understanding of the national and identifiable. Take the following two examples for instance. In the first she is commenting about the significance and importance of the dance in Africa.

> *When the daughter of the Bull*
> *Enters the arena*
> *She does not stand there*
> *Like stale beer that does not sell,*
> *She jumps here*
> *She jumps there.*
> *When you touch her*
> *She says 'Don't touch me!'* (p. 34)

The point being made here is that the dance is an expression of an individual as well as a communal meaning of life, an identification of life as opposed to being merely a 'type'. Lawino then unveils the wrappers of alienation in her description of ballroom dancing.

> *It is true, Ocol*
> *I cannot dance the ball-room dance.*
> *Being held so tightly*
> *I feel ashamed,*
> *Being held so tightly in public*
> *I cannot do it,*
> *It looks shameful to me!*
> *They come to the dance dead drunk,*
> *They drink white men's drinks*
> *As well as waragi.*[41]
> *They close their eyes,*
> *And they do not sing as they dance,*
> *They dance silently like wizards.*
> *Each man has a woman*
> *Although she is not his wife,*
> *They dance inside a house*
> *And there is no light.*
> *Shamelessly, they hold each other,*
> *Tightly, tightly,*
> *They cannot breathe!* (pp. 35–36)

This search for liberation of the physical, the emotional, and the spiritual is central to the identity of the African. It seems from a short experience that it cannot lie comfortably within the strictures of a 'national' identity as defined by western and eastern concepts. Okot p'Bitek thinks that the West, from which we wish to invent an identity and the expression of a 'nation', has

drained us of all the values that we had and that we cannot ever expect to have any until we reevaluate the miasms of confusion that we are in now. (51–53)
...

The same point of view on this theme of 'National Identity' is taken by Okello Oculi in his long poem *Orphan* (Nairobi: East African Publishing House, 1968). The search here is not for a 'national' flag, but for a nation's soul. The framework is already there – submerged like an iceberg – but the *Orphan* must find it through the cross as it were:

> *Orphan boy, you must learn to expect little*
> *From the generosity of the world,*
> *To grapple alone with the top of the earth* (p. 29)
>
> ...
>
> *Wake out of the soothe of tranquillisers,*
> *Sympathy, love*
> *Thin delicate threads for bridges cross*
> *The chasms and walls of silence*
> *Between letters in an alphabet,*
> *Between bricks in a wall claiming unity*
> *In sharing layers of cement and asserted*
> *Brickness fragmented to satisfy identity,*
> *Deriving a unity in the distributed presence*
> *In the wall's expanse;*
> *A fragile unity that crumbles in violent*
> *Confusion and panic at the tease of an*
> *Earthquake's casual belch,*
> *And falling back to calls of sympathy*
> *And the oneness in walls.* (pp. 36–7)

This brings me to the major novelists in East Africa. James Ngugi, in his three novels *Weep Not, Child; The River Between,* and *A Grain of Wheat* (London, Heinemann),[42] though on the surface concerned with the emergence of Kenya as an independent country, is basically concerned with the social problems of man in his human relationship with others. Grace Ogot's *The Promised Land* (East African Publishing House, 1966)[43] is a novel that examines the possibilities of patching up a tribal unit into a national unit – but once again the social comment is paramount. My own novel *No Bride Price* (East African Publishing House, 1967) is about the social and personal problems that face the young and ambitious young men in the postindependence period in urban and rural areas – i.e. the past, the present, and the future.

Whether East African writers will shape the new image of national creation and national identity I am not as yet able to judge. They are however being now widely read. And if censorship will continue to be as tolerant as it is at the moment they may well have some impact. Their major impact at the moment has been in schools, colleges, and the University. Maybe the new generation that has been exposed to them, when it comes to power eventually, will be influenced by some of the ideas in them and the influence of their ideas may seep through into the corridors of power.

But so far none of the East African writers have consciously attempted to write in ideological terms. That is to say, there has not been that kind of writing that consciously tries to evoke nationalistic fervour so as to lift the souls of men to heights of a new 'glory'. This type of writing may soon come when East Africa has found an ideology of any significance or spiritual power. At the moment it has not, with the exception perhaps of Tanzania. At the moment the writing is personally conceived, sensitive in execution, and one more concerned with the lot of what is called the 'ordinary man' and his 'fortunes' in the 'Brave New World'. (54–56)

B. *Englische Sprache und Literatur heute*

4. Die Landessprachen und das Englische

29. OBIAJUNWA WALI, *The Dead End of African Literature?* (1963)

Aus: *Transition* III, 10 (1963), 13–15. – O. Wali studierte an der University of Ibadan Englische Literatur, setzte sein Studium in den Vereinigten Staaten fort und unterrichtete dann an der University of Nigeria in Nsukka. In seinem 1963 veröffentlichten Aufsatz setzt er sich kritisch mit der "Conference of African Writers of English Expression" auseinander, die im Juni 1962 am Makerere College stattgefunden hatte und zum ersten Male afrikanische Schriftsteller nach dem Kongreß von Rom zusammenführte. Walis teilweise polemischer Artikel führte zu einer Flut von Reaktionen in den folgenden Ausgaben von *Transition*; sein Standpunkt, afrikanische Autoren sollten in ihren eigenen Sprachen schreiben – den er selbst in die Tat umsetzte –, spielt in der Auseinandersetzung um die afrikanische Literatur weiterhin eine Rolle.

Perhaps the most important achievement of the last Conference of African Writers of English Expression held in Makerere College, Kampala, in June 1962, is that African literature as now defined and understood, leads nowhere.

The Conference itself marked the final climax of the attack on the Négritude school of Leopold Senghor and Aimé Césire. For some time now, African writers of English expression like Ezekiel Mphahlele, Wole Soyinka, and Christopher Okigbo, have treated this kind of literature which expresses sterile concepts such as "négritude" or the "African personality"[1] with the utmost derision. One would say that negritude is now dead, judging from the confident tones of the remarks and decisions made at the Makerere conference.

Another significant event in the conference, is the tacit omission of Amos Tutuola. Not only was Tutuola, who undoubtedly is one of the most significant writers in Africa today, not present in the conference, but there was a careful exclusion of his works in the discussions of the conference. In fact, according to the Conference report, Tutuola's publishers protested at the implied questioning of their integrity in publishing this writer's works. One can guess that Tutuola received this kind of treatment partly because influential critics like Janheinz Jahn have repeatedly grouped him in the negritude school, and partly because he has gone out of line winning acclaim overseas for using that kind of English expression that is non-Ibadan, and non-Makerere.

With the now seeming defeat of the Negritude and Tutuola schools of African writing, what now represents African literature can be seen from these examples from some of the writings of the artists and critics who now dominate our literature. Una Maclean, reviewing J. P. Clark's play, *Song of a Goat*,[2] opens in the following fashion: "The author of this poetic melodrama possibly perceives himself as some sort of Tennessee Williams of the Tropics. Suddenly the sultry symbolism of the sex war seeps through the swamps, to hang like a horrid miasma upon the polluted air ... It is a simple and familiar tale, impotent man, ardent woman. But this cat on a hot tin roof had once known better times, for her partner had once given palpable token of his potency in siring a son."³

Christopher Okigbo in his acknowledgement prefixed to his poem, *Silences*, makes the following observations: "the author wishes to acknowledge his debt to those composers whose themes he has used or varied in certain parts of the present work. The INTROIT is a variation on a theme in Raja Ratnam's *At Eight-fifteen* in the Morning; the first three passages of the first movement are variations on a theme by Malcolm Cowley; "Sand banks sprinkled with memories" in the 4th passage of the same movement is a variation on Stephane Mallarmé's "Au bosquet arrose d'accords" in his *L'Apres-midi d'un Faune*; the 6th passage of the same movement is a variation on a theme in Rabindranath Tagore's *Stray Birds*."⁴

Ulli Beier, in his paper read to the Makerere conference, discussing the poetry of J. P. Clark, remarks, "John Pepper Clark is a very different poet. His background is similar to that of Okigbo ... He studied English, and what Ezra Pound is to Okigbo, Eliot and Hopkins are to Clark. As the case of Okigbo, one finds it occasionally disturbing to recognise the 'ready made' language."⁵

What these examples clearly show is that African literature as now understood and practised, is merely a minor appendage in the main stream of European literature. Both creative writers and literary critics, read and devour European literature and critical methods. The new drame of J. P. Clark is seen in terms not only of the classical past of Aristotle and the Greeks, but in the current present of Tennessee Williams, and the Absurds, leading to such crudities as Una Maclean's comparison of the simple and child-hungry Ebiere, to the sexual complications of Big Daddy's American family. In this kind of literary analysis, one just goes back to parrot Aristotle, and the current clichés of the English and American new critcs.

The consequence of this kind of literature is that it lacks any blood and stamina, and has no means of self-enrichment. It is severely limited to the European-oriented, few college graduates in the new Universities of Africa, steeped as they are in European literature and culture. The ordinary local audience, with little or no education in the conventional European manner, and who constitute an overwhelming majority, has no chance of participating in this kind of literature. Less than one per cent of the Nigerian people have had access to, or ability to understand Wole Soyinka's *Dance of the Forests*. Yet, this was the play staged to celebrate their national independence, tagged on to the idiom and traditions of a foreign culture. It is no wonder, that a poet like Christopher Okigbo, so readily resorts to Mallarmé's idea of an aristocratic and limited poetic community, for his impertinent remark, "I don't read my poetry to non-poets" is Mallarmé in paraphrase.

The purpose of this article is not to discredit these writers who have achieved much in their individual rights within an extremely difficult and illogical situation. It is to point out that the whole uncritical acceptance of English and French as the inevitable medium for educated African writing, is misdirected, and has no chance of advancing African literature and culture. In other words, until these writers and their western midwives accept the fact that any true African literature must be written in African languages, they would be merely pursuing a dead end, which can only lead to sterility, uncreativity, and frustration.

The conference itself, faced with the fundamental question of defining African literature, and the problems involved for an African writing in a language that is not native to him, came very near the truth: "It was generally agreed that it is better for an African writer to think and feel in his own language and then look for an English transliteration approximating the original."[6] This very conclusion, as naive and as misguided as it is, expresses the problem concisely and accurately, and it is from that we shall find a new direction for African literature, if we are really serious and sincere in what we are doing.

An African writer who thinks and feels in his own language *must* write in that language. The question of transliteration, whatever that means, is unwise as it is unacceptable, for the 'original' which is spoken of here, is the real stuff of literature and the imagination, and must not be discarded in favour of a *copy*, which, as the passage admits, is merely an approximation.

Of course all the old facile arguments would arise again – the multiplicity of African languages, the limitation of the audience to small patches of tribal groups, questions of orthography, and all the rest of them. Yes, but why not? I believe that every language has a right to be developed as literature. There is no part of the world where a false literary unity has been attempted in the way that we are doing today in Africa, not even in Europe. The problem has always been met by the technique of translating outstanding literary achievements into other languages, especially the more widespread and influential languages of the world. One wonders what would have happened to English literature for instance, if writers like Spenser, Shakespeare, Donne, and Milton, had neglected English, and written in Latin and Greek simply because these classical languages were the cosmopolitan languages of their times. Even though a man like Milton could write even more easily in Latin and Greek, he did his major works in his own mother tongue without playing to the gallery of international fame.

Literature after all, is the exploitation of the possibilities of language. It is the African languages that are in crying need of this kind of development, not the overworked French and English. There is, for instance, a good deal of scholarly work being done in the linguistic structure of several African languages, but there is practically no use being made of these in creative writing, simply because we are all busy fighting over the commonplaces of European literature. If linguistic science devotes so much energy and attention to African languages in spite of their tribal and limited scope, why should imaginative literature which in fact has more chances of enriching the people's culture, consider it impossible to adventure in this direction?

The criticism being done today in African writing in English and French, sounds so dull, drab, and flippant, mainly because there is no opportunity for original thinking. It is the same clichés over and over again – romantic and classic, realism, sentimentality, Victorianism, surrealism, and so on. There is no need for creative thinking in order to become a 'leading critic or authority' in African literature. Fraser, Freud, Darwin, and Marx, are, as in European literature, the necessary reading for the acquisition of fundamental critical tools.

What I am advocating here is not easy, for it entails a good deal of hard work and hard thinking, and what is more, a necessary casting overboard of hardened debris of the overblown ego. It would force some 'leading' critics to go in for the hard school of African linguistic studies, a knowledge of some of the important African languages, before generalising and formulating all kinds of philosophical and literary theories. Literature in Africa would then become the serious business that all literature truly is, reaching out to the people for whom it is meant, and creating a true culture of the African peoples that would not rely on slogans and propaganda, nor on patronage of doubtful intentions.

The basic distinction between French and German literature for instance, is that one is written in French, and the other in German. All the other distinctions, whatever they be, are based on this fundamental fact. What therefore is now described as African literature in English and French, is a clear contradiction, and a false proposition, just as 'Italian literature in Hausa' would be.

What one would like future conferences on African literature to devote time to, is the all-important problem of African writing in African languages, and all its implications for the development of a truly African sensibility. In fact, the secondary place which African languages now occupy in our educational system would be reversed if our writers would devote their tremendous gifts and ability to their own languages. Attempts have recently been made to include the study of African languages in the curriculum of some of the new African universities. This programme would certainly have no future, for all that is available even at the university level is the usual string of proverbs, a few short stories on the tortoise and the tiger, and a numer of inadequate grammar books written by untrained linguists. The student of Yoruba for instance, has no play available to him in that language, for Wole Soyinka, the most gifted Nigerian playwright at the moment, does not consider Yoruba suitable for *The Lion and the Jewel* or *The Dance of the Forests*.

The main reason for the study of a language is that it contains great literature or some form of literature. This was what led scholars like Eliot and Pound to the study of oriental languages in their poetic experiments early in this century. There is little doubt that African languages would face inevitable extinction, if they do not embody some kind of intelligent literature, and the only way to hasten this, is by continuing in our present illusion that we can produce African literature in English and French.

The last junketing at Makerere was good as far as it went, but it is a little scandalous to admit that its only concrete achievement is that it gave African writers and their patrons, the opportunity to get to know one another!

30. EZEKIEL MPHAHLELE, *Are We Going to Fold Our Arms and Wait for that Kingdom to Come?* (1963)

Aus: *Polemics,* [Letters to the Editor], *Transition* III, 11 (1963), 11–12. – E. Mphahlele (geb. 1919) setzt sich mit Walis Essay (cf. Text 29) auseinander und fordert die Freiheit für jeden Schriftsteller, sich das ihm gemäße sprachliche Medium zu suchen. Der in Südafrika geborene Autor verfaßte Kurzgeschichten, einen Roman mit deutlich autobiographischem Einschlag, eine Autobiographie, *Down Second Avenue* (London, 1959), und eine Reihe literaturkritischer Arbeiten. 1957 verließ er Südafrika, unterrichtete in Nigeria, Kenia und den USA. Er kehrte freiwillig aus dem Exil zurück und lebt in Johannesburg.

Let's try to extract something worth talking about from the tangle of Wali's thoughts, while wishing that he had, as a critic, brought us face to face with the *actual* texts he is referring to so that we didn't have to keep warding off the critics whom he is constantly thrusting upon us.

He is trying to say that because some of us Africans are writing in English or French, because our works echo this or that English or French author, our literature "lacks blood and stamina, and has no means of self-enrichment." Furthermore, "the whole uncritical acceptance of English and French as the inevitable medium for educated African writing, is misdirected, and has no chance of advancing African literature and culture. In other words, until these writers and their western midwives accept the fact that any true African literature must be written in African languages, they would be merely pursuing a dead-end..."

Let us agree that the best language for a creative writer to use is his own. This does not need belabouring. But why compare an African with Shakespeare, Milton, Spenser, who, as Wali says, did not neglect their own language simply because Latin and Greek were the cosmopolitan languages of their time. There was no need to abandon English because these writers were not committed in a struggle against colonialism, as we Africans are today: they were not discriminated against in the way a black man is today. The English did not need to organize a variety of tribes speaking different languages against a colonial or fascist power. Latin and Greek were not spoken by the man-in-the-street when Shakespeare and Milton wrote. These languages were scholastic fossils. English and French have become the common language with which to present a nationalist front against white oppressors. Where the white man has already retreated, as in the independent states, these two languages are still a unifying force. By stages, each of the various states will need to find an African official language for itself. The African languages will need to develop a technical terminology and a vocabulary that meets the needs of systematic analytic contemporary thought.

In the meantime, are we going to fold our arms and wait for that kingdom to come? The creative instinct always runs ahead of social, political, and economic developments; and the creative impulse cannot wait for such developments before it expresses itself. So we use English, French and Portuguese, which we know and have mastered.

So far, only some of the Bantu languages like Sotho, Zulu, Xhosa, Shangana-Tsonga (the four main languages of South Africa with Sotho having three dialects) and Swahili, possibly followed by Hausa, have the oldest literature in Africa. South African Bantu poetry dates back 90 years, Swahili poetry, in Arabic script, more than that. Furthermore, the South African languages have been subjects of study for more than forty years in local schools and universities and have a large body of adult poetry and prose fiction.

In spite of this, some writers have chosen to write in English. Why? It is surely a matter of choice for a writer. I believe a writer has a right to choose his medium, and it is hard on him to predict doom and a cul-de-sac for him when he has only just begun, relatively speaking. Why can he not be authentic simply because he is using a foreign medium? He is bringing to the particular European language an African experience which in turn affects his style. There will naturally be conscious and unconscious imitation in the beginning, but if he is worth his salt, he will continue to clean up his style and eventually evolve something of his own.

If, as Wali says, present-day criticism of African writing in English and French "sounds dull, drab, and flippant mainly because there is no opportunity for original thinking", are African writers in general to blame? Is Una Maclean's obtuse criticism to be laid at J. P. Clark's door, for instance? Again, if, as Wali says, the expression "African literature in English and French is a clear contradiction, a false proposition", is it the African writer's fault – because he writes in English or French? Is it not merely a convenient term? If Wali is so particular about the use of names or categories, what would he call literature produced by eastern Russians – European or Asian? What would he call literature produced in Hawaii – American? South Americans write in Spanish and Portuguese because these are the languages spoken in that part of the world. Would Wali quarrel if we called the literature from there South American writing in Spanish and Portuguese? These were not the original languages of the indigenous people of South America.

"The secondary place which African languages now occupy in our educational system" Wali concludes, "would be reversed if our writers would devote their tremendous gifts and ability to their own languages." Surely they were given secondary place by our past colonial masters. And it is not the writer alone who will redeem the situation. Wali should address himself to the education departments and universities of Africa. It is as much a pedagogical problem as a literary one. We have to wait a generation or two before more Africans outside South and East Africa can produce an adult literature in their own languages. But we as writers cannot be asked to leave off writing and engage in linguistics which are the basic concern of education authorities. Now we are also being told to produce Yoruba plays for the benefit of the student of Yoruba! This is exactly what missionary presses and the "literature bureaux" of East and Central Africa are promoting: writing for pupils. In South Africa, white presses that support the government have now also cashed in on the school market, because they will not publish a novel or poetry in the African languages that will appeal to the adult mind and therefore help in the process of politicisation. It is still only the missionary presses that publish this latter kind of literature. Furthermore, the government has decreed that the African languages shall be used as media of instruction right up to secondary school. The aim is obviously to arrest the black man's education, because the previous system whereby English was the medium after the first six years of primary education produced a strong educated class that has in turn given us a sophisticated class of political leaders and a sophisticated following – a real threat to white supremacy. South African non-white writers have always addressed themselves to their own public, not to an overseas audience, and because of this, they have been experimenting with styles of writing in English which are anything but "dull and drab". Others have continued to write in their vernacular languages. One of the ways in which literature can be kept on an infantile level is by promoting a school literature in such a way that the man who wants to write for an adult audience does not stand a chance of being published. We have to revolutionise publishing in Africa so that men writing in European or African languages – as they choose – may stand an equal chance of being read.

Supposing we met at Makerere to discuss African literature in the indigenous languages, what common language would we have which would help us understand the books being discussed? How many writers, even if they all wrote in indigenous languages, would have understood what was being talked about in connection with vernacular texts? What would be the common problems to talk about, such as we had as writers of English? And the problems we discussed are real, and are based on the reality that is African English literature, even although Wali thinks that it is an illusion to think of producing African literature in English and French. It is no use trying to wish this volume of writing out of existence. If it is argued that the get-together was a junket, that is a matter of opinion.

Inasmuch as a book in an African language can be translated into English or French, there is no reason why Chinua Achebe's *Things Fall Apart* cannot be translated into Ibo or Yoruba or Hausa, or Wole Soyinka's plays into any African language to enrich it. There will thus be no reason why any language should wait for its own people to write originally in it in order to develop it as a literary medium. A writer must choose the medium that suits him best, I must repeat.

31. GABRIEL OKARA, *African Speech... English Words* (1963)

Aus: *Transition* III, 10 (1963), 15–16. – Gabriel I. G. Okara (geb. 1921) aus dem südöstlichen Teil Nigerias wählte nach seiner Schulausbildung keine akademische Karriere, sondern wurde Buchbinder. Gedichte in englischer Sprache erschienen bereits in Anthologien und Zeitschriften der fünfziger Jahre. Der 1964 publizierte Roman *The Voice* erregte vor allem wegen Okaras experimenteller Sprachgebung Aufsehen und belebte die Diskussion um die Verwendung des Englischen in der afrikanischen Literatur. Im folgenden Text begründet Okara sein Vorgehen.

Trying to express ideas even in one's own language is difficult because what is said or written often is not exactly what one had in mind. Between the birth of the idea and its translation into words, something is lost. The process of expression is even more difficult in the second language of one's own cultural group. I speak not of merely expressing general ideas, but of communicating an idea to the reader in the absolute or near absolute state in which it was conceived. Here, you see I am already groping for words to make you understand what I really mean as an African.

"Once an African, always an African; it will show in whatever you write" says one school of thought. This implies that there is no need for an African writer to exert a conscious effort to make his writing African through the use of words or the construction of sentences. Equally it seems to say that the turns of phrase, the nuances and the imagery which abound in African languages, thinking, and culture are not worth letting the world know about.

As a writer who believes in the utilisation of African ideas, African philosophy and African folk-lore and imagery to the fullest extent possible, I am of the opinion the only way to use them effectively is to translate them almost literally from the African language native to the writer into whatever European language he is using as his medium of expression. I have endeavoured in my words to keep as close as possible to the vernacular expressions. For, from a word, a group of words, a sentence and even a name in any African language, one can glean the social norms, attitudes and values of a people.

In order to capture the vivid images of African speech, I had to eschew the habit of expressing my thoughts first in English. It was difficult at first, but I had to learn. I had to study each Ijaw expression I used and to discover the probable situation in which it was used in order to bring out the nearest meaning in English. I found it a fascinating exercise.

Some words and expressions are still relevant to the present day life of the world, while others are rooted in the legends and tales of a far-gone day. Take the expression "he is timid" for example. The equivalent in Ijaw is "he has no chest" or "he has no shadow". Now a person without a chest in the physical sense can only mean a Human that does not exist. The idea becomes clearer in the second translation. A person who does not cast a shadow of course does not exist. All this means is that a timid person is not fit to live. Here, perhaps, we are hearing the echoes of the battles in those days when the strong and the brave lived. But is this not true of the world today?

In parting with a friend at night a true Ijaw would say, "May we live to see ourselves tomorrow". This again is reminiscent of the days when one went about with the danger of death from wild beasts or hostile animals dogging one's steps. But has the world we live in changed so much? On the other hand, how could an Ijaw born and bred in England, France or the United States write, "May we live to see ourselves tomorrow" instead of "Goodnight"? And if he wrote "Goodnight", would he be expressing an Ijaw thought? Is it only the colour of one's skin that makes one an African?

In the Ibo language they say something like, "May dawn come", or "May it dawn". Once again it is a wish or a prayer. Isn't the grave sometimes likened to an endless night and is it not only the dead that go to the grave? The Ibos sometimes lighten this sombre thought with the expression, "You sleep like a rat while I sleep like a lizard." Because it is thought that rats never sleep, while lizards are heavy sleepers, this never fails to produce peals of laughter.

Why should I not use the poetic and beautiful, "May we live to see ourselves tomorrow" or, "May it dawn", instead of "Goodnight"? If I were writing a dialogue between two friends, one about to leave after visiting the other at night, I would do it this way:

"Are you getting up now?" said Otutu as he saw his friend heaving himself up with his two hands gripping the arms of the chair he was sitting on.

"Yes I am about walking now. The night has gone far", Beni his friend said, for he was a very fat man.

"May we live to see ourselves tomorrow", Otutu said after seeing his friend to the door.

"May we live to see ourselves tomorrow", his friend also said and walked panting into the night.

What emerges from the examples I have given is that a writer can use the idioms of his own language in a way that is understandable in English. If he uses their English equivalents, he would not be expressing African ideas and thoughts, but English ones.

Some may regard this way of writing in English as a desecration of the language. This is of course not true. Living languages grow like living things, and English is far from a dead language. There are American, West Indian, Australian, Canadian and New Zealand versions of English. All of them add life and vigour to the language while reflecting their own respective cultures. Why shouldn't there be a Nigerian or West African English which we can use to express our own ideas, thinking and philosophy in our own way?

32. CHINUA ACHEBE, *English and the African Writer (1964)*

Aus: Chinua Achebe, *Morning Yet on Creation Day* (London, 1975), 55–62; rev. ed. – Achebe (cf. Text 26) setzte sich wiederholt mit der Frage auseinander, ob afrikanische Autoren in englischer Sprache schreiben sollten. Im vorliegenden Text vertritt er die Auffassung, daß spezifische Umstände in einer grundsätzlichen Diskussion hierüber zu berücksichtigen seien, aber auch, daß das Medium der Autoren in der Weise zu verändern ist, daß es dem afrikanischen Kontext als angemessen erscheint.

What all this suggests to me is that you cannot cram African literature into a small, neat definition. I do not see African literature as one unit but as a group of associated units – in fact the sum total of all the *national* and *ethnic* literatures of Africa.

A national literature is one that takes the whole nation for its province, and has a realised or potential audience throughout its territory. In other words a literature that is written in the *national* language. An ethnic literature is one which is available only to one ethnic group within the nation. If you take Nigeria as an example, the national literature, as I see it, is the literature written in English; and the ethnic literatures are in Hausa, Ibo, Yoruba, Efik, Edo, Ijaw, etc., etc.

Any attempt to define African literature in terms which overlook the complexities of the African scene and the material of time is doomed to failure. After the elimination of white rule shall have been completed, the single most important fact in Africa in the second half of the twentieth century will appear to be the rise of individual nation states. I believe that African literature will follow the same pattern.

What we tend to do today is to think of African literature as a new-born infant. But in fact what we have is a whole generation of new-born infants. Of course if you only look cursorily one infant looks very much like another; but in reality each is already set on its own seperate journey. Of course, you may group them together on the basis of anything you choose – the colour of their hair, for instance. Or you may group them together on the basis of the language they will speak or the religion of their fathers. Those would all be valid distinctions; but they could not begin to account fully for each indidivual person carrying, as it were, his own little lodestar of genes.

Those who in talking about African literature want to exclude North Africa because it belongs to a different tradition surely do not suggest that Black Africa is anything like homogeneous. What does Shabaan Robert[7] have in common with Christopher Okigbo or Awoonor-Williams?[8] or Mongo Beti[9] of Cameroun and Paris with Nzekwu of Nigeria? What does the champagne drinking upper-class Creole society described by Easmon[10] of Sierra Leone have in common with the rural folk and and fishermen of J. P. Clark's plays? Of course, some of these differences could be accounted for on individual rather than national grounds but a good deal of it is also environmental.

I have indicated somewhat off-handedly that the national literature of Nigeria and of many other countries of Africa is, or will be, written in English. This may sound like a controversial statement, but it isn't. All I have done has been to look at the reality of present-day Africa. This "reality" may change as a result of deliberate, e.g. political, action. If it does an entirely new situation will arise, and there will be plenty of time to examine it. At present it may be more profitable to look at the scene as it is.

What are the factors which have conspired to place English in the position of national language in many parts of Africa? Quite simply the reason is that these nations were created in the first place by the intervention of the British which, I hasten to add, is not saying, that the peoples comprising these nations were invented by the British.

The country which we know as Nigeria today began not so very long ago as the arbitrary creation of the British. It is true, as William Fagg says in his excellent new book *Nigerian Images*,[11] that this arbitrary action has proved as lucky in terms of African art history as any enterprise of the fortunate Princess of Serendip. And I believe that in political and economic terms too this arbitrary creation called Nigeria holds out great prospects. Yet the fact remains that Nigeria was created by the British – for their own ends. Let us give the devil his due: colonialism in African disrupted many things, but it did create big political units where there were small, scattered ones before. Nigeria had hundreds of autonomous communities ranging in size from the vast Fulani Empire founded by Usman dan Fodio in the North to tiny village entities in the East. Today it is one country.

Of course there are areas of Africa where colonialism divided up a single ethnic group among two or even three powers. But on the whole it did bring together many peoples that had hitherto gone their several ways. And it gave them a language with which to talk to one another. If it failed to give them a song, it at least gave them a tongue, for sighing. There are not many countries in Africa today where you could abolish the language of the erstwhile colonial powers and still retain the facility for mutual communication. Therefore those African writers who have chosen to write in English or French are not unpatriotic smart alecs with an eye on the main chance – outside their own countries. They are by-products of the same process that made the new nation states of Africa.

You can take this argument a stage further to include other countries of Africa. The only reason why we can even talk about African unity is that when we get together we can have a manageable number of languages to talk in – English, French, Arabic.

The other day I had a visit from Joseph Kariuki[12] of Kenya. Although I had read some of this poems and he had read my novels we had not met before. But it didn't seem to matter. In fact I had met him through his poems, especially through his love poem, "Come Away My Love" in which he captures in so few words the trials and tensions of an African in love with a white girl in Britain.

> Come away, my love, from streets
> Where unkind eyes divide
> And shop windows reflect our difference.

By contrast, when in 1960 I was travelling in East Africa and went to the home of the late Shabaan Robert, the Swahili poet of Tanganyika, things had been different. We spent some time talking about writing, but there was no real contact. I knew from all accounts that I was talking to an important writer, but of the nature of his work I had no idea. He gave me two books of his poems which I treasure but cannot read – until I have learnt Swahili.

And there are scores of languages I would want to learn if it were possible. Where am I to find the time to learn the half-a-dozen or so Nigerian languages each of which can sustain a literature? I am afraid it cannot be done. These languages will just have to develop as tributaries to feed the one central language enjoying nation-wide currency. Today, for good or ill, that language is English. Tomorrow it may be something else, although I very much doubt it.

Those of us who have inherited the English language may not be in a position to appreciate the value of the inheritance. Or we may go on resenting it because it came as part of a package deal which included many other items of doubtful value and the positive atrocity of racial arrogance and prejudice which may yet set the world on fire. But let us not in rejecting the evil throw out the good with it. (56–58).

...

I think I have said enough to give an indication of my thinking on the importance of the world language which history has forced down our throats. Now let us look at some of the most serious handicaps. And let me say straight away that one of the most serious handicaps is *not* the one people talk about most often, namely, that it is impossible for anyone ever to use a second language as effectively as his first. This assertion is compounded of half-truth and half bogus mystique. Of course, it is true that the vast majority of people are happier with their first language than with any other. But then the majority of people are not writers. We do have enough examples of writers who have performed the feat of writing effectively in a second language. And I am not thinking of the obvious names like Conrad. It would be more germane to our subject to choose African examples. (59)

...

I do not see any signs of sterility anywhere here. What I do see is a new voice coming out of Africa, speaking of African experience in a world-wide language. So my answer to the question, Can an African ever learn English well enough to be able to use it effectively in creative writing? is certainly yes. If on the other hand you ask: Can he ever learn to use it like a native speaker? I should say, I hope not. It is neither necessary nor desirable for him to be able to do so. The price a world language must be prepared to pay is submission to many different kinds of use. The African writer should aim to use English in a way that brings out his message best without altering the language to the extent that its value as a medium of international exchange will be lost. He should aim at fashioning out an English which is at once universal and able to carry his peculiar experience. I have in mind here the writer who has something new, something different to say. The nondescript writer has little to tell us, anyway, so he might as well tell it in conventional language and get it over with. If I may use an extravagant simile, he is like a man offering a small, nondescript routine sacrifice for which a chick or less will do. A serious writer must look for an animal whose blood can match the power of his offering.

In this respect Amos Tutuola is a natural artist. A good instinct has turned his apparent limitation in language into a weapon of great strength – a half-strange dialect that serves him perfectly in the evocation of this bizarre world. His last book, and to my mind, his finest, is proof enough that one can make even an imperfectly learnt second language do amazing things. In this book *The Feather Woman of the Jungle*[13] Tutuola's superb storytelling is at last cast in the episodic form which he handles best instead of being painfully stretched on the rack of the novel.

From a natural to a conscious artist: myself, in fact. Allow me to quote a small example, from *Arrow of God*[14] which may give some idea of how I approach the use of English. The Chief Priest in the story is telling one of his sons why it is necessary to send him to church:

"I want one of my sons to join these people and be my eyes there. If there is nothing in it you will come back. But if there is something there you will bring home my share. The world is like a Mask, dancing. If you want to see it well you do not stand in one place. My spirit tells me that those who do not befriend the white man today will be saying *had we known* tomorrow."

Now supposing I had put it another way. Like this for instance:

"I am sending you as my representative among these people – just to be on the safe side in case the new religion develops. One has to move with the times or else one is left behind. I have a hunch that those who fail to come to terms with the white man may well regret their lack of foresight."

The material is the same. But the form of the one is in *character* and the other is not. It is largely a matter of instinct, but judgement comes into it too.

You read quite often nowadays of the problems of the African writer having first to think of his mother tongue and then to translate what he has thought into English. If it were such a simple, mechanical process I would agree that it was pointless – the kind of eccentric pursuit you might expect to see in a modern Academy of Lagado; and such a process could not possibly produce some of the exciting poetry and prose which is already appearing.

One final point remains for me to take. The real question is not whether Africans *could* write in English but whether they *ought* to. Is it right that a man should abandon his mother-tongue for someone else's? It looks like a dreadful betrayal and produces a guilty feeling.

But for me there is no other choice. I have been given this language and I intend to use it. I hope, though, that there always will be men, like the late Chief Fagunwa,[15] who will choose to write in their native tongue and ensure that our ethnic literature will flourish side by side with the national ones. For those of us who opt for English there is much work ahead and much excitement... I feel that the English language will be able to carry the weight of my African experience. But it will have to be a new English, still in full communion with its ancestral home but altered to suit its new African surroundings. (61–62)

33. J. O. EKPENYONG, *The Use of English in Nigeria* (1965)

Aus: John Press (ed.), *Commonwealth Literature: Unity and Diversity in a Common Culture* (London, 1965), 144–150. – Der Verfasser studierte in den USA und Kanada. Er lehrte an der University of Nigeria in Nsukka und fiel im nigerianischen Bürgerkrieg. Ekpenyong erblickt in der Weiterverwendung der englischen Sprache in Nigeria eher ein das Land einigendes Band als ein koloniales Relikt, das durch Dekret außer Kraft gesetzt werden kann. Darüberhinaus spiegeln die Varianten des Englischen, wie sie in Nigeria nachweisbar sind, deren kommunikative Rolle wider, die sie in unterschiedlichen sozialen Kontexten spielt.

Whatever was the motive behind it, it is doubtless true that the introduction of English as the official language is one of the greatest benefits of colonialism in Nigeria. How else could communication of whatever nature among a people speaking about 250 languages and dialects have been possible without the tedious, expensive, time-consuming and sometimes unreliable, process of interpretation? Had the early British officials and missionaries in Nigeria decided to learn the languages of the various national groups in the country and to administer them each in its own language, who knows whether the nationalist leaders could have been so successful within such a reasonably short time to reach all the national groups in the country with their agitation for independence? How could they have so easily made the national feeling of dissatisfaction with the colonial government in Nigeria known to the home government in a series of conferences which in the end brought pressure to bear on the British Government to grant independence to Nigeria? How could the task of reconstruction of the new Nigeria have proceeded so fast and so satisfactorily in less than half a decade of independence if there were no common language in Nigeria? These questions are difficult to answer now. Perhaps no answers may impress that fail to recognize that a common medium of communication is the greatest single factor of strength in nation-building.

Today Nigerian peoples move along with about 300 million peoples of the world in using English as their primary language, perhaps not for any love of England and America, but because English performs certain functions which none of the indigenous languages can, though better known by the majority in areas where they are spoken.

Public administration in Nigeria is done in English, teaching in the majority of the schools is in English, most of the business contacts are made in English of some sort, the major programmes of our radio and television are in English, because of intertribal and xenogamous marriages English is the first language in many homes in Nigeria. With the educated class, even the use of the vernacular is punctuated here and there with English words, phrases or sentences. In counting and other forms of verbal selfstimulation or thinking in words, English is the medium used by a large percentage of the Nigerian population. It may be safe to conclude that English, regardless of quality classification, is the essential and practical medium of communication in everyday life in Nigeria today. (144–145)

...

On the whole, the use of English in Nigeria seems to fall into the three streams in Allen Warner's article – "A New English in Africa?"[16] The categories are: the westernized, the folklore type and the new mad type. The English of most Nigerian professionals would fall within the westernized category. In writing the works of Achebe, Ekwensi, and Soyinka belong in this category. The folktale category is a cross between the westernized and the pidgin English. Either by intention or through academic deficiency, users in this category do not pay particular attention to grammar, nor do they pretend to use the language idiomatically. Since the material they handle is usually of the folklore type, they generally make a literary translation of the vernacular into English. The works of Tutuola and Etok Akpan[17] belong in this category. Though they may ignore grammar and idiom they often succeed in making quite a gripping impact upon the reader with their boldness in coining words and introducing new usages for familiar English words. Tutuola in *My Life in the Bush of Ghosts*[18] talks of ghosts and 'ghostesses'. Of course, the bid to find corresponding feminine forms for the masculine is quite common in Nigeria. The wife of a governor has often been referred to as 'governess'.

A race of pamphlet-writers whose English may be said to belong to the 'new mad type' has reccently sprung up round Onitsha. Anyone who makes a visit to Onitsha Market or crosses the River Niger from Onitsha to Asaba by the Inland Waterways Ferry will be astonished at the number of pamphlets written by these writers and stacked up in the stalls and hawked in the Ferry. These writers seem to feel that they have something to communicate and they find English the only satisfactory medium for communicating it. Their subjects range from 'professional' lectures on 'How to Speak and Write Good English' to philosophical and psychological discourses on love and wealth, and sundry other subjects between. Their tone is in keeping with the bold, vigorous and sometimes vulgar high-life rhythm of the new Nigeria. Though their expressions may be anything but orthodox, though they may 'wine and dine'[19] and call on a writer to 'pay another visit of his tongue to our young men (who) have started to walk and shake their waists like women',[20] they are bold, creative and original.

Formerly, pidgin English was reserved for the Police Force and the market place. But now it has become so respectable and well received that some parliamentarians find it more handy than formal English in debates; newspaper columnists consider it more effective for social satire, especially when spiced with poignant American slang; and radio stations, recognizing the unlimitedness of its coverage, have adopted it in their comedy programmes.

It is a strange paradox indeed, that when it is quite obvious that English has invaded all the social strata of the country and has asserted itself as the only sensible *lingua franca* that Nigeria can have, there has been a general cry in the country that English should be dropped as the offical language of Nigeria. The cry is due in part to embarrassing mimicry of the Nigerian use of English by some American and British critics (as an example the *Time Magazin* article of 5 December 1960); in part to the regulations of the West African Examination Council[21] (which until recently made success in the entire examination dependent upon the candidate's performance in English); and in part to the rapidly growing sense of nationalism in Nigeria. We seem to think that, after all, we are not really independent if after our colonial masters have left us to rule ourselves we still continue to use their language even in this process of ruling ourselves. This is understandable, for it appears that political freedom is a bedfellow to cultural freedom. Believing in this, Noah Webster, the American lexicographer, once cried out in rebellion against the British Standard of English: 'Let us seize the present moment and establish a national language as well as a national government.'[22] It becomes particularly annoying when a life's career is marred by failure to obtain mastery in a language not one's own. Under the circumstance we agitate for an act of Parliament to send the English language packing to the United Kingdom and the United States where it belongs.

It appears to me that a national language should not be determined by an act of Parliament, but rather by its international effect on commerce, diplomacy, science, and education. It may be that the agitators for an indigenous national language in Nigeria should borrow a leaf from India. In 1950 the Indian Parliament decided that Hindi should be the official language of India. It was discovered after a short trial that if English were done away with there would be no way for all the peoples of that huge country to communicate and that the work of reconstruction in the early years of independence would be slowed down very greatly. The very announcement of the calling off the Central Government's proclamation – that Hindi should be the official language of India – was made in English by Mr Nehru with a convincing tartness that remains memorable – 'English is the major window for us to the outside world.'[23]

In spite of the agitation of the failures in the West African School Certificate Examinations, and in spite of the bickering of the ultra-nationalists of the new Nigeria, I share Chinua Achebe's view expressed in his recent article – 'The English Language and the African Writer' – that 'the national literature of Nigeria and of many other countries in Africa is, or will be, in English'.[24] To levelheaded people, English does not seem to have a stiff competition with any indigenous language for election into the chair of offical language, for strictly speaking, it is not a foreign language in Nigeria. By the peculiar circumstance of her birth, Nigeria was born into English as the mother tongue. English has accomplished a lot for Nigeria already and has yet a lot more to do which cannot be done by any single indigenous language in Nigeria within the next fifty years. (147–149)

34. JOHN PEPPER CLARK, *The Legacy of Caliban* (1970)

Aus: John Pepper Clark, *The Example of Shakespeare. Critical Essays in African Literature* (London, 1970), 1–38. Clark (geb. 1935) aus Nigeria studierte in Ibadan und Princeton. Er veröffentlichte Gedichte und Dramen, betätigte sich als Herausgeber von Zeitschriften und übersetzte Literatur seiner Muttersprache, Ijaw, ins Englische. *Ozidi* (London, 1970), Clarks bekanntestes Theaterstück, wurde verfilmt. In "The Legacy of Caliban" setzt sich der Autor mit der Verwendung des Englischen in der afrikanischen Literatur auseinander und plädiert, ähnlich wie Achebe, für eine afrikanischen Themen angemessene Sprachverwendung. Clark lehrt Englische Literatur an der University of Lagos.

Dylan Thomas, announcing the phenomenon of Amos Tutuola's *The Palm-Wine Drinkard* to the British in 1952 wrote: 'a brief, thronged, grisly and bewitching story ... written in English by a West African'. The emphasis, one could suspect, falls on the final statement, 'written in English by a West African' who being a native should write in his own vernacular. It is the first public admission of this linguistic prejudice by a prominent literary figure in Britain.

The implication seems to be that the new African literary performance is unusual, that it is unnatural of the African to write in English, French or Arabic. A decade after, does the point still arise? A debate is running right now but let us not get drawn into it. That the African has taken over a number of European languages is a fact of history, probably the one permanent evidence of the love-hate relationship today at play between Europe and Africa. English, French, Portugese, and to a lesser extent, Spanish, and for an earlier period, Italian and German have become for Africans the language of government, business, education and indeed general communication, not simply between them and the wider world but in many cases among themselves at home as well as abroad. The situation is rather reminiscent of the earlier one in Europe when, before the formation of modern national states, her various peoples, with all their multiplicity of tongues, had for their common medium of expression Latin and Greek. But whereas the tendency then in Europe was towards homogeneous units, each adopting a vernacular as the language, the forces at work now in Africa have been for widely different groups to come together under one colonial flag and cosmopolitan language. Remove this dual experience of foreign rule and language and many of the new African states might well collapse without any help from military coups. Today each of these alien European tongues provides for many Africans the one ready vehicle for thought and even for dreaming. Recently there have been attempts to reverse the position, to replace the foreign with the vernacular tongue, notably in Tanzania where English has officially given way to Swahili. Elsewhere the African seems satisfied with having taken over a European tongue as he has the motor car, the radio, the refrigerator and all other articles of modern day living. After purchase, a ware becomes the *bona fide* property of the consumer.

There are a number of questions still to be answered. Having adopted a European language, how does the African writer use it, that is, with what sense of propriety? Does he fit the 'foreign' tongue to local subjects and characters? Is the language in his hands following the peculiar lie of the African situations that he depicts? As Hamlet would have put it, does the African writer in English or French 'suit the action to the word, the word to the action'? Or is there, as Mr A. Bodurin in *African Statesman* has charged, a dissociation of content from expression?[25]

This raises at once the old matter of verisimilitude. In the English or European novel and play there is observed a strict gradation of speech according to social class, which in turn determines to a large extent the level of education and thought of each character. Notwithstanding the liberalization of opportunities and the greater degree of mobility now prevalent among the classes as a result of the adoption by Europeans of one brand of socialism or another, the peasant in Europe still remains a peasant, the office worker an office worker, and the factory hand a factory hand in the general scheme of things, each retaining an attitude of mind almost as unshakeable as the sense of security felt by the Elizabethan in the world picture of his time. The European artist, working within a norm like this, generally strives to achieve a naturalistic if individual reflection of life as lived in a chosen society.

Apparently for this reason, the African or native character in English literature has posed for the English writer a peculiar problem. How does he fit into the structure of a society where class and education determine a man's manner of speech and by implication the level of his mind as well as the limits which his ambition may vault?

Shakespeare provides the supreme example. In delineating Caliban, 'as savage and deformed slave', the dramatist does not rely on the simple use of dialect but on the quality and content of imagery. 'Caliban', to fall back on Wolfgang Clemen, 'is a person who does not think in abstract terms but in concrete objects, which consequently abound in his language.' And this is language learnt in adulthood and at the hand of a king whose own 'language has the widest range' from 'the familiar, conversational, easy-flowing tones' to 'the solemn poetic diction which has in it something dignified and lofty'. Caliban, we must remember, is no simple yokel straight out of the English countryside. Scandalized as Prospero is by Caliban's advances to Miranda, a sense of shock and outrage shared by nearly if not all European readers, it must not be forgotten that Caliban, though deformed and savage, was actually his own king before Prospero arrived and subverted him (4–6)

...

A stress upon the study of language texture and leading themes as a means for indexing character and situation in the African novel, play and poem does not mean the complete dismissial of the more popular method exploited by the 'naturalists'. Graded speech which defines the relative superiority of social stations among characters, and perhaps their geophysical locations has in fact its own place in modern African literature. Where appropriately used, pidgin or broken English, for instance, serves to show up the new order of things, with differences of education and employment opportunites creating a variety of social classes among the polyglot populations ineluctably on the move today from the rural areas to the urban.

The novelist Mr Chinua Achebe combines both methods to great advantage. He uses in the main the Shakespearean approach, supplementing it with that of 'propriety' whenever necessary. But first it must be noted that Mr Achebe is eminently qualified for his task. Right from his first novel *Things Fall Apart* to his fourth uncanny work *A Man of the People*, he has found for himself a voice of balanced tones, adequate for his purposes, faithful to the facts, and fair to all sections of his readership. As a result, the text of each of his novels is an integrated piece, free of undue pressure from the personality of the artist who maintains all the time a medial distance between his subject and audience:

"Obierika was sitting outside under the shade of an orange tree making thatches from leaves of the raffia palm. He exchanged greetings with Okonkwo and led the way into his obi."[26]

This is a passage from *Things Fall Apart*. It shows how in a straight prose text, whether narrative, descriptive or expository, Mr Achebe can place things with surprising ease and brevity. This economy of expression and the impregnation of it with the spirit of the matter informing the subject is probably Mr. Achebe's contribution to the novel, and it is nothing less than a consummate use of imagery. (24–25)

35. SOLOMON ADEBAYE Q. BABALOLA, *The Role of Nigerian Languages and Literatures in Fostering National Cultural Identity* (1975)

Aus: *Présence Africaine*, 94 (1975), 53–83. – Babalola (geb. 1926) aus dem Westen Nigerias leitet das Department of African Languages and Literature an der Universität of Lagos. Neben seiner Lehrtätigkeit beschäftigte er sich vor allem mit der traditionellen Literatur seines Volkes, der Yoruba, und veröffentlichte *The Content and Form of Yoruba Ijala* (Oxford, 1966). Seine Aufgabe erblickt er in der Bewahrung und Förderung afrikanischer Sprachen und Literaturen, denn nur hierdurch bietet sich für die Zukunft die Möglichkeit der eigenen Identitätsgewinnung auch innerhalb des nationalen Kontexts.

... Our subject is the part that Nigerian languages and literatures can play and should be allowed to play in the process of getting our nation, Nigeria, to develop a personality characterised by a distinctive way of life which will make her stand out with dignity in the comity of nations.

Let us now consider the figure that Nigeria cuts in this regard at the present time. It is, in my opinion, a sorry figure cut by educated Nigerians. I am seizing on the educated Nigerians because they are the bearers of Nigerian national cultural identity; it is they who interact most of the time with foreign nationals in whose minds they create an image of Nigeria's personality as a nation. The impression that educated Nigerians, by and large, give at present is that they are imitation Europeans or Americans, speaking almost always in English or American, conversant with English Literature, American Literature, French Literature etc., but not with Literature in Nigerian Languages, and aware of music only in terms of European music or American music. It is necessarily a complex process – the process of replacing this image with the desired image of Nigeria as a nation whose people know their grass roots, know themselves and live as themselves, manifesting their African personality with proper pride: This paper is focused only on the role of Nigerian languages and literatures in that process.

What are the basic data about Nigerian languages and literatures? The estimated total number of Nigerian languages is about 250. There is literature in each language; hence the plural term "literatures". Literature, in our context, is the collection of all the high-quality works of the creative use of the imagination produced in a particular language. There is oral literature, otherwise called spoken art; there is also written literature to which the term "literature" is erroneously confined in the minds of many laymen.

Nigerian languages can play a crucial role in fostering national cultural identity and my plea is that they be allowed to play this role. Ideally, Nigeria's *lingua franca* should be a Nigerian language. National pride demands it. In the ideal situation then, all the communications of the Federal Government of Nigeria would be made in that *lingua franca* and therefore there would be the need for other nationals, especially members of the diplomatic corps, to learn the language. Such a *lingua franca* would highlight Nigeria's African cultural identity and would distinguish her from West Indian and other non-European nations using English or French. But this ideal is yet to be realised; it is to be worked for; at present, English is, for convenience, our limited *lingua franca*. It should be noted that it is merely the official *lingua franca* of Nigeria today; it is *not* a national *lingua franca* since it is spoken only by the educated citizens who probably constitute only about a tenth of the total population of our nation. The way forward to the ideal situation is through a multi-language policy for Nigeria to be adopted and implemented by the Federal Government.

The *raison d'être* for Nigeria's need to place a high premium on a national language may be succinctly given in the words of Fishman.[27]

"In the absence of a common, nation-wide ethnic and cultural identity, new nations proceed to plan and create such an identity through national symbols that can lead to common mobilization and involvement above, beyond and at the expense of pre-existing ethnic-cultural particularities. It is at this point that a national language is frequently invoked (along with a national flag, a national ruler, a national mission etc.) as a unifying symbol". (53–55)

...

An examination of the language situation in Nigeria today will show clearly that it poses a real challenge to the survival and development of the traditional cultures of our land. In the curricula of the primary and secondary schools, the status of the mother tongue is low. It is *not* a compulsory subject for the First School Leaving Certificate. It is *not* a compulsory subject for the West African School Certificate. The upshot is that the youth of Nigeria, nay, educated Nigerians by and large, are becoming indifferent to their mother tongue and are losing or disregarding the traditions of their indigenous culture. The average educated Nigerian is rapidly losing his African personality, for, as he throws away his mother tongue, he throws away along with it the associated indigenous culture.

Supporting evidence for this observation is quite abundant. For example, there is the fact that the average educated Nigerian performs poorly nowadays on traditional ceremonial occasions such as child-naming, wedding or funeral celebrations. His standard of oration in his mother tongue is very low; it usually turns out that when he is attempting to speak in his mother tongue he actually speaks a sandwich of English and the former!

I hope that the foregoing has clearly shown the importance of the mother tongue as a vehicle of acculturation. It follows from the argument that certain, reforms need to be carried out by the governments of our Federation in order to render satisfactory the language situation in Nigeria.

Our rulers must grasp the basic fact that it is through the use and cultivation of indigenous languages that the traditions and culture of the nation will be maintained and strengthened. Therefore, our rulers should see to it that the national educational system is properly balanced. At present, our national educational systems is imbalanced in that it is apparently aimed at satisfying only the national requirement of adequate and efficient manpower for the rapid modern development of the country in this international, scientific and technological space age. It is apparently not at all aimed at satisfying another major national requirement which is the proper acculturation of every Nigerian child into the African Nigerian Community.

Our children should be taught to speak and write in their mother tongue and to read and love both its traditional and modern literature. They should not be allowed to disregard these in favour of exclusive concentration on the European language through which higher education is available.

For the continuation and enrichment of the cultural tradition enshrined in the languages of our country, there is need for a considerable concentration of effort and capital expenditure by Government on (a) carefully designed language-teaching programmes; (b) the production of improved text books both for the mother tongues and for the English language; (c) the study of the massive tradition of oral literature and (d) the encouragement of writing in indigenous languages.

The Federal Government should formulate, adopt and implement a multilanguage policy if Nigerian languages and literatures are to be allowed to play their proper role in fostering our national cultural identity. It is because there are many ethnic groups in our country that the Nigerian national language policy has to be complex, just as our national cultural identity must be understandably complex and variegated.

For reasons already elaborated, selected Nigerian languages should be used as the official languages of the governments of not only the local districts, but also the various States of the Federation. And since the process of acculturation for the child in our country is now according to the practice of literate communities, the formal school system has to do the bulk of the acculturation task. Therefore Nigerian languages and literatures ought to be given a prominent place in the curricula of both primary and secondary schools.

At the local district level, the language of primary education should be the local Nigerian language – the people's mother tongue in the particular area. It should be a compulsory subject in the curriculum and the syllabus will range over the simple aspects of the oral literature in the language, customs and institutions of the people.

Another language (to be a compulsory subject) in the curriculum of the primary school should be the Nigerian language that is the official language of the State within which the school lies. If this State language is the same as the local language of the school's district, that is to be seen as a welcome coincidence.

In the secondary school curriculum in each State, four languages should be compulsory subjects: (a) the local language of the school's district; (b) the State official language; (c) the official *lingua franca* for Nigeria and (d) another Nigerian language which is a State official language within the Federation.

After about twenty years of implementating such a policy on language education, it should be possible to get one of the Nigerian languages selected by plebiscite as the national *lingua franca*. The ideal situation will then arrive with such an indigenous *lingua franca* highlighting Nigeria's African cultural identity. (57–59)

36. NGUGI WA THIONG'O, [*Afro-European Literature and African Literature*] (1980)

Aus: [Interview with Ngugi wa Thiong'o (Aarhus, 1980)]. – Der kenianische Schriftsteller Ngugi (geb. 1938) studierte am Makerere University College, Uganda, und in Leeds Englische Literatur. Er lehrte Afrikanische und Westindische Literatur in Nairobi und Evanston, USA. Als bekanntester ostafrikanischer Autor veröffentlichte er fünf Romane, von denen der bisher letzte, *Devil on the Cross* (1978), zunächst in Kikuyu, Ngugis Muttersprache, erschien. Daneben publizierte er Dramen, Kurzgeschichten und kritische Essays zur afrikanischen Kultur und Literatur. Nach der Aufführung des Theaterstücks *Ngaahika Ndeenda* wurde er Ende 1977 verhaftet und erst nach einem Jahr wieder freigelassen, ohne bisher seine Arbeit am Literature Department der University of Nairobi wieder aufnehmen zu können. Im folgenden Interviewausschnitt äußert Ngugi sich dazu, warum er nicht mehr in englischer Sprache schreibt.

I certainly make a distinction between literature written by Africans in European languages and a literature written by Africans in African languages. Literature written by Africans in European languages is what I now call Afro-European literature. In other words, we who have been writing in English, or French, or Portuguese have not been writing African literature at all; we have been writing that branch of literature that can only meaningfully go under the name of Afro-European literature. For those who write in French it is Afro-French literature and so on. This is to be distinguished very firmly from literature written by Africans treating African themes and written in African languages...

Now the question of language obviously is fundamental here as Frantz Fanon once said: to choose a language is to choose a world. In the same way, when you are choosing a language objectively you are choosing an audience. You cannot possibly write in English and assume that you are writing for, let us say, the African peasantry. There is no way, because the moment you write in English you assume a readership that can speak and read English, and this can only mean the African educated élite or foreigners who speak the language. This means your are precluding in terms of class the peasantry in Africa, or the workers in Africa who often do not read or understand these foreign languages.

Now, there are other aspects to language which can only be understood when they are seen in the colonial context. The colonizing people or nations or classes looked down upon African languages. In some cases African children in schools were given corporal punishment for speaking their own languages. Others were made to carry humiliating signs when being caught speaking African languages, signs like 'I am stupid' or 'I am an ass'. Now, what happens to the mentality of a child when you humiliate him or her in relationship to the particular language? Obviously he comes to associate that language with inferiority or backwardness, with humiliation and punishment. So he must somehow develop antagonistic attitudes to that language which was the object or the basis of his humiliation and punishment. And by extension he becomes uncomfortable about the people who created that language and the culture that was carried by it. On the other hand by education he comes to develop positive attitudes to the foreign language for which he is praised and thought intelligent once he speaks it well, and he also comes to respect and have a positive attitude to the cultures carried by the foreign languages. And, of course, he comes to have a positive attitude to the people who created the language which was the basis of the the high marks he was getting in school.

What does this mean in practical terms? It means that he comes to feel uncomfortable about the peasant masses and the working masses who are using that language. So we African writers who continue to write in European languages are in fact perpetuating a neo-colonial cultural tradition, no matter the attitude, the subject matter of our novels and plays and poems, no matter the attitude towards the classes in those novels, dramas and poems because if we are saying that these things can only be articulated within borrowed tongues it means that even at their progressive best, their radical best we are in fact continuing the neo-colonial tradition which we were setting out to oppose. So there we are involved in an immediate kind of contradiction.

What happens when you write in an African language? First, you are creating a positive attitude to that language. In other words, if a child can read a novel and feel that its language can carry its philosophical weight or can totally reflect his environment he will develop a positive attitude to that language, to that people who created that language and to the culture and traditions carried by it. And if he begins to have respect for his immediate language, be it Kikuyu, Luo, Yoruba or Ibo, by extension he will also have a respect for all the other languages that are related to his language. Or, to put it another way, if he hates his own immediate language, how do I expect him to respect other languages that are related to his?

To answer the question about my choice of the Kikuyu language, it was a very deliberate choice on my part, or rather it was a conscious decision although I was forced into it by peculiar historical circumstances in which I found myself. There is a further point I would like to add to his, i.e. that for a long time African languages and cultures, or rather cultures and languages of the different African nationalities, have not been communicating, have not been talking to one another. They have been communicating via English. In other words, I have a sense of Iboness in Achebe's novels; they are true, his novels in English, and I presume the same is the case with my novels. Now, the moment African writers start writing in their mother tongues some of the novels will be translated into other African languages as well as into English and into other foreign languages. The moment you get an Ibo novel translated into Kikuyu, let us say, or a Yoruba novel translated into Luo in Kenya, or a Luo novel translated into Hausa, you are getting these languages and characters talking and communicating directly and mutually enriching one another. So, far from being a divisive force these languages become an integrating force because they will be enhancing a respect for each other's languages and cultures as they are showing similarities between the various cultures and communicators who speak these languages ...

5. Autoren, Leser und die afrikanische Literaturszene

37. CHINUA ACHEBE, *The Role of the Writer in a New Nation* (1964)

Aus: G. D. Killam (ed.), *African Writers on African Writing* (London, 1973), 7–13 [repr. aus *Nigeria Magazine*, 89 (1966), 118–126]. – Achebe (cf. Text 26) sieht in diesem richtungsweisenden Aufsatz die Rolle des afrikanischen Schriftstellers als Interpreten der eigenen Kultur, dessen Aufgabe darin liegt, seiner Gesellschaft zu helfen, ihre Würde wieder zu erlangen. Damit verweist der Autor zugleich auf ein wesentliches Merkmal der in den fünfziger und frühen sechziger Jahren entstandenen afrikanischen Literatur.

For me, at any rate there is a clear duty to make a statement. This is my answer to those who say that a writer should be writing about contemporary issues – about politics in 1964, about city life, about the last *coup d'etat*. Of course, these are all legitimate themes for the writer but as far as I am concerned the fundamental theme must first be disposed of. This theme – put quite simply – is that African people did not hear of culture for the first time from Europeans; that their societies were not mindless but frequently had a philosophy of great depth and value and beauty, that they had poetry and, above all, they had dignity. It is this dignity that many African people all but lost during the colonial period and it is this that they must now regain. The worst thing that can happen to any people is the loss of their dignity and self-respect. The writer's duty is to help them regain it by showing them in human terms what happened to them, what they lost. There is a saying in Ibo that a man who can't tell where the rain began to beat him cannot know where he dried his body. The writer can tell the people where the rain began to beat them. After all the writer's duty is not to beat this morning's headline in topicality, it is to explore in depth the human condition. In Africa he cannot perform this task unless he has a proper sense of history.

Let me give one small example to illustrate what I mean by people losing faith in themselves. When I was a schoolboy it was unheard of to stage Nigerian dances at any of our celebrations. We were told and we believed that our dances were heathen. The Christian and proper thing to do was for the boys to drill with wooden swords and the girls to perform, of all things, Maypole dances. Beautiful clay bowls and pots were only seen in the homes of the heathen. We civilized Christians used cheap enamel-ware from Europe and Japan; instead of water pots we carried kerosene cans. In fact, to say that a product was Ibo-made was to brand it with the utmost inferiority. When a people have reached this point in their loss of faith in themselves their detractors need do no more; they have made their point.

A writer who feels the need to right this wrong cannot escape the conclusion that the past needs to be recreated not only for the enlightenment of our detractors but even more for our own education. Because, as I said, the past with all its imperfections, never lacked dignity.

The question is how does a writer re-create this past? Quite clearly there is a strong temptation to idealize it – to extol its good points and pretend that the bad never existed.

When I think of this I always think of light and glass. When white light hits glass one of two things can happen. Either you have an image which is faithful if somewhat unexciting or you have a glorious spectrum which though beautiful is really a distortion. Light from the past passes through a kind of glass to reach us. We can either look for the accurate though somewhat unexciting image or we can look for the glorious technicolour.

This is where the writer's integrity comes in. Will he be strong enough to overcome the temptation to select only those facts which flatter him? If he succumbs he will have branded himself as an untrustworthy witness. But it is not only his personal integrity as an artist which is involved. The credibility of the world he is attempting to re-create will be called to question and he will defeat his own purpose if he is suspected of glossing over inconvenient facts. We cannot pretend that our past was one long, technicolour idyll. We have to admit that like other people's pasts ours had its good as well as its bad sides.

This is why, in spite of my great admiration for Camara Laye as a writer I must still say that I find *The Dark Child*[1] a little too sweet. I admit that recollections of one's childhood tend naturally to be spread over with an aura of innocence and beauty; and I realize that Camara Laye wrote his book when he was feeling particularly lonely and home-sick in France. But I maintain that any serious African writer who wants to plead the cause of the past must not only be God's advocate, he must also do duty for the devil.

This is one of the things Wole Soyinka was saying in *A Dance of the Forests*. Those who want to resurrect an illustrious ancestor to grace their celebration may sometimes receive a great shock when the illustrious ancestor actually shows up. But, I think, it is still necessary that he should appear.

What I have said must not be understood to mean that I do not accept the present-day as a proper subject for the novelist. Far from it. My last but one novel is about the present day and the next one will again come up to date.[2] But what I do mean is that owing to the peculiar nature of our situation it would be futile to try and take off before we have repaired our foundations. We must first set the scene which is authentically African; then what follows will be meaningful and deep. This, I think, is what Aimé Césaire meant when he said that the short cut to the future is via the past.

I realize that some writers particularly from South Africa may object strongly to what I have said. They may say 'we are not tribal any more; we live in cities; we are sophisticated. Why should we beat the drums of the old gods? This is precisely what Verwoerd wants us to do and we have no intention to oblige him.'

Perhaps they are right to feel this way; I just don't know. It is for them to disvover how best to explore the human condition in their part of the continent. I speak for myself and this place and now. Sophistication is no substitute for a spiritual search for one's roots.

It is clear from what I have said so far that I believe the writer should be concerned with the question of human values. One of the most distressing ills which afflict new nations is a confusion of values. We sometimes make the mistake of talking about values as though they were fixed and eternal – the monopoly of Western civilization and the so-called higher religions. Of course, values are relative and in a constant state of flux. (8–10)

...

Anyone who has given any thought to our society must be concerned by the brazen materialism one sees all around. I have heard people blame it on Europe. That is utter rubbish. In fact the Nigerian society I know best – the Ibo society – has always been materialistic. This may sound strange because Ibo life had at the same time a strong spiritual dimension – controlled by gods, ancestors, personal spirits or *chi*,[3] and magic. The success of the culture was the balance between the two, the material and the spiritual. But let no one underrate the material side. A man's position in society was usually determined by his wealth. All the four titles in my village were taken – not given – and each one had its price. But in those days wealth meant the strength of your arm. No one became rich by swindling the community or (sic) stealing government money. In fact a man who was guilty of theft immediately lost all his titles. Today we have kept the materialism and thrown away the spirituality which should keep it in check. Some of the chieftancy titles and doctorate degrees we assume today would greatly shock our ancestors!

Let us mention just one more example of the crisis in our culture. Why is it that Nigerians are content with shoddy work? Put a man to sweep this room and in nine cases out of ten he will scamp through it leaving most of it unswept. Why? Because it is government work, and government is alien, a foreign body. When I was a boy, strangers from another part of Iboland were coming for the first time to our village during the planting season to work for the villagers for so much money and three meals a day. One day one of these strangers came to plant my mother's coco-yams. At the end of the day he received his pay, ate his last meal, and left. About two or three weeks later the coco-yams began to sprout and the whole village saw what this man had done ...

The writer in our society should be able to think of these things and bring them out in a form that is dramatic and memorable. Above all, he has a responsibility to avoid shoddiness in his own work. This is very important today when some publishers will issue any trash that comes out of Africa because Africa has become the fashion. In this situation there is a real danger that some writers may not be patient enough and disciplined enough to pursue excellence in their work.

That brings me to the linguistic question. In this discussion I am leaving out writers in the various Nigerian languages. It is not that I under-rate their importance, but since I am considering the role of the writer in building a new nation I wish to concentrate on those who write for the *whole* nation whose audience cuts across tribe or clan. And these, for good or ill, are the writers in English.

For an African, writing in English is not without its serious set-backs. He often finds himself describing situations or modes of thought which have no direct equivalent in the English way of life. Caught in that situation he can do one of two things. He can try and contain what he wants to say within the limits of conventional English or he can try to push back those limits to accommodate his ideas. The first method produced competent, uninspired and rather flat work. The second method can produce something new and valuable to the English language as well as to the material he is trying to put over. *But* it can also get out of hand. It can lead to *bad* English being accepted and defended as African or Nigerian. I submit that those who can do the work of extending the frontiers of English so as to accommodate African thought-patterns must do it through their mastery of English and not out of innocence. Of course there is the obvious exception of Amos Tutuola. But even there it is possible that he has said something unique and interesting in a way that is not susceptible to further development. I think Gerald Moore in his *Seven African Writers* is probably right when he says of Tutuola that he stands at the end of a fascinating cul-de-sac. For the rest of us it is important first to learn the rules of English and afterwards break them if we wish. The good writers will know how to do this and the bad ones will be bad, anyway.

In closing let me remind you of a theme that has been recurring in Sedar Senghor's thinking of late. He says that Africans must become producers of culture and not just its consumers.

African societies of the past, with all their imperfections, were not consumers but producers of culture. Anyone who reads Fagg's recent book *Nigerian Images* will be struck by the wealth and quality of the art which our ancestors produced in the past. Some of this work played a decisive role in the history of modern art. The time has come once more for us, artists and writers of today, to take up the good work and by doing it to enrich not only our own lives but the life of the world. (11–13)

38. JAMES NGUGI, HENRY OWUOR-ANYUMBA, TABAN LO LIYONG, *On the Abolition of the English Department* (1968)

Aus: Ngugi wa Thiong'o, *Homecoming* (Essays on African and Caribbean Literature, Culture and Politics) (London, 1972), 145–150. – Drei Lehrkräfte des English Department der University of Nairobi veröffentlichten Ende 1968 eine Stellungnahme, in der sie eine radikale Veränderung des Literaturunterrichts an der Universität forderten. Damit gingen sie noch über die Forderung der Konferenz in Freetown (cf. Text 4) hinaus, "that the literature of Africa should be included in the Literature Syllabuses of all universities in Africa and also in the work of schools".[4] Das an der University of Nairobi eingerichtete Literature Department verwirklichte wesentliche Punkte der 1968 erhobenen Forderung und erwies sich als richtungsweisend für Universitäten in anderen afrikanischen Ländern, die zur ehemaligen Kolonialmacht England gehörten.

1. This is a comment on the paper presented by the Acting Head of the English Department at the University of Nairobi to the 42nd meeting of the Arts Faculty Board on the 20th September, 1968.

2. *(a)* That paper was mainly concerned with possible developments within the Arts Faculty and their relationship with the English Department, particularly:
(i) The place of modern languages, especially French;
(ii) The place and role of the Department of English;
(iii) The emergence of a Department of Linguistics and Languages;
(iv) The place of African languages, especially Swahili.

(b) In connection with the above, the paper specifically suggested that a department of Linguistics and Languages, to be closely related to English, be established.

(c) A remote possibility of a Department of African literature, or alternatively, that of African literature and culture, was envisaged.

3. The paper raised important problems. It should have been the subject of a more involved debate and discussion, preceding the appointment of a committee with specific tasks, because it raises questions of value, direction and orientation.

4. For instance, the suggestions, as the paper itself admits, question the role and status of an English Department in an African situation and environment. To quote from his paper:

The English Department has had a long history at this College and has built up a strong syllabus which by its study of the *historic continuity of a single culture throughout the period of emergence of the modern west*, makes it an important companion to History and to Philosophy and Religious Studies. However, *it is bound to become less 'British', more open to other writing in English (American, Caribbean, African, Commonwealth) and also to continental writing, for comparative purposes.*

5. Underlying the suggestions is a basic assumption that the English tradition and the emergence of the modern west is the central root of our consciousness and cultural heritage. Africa becomes an extension of the west, an attitude which, until a radical reassessment, used to dictate the teaching and organization of History in our University.[5] Hence, in fact, the assumed centrality of English Department, into which other cultures can be admitted from time to time, as fit subjects for study, of from which other satellite departments can spring as time and money allow. A small example is the current, rather apologetic attempt to smuggle African writing into an English syllabus in our three colleges.

6. Here then, is our main question: If here is need for a 'study of the historic continuity of a single culture', why can't this be African? Why can't African literature be at the centre so that we can view other cultures in relationship to it?

This is not mere rhetoric: already African writing, with the sister connections in the Caribbean and the Afro-American literatures, has played an important role in the African renaissance, and will become even more and more important with time and pressure of events. Just because for reasons of political expediency we have kept English as our official language, there is no need to substitute a study of English culture for our own. We reject the primacy of English literature and culture.

7. The aim, in short, should be to orientate ourselves towards placing Kenya, East Africa, and then Africa in the centre. All other things are to be considered in their relevance to our situation, and their contribution towards understanding ourselves.

8. We therefore suggest:
A. That the English Department be abolished;
B. That a Department of African Literature and Languages be set up in its place.

The primary duty of any literature department is to illuminate the spirit animating a people, to show how it meets new challenges, and to investigate possible areas of development and involvement.

In suggesting this name, we are not rejecting other cultural streams, especially the western stream. We are only clearly mapping out the directions and perspectives the study of culture and literature will inevitably take in an African university.

9. We know that European literatures constitute one source of influence on modern African literatures in English, French, and Portuguese; Swahili, Arabic, and Asian literatures constitute another, an important source, especially here in East Africa; and the African tradition, a tradition as active and alive as ever, constitutes the third and the most significant. This is the stuff on which we grew up, and it is the base from which we make our cultural take-off into the world.

10. Languages and linguistics should be studied in the department because in literature we see the principles of languages and linguistics in action. Conversely, through knowledge of languages and linguistics we can get more from literature. For linguistics not to become eccentric, it should be studied in the Department of African Literature and Languages.

In addition to Swahili, French, and English, whenever feasible other languages such as Arabic, Hindustani, Kikuyu, Luo, Akamba, etc., should be introduced into the syllabus as optional subjects.

11. On the literature side, the Department ought to offer roughly:
(a) The oral tradition, which is our primary root;
(b) Swahili literature (with Arabic and Asian literatures): this is another root, especially in East Africa;
(c) A selected course in European literature: yet another root;
(d) Modern African literature.

For the purposes of the Department, a knowledge of Swahili, English, and French should be compulsory. The largest body of writing by Africans is now written in the French language. Africans writing in the French language have also produced most of the best poems and novels. In fact it makes no sense to talk of modern African literature without French.

12. *The Oral Tradition*

The Oral tradition is rich and many-sided. In fact 'Africa is littered with Oral Literature'. But the art did not end yesterday; it is a living tradition. Even now there are songs being sung in political rallies, in churches, in night clubs by guitarists, by accordion players, by dancers, etc. Another point to be observed is the interlinked nature of art forms in traditional practice. Verbal forms are not always distinct from dance, music, etc. For example, in music there is close correspondence between verbal and melodic tones; in 'metrical lyrics' it has been observed that poetic text is inseparable from tune; and the 'folk tale' often bears an 'operatic' form, with sung refrain as an integral part. The distinction between prose and poetry is absent or very fluid.

Though tale, dance, song, myth, etc. can be performed for individual aesthetic enjoyment, they have other social purposes as well. Dance, for example, has been studied 'as symbolic expression of social reality reflecting and influencing the social, cultural and personality systems of which it is a part'. The oral tradition also comments on society because of its intimate relationship and involvement.

The study of the oral tradition at the University should therefore lead to a multi-disciplinary outlook: literature, music, linguistics, Sociology, Anthropology, History, Psychology, Religion, Philosophy. Secondly, its study can lead to fresh approaches by making it possible for the student to be familiar with art forms different in kind and historical development from Western literary forms. Spontaneity and liberty of communication inherent in oral transmission – openness to sounds, sights, rhythms, tones, in life and in the environment – are examples of traditional elements from which the student can draw. More specifically, his familiarity with oral literature could suggest new structures and techniques; and could foster attitudes of mind characterized by the willingness to experiment with new forms, so transcending 'fixed literary patterns' and what that implies – the preconceived ranking of art forms.

The study of the Oral Tradition would therefore supplement (not replace) courses in Modern African Literature. By discovering and proclaiming loyalty to indigenous values, the new literature would on the one hand be set in the stream of history to which it belongs and so be better appreciated; and on the other be better able to embrace and assimilate other thoughts without losing its roots.

13. *Swahili Literature*

There is a large amount of oral and written classical Swahili Literature of high calibre. There is also a growing body of modern Swahili literature: both written and oral.

14. *European Literature*

Europe has influenced Africa, especially through English and French cultures. In our part of Africa there has been an over-concentration on the English side of European life. Even the French side, which is dominant in other countries of Africa, has not received the importance it deserves. We therefore urge for freedom of choice so that a more representative course can be drawn up.

We see no reason why English literature should have priority over and above other European literatures where we are concerned. The Russian novel of the nineteenth century should and must be taught. Selections from American, German, and other European literatures should also be introduced. In other words English writings will be taught in their European context and only for their relevance to the East African perspective.

15. *Modern African Literature*
The case for the study of Modern African Literature is self-evident. Its possible scope would embrace:

(a) The African novel written in French and English;

(b) African poetry written in French and English, with relevant translations of works written by Africans in Portuguese and Spanish;

(c) The Caribbean novel and poetry: the Caribbean involvement with Africa can never be over-emphasized. A lot of writers from the West Indies have often had Africa in mind. Their works have had a big impact on the African renaissance – in politics and literature. The poetry of Negritude indeed cannot be understood without studying its Caribbean roots. We must also study Afro-American literature.

16. *Drama*
Since drama is an integral part of literature, as well as being its extension, various dramatic works should be studied as parts of the literature of the people under study. Courses in play-writing, play-acting, directing, lighting, costuming, etc. should be instituted.

17. *Relationship with other Departments*
From things already said in this paper, it is obvious that African Oral and Modern literatures cannot be fully understood without some understanding of social and political ideas in African history. For this, we propose that either with the help of other departments, or within the department, or both, courses on mutually relevant aspects of African thought be offered. For instance, an introductory course on African art – sculpture, painting – could be offered in co-operation with the Department of Design and Architecture.

18. The 3.1.1.[6] should be abolished. We think an undergraduate should be exposed to as many general ideas as possible. Any specialization should come in a graduate school where more specialized courses can be offered.

19. In other words we envisage an active Graduate School will develop, which should be organized with such departments as the Institute for Development studies.

20. *Conclusion*
One of the things which has been hindering a radical outlook in our study of literature in Africa is the question of literary excellence; that only works of undisputed literary excellence should be offered. (In this case it meant virtually the study of disputable 'peaks' of English literature.) The question of literary excellence implies a value judgement as to what is literary and what is excellence, and from whose point of view. For any group it is better to study repre-

sentative works which mirror their society rather than to study a few isolated 'classics', either of their own or of a foreign culture.

To sum up, we have been trying all along to place values where they belong. We have argued the case for the abolition of the present Department of English in the College, and the establishment of a Department of African Literature and Languages. This is not a change of names only. We want to establish the centrality of Africa in the department. This, we have argued, is justifiable on various grounds, the most important one being that education is a means of knowledge about ourselves. Therefore, after we have examined ourselves, we radiate outwards and discover peoples and worlds around us. With Africa at the centre of things, not existing as an appendix or a satellite of other countries and literatures, things must be seen from the African perspective. The dominant object in that perspective is African literature, the major branch of African culture. Its roots go back to past African literatures, European literatures, and Asian literatures. These can only be studied meaningfully in a Department of African Literature and Languages in an African University.

We ask that this paper be accepted in principle; we suggest that a representative committee be appointed to work out the details and harmonize the various suggestions into an administratively workable whole.

James Ngugi
Henry Owuor-Anyumba
Taban Lo Liyong
24th October 1968

39. NGUGI WA THIONG'O, *The Writer in a Changing Society* (1969)

Aus: Ngugi wa Thiong'o, *Homecoming* (London, 1972), 47–50. – Die Entwicklung Ngugis (cf. Text 36) zu einem Schriftsteller, dessen Engagement für die Armen und Entrechteten seiner Gesellschaft immer deutlicher in seinen Werken zutagetritt, reicht bis weit in die sechziger Jahre zurück. Im folgenden Text, einer Rede, die er 1969 in Uganda hielt, formuliert er dieses Anliegen als Aufgabe afrikanischer Intellektueller, insbesondere aber der Schriftsteller.

A writer responds, with his total personality, to a social environment which changes all the time. Being a kind of sensitive needle, he registers, with varying degrees of accuracy and success, the conflicts and tensions in his changing society. Thus the same writer will produce different types of work, sometimes contradictory in mood, sentiment, degree of optimism and even world-view. For the writer himself lives in, and is shaped by, history.

We can see this in the work of the Malawian poet and novelist, David Rubadiri. In 1952 he wrote his famous poem *Stanley Meets Mutesa*,[7] in which he painted a picture of the fatal encounter between Africa and Europe and captured the mood of a continent. For this was a dominant theme in African writing. The period was also one of Africa's cultural and political assertion. Fourteen years later he was to write a novel, *No Bride Price*, which showed his distaste with the post-Independence era in Africa: the leaders of the anti-colonial struggle have become traitors to their peoples' cause and have sacrificed Africa on the altar of their own middle-class comfort. The disillusionment with the ruling élite is to be found in the recent works of most African writers: Okot p'Bitek, Leonard Kibera, Chinua Achebe, Wole Soyinka, Ayi Kwei Armah, to mention only a few. All of them are reacting to a situation very different from the one prevailing in the fifties.

I too must have changed since I started writing in 1960.

I was then a student at Makerere University College. I remember sending a shy little note to the Warden of my then Hall of Residence saying I wanted to be a writer. No doubt the note was a little hasty and rather self-conscious, because I had not then written anything. I had read a number of writers, African and West Indian, and I knew that what they told, the song they sang, was different from what I had heard from the British writers who had been crammed down my throat in schools and at the University. The African writers spoke to me, they spoke about my situation. What was my situation?

I grew up in a small village. My father with his four wives had no land. They lived as tenants-at-will on somebody else's land. Harvests were often poor. Sweetened tea with milk at any time of day was a luxury. We had one meal a day – late in the evening. Every day the women would go to their scruffy little strips of shamba. But they had faith and they waited.

Just opposite the ridge on which our village was scattered were the sprawling green fields owned by the white settlers. They grew coffee and tea and pyrethrum.[8] I worked there sometimes, digging the ground, tending the settlers' crops, and this for less than ten shillings. Every morning African workers would stream across the Valley to sell their sweat for such a meagre sum of money, and at the end of the week or month they would give it all to the Indian trader who owned most of the shops in our area for a pound of sugar, maize flour, or grains, thankful that this would silence the children's clamour for a few days. These workers were the creators of wealth but they never benefited from it: the products of their collective sweat went to feed and clothe the children of the Indian trader, and those of the European settlers not only in our country but even those in England. I was living in a village and also in a colonial situation.

One day I heard a song. I remember the scene so vividly: the women who sang it are now before me – their sad faces and their plaintive melody. I was then ten or eleven. They were being forcibly ejected from the land they occupied and sent to another part of the country so barren that people called it the land of black rocks. This was the gist of their song:

> And there will be great great joy
> When our land comes back to us
> For Kenya is the country of black people.
> And you our children

> Tighten belts around your waist
> So you will one day drive away from this land
> The race of white people
> For truly, Kenya is a black man's country.

They were in a convoy of lorries, caged, but they had one voice. They sang of a common loss and hope and I felt their voice rock the earth where I stood literally unable to move.

Their words were not the platitudes of our university philosophers who use words as shields from life and truth: these women had lived the words they spoke. There was at once a fatalistic acceptance of the inevitable and also a collective defiance. 'We shall overcome', they seemed to say. The women had taken a correct political stand in the face of an oppressive enemy.

In 1923 such a stand had cost the lives of twenty-three people in Nairobi when men and women collected and demanded the release of their leaders.[9] That stand also cost the lives of our early heroes of resistance, like the Laibon of the Kalenjin people, who led a violent peasant resistance against the early British occupation. In 1952 that dogged collective resistance cost Kenya even more lives; the peasants had taken to the forest to defend their lives and property and for four years were able to withstand the military might of British imperialism.[10]

That song I heard as a child then spoke of things past and things to come. I was living in a colonial situation but I did not know it. Not even when I went to school. I went to a missionary school where we were told over and over again that we were potential leaders of our people. We were being trained to be good responsible leaders. Education was not aimed at a knowledge of self and the reality of the black man's place in the world. What we did not know was that we were being groomed to become a buffer state between the propertied white rulers and the harsh realities under which the African peasants and workers lived. The idea was something like this. They, the African workers and peasants, would see their selected few brothers and sisters living in relative comfort and fraternizing with whites and they would be contented: they would have a we-have-almost-arrived kind of attitude – 'we are getting equality bit by bit'. Our schools and universities – I am not sure if they have changed much – were monuments of lies and half-truths. That which was most admired was a search for truth, meaning a life devoted to the truth that only rationalized the *status quo*, that conferred on nationally stolen property – stolen that is from the masses – the aura of sanctity. While we were at our bourgeois schools and universities searching for that truth in books written for us by our imperial conquerors, the peasant masses, those women I once heard sing, had collectively rejected the white seizure of the land.

It was they who fought for Uhuru.[11] It was the united strength of the peasants and workers that made British imperialists retreat, even though they later returned through the back door.

What have these peasants gained from Uhuru? Has our ruling élite tried to change the colonial social and economic structure? Are the peasants and workers in control of the land they fought for?

When I look around me, I see sad faces, I see unfulfilled hope and promise. We who went to schools and colleges and had regular salaries were quickly able to buy positions among the middle classes. With our cars, lands, and mansions, we forget that we are only joining our European and Asian counterparts in living on the sweat of millions. We entered the race to fill some of the vacant places, silencing protest by assuring our followers that we were only getting the national cake – for the tribe. Even the pretence of a national ideal has been abandoned by the ruling élite. When hungry, unsatisfied voices clamour around us we only say: 'Hush! you might ruin our tribal chances of a bigger share in the national cake.'

The Biafran-Nigerian conflict, where ordinary men and women who had not in any case gained much from Uhuru were made to slaughter one another, with guns supplied by competing Western powers who had for centuries ravished the continent, is today's African reality: the potential of a Biafran type of conflict exists in every African country that has doggedly refused to dismantle capitalism and colonial economic structures, to correct the legacy of an uneven geographic and social development.

I believe that African intellectuals must align themselves with the struggle of the African masses for a meaningful national ideal. For we must strive for a form of social organization that will free the manacled spirit and energy of our people so we can build a new country, and sing a new song. Perhaps, in a small way, the African writer can help in articulating the feelings behind this struggle.

40. E.S. ATIENO-ODHIAMBO, *Historical Sense and Creative Literature* (1971)

Aus: Andrew Gurr and Pio Zirimu (eds.), *Black Aesthetics*. Papers from a Colloquium held at the University of Nairobi, June 1971 (Nairobi, 1973), 81–103. – Der kenianische Historiker Atieno-Odhiambo nimmt im folgenden Text kritisch zur bisherigen Leistung ostafrikanischer Schriftsteller Stellung: allzu häufig ließen sich Autoren von europäischen Verlagsinteressen lenken, statt ihr Augenmerk auf Bedürfnisse des eigenen Volkes zu lenken.

What is the record of East African writers?

Creative writing on a large scale in the English language by East Africans is a recent phenomenon. Sometimes the excuse is given that during the colonial era we were too busy fighting for independence to write. It may well be that we were simply too confused or too illiterate to write. The kind of writing that we did during the colonial period was of the protest type, protesting largely against colonialism and its cultural imperialism. Essentially this was a "backward looking"[12] move and the effort was directed towards the past in the hope of invoking the ancient societal liberties. Typical of this output was Jomo Kenyatta's *Facing Mount Kenya*. Published in 1938, the book is dedicated to "Moigoi and Wamboi and all the dispossessed youth of Africa: for perpetuation of communion with ancestral spirits through the fight for African Freedom, and in the firm faith that the dead, the living, and the unborn will unite to rebuild the destroyed shrines."[13]

The exercise was one of assertion and of hope; of asserting that the African *did* have a culture; of hoping that the historical cord of continuity would not be permanently severed by colonialism, so that the dead, the living and the unborn would one day reunite in an African cultural Parousia. This kind of literature was geared towards the contemplation, examination, and criticism of the *outsider* i.e. the colonial forces. It was the kind of literature that had a revolutionary dimension to it, revolutionary in the sense that it wanted to overthrow the imposed social structures of the white man, and substitute for them something authentically African. A second dimension of this literature was that it was *mass orientated.* The creative writer, significantly in the minority, carved out for himself a role, and that role was that of a representative of his people. The issue of commitment naturally loomed large in this self-chosen task.

Came independence. And more authors. Came independence and different ruling elites. Instead of the white rulers East Africans found themselves apparently being ruled by fellow blacks. We have been faced with the birth pangs of nationhood, with problems of modernization, with issues of development, with problems of self-realization, and the paradoxes of frustration at communal and individual levels. The East Africans have glimpsed, heard, observed, and written. But written what? Here our task shall not be to individually review all the available literature. Rather we shall attempt to discern some of the motifs and patterns that dominate this productivity and push the line of a general critique.

Generally the East African writer has since independence been a bitter, sometimes critical mind. He has been angry. This angry writer has had his anger very well focussed. He knows against whom he is bitter – against the bureaucracy, its corruption, its despotic narrow-mindedness, its lack of concern for culture, and (ironically) its lack of tutelage over East Africa's intellectual and artistic life. And yet at the same time this bitterness has been articulated either at a very general superficial level or alternatively at a very limited narrow level. When it is articulated at the general level, one inherently as a reader is confronted with the same motifs, same patterns – poverty, the Hilton, beggars, prostitutes, freedom fighters, the police, big cars, inefficiency, corruption – to suggest just a few. This in itself has its limitations. How general is the general motif the writer has selected? To what extent does his motif capture the central forces and the complexity of emotions and the factors that lie behind these emotions? There is also the bandwagon tendency, one fears, to associate being a writer with writing about these motifs. The accuracy of the focus of anger does not necessarily make a work of art artistically effective. To put it differently, the presumed social significance of a theme or a subject does not necessarily make a write-up on it a piece of *artistic significance.* Let us push this line further. The time for apologetics on African culture is past. What we need is a serious literary treatment as it relates to development or non-development. One hundred poorly sketched Lawinos are not going to make us culturally richer. And just as the time for apologetics on past cultures is over so also is past the time for bandwagon condemnation of the colonial and independence regimes. Take issues like corruption and prostitutes. A lot of poems, songs and novels have been written simply condemning in clear and obscure languages these *items* in our society. But the politicians are doing the same, in fact a lot more articulately. What would be a far more fruitful exercise – since the writers have taken it as their self appointed task to "educate" (hence the often heard desire of the writers to "communicate") – would be for the writers to study carefully just what has made possible the existence of some of these items. Given the colonial experience of East Africa, it was inevitable that slums, prostitutes, and corrupt politicians would emerge in our society. Quite seriously one does not know what to do with some of the books and manuscripts after one has read them. After the predictable laughter, one is almost always posing the question: So what? Sometimes one gets the feeling that people are just writing, in the words of Taban[14] and Okot, "to flood the market". This situation raises fundamental issues. One asks "is it a question of language?" In the past the question has been raised as to whether the media of prose and poetry in the English language at large can express adequately the experiences of our generation. This issue has been discussed along the lines of English being a foreign language (and in our case Swahili being indigenous), with the end result that the benefit of the doubt has always been given to the writer. One feels that we have come to a stage when we can discuss this issue quite outside that parameter. Reports from the editors' desks suggest that a lot of the work being produced is still downright shoddy. One detects a tendency of being in a hurry to be published for it has come to be associated with *social recognition*. In the words of the Kenyan poet Joe Mutiga: "It is a time of opportunity when one line makes a poet."[15] It is a question of really being in a hurry, and part of the shoddiness is a consequence of simple *shortwindedness*. And this is where the question of the historical sense again looms large. Oftentimes because of insufficient preparation we run short of breath, and just when our audience is prepared to hear us fully we cut off the dialogue, *gasping*. As a result, we remain for a long time on the list of *promising* but not yet fulfilled artists.

Connected with this problem of shortwindedness and literary gasping, and indeed a possible cause of it, *is the problem of the illiterate artist*. Here one is faced with a situation where the writer is a product of a single track education. Thus one trained in literature hardly knows the problems of architecture, and how it relates to the problem of development; probably has no knowledge of rural economics, let alone the geography of the country as a whole, nor is he competent to evoke in himself sophisticated anger about, say, the unrealized industrial potential of a country. Thus the author deals with aspects of problems, rather than with problems in their totality, because, to put it crudely, he has no perspectives in the historical movement of the society. Quite often one is charmed by one's own semantic prowess and may well be arguing fascist ideas for example without knowing that they have been Fascists who have expressed these same ideas elsewhere, earlier and because of similar circumstances. Another way of looking at it is to regard a particular artist as having a dialogue with himself. A possible end product of this stance is naiveté, for the individual who has an ignorant dialogue with himself may well think he is being critical and even cynical when at a comparable level with authors elsewhere all he is doing is being simplistic. The point is that to be cynical one has got to have the experience of living. Having chosen to be the spokesman of a people one must undertake the task with seriousness. One must know the people. Tom Mboya put it glaringly to the students of Nairobi in February 1967:

"My point is that service through involvement means contact with the people. I also want to emphasize that the intellectual who wants to write about the people or provide answers to their problems and thereby help the country move forward must maintain constant touch with the people."[16]

And by the people, for the Kenyan, we mean the farmers of Kirinyaga, the nomads of Isiolo, the peasants of Malindi, the small farmers of Kakamega, the charcoal trader in Mbotela, the messenger in Jogoo House, and the lorry driver in Kisii – *all together taken to constitue the people of Kenya living in the objective environment that constitutes Kenya.*

In the realm of thought, the challenge that is being posed to the creative writer is to know the subject matter, employ historical sense and translate the existential into the dialectical. This means in terms of effort a marriage of the past, the present, and the *logical* future. One has got to avoid being simply didactic about an imagined present. Let us illustrate what we mean. A lot of ink and breath has flowed and spouted over Taban lo Liyong's The Last Word.[17] Taban was ungrateful enough to borrow from Nkrumah without acknowledgement. Kwame Nkrumah wrote his philosophical treatise *Consciencism*,[18] to give direction as to what Africa is to do in order to face the realities of the twentieth century. Taban followed on by fangling a similar-ringing motion, *synthesism*, as the last word in culture. Where Nkrumah was distinctly historical Taban was singularly imaginatively undisciplined. Taban looked at the present and saw Africa *technologically* behind Europe and North America. Taban got frightened. He mistook technology for total culture. He mistook superior technology for superior culture. Taban therefore prescribed a predictable cure for Africa: "catch up with Europe technologically or Africa is doomed", he proclaimed. What history Taban omitted was first that there are very specific reasons why we are not technologically at par with Europe; secondly that technology is not necessarily an answer to Africa's problems – our scientists are telling us that all the time; thirdly that technological achievement is not a panacea for man's ills. – Taban failed to notice the neurosis it has bred in Western Europe and North America, another case of failure to appreciate comparative history; fourthly that with the resources we have got his project may not be immediately feasible if we are to take care of the contemporary present; fifthly that intelligent technological advance needs to be related to the rest of the social movements in society; sixthly that international political practice may well not allow Africa even to move technologically – otherwise what is neo-colonialism all about? In a word Taban's thesis lacks the existential correlative we are so concerned about in this paper.

Taban's thesis is symbolic also of what is another emergent trend in the East African literary scene; this is the problem of individualism. We have looked at this issue earlier along the line of ignorant authors. There is also the assumption by a writer that his personal experiences are representative of his fellow men and women. Sometimes the author suffers incidents like imprisonment, venereal disease, death, or accidents. When he emerges from these experiences he poses as a scapegoat on behalf of the people. Which people? We hasten to add that the author may genuinely be trying to use these experiences as literary symbols. But quite often, and this is revamping our earlier point, shortwindedness and gasping take the upper hand and the symbolism fails. Individualism must also have an existential correlative, otherwise it amounts to failure to participate in understandign the problems of the peoples of East Africa. We should cry for those our friends who die in coups but we shall serve them, the living and the unborn, even better by discerning those conditions and underlying trends that will enable a people to avoid other coups.

The burden of this paper is to plead with the East African writers to exert themselves fully in the effort of understanding East Africa, towards the execution of our prime duty, *the duty of serving the people as a whole.* Such social relevance can only spring from the roots of our total historical experience. (96–102)

41. S.I.A. KOTEI, *Some Cultural and Social Factors of Book Reading and Publishing in Africa* (1973)

Aus: E. Oluwasanmi, E. McLean and H. Zell (eds.), *Publishing in Africa in the Seventies* (Ile-Ife, 1975), 174–208. – S.I.A. Kotei arbeitet als Senior Lecturer am Department of Library Studies der University of Ghana. In seinem Beitrag zu einer Konferenz über das Verlagswesen in Afrika, die 1973 an der University of Ife in Nigeria stattfand, schätzt er das sowohl mangelnde wie auch einseitig auf Unterhaltungsliteratur gerichtete Interesse des verhältnismäßig kleinen Lesepublikums in Westafrika sehr realistisch ein und entwickelt Vorschläge zur Verbesserung der gegenwärtigen Situation.

As has often been said, it is authors, and not books, which sell. Hence for many publishers the bestselling writers are able to "carry" works which are less profitable, although they may have greater academic and literary merit. This is particularly true of imaginative writers. The sucessful writer is both the image and mirror of the values of his society, accordingly he is endowed with a hyper-sensitive perception of the socio-cultural milieu and an awareness of the spiritual, intellectual and aesthetic forces of his environment; he has the ability to articulate ideas in language which makes emotional and mental appeal at one and the same time. The following paragraphs try to see whether in fact the African creative writer is in tune with his audience.

One need not conduct an elaborate scientific survey to discover that the small minority who read fiction for subjective reasons are mostly attracted to novels written in the romantic vein. In this context "romance" means the kind of themes variously described as "bust and lust", "breast-seller", "light love" and "highly immoral to the point of perversity", novels and others in which "mostly nasty people do nasty things". In this and other regards, the Onitsha market writer seems to have excelled others in capturing the predominant mood of the day and capitalising on it. This is no derogatory comment, on the contrary he appears to be more socially sensitive than his highbrow counterpart about whom we shall venture an opinion in due course. The next group of writers might be termed the religious, sentimental novelist, including a number of foreign writers, the archpriestess of whom is the incomparable Marie Corelli.[19] A third identifiable group consists of those who write sociological/anthropological novels, depicting themes ranging from the most serious political issues of the day to corruption in high places, subjects which seem to give vicarious pleasure and a sense of self-righteousness to many readers. The scions of African creative writing belong to this group, but seem not to be aware of the fact that they are beginning to repeat themselves. There is now a stereotype novel which deals with one or more of the following themes – the human problems of rapid social change, the conflicts which arise from a confrontation of tradition with modernity, the dissipation of rural values by city lights, the schizophrenia of the evolue, mixed-marriage motifs and that sort of thing.

The best description that I can find for the last, but by no means the least popular, set of writers is "tradition and culture novelists". It is the group whose writings arouse the most spontaneous emotional response from our readers, probably because they are able to make an appeal to our inner cravings, having borrowed from those folk narratives which gave us our first lessons in literary appreciation. Their popularity may be due also to the fact, as Anand[20] reminds us, that despite the inevitability of culture change "there is an enormous number of oral traditions concerning psycho-social phenomena which reveal an understanding of man's inner life, not available in the rational thought of the modern world . . . in the grim face of modern technology men everywhere must turn to their own" inner reality. The point is particularly of interest in recreational reading, for once the utilitarian urge is satisfied, emotional reactions become of increasing significance in the reader's choice of reading matter. Consequently, creative writers and publishers are often reminded[21] to always look out for "interest content".

To a large extent the anti-colonial sentiments, so vigorously expressed by a number of political radicals after the Second World War, may have given a new lease of life to our traditional oral literature. The ideology of African Personality which they propounded was both a political and cultural revivalist movement. Together with Negritude, the new ideology assaulted Western value concepts. Léopold Senghor's earlier poetic evangelism called for a return to our cultural, religious, political and literary roots in order to assert the vitality of Africanness. Responding to the call, the Diop brothers produced literature whose immediate acceptance proved that African audiences would much prefer to read literature which mirrored their indigenous social mores. Ousmane Socé Diop's *Karim*[22] is as widely popular as Birago Diop's *Stories of Amadou Koumba*.[23] And Cheikh Anta Diop's *Nations Nègres et Culture*[24] has attained the eminence of a Bible among young Senegalese. A reading survey carried out in Chad and Senegal has confirmed[25] that these tradition and culture novels are among the most popular books.

A number of other novelists have made equally effective use of the ethic, imagery, idiom and myth of the folklore. It is for this reason that Amos Tutuola, Camara Laye and veteran D. O. Fagunwa are better appreciated by some critics than those they describe as "neo-African".[26] The remarkable thing about the grass-roots writers is that their works have been translated into a number of European languages, which shows that the authentic African writer can be successful without pandering to Western tastes or standards. But the main point of these perfunctory remarks is that many more people are prepared to buy and read Camara Laye and Tutuola than, say, Ayi Kwei Armah! It is safe to predict, then, that the grass-roots novel will not lose favour with the reading public in the forseeable future, in spite of its denigrators. Characters are set in dream sequences reminiscent of William Blake and the dreary subterranean world of Pluto, but they also depict states of existence in which mortals commune freely with supernatural beings; a generous mixture of fact, fable and fantasy, of mystery and magic is the stuff of which African traditional literature is made, and appreciated.

If the above and following assumptions are at all plausible, we need to ask whether the trend of writing and publishing today does conform to the demand, or whether the false standards which we shall mention presently are frustrating popular demand. To begin with let us ask why there are comparatively fewer folktales – both original and adapted versions – on our bookstalls than other kinds of literature?

Another popular set of reading matter among urban dwellers is what might be called psychological magazines and sentimental novels. In 1955 Helen Kimble,[27] assisted by Gustav Jahoda, carried out the first subjective study of recreational reading among a number of library users in Accra. First it was discovered that Marie Corelli (1855–1924) was the most sought-after novelist, probably because she articulates the African's deference to supernatural forces. Similarly Christoph von Schmid's *Basket of Flowers* and Bertha Clay's *Beyond Pardon*[28] express the concern for the preservation of good human relations, truth and justice.

Equally popular were magazines like *Prediction, Fate, Occultist* and *Psychology Magazine* about which Mrs Kimble expressed some consternation. Did these preferences indicate "a fundamental sense of insecurity among the emerging educated classes?" she asked. Had the educated person become "a man of two worlds" who had "turned his back on traditional forms of society, and yet felt that he had lost the magic key to prosperity and success in the Western way of life?" These are possible explanations, for it is accepted that drastic change from the traditional to an urban environment creates a sense of insecurity. It would appear, then, that the reader of these pseudo-psychological magazines is searching for means to restore his emotional balance in a world of conflicting values. By practising the corrective therapy so lavishly prescribed by these magazines the reader hopes to create a psychic link between his "two worlds". Failing a complete cure, such reading could at least provide avenues of escape from reality, or a means of socialising with the self in compensation for the isolation and individuality of urban life. (188–191)

...

It is probably in the pursuit of economic gain that many writers today are tempted to play it up to a foreign gallery. Anand[29] remarks that the vast majority of writers since the turn of the century have been driven by the "values of the cash nexus". Particularly in the field of imaginative writing, there have been more "commercial books than honest grass-roots entertainment". Among African writers it is believed that commercialisation of art became rampant in the 1960s[30] when the better-known authors were writing almost exclusively for Europe and America from which they were assured of lucrative cash returns. Those who at the same time wished to satisfy a local audience succeeded in creating a literature "with a hybrid character and the stamp of cultural interbreeding".

Let us concede that financial gain may be an attractive incentive, but it is by no means the only one. Every writer is anxious to be read by as many people as possible, irrespective of whether they are Americans, Europeans, or Africans. The fact, however, is that six countries in Africa have no more than 300,000–400,000 inhabitants and only sixteen have a population of more than five million, eighty percent or more of whom are illiterate. In terms of size of reading population the only countries that can sustain a viable industry are those with a population of more than ten million or so, namely, Nigeria, the Sudan, the Republic of South Africa and Egypt. More than two-thirds of this number, although literate, do not read books unless they must. The writer, conscious of this limitation, is constrained to adapt his style, characterisation, language, etc., to a foreign, albeit larger and appreciative, audience. Ultimately this means that he has not reached the full potentials of his abilities, either as an artist or social commentator, for although he is capable of doing so he cannot utilise material which would have appealed solely to the silent, unresponsive, and undemanding local population. The prevalence of the so-called anthropological novel may even be said to have been influenced by those who call the tune of African writing. The danger here is that in trying to delineate the socio-cultural background from which his characters have emerged the writer more often succeeds in displaying his scholarship than his artistry as a storyteller.

One other reason why the more serious authors may prefer foreign publishers, irrespective of financial considerations, is the recognition that scholarship is an international commodity. Thus, for example, Fourah Bay College has sought affiliation with Oxford University Press because of the latter's international connections. Similarly Kwame Nkrumah having founded a State Publishing Corporation for the encouragement of local authorship, yet found it necessary to enlist Macmillan, Heinemann, Nelson, Lawrence and Wishart, Inostrannoi Literary and Panaf Publications, among other publishers, so that his cherished ideas might gain international stature. (192–193)

42. ANGUS CALDER, *Some Practical Questions* (1974)

Aus: Andrew Gurr and Angus Calder (eds.), *Writers in East Africa* (Nairobi, 1974), 79–93. – Angus Calder (geb. 1942) aus England unterrichtete Englische Literatur am Literature Department der University of Nairobi und lehrt jetzt in Edinburgh. Er veröffentlichte Gedichte und eine Geschichte des 2. Weltkriegs. In einer Reihe von Aufsätzen beschäftigte er sich mit der Entwicklung der ostafrikanischen Literatur. Im folgenden Text richtet er sein Augenmerk auf das Verhältnis von Autor – Leser – und Verleger.

Besides ruling out the prospect of a full-time career in writing, the current situation must pose for all writers the problem of audience in an especially acute form. I mean, the problem of whom one writes for. The reading public in East Africa is a small class of highly-educated people. Such people also form the bulk of the local bourgeoisies, and would seem on all available evidence to prefer the sick fantasies of James Hadley Chase or the meaningless romances of Anya Seton to novels about real local conditions by local writers.

Let me give two ominous examples. In two successive years (1968 and 1969) I asked the first year class of students taking literature – about forty in the first case, thirty-five in the second – how many of them had read *A Grain of Wheat*, which was already available in paperback. One hand went up the first time; not one the second. I suspect that any James Bond story would have scored higher. Then, more recently, a young man who was writing poetry sent me some work. I thought it showed promise and met him to discuss it. His total reading in poetry so far consisted of *Song of Lawino* and Angira's *Juices*,[31] he had made pretty good use of it. But his favourite writer was Harold Robbins. East African books do not seem to circulate widely even amongst the people who have the keenest interest in literature. Better libraries would help to improve matters. Bookshops are still disgracefully few and badly stocked, and second hand bookshops (which would bring prices down for the poorer student or reader) are not often seen. By more vigorous salesmanship aimed at the general public, not just at schoolteachers who might buy class sets, publishers could help. But there is a problem of attitudes which won't be so easy to get over; represented by the Nairobi clerk who told me that he preferred Fleming to Ngugi because Africans couldn't write good English; represented by the total absence of all books from the living room of one young executive (I think he had a few technical manuals in the next room); and the pride of place given to Churchill's *History of the Second World War* in the bookshelf of another such man.

The writer, in short, is confined to addressing a small section of the community which is probably, of all sections, least interested in a really radical message or a really subtle criticism of contemporary manners. A writer who saw his novels as blows for the cause of humanity, and who wanted to move a large public, would find no large public to move. It may be that films, which communicate to the untaught, and can scramble across language barriers, are an apter medium for the committed artist than novels; it is again symptomatic of something badly wrong that the films made by that fine Senegalese novelist Sembene Ousmane[32] have not been screened in Kenya; but now that Hilary Ngweno[33] is trying to mobilise a local film industry, some writers at least may be attracted to its possibilities.

Irrespective of political commitment, the writer has problems of identity in relation to his public. If his work has a tribal background, he will have to explain many things to those who do not share it, at the risk of boring those who do. I suspect that the general ignorance of the customs of other African peoples is such that the author who explains his material adequately to Africans will have to go no further to accommodate an international audience; but a consciousness of that latter audience may bring further problems of tone, style and form – do you write English for critics in London, or for laymen in Nairobi? I am not merely theorising when I say that the problem of selecting the right presentation of material for the audience one is addressing can be nerve-wracking, expecially if one doesn't have too clear an idea of the composition of that audience – I know this from my own experience as a British writer producing for various British audiences. The ideal is to find a voice which is truly and frankly one's own, and yet suitable for all purposes – for newspaper pieces as well as for scholarly articles. I haven't succeeded in this quest. In East Africa, the fact that school students form a dominant section of the local market for books must affect the attitudes of both writers and publishers towards style. It must certainly tend to discourage the latter from accepting books which use a local variety of English rather than the standard form. I remember, when a local publisher asked me to comment on a certain novel in manuscript, finding it very hard to decide whether it was publishable or not. The English was unorthodox; it was generally, but not always, quite clear and comprehensible. Should one send the book back for complete rewriting? Or tidy up the style throughout to make it conform to standard usage? Or make just a few alterations? Or print it as it stood? It will be a great pity if the pressure to conform to school requirements, or the fear of seeming naïve to a London critic, can prevent the publication of books which use the idiom of East Africa rather than that of Oxford.

But there is no clear sign yet of a forceful and consistent East African idiom in English; a few common departures from standard English don't amount to a freshly vital literary medium. (I do not mean that East African writers are not distinctive, but each is distinctive in his own way.) In any case, everyone is agreed in theory that mother tongue is the best medium for any writer; and if a *lingua franca* is to be adopted many people (though not quite all) would see Swahili as preferable to English. But there is a marked, and possibly unhealthy, gap between theory and practice.

The few years since the publication of *Weep Not, Child* and *Song of Lawino* have seen a rapid and accelerating growth of creative writing in *English* from East Africa. Only in Tanzania has Swahili seemed likely to supplant English, but Tanzania has been markedly less productive than Kenya or Uganda. My dominant impression has been of enormous enthusiasm, with no major local writer much older than forty and a tremendous upsurge of talented writers, especially of poets, who are still in their early twenties. A Kenyan writer who had been abroad for three years or so told me when she returned that she was amazed to find out how much had been going on. But it seems to me that in Kenya and Uganda at any rate, this enthusiasm is almost all directed towards writing in English; those writers who have tried their hand in Swahili for a change haven't been satisfied with the results sufficiently to continue. Meanwhile, the production of good work in English is creating a "snowball" effect; the more there is of it, the more there is likely to be as the ball gathers snow and momentum down hill, though snowballs, of course, can melt with great suddenness.

The young man or woman who is starting to write has before him the examples of numerous imposing local talents, all of them apparently committed to writing in English – and all of them with thirty, forty or fifty years of writing ahead of them, assuming that they attain the biblical three score years and ten; it is likely that most of them will still be producing good work in English in the year 2000. To name the most prominent: Okot, Taban, Okello, Serumaga, Seruma,[34] Bukenya,[35] Ntiru[36] from Uganda – David Rubadiri from Malawi – Ngugi, Grace Ogot, Kibera,[37] Mangua,[38] Angira from Kenya – Peter Palangyo[39] from Tanzania. Aspiring writers, reading the books of these heroes in their schools, where English is still the main medium of instruction, are overwhelmingly likely, for the time being, to emulate their elders in English. The more good books come out in English, the more likely this process is to continue. Any switching of languages at the moment seems to be in favour of English; thus Okot no longer writes in Acoli first, and Stephen Ngubiah, I gather, turned to fiction in English after failing to interest publishers in his fiction in Kikuyu.

Only in drama, perhaps, is there much immediate prospect of a turn to the vernaculars and Swahili. There are two reasons. Even a "drawing room comedy" gains in freshness from being given in the language which the characters actually speak – drama, of course, is all speech. And drama needs an immediate audience to give it funds and meaning, and will tend to adopt the language which its audience actually speaks.

As I said, snowballs may melt; it would perhaps require only two or three outstanding books in that language to set up a counter-current in favour of Swahili, and maybe Tanzania will soon produce them. But for the moment not only authors, but publishers, are vesting their interests in English. It is very unlikely that any purely commercial initiative will change the picture; and only the most vigorous implementation of pro-Swahili or pro-vernacular language policies by the governments of Kenya and Uganda would suffice.

Let us consider in this context the structure of relationships between publishers, writers, and profits. The fourteen leading writers I have named fall into two categories. Five (Ngugi, Taban, Serumaga, Palangyo, and shortly, Angira) are published by Heinemann Educational Books, pioneers and still leaders in the field of African creative writing, but based in London, whither, as one of their directors ruefully told me, writers fly in upon them like stray birds of passage, expecting, them to provide free beds. Four of the five writers have also given work to local publishers, but their international and Pan-African reputations reflect the wide distribution provided by Heinemann. (EAPH use Heinemann's network to distribute abroad but not, I gather, with very striking results, and EALB's overseas operations are so far small.)[40]

Rubadiri, whose collection of poems was published by Pergamon in England; but whose novel appeared from EAPH, is another bird of passage. But the remaining eight writers have published only locally, except in anthologies. At least three of them, to my knowledge have sold extremely well; and rumours that Okot is the main money-spinner for EAPH among all their writers, including writers of nonfiction, have never been contradicted; sales of poetry in East Africa *are* quite extraordinary.

But observe how the scales drop for English. Heinemann, and their British-linked rivals OUP and Longmans, are interested in the widest possible market, which means that fiction in English will be more useful to them than fiction in Swahili. EAPH on the other hand now have a long, and in part very profitable, backlist of titles in English which they will wish to continue to sell for many years to come. The other significant local publishers, EALB, Equatorial, Uganda PH, simply don't have enough prestige to sway the balance, even if they all started boosting Swahili simultaneously. I am not trying to suggest that publishers, even foreign ones, are not responding to the claims of nation-building; all of them publish in Swahili. But books for schools and works of nonfiction in Swahili do not alter matters so far as prose fiction is concerned. Heinemann have broken new ground by publishing Ngugi in a Swahili translation, and OUP have brought out the play *Kinjeketile*[40] simultaneously in both Swahili and English versions. But only a really drastic change of policy by all publishers simultaneously would make much difference in the foreseeable short-run, and meanwhile the snowball gets bigger. I should add that even if writers and publishers committed themselves, now and finally, to African languages, the readers would still be able to buy fiction in English published abroad, and they might prefer it to local produce for the usual bad reasons. If a writer begins with imitation, as most do, he will still be attracted by Achebe, by Conrad, or by Dostoevsky in English translation, and the chances are that he will imitate them in English. In poetry, the influence of Soyinka, Okigbo, Eliot – or, for that matter, of Okot – will be even more decisively persuasive. (83–89)

43. KOLE OMOTOSO, *The Indigenous Publisher and the Future of Culture in Nigeria* (1976)

Aus: G. O. Onibonoje, Kole Omotoso, O. A. Lawal (eds.), *The Indigenous for National Development* (Ibadan, 1976), 59–70. – Kole Omotoso (geb. 1943) aus Nigeria studierte Arabisch und Französisch in Ibadan und promovierte in Moderner Arabischer Literatur an der University of Edinburgh. Er lehrt an der University of Ibadan. Omotoso veröffentlichte Gedichte, Kurzgeschichten, Romane, und Dramen. Für den Onibonoje Verlag in Ibadan betreut er eine für den Schulgebrauch bestimmte Literaturreihe. Im folgenden Textauszug vertritt er die Auffassung, daß die Existenz englischsprachiger Literatur gegenüber der einheimischen den Klassengegensatz zwischen europäisierter Elite und der Masse der Bevölkerung widerspiegelt. Aufgabe des afrikanischen Verlegers ist es, Literatur und Kultur der Mehrheit in deren eigenen Sprache zu fördern.

If the cultural situation is also dual in Nigeria, it is directly derived from the political and economic duality which has been referred to above. The cultural duality is emphasised by the duality of the languages involved and the media consequent on these. On the one hand the educated élite expressed its culture, both what it has inherited from the colonialist as well as the dregs of its own tradition, in the European language which happens to belong to its colonising master. On the other hand, the majority of the people express their culture in their own language, a language which has begun to reflect its contact with Europe. The medium of the expression of these cultures are for the elite, written and for the majority of the people, oral. For the élite there are the various publishing firms bringing out each day novels, plays and collections of poetry in the European languages. For the majority of the people we have the recording studios and the broadcasting aspects of the mass media relaying extracts from novels in Nigerian languages, plays and poetry. The powerful influence of Yoruba actors such as Baba Sala (Mr. Adejumo of Alawada Theatre) and Yoruba poets such as Olanrewaju Adepoju are cases in point.

For twenty years, African writing has been published mainly for the outside world. The speakers for the country have been elected by foreigners who had specific aims in mind, aims which while coinciding with the aims of the local élite had no notion of the local majority.

It is obvious that the culture of which we speak in this essay is the culture of that neglected, politically repressed majority rather than the client culture of those who happen to wield political power as well as economic domination in the country. This is the culture whose future one must be concerned with. This concern must be expressed in political action since culture is not born in a vacuum.

To some extent, the powerful minority inheritors of colonial powers and collaborators with neo-colonialists have realised this. This is the reason behind the so much publicised cultural revival. Under the guise of this cultural revival, villages are rampaged periodically to bring to the urban areas the cream of the rituals, the most profound of the oral literature for the entertainment of the same élite. By the nature of this periodic association with their sources, no effects of these rituals are possible on the élite. Rather they continue to collaborate in the exploitation of the masses of the people, an aspect of which exploitation this particular cultural revival becomes. The myth and the being, the aspects of these cultural manifestations which have always stood the practitioners in good stead in the process of nation-building is lost on the élite. Doubtful of its own influence on the city élite, the people move back to their villages with their rituals, with these aspects of their culture which they need not revive since it lives with them and they in it.

It is obvious that this culture has no political backing to reassert itself. From this realisation one must wonder how it was so easy in the first place for the educated élite to take over everything so completely to the disadvantage of the masses of the people and the denigration of the culture of the people. Furthermore, one must wonder if it would ever be possible for the masses of the people to find enough representatives who will fight their fight with them and aid them in the process of reasserting this culture not only for themselves but also for the deluded hybrid inheritors of and collaborators with imperialism.

It is within the sphere of fighting with the masses of the people that I see the role of the indigenous Nigerian publisher. It is not an easy role to play. But it is easy to misinterpret what is expected of the indigenous publisher or any one for that matter who claims to have a conscious awareness of the awkwardness of our Nigerian society, easy for such people to fight for the people instead of fighting with them. Many of our present day avowed socialists are merely prepared to fight for the masses of the people. They publish journals in foreign languages addressing their fellow élites while the masses of the people for whom they express such verbally profound feelings know not what their fight is all about. He who must fight with the people must first and foremost, commit them to a programme of literacy. The role of the indigenous publisher is obvious in such a programme. There is no doubt that the culture of the masses itself would undergo a profound alteration during this process of literacy campaign. The accretions from the élite culture would be washed away from it if it is to be capable of replacing the culture of the élite and providing for the cultural nourishment of all the peoples of the country. Besides this process of washing off the dross of élite culture from the cultures of the peoples, there is also a crying need for profound alteration in the so-called traditional culture itself. For the revolutionary must not be dragged into the same mistake as some of our historians who have been enmeshed into the issue that 'tradition' is fixed and at no time absent from the time scale of the indigenous society. The word tradition has been used to excuse such anomalies as secret cults in present day Nigeria without questioning the basis of such a group in a free and egalitarian society supposedly the dream of this country. Many traditions are in fact opposed to the achievement of a free and just society and such traditions must be changed. The institution of Obas, Emirs, Obis and all the gradations of the chieftaincy titles must be done away with if indeed a just, egalitarian and free society is to be established. Thus the process of converting the present oral cultural manifestations of the masses of the people into writing must witness radicalizing programmes rather than simply educating them into the existing world-order which is itself discreditable.

To do this successfully, literacy campaigns must be conducted in the first language of the people. Little has been achieved from the many years of half-hearted literacy campaigns which have been carried out in this country. Even when there had been some measure of success, the programme had been so conservative in content as not to make any difference to the situation of the man who has acquired the literacy. What is meant here is that literacy campaigns must be seen as a cultural action for the freedom of the masses of the people rather than a weapon to aid the oppressed majority in the imitation of their oppressors.

The indigenous publisher can render much service if he is prepared to fight with the oppressed majority. But the contradictions are many and he must be prepared to face these contradictions and decide one way or the other. To begin with he is committing class suicide when he identifies with the oppressed majority and accepts to fight with them using the effective weapons he, on behalf of the people, controls. But he dies in his class to resurrect in a better, less stratified society. Moreover he does not really lose everything as compared with those who will range themselves on the side of the enemies of the oppressed masses until the tide of the anger of the people drowns them along with the enemy. By making an initial choice on the side of the people he pre-empts a historical foolishness which makes people fight against the inevitable march of history instead of seeing its trend and lending their weight to keep it on the revolutionary path for the good of all.

Another contradiction which the indigenous publisher must be, and in fact cannot but be, aware of is that profit cannot really be excessive in such an enterprise as this. In our type of incompetent capitalist society, how does one appeal to a man who has invested his money, time and talent in an enterprise, not to take advantage of the situation and enrich himself beyond the recognition of his society? This is a difficult question because it is not a theoretical one. Yet if such a publisher were well grounded on the theoretical aspects of the struggle of the people, he would know that the people's profit is his gain on the long run.

In this connection one must comment on the present trend of book pricing in Nigeria. There are generally two ranges of prices of books in the market. There are those books which are cheap and easily available. They usually sell under fifty kobo but never above seventy-five kobo. Such books are in subject matter and cultural content unsuitable for the people who find them the most financially accessible of books. The only books of any use in this group are books imported from Socialist countries. These are not yet available in numbers as to make any difference to the market. Religious books also come under this category. On the other side are the books which would be useful but which are completely out of the financial capabilities of most people, including sometimes the élite themselves. This pricing situation is understandable in the declining capitalist countries where every aspect of the book trade is unionised and the resultant increase in production cost, in order to safeguard the profit of the publisher, is passed on to the reader. In such a country, books are no longer cultural materials but articles of trade whose cultural role in society is irrelevant to the publisher.

The type of atmosphere in which the indigenous publisher can conveniently fulfil his role does not, as yet, exist in Nigeria. But the indigenous publisher, as a conscious member of the society must help towards the creation of such a society, a society in which books, like garri and plantain, will not only be made available but also made available as cheaply as possible. (65–70)

6. Afrikanische Literatur im Spannungsverhältnis zwischen nationaler Verpflichtung und internationaler Anerkennung

44. MARTIN TUCKER, The Headline Novels of Africa (1962)

Aus: *West Africa* (July 28, 1962), 829. – Der Literaturwissenschaftler M. Tucker (geb. 1928) unterrichtete in Afrika und verfaßte einen der ersten Überblicke über die englischsprachige Literatur des Kontinents: *Africa in Modern Literature: A Survey of Contemporary Writing in English* (New York, 1967). In einer der frühesten Stellungnahmen zur literarischen Qualität afrikanischer Literatur bemängelt Tucker ihre oft vordergründige Thematik und rief damit seinerseits die Kritik afrikanischer Literaten und Wissenschaftler hervor.

Topicality is ruining the modern novel written in English about Africa. The English and American commentators are mostly to blame, but the West African novelist must share in the blame. Today the most important development in the English novel about Africa lies in the emergence of a new group of African writers, educated usually in England and living mainly in West Africa. These writers are expected to play the major role in a new African literature springing from native roots and concerned with contemporary issues. Indeed, every liberal thinker is waiting for a literature of achievement to emerge from this group.

Yet it is this very speed with which novelists are rushing into the act that is turning the novel about Africa into a political and sociological pamphlet. In the past the novels by English and American writers have seemed too hurried, too journalistic; the novels by South Africans too much involved in their régime's ambivalent attitude to its Black and Coloured citizens. Today the West African novelists are only beginning to tackle the problem of individual characterisation in a contemporary world.

In general, modern fiction in English about Africa has concentrated obsessively on the issue of race relations. Such an issue is no stranger to other national and regional literature, but African fiction, whether by white or black, new or old, has a puritanical, instructional quality that mars its artistic achievement. From the nineteenth century through the present, English writers have looked on Africa as a school for experience rather than an experience fulfilled in its passing. Certain exceptions come to mind immediately – Olive Schreiner,[1] Joseph Conrad,[2] H. Rider Haggard[3] – but these are the few great writers in the field. The rest find it necessary to make of Africa a justification for the personal development of the ego or the political and social development of a people.

What is needed in novels about Africa is a new approach. This is of course a plea to be found in any criticism of a national or topical literature. Yet the demand is immediately relevant to fiction about Africa. For while such a phenomenon as 'the Great African Novel' may never be written (or written many times by various writers), the need exists for writers to get above their material and to worry less about the immediacy of their fictional milieu. Not surprisingly, the

West African novelist, secure in his roots, has been less prone to make of his novel a tract, but he is still a servant of the social rather than the aesthetic spirit.

Two West African novelists, Chinua Achebe and Onuora Nzekwu, have at moments surpassed the topicality of their fictional milieu to write a work of universal compassion, but even in the work of Chinua Achebe there are signs that the social issues are warping the artistic shapes of his work. Achebe's first novel *Things Fall Apart* dealt with that period of time which most Nigerian novelists (Cyprian Ekwensi, T. M. Aluko, Nzekwu) have employed for their first-published novels – the moment just before and after the white man and his civilisation arrived in Africa. Although critical of the Europeanising of Africa, and of missionaries who failed to leaven their teachings with an understanding of African customs and beliefs, Achebe's novel revealed the mind and character of its hero Ononkwo (sic) so that he became an individual struggling with a world slipping from his grasp. Ononkwo was not idealised but made real. What destroyed him was his unyielding pride, his failure to adapt to the new era he found so distasteful. The tragedy was that Ononkwo was the best man in the village.

Achebe's secon novel *No Longer at Ease* is set in that period so familiar to readers of African novels – the contemporary world of political, racial and social struggle. The action is placed in Lagos where an African who has squandered his great intellectual and spiritual potential is on trial for accepting a bribe. The novel is a flashback, an illuminating descent, into the causes of Obi's fall. Yet while the novel presents realistic, graphic scenes of Nigerian corruption, the characters are more symbolic than real. Obi is the familiar hero trapped in the transition between an old and modern Africa. He cannot resolve the conflict between the propriety of the past and the allurements of the present; he is paralysed into decadence.

Things Fall Apart is the best example of a West African novel of its type, yet ultimately it is a failure as a novel for concentrating too heavily on the social situation (and the sociological causes for that situation) rather than on the individuals caught within its bounds. Another West African novelist who utilises the same topical milieu but without the skill of Achebe is Cyprian Ekwensi, who in his first two full-length novels used Lagos as the hell which burns out the spirits of its inhabitants. Ekwensi idealised a whore in *Jagua Nana* who has to leave the capital city where murder, robbery, prostitution, and other forms of corruption are part of the social-political life, in order to regain her joy of life. His first novel *People of the City* was a proletarian diatribe against the evils of urban culture.

Ekwensi's novels read like journalistic exposés: they are filled with the cluttered accuracy of surface details, but they remain a series of scenes without an artistic climax. Yet the fault lies not so much in the skill, or lack of it, exhibited by Ekwensi (and by William Conton in *The African* and T. M. Aluko in *One Man, One Wife*[4]) as in the emphasis by these novelists on social and topical issues to the detriment of human characterisation. Topicality and nationalism, and the need to argue a cause, become more important than the joy and suffering of an experience.

Generally, West African novels in English have employed two time periods for their settings – the end of the nineteenth century when the white, Western forces asserted their technological superiority to submerge a native culture; and the present decade when a black, African culture won its rightful place in an independent land. Yet, by emphasising these two periods, the novelists have largely ignored the individual coming to grips with his personal matter. In choosing a time of conflict, the conflicts within the individual have become lost in the larger areas of battle, and individuals have become stereotyped in the war between black and white, progressive and reactionary, conservative and nationalistic, proud and corrupt. The individual becomes more important for the side he chooses, than for his personal beliefs. Even William Conton's novel *The African* which tries to give a many-levelled portrait of a political leader not unlike Kwame Nkrumah, is overloaded with the factual details of a tribal-national clash. And the hero of *The African* is not rendered any more precise by the narration of his political beliefs and programmes; only in the two acts of love – one with a South African girl in England, and the other in forgiving the South African racist who murdered her – does Conton's hero become alive and illuminated.

English and American writers are much more guilty of exploiting Africa than these West African novelists, but Achebe, Nzekwu, Ekwensi, Conton and Aluko face the same dangers in the dilemma between art and propaganda. The West African novelist cannot avoid dealing with issues unless he wants to create a lifeless art, but topicality can vitiate a novel just as surely as fastidiousness. The West African novelist, in dealing with issues, must be careful to create a literature with the proportions of art.

45. JOSEPH OHIOMOGBEN OKPAKU, *African Critical Standards for African Literature and the Arts* (1967)

Aus: *Journal of the New African Literature and the Arts* (Spring 1967), 1–7. – Als einer der rigorosesten Verfechter vertrat Okpaku (geb. 1935) Ende der sechziger Jahre immer wieder den Standpunkt, daß nur afrikanische ästhetische Kategorien zur Beurteilung afrikanischer Literatur und Kunst heranzuziehen seien. Als Herausgeber der o. a. Zeitschrift wie als Förderer schwarzer Literatur versuchte er, die im folgenden Textauszug angestellten programmatischen Überlegungen in die Tat umzusetzen. Okpaku veröffentlichte die Beiträge der Zeitschrift 1970 in einem Sammelband unter dem gleichen Titel, schrieb Theaterstücke und einen Roman und leitete den nur von Schwarzen betriebenen Verlag *The Third Press* in New York.

Critical standards derive from aesthetics. Aesthetics are culture dependent. Therefore critical standards must derive from culture.

In order for African literature and other creative arts to be valid *per se*, they must be valid within the context of African culture. The corollary is also true: if they are valid for Africa, then they are automatically valid *per se*. How then do we judge this validity? The present practice of judging African literature by Western standards is not only invalid, it is also potentially dangerous to the development of African arts. It presupposes that there is one absolute artistic standard and that, of course, is the Western standard. Consequently, good African literature is taken to be that which most approximates Western literature. The fallacy in this is twofold. One, it presupposes that there is one and only one artistic evolutionary process and that in that process Western art stands at the leading point through which African art must inevitably and necessarily pass. Two, it erroneously assumes that what the West considers "good" art must necessarily be considered the same by the non-Western world, unless they are not "sufficiently sophisticated" to appreciate good art.

There is no universal aesthetic, and if there were it would be most undesirable. The greatest value of art lies in the very fact that there are at least as many different and sometimes conflicting forms as there are different cultures. This is the basis of the wealth and richness of art. To fully enjoy art, it is not necessary that all art be reduced to a single form (the Western form) in order to make it easily comprehensible and acceptable to the Western audience and to all those who have acquired its taste (by "proper education"), but rather that the would-be connoisseur must make an effort to learn to appreciate different art forms.

Art is communication. Communication implies the awareness, by the artist, of an audience. The "ways" and means – that is, the "language" of communication – must be determined by the particular audience for which the artist performs. By "language" is meant not only the particular language used (whether English, French or Swahili) but also the imagery, symbolism, style, etc. Thus, some cultures dwell on subtleties, implications and understatements while others are more explicit and obvious. And even within the same culture the language used in addressing children is not the same as that used for adults. There are even variations within the second group depending on the "level of sophistication" of the particular adult audience. Thus we must affirm precisely that which many African writers have denied; namely, that a writer, and in particular a good writer, must bear in mind, consciously or subconsciously, the particular audience he seeks to address. Failure to do this results in a "hodgepodge" literature which is supposedly universal but without serious meaning to any audience.

Thus, in African literature many writers have denied themselves the advantages of bearing in mind an African audience and have sought, in spite of their denials, to make themselves intelligible primarily to the Western reader. Consequently, we have countless pages of explanations which, though they might contribute to the Western reader's comprehension, destroy the artistic qualities of the works and tend to make them boring to the African reader who, as an African, does not need all that description of his own culture. The novels of Onuora Nzekwu (for example, *Wand of Noble Wood*) and Francis Selormey's *The Narrow Path*[5] are cases in point. Even Achebe is not free from this. One gets the impression, in fact, that the London publisher goes through the manuscript, underlines all that needs to be explained (of course to the Western reader) and then returns it to the writer for clarification.

It is not intended to imply that art can or should be comprehended only within its culture. However, it is essential for the development of any art that it concern itself primarily with being valid, relevant and comprehensible, aesthetically as well as in its meaning within its cultural context. Then, if somebody outside of the culture wishes to fully comprehend that art, he should study the culture itself. This is the primary role of books on sociology and anthropology and not of the creative artist. When Shakespeare wrote he did not bear in mind the importance of being intelligible to Africans. He wrote consciously for England and its Western cultural extensions. In order, therefore, for us to fully understand him we have to study English culture, especially the state of that culture contemporary to Shakespeare's times. By the same token, the African writer should concern himself with producing beautiful and meaningful art for his African audience. Then the non-African who is interested in appreciating and comprehending that art should make the necessary effort to study and understand African culture.

What then is good African art? In particular how do we judge African arts? First let us define what we mean by African art.

Okigbo tells us that an African work "must have its roots deep in African soil, must take its birth from African experience, must pulsate with African feeling."[6] This is characteristic of the double-talk and nonsensical pseudo-profound speculation that permeates the world of African writers today – especially that of my fellow Nigerians. By Okigbo's definition, an African writing about a non-African experience does not qualify as an African writer.[7] As for "deep roots in African soil" and "pulsating with African feeling", it would be nice to know what he means. If one followed Okigbo, one would have to throw out J. P. Clark's *America, Their America*.[8] The same for all of Senghor's works inspired by his experiences of existential contradiction while living an alien life in Paris.

Others have said that "theme" is the determinant; the theme must be African. This would rule out Obi Egbuna's hilarious and beautifully written play *The Anthill*.[9] Perhaps that is why he felt the need to introduce a little culture conflict at the end in order to qualify. This would classify Conrad, Gide, and others as African writers. Certainly the Tarzan stories would belong. Silly as this definition is, it has been the basis of operation of many a publisher and writer. For a work to be authentically African its setting must be in Africa. Janheiz Jahn's approach in his *Bibliography of African and Neo-African Literature*[10] is an extreme and extremely ridiculous extension of this position.

There is, it seems, only one valid definition of African literature. AFRICAN LITERATURE IS THE ENTIRE BODY OF LITERARY WORKS WRITTEN BY AFRICANS. This is so simple that I'm surprised it has not been regarded as self-evident, which it is. This is a common sense definition. It makes sense – and what is more, it *works*. This definition has several far-reaching implications which are worth mentioning in brief. By "Africans" it is meant all those who are citizens or natives of all those territories which are clearly defined in geography as Africa. This would include the Arab North as well as the problematic South. This would include all immigrants no matter their race or national origin. On the other hand it would exclude all African emigrants (not exiles) no matter their race or national origin.

The primary criticism of African arts must come from Africans using African critical standards. We cannot accept either of the existing two approaches to criticism of African literature. It is as undesirable to plead for leniency in criticising African works as it is absurd for Lewis Nkosi[11] to ask that Western critical standards be used. Western critical standards are developed in the Western tradition and are applied by Western critics to interpret and criticise Western literature to the Western audience. Thus, when a critic says of the Western writer that he smacks of Conrad, he immediately invokes a whole concept of Conradism with which the Western reader is acquainted as part of his cultural education. So, when the Western critic looks at African work he immediately tries to find out which Western works it best resembles so he can use this to establish communication with the Western reader. His comparisons are made against the background of Western literature and therefore Western culture. By the same token, an African critic trying to relate African literature or any other literature to Africans must do so against the background of African culture. He must draw upon the patterns of the African aesthetic. In other words, he must use African critical standards.

Clearly the role of the Western critic of African literature differs from that of the African critic. The Western critics' only valid job is to interpret African literature and the other arts to Western audiences. Except in a very unusual case, his views will at best be only "interesting" to the African reader. To play this role, he should study African culture, and the aesthetic and philosophical implications of the particular piece in question within the context of that culture. Then with this understanding he can recast the meaning and profundity derived, into his own Western cultural context in order to make it relevant to his own culture. On the other hand, the role of the African critic is to interpret and criticize African arts for African readers. To do this he must use the means common to both critic and audience, namely, African culture.

What then are these African critical standards? The logical place to go in search of them is the African aesthetic. In particular, we shold examine our traditional artistic forms as well as genuine (not "studied") contemporary African tastes and attitudes towards the various art forms. That African tastes often differ from their Western counterpart cannot be disputed. Except for the alienated ones, it is evident that most Africans insist upon rhythm as a basic requirement in music. Consequently, many would consider a great number of classical pieces as "noise". An examination of the folk literature will reveal an African concept of literature as being more than the written word. Not only is the musical accompaniment (voice and instrumental) often a necessary part of it, the use of the voice by the narrator, the tonal variations and the histrionics are also central and vital to sustain the interest of the audience. This will suggest in African novels an emphasis on the beauty of the voice as a natural development from the oral traditions. More important it will suggest the very form of the novel as inadequate for the fullest expression of African literary talent. One suspects that drama, opera, ballet or film would lend themselves better.

The next place to search for these standards would be an examination of those common aspects of life most frequently dramatized in the arts. This would include love, life, hate, honor, duty, death, destruction, pride, prejudice, friendship, fear, violence, birth, and reality amongst others. Different cultures not only have different conceptions of these but have different attitudes to them. Not only that, they give them different emphases. All these different conceptions, attitudes, emphases, tastes and preferences constitute the basis on which to build criticism. This is where the search for African critical standards must begin. (1–4)

...

Thus, by examining, from the point of view of African culture and aesthetics, aspects of life and death which writers often dramatize, we can proceed to build a body of African critical standards for not only African literature, but all literature. Then, by applying these standards responsibly, critically, and with sharp insight – and always with an adequate sense of humor – we can then hope, as critics, to help bring about the creation of a body of literature that best satisfies the literary and aesthetic tastes of Africans.

That the West has always taken a pejorative attitude to Africa is self-evident. That some have modified this to an often condescending always reprehensible patronage exhibited through "defenses" of Africa, is perhaps not quite so apparent. But what does seem so clear is the glaring fact that most of us so-called African intellectuals have consciously or unconsciously swallowed this same prejorative attitude towards Africa. Our literature, our politics, our scholarship, our language – what does not show it? So at Dakar, Wole Soyinka said he prefers to be called a writer, NOT an African writer. It is true of course that when the Englishman talks of an "African writer" he implies inferiority. But it is also true that when Soyinka says therefore don't call me an African playwright, he also accepts this implicit inferiority. What Soyinka forgets is that when the Western man talks of a writer *per se,* he means a Western writer. Yet I am sure Soyinka will deny that he wants to be called a Western writer.

Perhaps as a prescription to Soyinka's problem, we may emphasize that the important thing is to be a *good* African playwright. The moment he achieves this, and is acclaimed by African critics using African critical standards, then the world, if it has any respect for African culture and aesthetics, must automatically accept him as a playwright *per se;* or in refusing to do so, must not attempt to tell Africans what a good playwright should be. The problem is not, as Soyinka thinks, that being a good African writer is bad, but that there has not been a good African writer by African standards in recent times.

The movement we call for, one which is crucial and inevitable if African culture is to remain valid and meaningful and to survive the existing pressure for Westernization based on an erroneous concept of progress and resulting in that curious product – the alienated African – is a movement which demands that we relate ourselves, our writings, our scholarship, and our academicism first to ourselves and to our people; to the social, political and cultural realities and tastes of Africa. It is only in this way that we can have any claim to validity as Africans. (6)

46. ELDRED DUROSIMI JONES, *The Decolonization of African Literature* (1968)

Aus: P. Wästberg (ed.), *The Writer in Modern Africa* (Uppsala, 1968), 71–76. – Jones' (cf. Text 25) kritische Bestandaufnahme der Leistung afrikanischer Schriftsteller, die häufig geneigt schienen, ein allzu idyllisches Bild vom Afrika vorkolonialer Zeit zu zeichnen, verstellt ihm nicht den Blick auf jene Werke, die sich realistisch mit der eigenen Vergangenheit auseinandersetzen und die Totalität einer widersprüchlichen Geschichte und Gegenwart literarisch gestalten.

The most obvious sign of the influence of Europe on African literature is in the language of African literature. Although there have been, and still are, writers who write in African languages, the late Yoruba novelist Fagunwa, for example, the best modern African writing is written in European languages – predominantly French and English – but also in Portuguese. There are obvious drawbacks arising from this situation. It takes a great deal of time and effort to master a second language well enough to produce in it a work of art which is not at best a literary curiosity, tolerated because it is produced by someone from whom the world expected nothing and so is pleasantly surprised to get anything at all. This means that many artistically gifted persons may not have direct access to a world audience. The drawback is not, however, total. It is possible to write in an African language and get the work translated into a world language. This has actually happened to a few authors.

The great advantage for a writer who masters his language of adoption is the obvious one of direct access to a large number of his fellow Africans, whom he can only reach through a European language, and direct access to a large part of the rest of the world as well. This is why all who can will, I believe, write in a European language.

It has been shown by several African authors that a work can be written in a European language and still convey something of the African experience in artistic form. Senghor's poems are written in excellent French but are so imbued with African images conveying the spirit of Africa that he can be said to have added a new dimension to the language of his adoption. An English critic has acknowledged a similar repayment of Wole Soyinka's debt to English. Penelope Gilliatt, writing in *The Observer* (London) of September 19, 1966, wrote:

"Every decade or so, it seems to fall to a non-English dramatist to belt new energy into the English tongue. The last time was when Brendan Behan's *The Quare Fellow* opened at Theatre Workshop. Nine years later, in the reign of Stage Sixty at the same loved Victorian building at Stratford East, a Nigerian called Wole Soyinka has done for our napping language what brigand dramatists from Ireland have done for centuries – booted it awake, rifled its pockets and scattered the loot into the middle of next week."

What Miss Gilliatt is saying in her own, rather tough, brigand imagery is that Soyinka is employing his adopted language with such originality that he is contributing to its enrichment. The use of the foreign language then need not embarrass the African or the European. As everyone knows, English and French are the two foremost African languages.

The African writer need not therefore be dominated by the language of his adoption, though it is perfectly possible that he may be. It is possible that with the adoption of his new language he may become mesmerised by the material in it and quite unconsciously reflect ideas and attitudes not really his own. This, of course, really means that a person who is so mesmerised cannot be a really successful artist. For the true artist learns from all he meets but distils it in his own imagination and makes something new and original out of it. This should be the aim of the African writer. To be faithful to his own imagination, whatever language and whatever medium he happens to be using.

Writers themselves have examined the means by which the character of African speech can be conveyed in a foreign language. I have elsewhere (in *African Forum*, No. 4, 1966) quoted Mr Chinua Achebe's words of the subject, as well as the excellent illustration he gives from his own work.

Other authors have sought to use the very syntax of African languages, while employing the words of the foreign language. This is the basis of Gabriel Okara's style in *The Voice*. Yet others have used the standard version of the foreign language. The success of each work has to be judged individually, in so far as it fulfils the author's purpose and is an artistic success.

Much more fundamental than the mere reproduction of syntax is the conveying in its totality of an experience in a way that reflects its environment without precluding it from general applicability. In looking at the African author's work we may be able to recognise its Africanness; we must be able to see its universality. Fortunately the two things often go together. A work which succeeds in realising its environment to the full often achieves this universality. The happy paradox is that, to be truly universal, one must be truly local.

In one sense African literature has been unduly influenced by the fact of colonisation. Necessarily so, since artists and intellectuals tend to be very sensitive to restrictions of any kind. Because colonization itself was a form of suppression, there was a great outcry against it. It therefore became a recurring theme in the work of African writers. The voices of Anglophones and Francophones merge here in a strong unison. (71–73)

...

The African writer can now, I feel, shake himself free of this indirect limitation and take a total and unembarrassed view of his Africa – the Africa of the present and the past. The resulting picture may be unromantic, it may be disillusioning. The only rule should be that it must reflect the total situation.

This is already happening. I have mentioned Mr Achebe in relation to the novel of the past. He has, of course, looked quite searchingly around him at our own Africa in *No Longer at Ease* and more recently in *A Man of the People*. Wole Soyinka's *The Interpreters*[12] and Easmon's *The New Patriots*[13] do not gloss over the glaring and frightening imperfections of modern Africa. The second instalment of Camara Laye's autobiographical work *Dramouss*[14] also hints at some of the mixed consequences of political decolonization.

One of the most interesting antidotes to the over-romanticised view of old Africa is Soyinka's *A Dance of the Forests*. First of all, the play works in two areas of time, since the past illuminates the past. The play looks back at one of the great empires of the past, not so much as a symbol of greatness, but as a community of people – people, rather than shadowy historical giants or massive saints. The play shows people with the familiar urges, drives and motives which make up our own world, and which, unless human nature has dramatically changed, must have governed people then in Mali, Songhai, Ghana or any of the great kingdoms. Thus, in clearing away the false romance of the past, the play puts us on our guard against any illusions about our present.

War in the past probably found its blind adherents, like the Historian of Soyinka's play, who is a forerunner of the academic lackey who uses his intellect to defend ideas and policies which he knows are wrong. This is not a particularly African character, although Africa has its own supply of them. The play breaks out of the dimension of the past and out of the boundaries of Africa when Soyinka portrays the glorification of war in these dramatically ironical words of the Historian:

"I would show you the magnificence of the destruction of a beautiful city. I would reveal to you the attainments of men which lifted mankind to the ranks of gods and demi-gods. And who was the inspiration of this divine carnage? Helen of Troy, a woman whose honour became as rare a conception as her beauty. Would Troy, if it were standing today, lay claim to preservation in the annals of history if a thousand valiant Greeks had not been slaughtered before its gates, and a hundred thousand Trojans within her walls?"

The specious arguments of the prostituted intellectual carry the day. Mata Kharibu, the tyrant, has his way, and the slave dealer (not European) has a new and unexpected source of merchandise. African artists can produce great works but, as men, they are as subject to jealousy as Demoke is to vertigo. All this is not to say that the empires of the past were not great or that Africa today is not potentially great, but it is to say that the human element in politics, as in art, is just as uncertainly poised on the brink of triumph or disaster now, as then. When artists look at their material like this, they are likely to write great and abiding literature, and they would have overcome the limitations of colonization.

Africa has a wealth of tradition, but it is also a new and dynamic continent. It is a land of quiet villages and throbbing cities, of skyscrapers and mud huts, of honour as well as corruption, of benevolence as well as of tyranny, of beauty as well as ugliness. This is the total picture. We must look at it all. (76–77)

47. ERNEST EMENYONU, *African Literature: What does it take to be its Critic?* (1971)

Aus: E. D. Jones (ed.), *African Literature Today,* 5 (1971), 1–11. – Der nigerianische Literaturwissenschaftler Emenyonu nimmt innerhalb der Debatte um die afrikanischer Literatur angemessenen Kriterien eine Position zwischen den Befürwortern einer „black aesthetic" ein und jenen, die von Universalien auszugehen fordern. Nichtafrikanischen Kritikern wirft er allerdings oft mangelnde Kenntnisse über afrikanische Kultur und Geschichte vor, die zu ungerechtfertigten Urteilen führen. Emenyonu unterrichtet an der University of Calabar, Nigeria.

African literature has come to mean several things to several people. To some it is a tool for the literate African's arrogation of the essence of his cultural heritage – an assertion and at times an imposition of the contents and excellence of a black culture, on a white dominated world. To others African literature means 'a new literature of the world' with its authentic and original genre, themes, and message. To a few, it is simply a political document of protest against the assumptions of colonialism and imperialism as they relate to the world of the black man. To yet other people, African literature in all its ramifications represents a mere appendage to British or French literature since most of the African writers write chiefly in English or French.

It would appear that the literary world was not prepared for the emergence of African writing when it did. Those who posed as its 'judges' knew little or nothing of the existence and depth of oral literature in Africa, and therefore, little or nothing of the true roots of written African literature. Some of them were gaining their first insight into the African social scene, and approached African writing for its sociological rather than its literary interest. Criticism of African literature, therefore, centred around the discovery of the degree of new information on African primitive ways which each subsequent work revealed.

Some of these people were quick to rush to the conclusion that they would soon get bored with the content of African writing. When Chinua Achebe's second novel *No Longer at Ease* appeared in 1961, many critics had no further doubts in their minds that the African novel of the second half of the twentieth century was simply the sociological document that they suspected it of being from the start. When *Arrow of God* (Achebe's third novel) emerged, this conclusion became absoute. But when further works from African pens (including Achebe's) came out with emphasis on other things apart from 'primitive' social idiosyncrasies of remote Africa, the critics' dilemma and unpreparedness showed in their approach to the works. In the Western world some universities quickly dichotomised African literature into the traditional, meaning oral, and the modern, meaning written. Critics had little to say about the former because as Dr. Edris Makward has pointed out: 'Literary criticism as a separate and autonomous specialty or genre had no place in pre-colonial Africa, where the best qualified and reliable critics were indeed the public itself.'[15] In spite of this, however, some teachers have still engaged in the task – helped by two or less years of graduate study in an African language – of translating African folk tales and assigning their students to read the printed word and 'discover' the qualities of a good African folk-tale.

The critics of the so-called 'modern' African literature became more confused in their purpose and approach than some college departments who wanted to see in African literature a steady source for the ethnographic data of the 'old Africa rediscovered'. Some of them only began then to do what they should have done from the beginning – recognise that the novel is a Western form, and therefore, concern themselves with what the African novelists 'have done to their derived form instead of the amount of traditional ritual and modern rottenness and rheum that is to be found in them'.[16]

Some did not see this exercise as worth anything because a novel by an African in the English or French language must in the final analysis have nothing noble enough to recommend its form. A British critic did not equivocate in a London newspaper when he said:

"We are in for a spate of 'quaint' books from Africa written in what almost amounted to 'pidgin English' – this is the new writing of Africa and the only true way in which the African can speak his mind and convey his emotions and environment in the English language."[17]

But the non-'quaint' books from Africa sounded too good to have their sources in Africa. So critics began to find godfathers for the successful or popular African writers. If a book became successful then it must be because the author had an as-yet-undiscovered root in a Western literary tradition, or had all his life been reading the works and philosophies of great Western literary figures, and this is the discovery that the critic made. If it was unsuccessful or it contained the looked-for fetish, then, of course, it became truly African.

In a loosely written book entitled *African English Literature,* Anne Tibble, not satisfied with finding in Amos Tutuola's *Palm Wine Drinkard* episodes which reminded her of 'the money-changers whipped from the Temple' by Jesus, or the 'story of Gomorrah', and 'the Food in reverse', concluded that Tutuola's: "mixing of modern wonders, radios, telephones, guns, and bombers, with Crusoe-Anderson-Treasure Island gnomes, imps, goblins, cudgels, cutlasses, and jungles, openly states his debt to previous tale-tellers. Clearly he has read a great deal of non-African folk and fairy tale. But his mixture of ancient and modern is an added part of his fascination for the young."[18]

Anybody who knows anything about Amos Tutuola's literary background knows that it is misleading to suggest that Tutuola 'clearly has read a great deal of non-African folk and fairy tale' before writing *The Palm Wine Drinkard.* The same is true of Tutuola's 'mixing of ancient and modern'. If one is able to see African literature as a cohesive piece of study which is made more interesting by the changes that it undergoes in its complexion and emphasis as a result of the cultural, historical and social circumstances which act on its existence, then such things as the 'mixing of ancient and modern' would not be difficult to explain. As Okogbule Wonodi pointed out:

"Folk tales are elastic and progressive changes in the modes of behaviour and values are continually filtering into age-old tales ... Age-old stories about oppressed orphans now have the added injustice of the orphans not being sent to school. The moneys used in the tales are no longer cowries but pounds, shillings, and pennies, but by the end of the story, we are back in our familiar world of present-day Nigerian coinage."[19]

It is not because Wonodi is African that he is able to know this. If Anne Tibble had looked to African (indeed Yoruba) oral literature as Tutuola's source and not 'non-African folk and fairy tales' perhaps she could have come to such a simple deduction. Compare Anne Tibble's discussion with E. N. Obiechina's in *Presence Africaine*, No. 65, 1968. But Anne Tibble is not alone in this search for the roots of African literature initiatives outside Africa. Because Chinua Achebe derived the title of his first novel from a poem by W. B. Yeats, Miss A. G. Stock has recently written an article showing the connection between the theme of Achebe's novel and Yeats' vision of history 'as a succession of civilisations, each giving way to another through its own inability to embrace all human impulses satisfactorily within one closed order.'[20] Having made her point, Miss Stock then tries to make token appreciation of Achebe's literary abilities as an original writer within the 'African' context! What can one argue against this case – that *Things Fall Apart* is not the story of Umuofia society (or African civilisation for that matter) giving way to the Western civilisation because of the former's inability to embrace all the indigenous and foreign human impulses satisfactorily within one closed order? Or is one (besides Achebe himself) to argue that Achebe has never been a disciple of Yeats in thought or deed, which is the 'discovery' that Miss Stock has made.

In the same way, J. P. Clark is said to echo the Greek visions of tragedy and reminds many people of T. S. Eliot. Other established African writers possess declared and undeclared 'godfathers' while the emerging ones are waiting to have the critics announce their forebears. It is indeed surprising that no one has made any 'discovery' yet about the connection between African writers and the big grandfathers in American, German, Russian, and Chinese fiction. Would it not be worth while for instance 'discovering' how much Wole Soyinka owes to Neil Simon or Peter Abrahams to Leroi Jones and James Baldwin? (1–4)

...

What many Western critics issue on African literature is a reflection of a profound lack of knowledge about African cultural tradition coupled with an ignorance of the existence, nature and depth of the heritage of African oral literature. In most cases some vague literary background or a landing on an African soil has not been enough to correct this intellectual imbalance.

In spite of some of the consequently unsound views expressed by such critics, African literature has its roots in Africa and is neither an appendage to French or British literature nor yet an African replica of popular Western authors. It should be looked at objectively or not at all.

All this is not to say that African critics are setting themselves up to be the judges here qualified to assess the works of African authors. But perhaps they may be more disposed to offer their views on an African work in order solely to help the reader towards gaining a proper perspective in the author and the realities of his work. The situation as it now exists seems to be that a Peace Corps sojourn, a spell of field work in Africa, a conference on African literature, a graduate studentship in African literature in a Western university, any of these is enough to qualify one as an authority on African literature.

The inescapable consequence of this approach is a literary criticism which has not much to recommend it but either a feeling of smug patronage or outrage towards the African writers – what J. P. Clark has described as 'the jaundice of prejudice and injured pride ... which, because it is a disease comes on the critics without their knowing it'.[21]

Judging from what comes often from the pens of some of these critics, one cannot help but agree with Clark that 'between great learning and great ignorance, the gap is indeed thin'. It may sound like saying that African writers are very sensitive about outside criticism, but it may be best to close here with Chinua Achebe's reply that:

"We are not opposed to criticism but we are getting a little weary of all the special types of criticism which have been designed for us by people whose knowledge of us is very limited."[22] (9–10)

48. SOLOMON O. IYASERE, *Cultural Formalism and the Criticism of Modern African Literature* (1976)

Aus: *The Journal of Modern African Studies*, XIV, 2, (1976), 322–330. – S. O. Iyasere lehrt Englische Literatur in den USA. In der Diskussion um eine angemessene Beurteilung der afrikanischen Literatur konzipiert er im folgenden Text den Begriff des "cultural formalism": Aufgabe des Kritikers ist es, seinen Blick nicht nur dem Kunstcharakter eines literarischen Werkes zuzuwenden, sondern die spezifisch kulturellen Elemente, die in es eingebettet sind, auch der Analyse zu unterziehen. Herausragende Beispiele afrikanischer Literatur halten einer solchen Untersuchung stand.

Our modern, individually inspired literature has evolved from an oral tradition of communal, spontaneous authorship, in which the act of performance was the moment of composition. Nowadays, working in isolation, deliberately rendering and shaping his own vision of a complex social reality, the modern author is free of the demands, limits, and pressures of immediate production, and can revise, collate, and edit his manuscript before presenting it as a fixed text. Creative productions have become, for the most part, individual (if not commercial) activities, with writers employing the impersonal medium of print to reach a wider, more diversified, and unseen audience.

As Adrian Roscoe puts it, 'To persuade with the written word is basically different from persuading with the spoken word and the leap from the oral tradition to the "Gutenburg Galaxy"-bristles with problems'.[23] The direct interplay between audience and artist, between performance and criticism, has become a thing of the past. Contemporary literature has become more formal, more specific, and more complex in both theme and form as authors incorporate their own private, charged, non-referential images and symbols, rather than the discursive, conventional patterns of communal art. Yet, the movement from oral to written literature is only a shift, not a schism.

Creative writing in Africa today is still strongly influenced by the literary traditions of the oral past. As I have stated elsewhere, 'The modern African writer is to his indigenous literary heritage as a snail is to its shell. Even in a foreign habitat, a snail never leaves its shell behind.'[24] Or to put it differently, the African is writing in the modern world with 'one ear bent to the sleeping centuries along the dark road of time'. Consequently, mature writers, such as J. P. Clark, Wole Soyinka, Yambo Ouologuem,[25] Ayi Kwei Armah, and Amos Tutuola, who have produced works of significance, have attached themselves to their own literary heritage in order to give internal integrity and unique form to their fiction.

Thus, the native character of the literature, the 'habit of the works', must be considered in order to determine the nature of the criticism to be applied, especially when this must evolve alongside the literature. A scholar does not merely use a critical technique, but frequently spends a good deal of time reshaping and refining this in response to the new creative challenges encountered. Only through the employment of an appropriate approach can he be able to account for the optimum number of details at their maximum level of significance, and so avoid the pitfall of misinterpreting the universal by misunderstanding the particular. This is one of the greatest weaknesses in much of the criticism of African literature at this time. In his discussion of Amos Tutuola, for example, Gerald Moore simply dismisses the author's use of traditional verbal art, perhaps because an essentially Eurocentric approach cannot account for these uniquely African features.[26]

At times, what seems a flaw in the literature is more accurately a failure in the approach. *The Beautyful Ones Are Not yet Born*[27] appears 'plotless' until we view it in structure and content as an elaborate parable, an artistic device native to the African oral tradition. Furthermore, the maximum intensity of Ayi Kwei Armah's satire is lost without recognition of his use of another technique. Roscoe makes the point that 'Africans have a familiar way of personifying anything, a device which can always be relied on to give flesh and blood life to phenomena otherwise abstract and rather dull'.[28] Armah uses personification in precisely this way, to give flesh and blood life to Koomsoon's corruption:

"His mouth had the rich stench of rotten menstrual blood. The man held his breath until the new smell had gone down in the mixture with the liquid atmosphere of the Party man's farts filling the room. At the same time Koomsoon's insides gave a growl longer than usual, an inner fart of personal, corrupt thunder which in its fullness sounded as if it had rolled down all the way from the eating throat thundering through the belly and the guts, to end in further silent pollution of the air already thick with flatulent fear."[29]

E. N. Obiechina provides the analysis: 'In this brief passage, Koomsoon's corruption is no longer a simple, abstract moral issue. It is corruption given a body, a physical phenomenon which is the more oppressive because the more concrete and all-pervasive.'[30] In similar fashion, other devices borrowed from the oral tradition – such as repetition, proverbs, folk tales, fables, and chants – also control and shape the artistry of *Things Fall Apart* by Chinua Achebe, *The*

Voice by Gabriel Okara, *The Trial of Christopher Okigbo* by Ali Mazrui,[31] and *This Earth, My Brother* by Kofi Awoonor.[32]

Plays, perhaps more than novels, owe heavily to the oral heritage of their authors. *The Strong Breed* by Wole Soyinka, *Three Plays* by J. P. Clark, *Three Yoruba Plays* by Duro Ladipo, and most recently *The Sudden Return and Other Plays* by Martin Owusu,[33] articulate modern dilemmas through the voices of tribal myths, dramatised story-telling, magical ceremonies, religious practices, and historical sagas. While these modern plays maintain a universality of appeal, their particularities, which developed outside the western literary milieu, are a testament to the richness of the dramatic tradition of the African culture. Quite often, the standard western elements of unity of action, balanced plot, or progressive development of characters may be absent. To search for them – let alone to insist on their presence – in all African plays is to miss the point.

For the most part, African drama was not 'staged' as in the West; rather, it was a spontaneous activity in which 'the entire community is the cast and the village square the stage', a traditional mode incorporated by J. P. Clark for the opening of *Ozidi*. Clearly, what is true of plays from Europe may not be true of those from Africa. Aristotle had neither *The Imprisonment of Obatala* nor *The Murder of Adesua*[34] in mind when he conceived *The Poetics*; we cannot presume that any African writer had Shakespeare in mind when he conceived his play. Contrary to established critical views, the general plot and motivation of great tragedies are not the same everywhere, for human nature is not identical the world over. Certainly the Tivs of northern Nigeria are reported to have found Shakespeare's *Hamlet* unintelligible and the Prince of Denmark an object of ridicule.[35]

African literature today is then an amalgamation, a syncreticism, of past and present. The criticism should be the same.[36] The Eurocentric approach did help to establish the importance of African writers by educating the public to the general value of their literature and liberating this from the strong grasp of the cultural anthropologist. For example, initial responses viewed *Things Fall Apart* by Chinua Achebe as only the curious, ethnic reportage of quaint, antique customs. Later, the literary critics called attention to the artistic elements of the novel, and demonstrated that it was a significant work of art. Similar points can be made about *The Palm Wine Drinkard* by Amos Tutuola or *The Interpreters* by Wole Soyinka. For this reason, we ought not discard the benefits which this approach provides. After all, 'one hand cannot wash itself clean; it needs the help of the other'.

What we need in our evaluation of African literature is an approach which encourages what I call 'perceptivism' – a process of getting to know a literary object from a diachronic as well as a synchronic point of view. *Cultural formalism* entails treating African literature as works of art, demanding attention to the formal elements, the *nsaasia* as the Turu would say, while simultaneously forcing the critic, whatever his nationality, to account for the cultural, referential properties embodied in the piece. To do both involves an ongoing education and heightened sensitivity to traditional African literary culture. Any other approach may well lead to the subversion of the specificity of the literature and, consequently, to a bland, commonplace, if not erroneous, evaluation.

Let us consider, for example, the opening lines of Kwesi Brew's poem, 'The Vulture':

> The broken bone cannot be made whole!
> The strong had sheltered their strength
> The swift had sought life in their speed
> The crippled and the tired heaped out of the way.
> Onto the ant hills . . .[37]

Lack of familiarity with the indigenous rhetorical devices of Ghana can lead a critic to view this poem as a mere collection of pithy statements, loosely strung together without coherence or form. Here, however, is a tight if extended proverb, whose central idea is the despairing state of affairs in Ghana. Rather than use straightforward description to convey his vision of social reality, the poet uses situation – again a literary device characteristic of African oral literature – to define and explore the contemporary context. The first line tells of despair if not nihilism, as juxtaposed against the selfishness articulated in line two; the initial hopelessness is then further reinforced by the loss of courage, the death of love and compassion, and the image of the wasteland. The social landscape has both internal integrity of form and effective dramatic development.

Brew's mode of rendition is quite similar to the traditional Yoruba *oriki:* consider, for instance, this extract on the *Ogoga* or King of Ikerre:

> However small the needle, the hen cannot swallow it.
> The toad jumps about happily in the face of the cook.
> Two hundred needles do not equal a hoe, two hundred
> stars do not make a moon.
> The white hair of an albino cannot be dyed,
> A good rider will not be thrown off his horse.[38]

What is striking about this Yoruba poem is its diaphoric structure, what would be to a westerner its unconventional mode of presentation. The central idea, the invulnerability and almost supernatural power of the *Ogoga* of Ikerre, is articulated progressively, but may seem to lack dramatic development and climax in the western sense of those terms. Each verse seems to have no connection with the others, as if needle, hen, toad, cook, moon, albino, rider, and horse were images carelessly thrown together.

On closer inspection, and with an awareness of the poem's traditional function, it is seen to be both well structured and consistently meaningful. All the thoughts are bound together, synthesised into a cohesive whole by the implied referent, the *Ogoga* himself, whose enemies can no more overcome him than the hen can overcome the needle or the cook the toad. Continuing its metaphoric praise, the poem indicates that as 200 needles do not make a hoe, nor 200 stars a moon, so 200 warriors are no match for the *Ogoga*. And it is as impossible to depose him as it is to give colour to an albino's hair or to throw a good rider from his horse.

The formal, traditional elements of these two works give them their aesthetic power and poetic dignity, in addition to their extra-aesthetic authority. An awareness of the function of the rhetorical elements drawn from the oral tradition reveals that these poems are not merely pithy utterances, but deliberate artistic creations.

Cultural formalism, when judiciously and imaginatively employed, can be a penetrating and discriminating tool, albeit with limitations, especially in the hands of the neophyte or the over-zealous ancestralist. This approach can degenerate into merely tracking down and cataloguing the vestiges of the oral tradition, without demonstrating how these elements shape and inform the imaginative life of the work itself. Such is the case with E. Ofori's article on 'Traditionalism in African Literature' which focuses on *Ozidi* by J. P. Clark.[39]

The point we need to bear in mind – seemingly missed by many critics – is that a writer who draws upon the oral tradition does not necessarily make a satisfying artistic creation. Like all formal elements in an original composition, the traditional features must declare their own artistic significance, their own forms, and their own purpose in order to justify their inclusion. Along with the generic and selective fallacies which any abuse of this approach may engender, we must caution ourselves against eclecticism and its inadequate regard for the specificity and integrity of a work.

Nothing useful can be said about a literary piece until we have fastened down the question of its making, its formal particularities, and it is in this pursuit that cultural formalism is best applied. Here we have a valid and responsive approach to the study of African literature. Its successful employment in bringing to readers that heightened sense of understanding – that 'Oh, I can see it now' experience – depends ultimately on the critic's intelligence, his cerebral competence, learning, aesthetic sensibility, judgement, and, above all, his love of literature. (326–330)

49. BRUCE KING, *Thoughts on African Literature* (1976)

Aus: *West African Journal of Modern Languages*, 2 (1976), 11–17. – Bruce King (geb. 1933) aus den USA studierte an der Columbia University und erwarb seinen Doktorgrad an der Leeds University. Er unterrichtete Englische und Commonwealth Literatur in England, Frankreich, Kanada, Nigeria und Neuseeland. Neben Veröffentlichungen über die englische Literatur des 17. Jahrhunderts edierte er drei Sammelbände über afrikanische und westindische Literatur sowie *Literatures of the World in English* (1974). Im folgenden Text argumentiert King, daß die afrikanische Literatur in englischer Sprache vor allem aus dem Widerspruch zwischen der durch westliche Technologie geprägten neuen Elite, der die Autoren angehören, und ihrer Ideologisierung der afrikanischen kulturellen Vergangenheit ihre Dynamik bezogen hat.

The current view of African literature is that it results from cultural contact with the West and is a protest against colonialism and its effects. There are several versions of this theory. There is the historical approach which sees early African writing as apprentice work which later goes through such developments as protest writing, the literature of the independence movement and the postindependence novels of disillusionment. Another version has it that the themes of African literature reflect cultural conflict by showing the various stages of contact with European civilization, although these stages did not necessarily appear sequentially in the development of African literature, but can appear at any time. As in the first version, African literature is seen as moving away from a conscious historical role after political independence freed the African from the burden of colonialism. Both versions assume that an African aesthetic developed along with protest literature, although the second version assumes that such a development is no longer relevant. Thus the contemporary African novel will be similar to the European novel. The trouble with both positions, with which Janheinz Jahn and Charles Larson[40] are identified, is that protest themes are perhaps more prevalent now than ever, although they would seem to be less relevant to the actual political situation. Recent African writing continues to proclaim African values and even more consciously expresses an African aesthetic. We need to account for this.

The first step is to forget our assumption that African literature has to do with black and white cultural and political contact. While I cannot deny that much writing especially of the period before independence has such subject matter, it is absurd to assume that colonialism and its effects is the continuing dynamic behind African literature. The continuing effect to Europe on Africa is technological; it is technology that changes society and culture.

We need to bear in mind that modern printed writing is a foreign technology which has been mastered by a westernized African elite. Many of the tensions and the dynamism of African writing have their origins in this fact. In a sense, modern African literature, especially if written in European languages, is a reflection of a rising class that by mastering western technology and ideologies became the founders and the masters of the new African national states. Such a statement of course, needs a good deal of qualification of a kind that is impossible to make here. I am conscious that such a view does not take into account the influence of oral literature on African poetry. But the fact remains that the modern African novel, poem or drama is a product of a mind strongly influenced by western literary forms and goals even when the work itself does not have a western significance. The very act of mastering writing, whether in English or a vernacular language, and creating a manuscript for a printer means the internalization of cultural changes. Tutuola's novels are, along with the Onitsha chap books, evidence of such cultural transition at a lower social level.

That modern African literature has developed alongside a governing class can be shown by considering the number of writers who have also been political leaders. From the eighteenth century onwards, the movements towards reassertion of African cultural and political identity – whether in the resettlement movements, the Victorian nationalists, or the twentieth century Negritudists – could only be effective within a European political context and demanded propaganda aimed at the western conscience. Similarly, within Africa the leaders of the mass movements had to appeal to westernized concepts of nation, race, equality and freedom, rather than tribal and community identity. Political effectiveness could only be achieved by those with western education. This produced writers who were also politicians, many of whom are now respected and sometimes rejected fathers of modern Africa. Neto[41] is perhaps the most recent example of a writer who is also a political leader.

An elite creates an ideology; an ideology often disguises reality. The westernized elite proclaimed the value and nature of African culture, although it was often foreign to or only partly at home with such traditions. The ideology had the advantage both of offering resistance to colonialism, with its assumption of cultural surperiority, and enlisting into supporters of the elite those who were making the transition from traditional to modern society. Thus there was a basic paradox within the growth of African literature. Only a westernized elite could lay the foundations for independence and create the concept of a modern state and run it. Its power was based on mastery of western processes and on enlisting growing westernized urban masses. At the same time its ideology had to speak of a return to African values, traditional life, the rejection of western influence. The elite and those it enlisted thus assumed an opposition between African and western modes while in fact showing their compatibility.

This paradox, I suggest, is the basic tension at the heart of African literature. It provided the dynamic for its growth, which has largely been new movements growing out of seeming contradictions within the older movements, and which in turn will give birth to newer movements shaped by the same paradox. These new movements represent different generations recruited into an increasingly industrialized society. Thus each generation will catch the discrepancy between what is said and what is done by its elders. It will be both more at home with foreign technology, expect what were once western luxuries, and will insist upon greater African authenticity, often accusing its elders of failure or corruption. (11–12)

...

It is tempting to speak of the development of recent African literature in terms of class and politics. Thus the growing bourgeoisie led the populace to throw out the colonialists, but the bourgeoisie upon gaining power failed to meet the aspirations of the populace and became the new colonialists. In this situation the writer, as a voice of the nation, becomes alienated and a critic of the new Africa. While such an analysis throws some light on the recent literature of disillusionment, it does not take into account that the writers themselves are part of the elite and bourgeoisie. Perhaps only Sembene Ousmane expresses the views of a labouring class growing into greater political awareness. In most other writings we are aware of a growing individualism and alienation, mixed with a vague desire for authenticity. (13)

...

Two major themes of African literature, besides the attack on colonialism and neocolonialism, are national corruption and the corrupting desire for western material objects which destroys African spiritual values. These themes are related and are a result of contact with western technology and its effects on traditional values. It is, however, obvious that the modern African state is committed to satisfying the demand for 'things'. The modern African writer is not a rich business man or a politican, but as a member of the elite, he is also a product of a culture increasingly concerned with luxuries. The traditional theme of the corruption of African values by western things (whether in *The Beautyful Ones Are Not Yet Born, Ambiguous Adventure*,[42] or *No Longer at Ease*) should be seen as reflecting a crisis of conscience (both moral and of awareness) within the elite.

Because of p'Bitek and Achebe we commonly speak of the African writer's roots in the oral communal tradition. But the African writer is an individual who adopts the communal pose both as a literary technique and for an ideological purpose. In a sense he is similar to the Europe intellectuals who have since the early nineteenth century opposed the cultural and social effects of industrialization by either idealizing a harmonious agricultural society of the past or by envisaging some future Utopia. It is noticeable that in European writing the same basic criticism of the effects of industrialization may make a writer conservative (praising the past) or radical (envisaging a future Utopia). Often both kinds of values exist side by side. A future communal or communist society is seen as a recreation of past values. In Africa there is a similar pattern; the nostalgia for an idealized communal past is held simultaneously with a political radicalism that envisages a future socialist society on a continental scale. Somehow the values of the villager tribe are to be recreated through industrialization and a highly complex structuring of society. While it is good that such a vision should be posited as an African authenticity in contrast to the worship of individualism and material wealth it may also show part of the elite becoming alienated from its own class values. If so the radical African writer is analogous to the European bourgeois rebel.

Looked at in this way, modern African literature can be seen as an expression and criticism of the new elite, the growing middle class and the westernized city dwellers who as a result of the colonial experience have become the rulers and set the style of modern Africa. However there is a fundamental contradiction between the ideology expressed by most writers and their own position as artists. The dominant ideology has claimed to represent the community, but the writer himself as part of the western educated elite is separate from the masses he claims to represent. Indeed the writer has seen his job as creating the consciousness of the African people, which means transforming it into an identity desired by intellectuals. If, as seems likely, popular aspirations are for westernized luxuries and individual social advancement within a developing industrial society, the writer, committed to a nostalgic view of the past, cannot help but become a critic of his society. Thus the alienation we notice in recent African literature. Yet, this alienation is, ironically, in itself western (in contrast to communal African social values) and no doubt influences the increasingly strident calls for a return to authenticity, communal values, and an African socialism. These contradictions can be traced at least as far back as E. Casely-Hayford's *Ethiopia Unbound* (1911), which both praises traditional village life and calls for the establishment of an African university to train new leaders of society. If such an observation is correct, the moral crisis of the African writer will produce a continuing desire for authenticity, sporadic idealizations of the past, a growing alienated individualism, increased criticism of existing institutions and a radical political stance. (13–14)

...

I do not think the increasing influence of foreign technology on society and culture will result in African literature being like that found elsewhere. Besides treating of the past and of future hopes, African literature will be concerned with the specifics of how a society develops, as living cultural traditions come under new pressure. It is the tension between the new and the old, whether in explicit or implied values, which is likely to be a rich area for the literary imagination. The recognition of such tension, with its opposing claims, is not the same as the idealization of the past. This provides us with a rule. Modern African literature set in the past should be seen as fictionalized transformations of contemporary problems or, if idealizations, as related to contemporary ideological needs. Thus *Things Fall Apart* reflects many of the same social tensions as *No Longer at Ease*. The portrayal of village life in *The Great Ponds* and the irony of its ending may be said to express both nostalgia for the past and an awareness that such a society is impossible for modern Nigeria.

...

When will this process end? It is doubtful that it will in the near future. The reaction against industrialization has continued in western literature for two centuries as has the development of symbolism and various formalistic techniques that reflect, if only by protest, the growth of urban industrial society and its effects on the individual and community. It is, however, probable that another literary tradition will develop alongside the patterns we have noticed. While it is necessary to record traditional Africa before it has been transformed beyond memory by the growth of a modern industrial Africa, the continuing emphasis given the past is in itself reactionary. There is a modern Africa of industrial workers, professionals, soldiers, businessmen, civil servants, intellectuals, politicians, teachers and villagers making the transition from traditional to modern society. If art is an imitation of nature, the problems, conflicts, decisions and lives of such people would seem logical subjects for a contemporary African literature. Such an art would require a different, more realistic aesthetic from that which has prevailed. While the main line of modern African literature has been the pastoral nostalgia of Senghor, Laye, and Achebe, it is possible that in the near future authors will learn their craft from such classic writers but will see their subject-matter as a development of the territory explored by the Onitsha pamphlet, Ekwensi and Ousmane. There is no assurance, however, that such writing will be better. The great modern classics of European literature are less often shaped by realism than by reactionary mythologies. It is possible that the realistic aesthetic will develop in television plays rather than novels and poems. (16–17)

50. FEMI OJO-ADE, *Subjectivity and Objectivity in the Criticism of Neo-African Literature* (1977)

Aus: *African Perspectives*, 1 (1977), 43–54. – Ojo-Ade (geb. 1943) aus Nigeria studierte in Nigeria und Kanada und unterrichtete in den USA, Kanada und Nigeria. Er publizierte Essays und Bücher über Schwarze Literatur und Kultur. Im folgenden Text vertritt er die Auffassung, daß sich die afrikanische Literatur in Englisch nach nur kurzer Zeit einen Platz innerhalb der Weltliteratur erobert habe.

Neo-African literature has won a battle – the battle for survival and for recognition. Its identity as an important continental literature having its own autonomous existence with distinct qualities of its own has been fairly well established. It is reviewed and analysed in learned journals and papers along with literatures from other continents. It has its own specialized journals in and outside Africa.[43] It has found its way into the curricula of African and non-African schools and Universities. In most Universities in Africa, America and Europe, it now has its own autonomous departments.[44]

The stereotyped ideas and disparaging myths held about Africa, which had formed the ugly basis upon which the first European critics had assessed African literature are gradually disappearing. The Black or African prototype – the barbaric, the exotic, the intuitive, the naive, the intellectually defective – invented and propagated by European negrophobists which has, for quite a time, influenced the appraisal given of African writers and their works and which seems to have dominated the creative writings on Africa by most non-Africans has now been reversed.[45] African writers and the characters created by them are now seen to be dynamic social beings with basic human qualities and complexities. The one-sided and inferior standards, (as compared with the critical parameters used by Western critics in evaluating and judging Western authors) built on a feeling of superiority which pushed the first metropolitan critics and reviewers to condemn excellent writers, to award exaggerated accolades to inferior writers, to accord blanket critical acclaim to second-rate novels and which made certain Western critics to consider such a writer as Tutuola as writing 'a naive non-English', 'a sort of young English' judged to be 'delightfully fresh and admirable', – all loose and weightless euphemisms – have now been thrown overboard. Tutuola's style, which was considered in the fifties by reviewers (cf. Lindfors 1975a)[46] to be the stylistic pattern of future Anglophone African writers, has been proved to be distinctly 'Tutuolan', so too has the creative independence of African writers been fairly well established. Paternalistic, condescending and sympathetic criticism is gradually becoming a thing of the past and is being displaced, especially on the part of non-African critics, by a more honest and a more open-minded approach which strives to take cognizance of the specificity and the internal characteristics of the African literature.

It is gradually being acknowledged too that, as in every authentic literary experience, every African writer, whatever his indebtedness to metropolitan writers and whatever his structural or stylistic borrowings from these literary 'giants' has a style, a creative approach and a conception of life quite distinct from these writers. Every African writer deals with specific themes which are dependent on his conception of man and society, his convictions and his interests, and which are given a distinctive pattern that is shaped by his literary and intellectual background, his linguistic competence and his creative ability. Very often, the same author gives new dimensions to his techniques and style in subsequent writings. Early Okigbo is not the same as later Okigbo; early Soyinka differs from later Soyinka. So too it is with many other African writers. Social awareness, the dynamics of politics, creative maturity and value-judgements of critics are some of the factors which influence these new orientations.

Instead of having to set African writers against non-African models or literary fore-fathers as it was most often done until about a decade ago when the comparison of techniques was generally established with non-African writing, African writers can now be compared one with another (though it will be foolhardy to say that consideration should not be given to the influence of European writers on African writers). The diversity, vitality and number of writings coming out daily from Africa, especially since the early fifties, allows this comparison.[47] Moreover, individual writers are now evaluated in terms of what they create and what they attempt as can seen in monograph studies of individual writers which combine factual materials especially biography with evaluation and analysis.[48] This evaluation is often made against the regional peculiarity, the ethical and cultural idiosyncracies which furnish the writers with their raw materials and which show how every region and indeed every ethnic entity of Africa is beginning to produce a literature with distinctive energies of its own, fully conditioned by all the multifarious facets of life, manners of expression, the world-view and the existentialist consciousness of the community to which each author belongs. This unity in diversity confirms Achebe's definition of African literature as 'the sum total of all the national and ethnic literatures of Africa.'

In the assessment of these literatures, reasonable elasticity is being given to the peculiarity of the African writer who is first and foremost a bilingual or even trilingual writer having most often to convey his literary experience in a foreign language in which limited competence reflects less than half of his total linguistic and cultural experience. This situation reveals concomitant effects on style – syntax, fluency, transference into European language of local imagery, figures of speech and of local expressions like proverbs, idioms, slangs and riddles. The literary accuracy and effectiveness of the style of such a non-monolingual writer, his use of pidgin English (or of any bastardized version of any other European language), his ability or inability to produce the right register in English for a character who, in certain situations, is naturally expected to speak an African language are some of the factors taken into consideration in assessing the literary quality of the African writer. Also considered is the impact on African written literature, especially the works of the first generation of writers, of oral literature which is defined by its own aesthetics and which among other features embraces oral poetry, non-oral poetry, ritual and secular drama, narratives, proverbs, palavers, folklore, legends and myths which define the African's mental landscape, cultural resources and also his traditional life. While a critic like Roland Christ (1967) felt unhappy at Achebe's use of proverbs which for him are meaninglessly used, another non-African critic, Gerald Moore, had earlier on expressed a contrary view when he stated that Achebe uses oral tradition, including proverbs, 'to make life before us more actual, to surround it with its own dignity, beauty or cruelty in its own moment of time and place.'[49]

For a fuller understanding of Neo-African literature, the need has been felt to be very intimated with the socio-cultural or the politico-cultural backgrounds from which the work springs, since every work of art, as Malcolm Bradbury (1970 : 17)[50] aptly says, is 'a resonant centre of substantiated and lived-through values', and so grows out of the collective experience, the reservoir of ideas and experiences of the total consciousness of the society in which the author lives. It is therefore the customs, superstitions, attitudes, outlooks and psyche of the Africans in the society from which the work originates which supply the socio-cultural atmosphere to the creative work and which illuminate African literary phenomena.

Again, in addition to the non-African critics who dominated the criticism of African literature up to the early sixties, Africans who see the works of their fellow Africans from inside and who live some of the experiences portrayed in the work are now producing illuminating in-depth studies on the cultural peculiarities implicit in the works as well as on the stylistic and technical devices adopted by each author (see Obiechina 1975)[51]. Even those other Africans who do not share identical ethnic backgrounds with particular writers but who understand the African psyche more than those who depend solely on written documents to understand the African mind have also been producing excellent critical materials. Moreover, it has now been revealed that in African Universities particularly, more than half of those who had originally specialised in non-African literature have crossed over to African literature. This 'desertion' has produced beneficial results for African literature. Africans are therefore getting more and more deeply involved in the assessment of their own literature and have been helping the public (both African and non-African) to move nearer to the understanding of what African literature is saying and the way the authors have been saying it.

Apart from winning for itself a pride of place in the world of literatures, establishing its stylistic and socio-cultural distinctness and showing its own laws and devices, African literature has somehow established its thematic pattern. Pre-independence anti-colonial literature has shown its thematic preoccupations as centering around the assertion of cultural identity, socio-cultural alienation and conflict, propaganda and revolt. This literature of protest, which is interpretative, analytical and satirical, differs a little bit from post-independence literature in the sense that while the former is directed against colonialism and its agents, post-colonial literature is directed against Africans themselves by concentrating on internal political and social problems – corruption, tribalism, greed and bribery and by seeking to examine African psyche and institutions. In the main, this has been a literature of self-examination and self-questioning (cf. Lindfors 1971a; Obiechina 1969).[52] (43–46)

ANMERKUNGEN

Anmerkungen zur Einleitung

[1] Janheinz Jahn, *Geschichte der neoafrikanischen Literatur* (Düsseldorf, 1966); *A History of Neo-African Literature* (London, 1968); Gerald Moore, *The Chosen Tongue* (London, 1969); Kofi Awoonor, *The Breast of the Earth* (Garden City, 1971); O. R. Dathorne, *The Black Mind* (Minneapolis, 1974); repr. *African Literature in the Twentieth Century* (London, 1976); Joachim Fiebach, *Kunstprozesse in Afrika* (Berlin-Ost, 1979); repr. *Literaturen der Befreiung in Afrika* (München, 1979)

[2] Etwa 95% der rund 1000 Autoren, deren Werke seit Ende des 18. Jahrhunderts bis 1970 erschienen, "made their debut after 1920". Per Wästberg, "Themes in African Literature Today", *Daedalus*, CIII (Spring 1974), 136

[3] G. Moore, *The Chosen Tongue* (London, 1969), XII

[4] Cf. Text 15

[5] Edward Wilmot Blyden, "Inaugural Address as President of Liberia College", in: Wilfred Cartey and Martin Kilson (eds.), *The African Reader.* Independent Africa, vol. 2 (New York, 1970), 44

[6] Cf. Text 24

[7] Eine Textsammlung legte vor: O. Mezu (comp.), *Igbo Market Literature*, 5 vols. (Buffalo, 1972); eine Auswahl edierte: E. N. Obiechina, *Onitsha Market Literature* (London, 1972); Cf. Text 9

[8] Cf. Text 37

[9] Wole Soyinka, "The Writer in an African State", *Transition*, VI, 31 (1967), 12; "From a Common Backcloth", *American Scholar*, 32 (1963), 390. Soyinka, Dramatiker, Dichter, Romancier und Literaturkritiker leitet das Drama Department der University of Ife. Inhaftiert von 1967–1969 veröffentlichte er nach der Freilassung *The Man Died* (London, 1972; repr. 1973, 1974)

[10] Cf. Text 10

[11] Cf. Text 38

[12] Cf. Bernth Lindfors (ed.), *Critical Perspectives on Amos Tutuola* (Washington, D. C., 1975), 29 ff.

[13] Cf. Lindfors, *op. cit.*

[14] Duro Ladipo, *Three Yoruba Plays* ("Oba Koso", "Oba Waja", "Oba Moro") (Ibadan, 1964); cf. Ulli Beier (ed.), *Three Nigerian Plays* (London, 1967; repr. 1970)

[15] Cf. Text 25; cf. Arthur Ravenscroft, African Literature V: "Novels of Disillusionment", *The Journal of Commonwealth Literature*, 6 (1969), 122–137

[16] Cf. Texte 26, 39 und 40

[17] Christopher Okigbo, *Labyrinths with Path of Thunder* (London, 1971)

[18] Aíyetoro (= everything is at peace) ist eine Kommune, die 1947 von Fischern im Südosten Nigerias gegründet wurde. Auf ihre zentralen wirtschaftlichen, religiösen und sozialen Ideen greift Soyinka in seinem Roman zurück. Cf. [Anon.], "Aiyetoro", *Nigeria Magazine*, 55 (1957), 356–386

[19] Cf. Kanti, C. G. (ed.), *Modern Poetry from Zambia* (Lusaka, 1975); Dep. of English, Univ. of Malawi, *Theatre in Malawi 1970–1976* (1978); Okpure, Obuke O., "Characterization in Zambian Literature", *Busara*, VIII, 2 (1978), 68–80; cf. auch die Zeitschrift *Outlook* aus Malawi

[20] J. P. O'Flinn, "Towards a Sociology of the Nigerian Novel", in: E. D. Jones (ed.), *African Literature Today*, 7 (1975), 34–35; D. Riemenschneider, "Die anglophone Literatur der siebziger Jahre", *Zeitschrift für Kulturaustausch*, 29, 2 (1979), 167–182

Anmerkungen zu Kapitel 1

1 Mulk Raj Anand (geb. 1905) aus Indien ist einer der produktivsten Autoren in englischer Sprache. Veröffentlichte Romane, Kurzgeschichten und Essays, u. a. *Untouchable* (London, 1935) und *Coolie* (London, 1936)
2 Lin Yu Tang (geb. 1895) aus China veröffentlichte u. a. *The Red Peony* (1962)
3 Phebean Iyatemi and P. Gurrey (eds.), *Folk Tales and Fables* (London, 1959)
4 There have been few general studies of written African prose, though articles have appeared, from time to time, in the French periodical *Présence Africaine*, which deal with literature within the general framework of *négritude*. Articles and detailed reviews of books by African authors also appear in the periodical *Black Orpheus*. See also *Approaches to African Literature*, by J. Jahn und J. Ramsaran. Jahn's contribution is expanded somewhat in his *Muntu*, Faber (English version), 1961 [Anm. im Text]
5 Even to-day in some African territories "suitability for schools" is still one of the most potent means of securing publication. [Anm. im Text]
6 S.P.C.K.: Society for the Promotion of Christian Knowledge, gegründet 1698 in London
7 The main works of these authors to date are as follows: A. Tutuola, *The Palm-Wine Drinkard*, Faber, 1952; *My Life in the Bush of Ghosts*, Faber, 1954; *Simbi and the Satyr of the Dark Jungle*, Faber, 1955; *The Brave African Huntress*, Faber, 1958; D. O. Fagunwa, *Ogboju-ode-ninu igbo Irunmale*, Nelson, 1939; *Igbo Oludumare*, Nelson, 1946 (?); C. O. D. Ekwensi, *People of the City*, Dakers, 1954; *Jagua Nana*, Hutchinson, 1961; C. Achebe, *Things Fall Apart*, Heinemann, 1958; *No Longer at Ease*, 1960. [Anm. im Text]
8 Richard Rive (geb. 1931) studierte in Südafrika, den USA und England. Er veröffentlichte Romane und Kurzgeschichten und edierte *Modern African Prose* (London, 1964); repr. 1965–1978
9 Graham Greene, *The Heart of the Matter*, (London, 1948)
10 Donatus Nwoga (geb. 1933) lehrt Englische Literatur an der University of Nigeria in Nsukka und veröffentlichte eine Reihe kritischer Studien zur afrikanischen Literatur
11 Joyce Cary (1888–1957) veröffentlichte in Afrika spielende Romane, u. a. *Aissa Saved* (1932), *The African Witch* (London, 1936) und *Mister Johnson* (London, 1939)
12 Arthur Ravenscroft lehrt Englische Literatur an der University of Leeds und edierte *The Journal of Commonwealth Literature*
13 Gerald Moore (geb. 1924) studierte in Cambridge, lehrte in Nigeria, Uganda, an der University of Sussex, publizierte Essays und Bücher über afrikanische Literatur und übersetzte afrikanische Romane aus dem Französischen ins Englische
14 Doris Lessing, (geb. 1919) aus Südrhodesien (Simbabwe) lebt seit 1949 in England. Ihr erster Roman *The Grass is Singing* (London, 1950) spielt in den dreißiger und vierziger Jahren in Südrhodesien
15 Joseph E. Kariuki (geb. 1931) aus Kenia studierte in Uganda und England und veröffentlichte Gedichte
16 Alfonso Álvares veröffentlichte Werke in portugiesischer Sprache im 17. Jh.
17 Gerald Moore, *Seven African Writers* (London, 1962), 46 ff. [Anm. im Text]. Moores Buch ist die erste umfassende Studie einiger afrikanischer Autoren (u. a. Tutuola, Achebe und Mphahlele)
18 See the article "African Twilight: Folktale and Myth in Nigerian Literature" in *Ibadan*, No. 15, March 1963, pp. 17–19. John Ramsaran is of course right but it ought to be stated that the prejudice against the folk-tale as oral literature (or its not being recognized as such) until six or seven years ago was entirely due to its close association with social anthropology and European interest in Africana exotica. Now that old resentments have given place to more positive reassessments, young African writers are finding that anthropology far from being an enemy could be turned into a useful friend. In

Anmerkungen zu Kapitel 1   209

no aspect of African life is this more demonstrable than in the field of oral tradition. [Anm. im Text]
[19] See: *The Long Revolution,* 64 ff. [Anm. im Text]
[20] A conference of teachers of English held in the Institute of Education and the Department of English, University of Ibadan, between 26 April and 1 May, 1965 came to the conclusion that "traditional material of folk tale, myth and legend is so intimately connected with the life of Africa, that some knowledge of it is necessary to an intelligent understanding of certain areas of African creative writing" and that "quite a few of the writers of today must be influenced consciously or otherwise by the work of traditional artists like story tellers and praisesingers". See *Cultural Events in Africa,* No. 6 of May, 1965, for Professor D. E. S. Maxwell's account of the Conference. [Anm. im Text]
[21] *Op. cit.,* 335 [Anm. im Text]
Goody and Watt, "The Consequences of Literacy", Jack Goody (ed.), *Literacy in Traditional Society* (Cambridge, 1968), 27–68
[22] Das East African Literature Bureau wurde 1948 gegründet, war der East African Community unterstellt und verfügte über Zweigstellen in Dar-es-Salaam und Nairobi
[23] East African Publishing House, gegründet gegen Ende der vierziger Jahre, ein afrikanisches Unternehmen, veröffentlichte bis 1975 vierhundert Titel
[24] Grace Ogot (geb. 1930) aus Kenia studierte in Uganda und England, arbeitete in staatlichen Institutionen und für B.B.C. Sie veröffentlichte den Roman *The Promised Land* (Nairobi, 1966) und eine Sammlung von Kurzgeschichten, *Land Without Thunder* (Nairobi, 1968)
[25] Die Acoli leben im Norden Ugandas. p'Bitek schrieb seinen ersten Roman, *Lak Tar* (1953) in seiner Muttersprache Acoli
[26] *Equiano's Travels* (London, 1789), abridged edition edited by Paul Edwards (London, 1967) [Anm. im Text]
[27] Samuel Crowther, *Experiences with Heathens and Mohammedans in West Africa* (SPCK, 1892) [Anm. im Text]
[28] Alex Quaison-Sackey, *Africa Unbound: Reflections of an African Statesman* (London, 1963) [Anm. im Text]
[29] T. M. Aluko (geb. 1918) aus Nigeria studierte in Ibadan und London. Er arbeitete als Beamter in Nigeria. Bisher veröffentlichte er fünf Romane, u. a. *One Man, One Matchet* (London, 1965) und *His Worshipful Majesty* (London, 1973)
[30] Akiki Nyabongo, *Africa Answers Back* (London, 1936) [Anm. im Text]
[31] Stanlake Samkange, *On Trial for My Country* (London, 1966) [Anm. im Text]
[32] It is perhaps worth noting that most of these writers took up some form of editorial work later in their career. Michael Echeruo was responsible for the first and only number of *The African Writer* in 1962, and a special issue of *The Conch* in 1971. *Black Orpheus* had as co-editor Wole Soyinka from 1960 to 1963, and J. P. Clark from 1968 to 1972. Chinua Achebe edited a campus radical magazine called *Nsukkascope* at the University of Nigeria during 1971–2, and is still responsible for *Okike,* a literary magazine he founded in 1971; he has also served for a decade as an advisory editor for Heinemann's African Writers Series. [Anm. im Text]
M. J. C. Echeruo (geb. 1937) aus Nigeria lehrt Englische Literatur an der University of Ibadan und veröffentlichte eine Gedichtanthologie, *Mortality* (London, 1968)
[33] For an early article on these publications, see Anon. (J. A. Ramsaran), 'Nigerian School Journals: key to nationhood', *The Times Educational Supplement* (London, 25 April 1968), 639. I was able to consult many of these journals at the library of the University of Ibadan while doing research in Nigeria during 1972–3 on a Fellowship from the National Endowment for the Humanities. [Anm. im Text]
[34] This estimate is based on information in *Nigerian Periodicals and Newspapers, 1950–1970* (Ibadan, 1971), 49. Information on other journals cited in this article can also be found in this source. [Anm. im Text]
[35] T. I. Olorunyomi, *The Andrian* (January 1964), 9–10 [Anm. im Text]

³⁶ John K. Jegede, "School Magazines", *The Oyemekun*, 1,2 (1957), 9–10 [Anm. im Text]
³⁷ Willspeare, "'Julius Caesar' in Sinemascope", *The Beacon*, 1,2 (1957), 9–10 [Anm. im Text]
³⁸ Martin Banham and Clive Wake, *African Theatre Today* (London, 1976) enthält einen knappen Überblick und eine Bibliographie über das moderne afrikanische Theater
³⁹ Aig Higo publizierte Gedichte in verschiedenen Anthologien. Er arbeitet für den Verlag Heinemann in Nigeria.
Frank Aig-Imoukhuede (geb. 1935) veröffentlichte Gedichte in verschiedenen Anthologien
Abiola Irele (geb. 1936) lehrte Französische Literatur in Ghana, Nigeria und Senegal und ist einer der profiliertesten Kritiker afrikanischer Literatur
Kalu Uka aus Nigeria leitete eine Theatergruppe und veröffentlichte Gedichte in *Okike*
Omolara Leslie lehrt Englische Literatur an der University of Ibadan
Okogbule Nwanodi (geb. 1936), *Icheke and Other Poems* (Ibadan, 1965)

Anmerkungen zu Kapitel 2

¹ Col. Ord's Report on the Condition of the British Settlement, West Coast of Africa – Sierra Leone. [Anm. im Text]
² Das "East African Protectorate"(E.A.P.) wurde 1895 etabliert und umfaßte das Gebiet vom Rift Valley bis zur Küste. 1920 erhielt es die Bezeichnung "Kenya"
³ Freretown, eine Gründung der C.M.S. für befreite Sklaven in der Nähe von Mombasa
⁴ "shamba" = Feld
⁵ Bishop Crowther (ca. 1807–1891); nach seiner Befreiung als Sklave 1822 erhielt er eine Ausbildung in Theologie und wurde der erste afrikanische Bischof
Bishop Oluwole aus Nigeria leitete die Lagos Grammar School
⁶ Hampton Normal and Agricultural Institute in der Nähe von Richmond, Virginia, wurde 1868 gegründet und diente der Ausbildung ehemaliger Sklaven
⁷ Tuskegee Normal and Industrial Institute wurde 1881 von Booker T. Washington (1856–1915) gegründet und diente der industriellen Ausbildung der schwarzen Bevölkerung in den USA
⁸ Count Gobineau (1862–1882), *Essai sur l'égalité des races humaines*, 4 vols. (Paris 1853/1855)
Benjamin Kidd, *Social Evolution* (London, 1894)
Lothrop Stoddard, *The Rising Tide of Color Against White World-Supremacy* (London, 1922)
⁹ Gordon Memorial College, Khartoum, gegründet als "Primary School" 1902, wurde 1911 die erste sudanesische "Secondary School"
¹⁰ Jack Woddis, *Africa, the Roots of Revolt* (London, 1960), 157 [Anm. im Text]
¹¹ *ibid.* [Anm. im Text]
¹² Leonard Barnes, *Empire or Democracy?* (London, 1939), 141 [Anm. im Text]
¹³ Frantz Fanon (1925–1961) veröffentlichte u. a. *Peau Noire, masques blancs* (Paris, 1952), *Les damnés de la terre* (Paris, 1961) und *Pour la Révolution Africaine* (Paris, 1964)
¹⁴ Michael Young's *The Rise of the Meritocracy* (Penguin, 1958) is a brilliant satire and analysis of the consequence of socialist and "progressive" educational reforms in Britain. His structures apply even more forcibly to the Third World and the "people's democracies" where intellectual criticism exists in much purer form than in "capitalist" countries. France is probably the only capitalist country where the technocratic and bureaucratic intelligentsia has consistently payed a major leadership role during the last century. [Anm. im Text]
¹⁵ Paul Theroux, "Hating the Asians", *Transition*, 33 (1967), 46 [Anm. im Text]

¹⁶ See Chapter V for discussion of the early years at Ibadan University College [Anm. im Text]
¹⁷ Ashby, *Universities: British, Indian and African*, (Harvard, U. P., 1966), 246–247 [Anm. im Text]
¹⁸ *Report of the Conference on the Development of Higher Education in Africa*, UNESCO Conference, Tananarive, September 3rd–12th, 1962, (UNESCO, 1963), 49 [Anm. im Text]
¹⁹ Die Ashby Commission legte 1960 einen Bericht über "post school certificate and higher education in Nigeria" vor, in dem u. a. die Gründung von Universitäten vorgeschlagen wird
²⁰ See Chapter VIII for the recommendations of the Ashby Commission [Anm. im Text]
²¹ See Chapter XII for details of the inadequacy of the sixth form [Anm. im Text]

Anmerkungen zu Kapitel 3

¹ Prince of Wales College, Achimota (Ghana), gegründet 1925. King's College, Lagos, gegründet 1909
² "avatar" (Sanskrit avatara): Inkarnation einer Gottheit; im Hinduismus bes. Vishnus
³ Cf. Beaubrun, Theodore [called Languichatte], *Anna*; comédie locale en 2 actes (Port-au-Prince, Haiti, 1962)
⁴ Voodoo: cf. Janheinz Jahn, *Muntu* (New York, 1961), 28–39
⁵ Ghana Association of Writers wurde 1875 gegründet
⁶ B. W. Vilakazi (1906–1947), "In the Gold Mines"; veröffentlichte Gedichte in verschiedenen Anthologien
⁷ David Diop (1927–1960) aus Senegal veröffentlichte einen Gedichtband *Coups de pilon* (Paris, 1961)
⁸ Thomas Mofolo (1875?–1948) aus Lesotho publizierte in Sesuto *Chaka: an Historical Romance* (engl. Ausgabe, London, 1931), sowie Erzählungen
Benjamin Akiga aus Nigeria schrieb in Tiv *Akiga's Story: the Tiv Tribe as Seen by One of its Members*, (engl. Übersetzung, London, 1939)
⁹ D. O. Fagunwas (1910–1963) Yorubasage erschien in englischer Übersetzung als *The Forest of a Thousand Demons* (London, 1968)
¹⁰ L. S. Senghor (geb. 1906) aus Senegal, „Mitbegründer" der Négritude, publizierte u. a. *Chants d'Ombre*, (Paris, 1945), *Nocturnes* (Paris, 1961) und *Éthiopiques* (Paris, 1956). Er edierte die wegweisende *Anthologie de la nouvelle poésie nègre et malgache* (Paris, 1948)
Camara Laye (1928–1980) aus Guinea publizierte Romane, u. a. *L'enfent noir* (Paris, 1959), *Le regard du roi* (Paris, 1965) und die Autobiographie *Dramouss* (Paris, 1966)
Birago Diop (1906–1980) aus Senegal veröffentlichte Gedichte und traditionelle Geschichten, die er ins Französische übersetzte
¹¹ William Conton (geb. 1925) aus Gambia veröffentlichte den Roman *The African* (London, 1960)
¹² Peter Abrahams (geb. 1919) aus Südafrika verließ seine Heimat 1939. Seine bekanntesten Romane sind *Mine Boy* (London, 1946) und *A Wreath for Udomo* (London, 1956). 1954 erschien die Autobiographie *Tell Freedom* (London)
¹³ "Language and Theme in *Things Fall Apart*", *A Review of English Literature*, Vol. V, no. 4 (October, 1964), 153 [Anm. im Text]
¹⁴ Ademola, Frances (ed.), *Reflections* (Lagos, 1962)
¹⁵ V. S. Naipaul (geb. 1932) aus Trinidad: *Mr. Stone and the Knights Companion* (London, 1963)
¹⁶ Joyce Cary (1888–1957), *Aissa Saved* (London, 1932), *Mister Johnson* (London, 1939); Margaret Laurence (geb. 1926) aus Kanada: *The Tomorrow Tamers* (Toronto, 1963), *This Side Jordan* (Toronto, 1960). Außerdem publizierte Laurence *Long Drums and Cannons: Nigerian Dramatists and Novelists 1952–1966* (London, 1968)

[17] Wole Soyinkas Gedicht "The Other Immigrant" findet sich in deutscher Übersetzung in Janheinz Jahn, *Schwarzer Orpheus* (München, 1973); "Telephone Conversation" in G. Moore and U. Beier (eds.), *Modern Poetry from Africa* (London, 1963)
[18] John Ekwere aus Nigeria veröffentlichte Gedichte in verschiedenen Anthologien
[19] C. Ekwensi, *Jagua Nana* (London, 1961)
[20] Chinua Achebe, *A Man of the People* (London, 1966)
[21] Wole Soyinka, *Before the Black-out* (Ibadan, n. d. [1965])
[22] Hubert Ogunde (geb. 1916) aus Nigeria ist einer der Pioniere der Yoruba "folk opera". Achebe bezieht sich auf *Yoruba Ronu* (Lagos, 1964). Das Stück wurde in Westnigeria verboten
[23] Chief S. Akintola war Premierminister der Westregion bis zum Militärputsch 1966
[24] Premierminister Nigerias war N. Azikiwe von 1963-1966; cf. Text 19
[25] In der Ostregion Nigerias stellen die Ibos den größten Bevölkerungsanteil
[26] David Diop, "The Time of Martyrdom" in: David Mandessi Diop, *Hammer Blows* (London, 1973), 41
[27] There were romours at this time that Soyinka had died in prison. [Anm. im Text]
[28] Biafra, die Eastern Region Nigerias, erklärte 1967 einseitig ihre Unabhängigkeit und ergab sich nach zweieinhalbjährigem Krieg 1970 der Zentralregierung von Nigeria
[29] Onuora Nzekwu (geb. 1928) aus Nigeria veröffentlichte Kurzgeschichten und Romane, u. a. *Wand of Noble Wood* (London, 1961) und *Highlife for Lizards* (London, 1965)
[30] Nkem Nwankwo (geb. 1936) aus Nigeria schrieb die Romane *Danda* (London, 1964) und *My Mercedes is Bigger than Yours* (London, 1975)
[31] John Munonye (geb. 1929) aus Nigeria ist neben Ekwensi und Aluko einer der produktivsten Romanciers seines Landes; u. a. erschienen *The Only Son* (London, 1966), *A Wreath for the Maidens* (London, 1973), *Bridge to a Wedding* (London, 1978)
[32] V. C. Ike (geb. 1931) aus Nigeria veröffentlichte eine Reihe von Romanen, u. a. *Toads for Supper* (London, 1965), *The Naked Gods* (London, 1970) und *The Chicken Chasers* (London, 1980)
[33] Flora Nwapa (geb. 1931) aus Nigeria schrieb 2 Romane: *Efuru* (London, 1966) und *Idu* (London, 1969)
[34] Frank K. Parkes (geb. 1932) aus Ghana veröffentlichte die Gedichtanthologie *Songs from the Wilderness* (London, 1965)
[35] Efua Morgue [Efua Sutherland] (geb. 1924) aus Ghana gründete eine Theatergruppe und das Ghana Drama Studio, 1962, und veröffentlichte Theaterstücke: *Foriwa* (Accra, 1967), *Edufa* (London, 1969) und *The Marriage of Anansewa* (London, 1975)
[36] Michael F. Dei Anang (1909-1978) aus Ghana lehrte Geschichte, gehörte zur ersten Generation afrikanischer Dichter und veröffentlichte u. a. die Anthologien *Wayward Lines from Africa* (London, 1946) sowie *Africa Speaks* (Accra, 1959)
[37] Adebayo Bablola [Babalola] (geb. 1926) aus Nigeria, cf. Text 35
[38] Cf. Text 1
[39] Dwabena Nketia (geb. 1921) aus Ghana leitet das Institute of African Studies der University of Ghana und veröffentlichte Geschichten in Tvi und Studien zur afrikanischen Musik: *African Music in Ghana* (London, 1962); *Folk Songs of Ghana* (London, 1963)
[40] Akan: ein in Ghana lebendes Volk
[41] "Waragi"; alkoholisches Getränk, das aus Bananen zubereitet wird
[42] Ngugi wa Thiong'o [ehem. James Ngugi], *Weep Not, Child* (London, 1964); *The River Between* (London, 1965); *A Grain of Wheat* (London, 1967)
[43] Grace Ogot, cf. Anm. 24 zu Kap. 1

Anmerkungen zu Kapitel 4

1. Ezekiel Mphahlele, *Press Report,* Conference of African Writers of English Expression, MAK/V(2) (Makerere, 1962) [Anm. im Text]
2. John Pepper Clark, *Song of a Goat* (Ibadan, 1962)
3. Una Maclean, "Song of a Goat", *Ibadan* (October, 1962), 28 [Anm. im Text]
4. Christopher Okigbo, "Silences", *Transition,* 8 (March, 1963), 13 [Anm. im Text]
5. Ulli Beier, "Contemporary African Poetry in English, Conference of African Writers Report, MAK/II(4) (Makerere, 1962) [Anm. im Text]
  Ulli Beier (geb. 1922) lehrte in Nigeria und New Guinea. Begründer der Zeitschrift *Black Orpheus,* förderte zahlreiche Künstler und Autoren und veröffentlichte eine Vielzahl von Werken über afrikanische Kunst, Literatur und das nigerianische Theater. Beier edierte *Introduction to African Literature* (London, 1967)
6. Ezekiel Mphalele, *op. cit.* [Anm. im Text]
7. Shabaan Robert (1909–1962) aus Tanzania schrieb Gedichte, Romane und Essays in Suaheli
8. Kofi Awoonor (George Awoonor-Williams) (geb. 1936) aus Ghana ist Dichter, Romancier und Literaturwissenschaftler
9. Mongo Beti (geb. 1932) aus Kamerun lehrt in Frankreich. Beti ediert eine Zeitschrift und veröffentlichte Romane, u. a. *Le pauvre Christ de Bomba* (Paris, 1956) und *Perpétue et l'habitude du malheur* (Paris, 1974)
10. Sarif R. Easmon (geb. 1925) aus Sierra Leone, Arzt, schrieb Dramen, u. a. *Dear Parent and Ogre* (London, 1964) und *The New Patriots* (London, 1965)
11. William Fagg, *Nigerian Images* (London, 1963)
12. Joseph M. Kariuki (1929–1975) aus Kenia schrieb Gedichte und die autobiographische Schilderung *Mau Mau Detainee* (London, 1963); wurde 1975 in Kenia ermordet
13. Amos Tutuola, *The Feather Woman of the Jungle* (London, 1962)
14. Chinua Achebe, *Arrow of God* (London, 1964)
15. Chief D. O. Fagunwa, cf. Anm. 9 zu Kap. 3
16. *A Review of English Literature,* Vol. V, no. 2 (April, 1963) [Anm. im Text]
17. Ntieyong Udo Etokapan [Ntieyong Udo Akpan] (geb. 1924) aus Nigeria, *The Wooden Gong* (London, 1965)
18. Amos Tutuola, *My Life in the Bush of Ghosts* (London, 1954)
19. Marius Nkwoh, *Talking About Love* (1963), 61 [Anm. im Text]
20. *op. cit.,* 8 [Anm. im Text]
21. Das "West African Examination Council" wurde 1952 eingerichtet und legt die Prüfungsbestimmungen für die Schulen im ehem. brit. Westafrika fest
22. Quoted by Stuart Robertson and Frederic A. Cassidy, *The Development of Modern English* (2nd ed. 1954), 377 [Anm. im Text]
23. Quoted from *Readers Digest* (Nigerian Edition) (November, 1963) [Anm. im Text]
24. Spear: *Nigeria's National Magazine* (July, 1964) [Anm. im Text]
25. *African Statesman,* I, 1 (Oct.–Dec., 1965) [Anm. im Text]
26. *Things Fall Apart* (London, 1958) [Anm. im Text]
27. Fishman, J. A., C. A. Ferguson & J. Das Gupta (eds.), *Language Problems of Developing Nations* (1958) [Anm. im Text]

Anmerkungen zu Kapitel 5

1. Camara Laye, cf. Anm. 10 zu Kap. 3
2. Chinua Achebe, cf. Anm. 20 zu Kap. 3
3. "Chi": " . . .a person's *chi* [is] his other identity in spiritland . . .", Chinua Achebe, "*Chi* in Igbo Cosmology", in: ders., *Morning Yet on Creation Day* (London, 1975), 93
4. Gerald Moore (ed.), *African Literature and the Universities* (Ibadan, 1965), 147

⁵ "Then University of East Africa with three constituent Colleges at Makerere, Dar-es-Salaam, and Nairobi. Since then the three have become autonomous universities." [Anm. im Text]
⁶ "This is a course for those who want to specialize in literature: 1st year – three subjects; 2nd and 3rd years – literature only." [Anm. im Text]
⁷ D. Rubadiris Gedicht "Stanley Meets Mutesa" wurde wiederholt in Anthologien aufgenommen. Cf. J. Reed and C. Wake (eds.), *A Book of African Verse* (London, 1964), 68–70
⁸ "pyrethrum": Chrysanthemenart, aus deren getrockneten Blättern ein Insektenvernichtungsmittel hergestellt wird. P. wurde als Monokultur in Kenia eingeführt
⁹ Während einer Demonstration gegen die Verhaftung von Harry Thuku, Mitbegründer der Young Kikuyu Association, wurden 25 Afrikaner 1922 in Nairobi erschossen
¹⁰ Ngugi spricht hier die Mau Mau Bewegung an.
¹¹ "uhuru" (Suaheli) = Freiheit, Unabhängigkeit
¹² B. A. Ogot, "Reintroducing the African Man into the World", *East African Journal* (December, 1967), 32 [Anm. im Text]
¹³ Jomo Kenyatta, *Facing Mount Kenya* (London, 1968), V; [Anm. im Text]. Erstausgabe London, 1938
¹⁴ Taban Lo Liyong (geb. 1939) aus Uganda, lehrte Englische Literatur in Kenia und Neuguinea, lebt im Sudan. Neben Gedichten und Erzählungen veröffentlichte Liyong vor allem kulturkritische Essays
¹⁵ Joe Mutiga (geb. 1940); "In the City" erschien in: Lennard Okola (ed.), *Drum Beat* (Nairobi, 1967), 94–95
¹⁶ T. J. Mboya, "Kenya Intellectuals and the KANU Goverment", *The Challenge of Nationhood* (London, 1970), 109 [Anm. im Text] Tom J. Mboya (1930–1969), einer der politischen Führer Kenias im Unabhängigkeitskampf; er wurde 1969 ermordet
¹⁷ Taban Lo Liyong, *The Last Word, Cultural Synthesism* (Nairobi, 1969)
¹⁸ Kwame Nkrumah, *Consciencism* (London, 1964)
¹⁹ Marie Corelli (1855–1924), populäre englische Autorin in den Kolonien; u. a. *The Sorrows of Satan* (London, 1895)
²⁰ Mulk Raj Anand, "By mouth or by book", TLS (12 May 1972), 552 [Anm. im Text]
²¹ L. J. Lewis, "Some principles of writing for new literates in Africa", *Development of Public Libraries in Africa: the Ibadan Seminar* (Paris: Unesco, 1954), 82–87 [Anm. im Text]
²² Ousmane Socé Diop (geb. 1911) aus Senegal; *Karim* (Paris, 3/1948); Erstveröffentlichung 1935
²³ Birago Diop, *Les contes d'Amadou Koumba* (Paris, 1947); engl. Übers. London, 1966
²⁴ Cheikh Anta Diop (geb. 1913) aus Senegal. Er veröffentlichte seine Doktorarbeit über *Nations Nègres et Culture* (Paris, 1954)
²⁵ Unesco, *Books in the Promotion of Development in Africa, Unesco Meeting of Experts on Book Development in Africa, Accra, 13–19 February 1968* (mimeo.), 6 [Anm. im Text]
²⁶ Janheinz Jahn, in a series of lectures given at the Institute of African Studies, University of Ghana, Legon, in 1965, refused to ascribe any authenticity to the work of writers who adopted European styles. [Anm. im Text]
²⁷ H. Kimble, "A reading survey in Africa", *Universitas* 2,3 (June, 1956), 77 [Anm. im Text]
²⁸ Christoph von Schmid, *Basket of Flowers;* [Übersetzungen von Kindererzählungen des deutschen Autors (1768–1854)]
²⁹ Mulk Raj Anand, *op. cit.* [Anm. im Text]; cf. Anm. 1 zu Kap. 1
³⁰ M. Kane, "The African writer and his public", *Présence Africaine* 58 (1956), 10–33 [Anm. im Text]
³¹ Jared Angira (geb. 1947) aus Kenia. *Juices* (Nairobi, 1970), die erste Gedichtanthologie des Autors
³² Sembene Ousmane (geb. 1923) aus Senegal veröffentlichte Romane, u. a. *Le docker noir* (Paris, 1956), *Le Mandat* (Paris, 1965) und *Xala* (London, 1976), sowie Kurzgeschichten. In jüngster Zeit betätigte er sich vor allem als Filmregisseur

³³ Hilary N'gweno (geb. 1938), *The Men from Pretoria* (Nairobi, 1975)
³⁴ Eneriko Seruma, (geb. ca. 1940), *The Experience* (Nairobi, 1970)
³⁵ Austin Bukenya, (geb. 1944) aus Uganda veröffentlichte *The People's Bachelor* (Nairobi, 1971)
³⁶ Richard Ntiru (geb. 1946) aus Uganda veröffentlichte die Gedichtanthologie *Tensions* (Nairobi, 1971)
³⁷ Leonard Kibera and Samuel Kahiga, *Potent Ash* (Nairobi, 1968), Kurzgeschichten
³⁸ Charles Mangua, *Son of Woman* (Nairobi, 1971) und *A Tail in the Mouth* (Nairobi, 1972)
³⁹ Peter Palangyo (geb. 1939), *Dying in the Sun* (London, 1969)
⁴⁰ EAPH = East African Publishing House; EALB = East African Literature Bureau
⁴¹ Ebrahim Hussein, *Kinjeketile* (Dar-es-Salaam, 1969)

Anmerkungen zu Kapitel 6

1. Olive Schreiner (1855–1920) aus Südafrika schrieb den ersten südafrikanischen Roman, *The Story of an African Farm* (Chicago, 1883); u.a. *God's Stepchildren* (London, 1924)
2. Joseph Conrad (1857–1924), *Heart of Darkness* (London, 1899)
3. H. Rider Haggard (1856–1925), *King Solomon's Mines* (London, 1885), *Ayesha, or the Return of She* (London, 1905)
4. T. M. Aluko, *One Man, One Wife* (Lagos, 1959)
5. Francis Selormey, *The Narrow Path* (London, 1967)
6. B. Fonlon, "African Writers Meet in Uganda", *Abbia*, 1 (February 1963) [Anm. im Text]
7. By "African Experience" Okigbo certainly does *not* mean an "African's experience." If he did, there would be no need for the rest of his above definition. [Anm. im Text]
8. John Pepper Clark, *America, Their America* (London, 1964)
9. Obi Egbuna (geb. 1938), *The Anthill* (London, New York, 1965)
10. Janheinz Jahn and Claus Peter Dressler, *Bibliography of Creative Writing* (Nendeln, 1971) Erstausgabe: *Die neo-afrikanische Literatur: Gesamtbibliographie* (Düsseldorf, Köln, 1965)
11. Lewis Nkosi (geb. 1936) aus Südafrika, lebt seit 1961 im Exil. Er veröffentlichte vor allem Aufsätze zur afrikanischen Literatur, u.a. in *Home and Exile* (London, 1962)
12. Wole Soyinka, *The Interpreters* (London, 1965)
13. S. Easmon, cf. Anm. 10 zu Kap. 4
14. Camara Laye, cf. Anm. 10 zu Kap. 3
15. Edris Makward, 'African Approach to African Literature', a paper delivered to the African Studies Association in Los Angeles, 1968 [Anm. im Text]
16. J. P. Clark, "Our Literary Critics", *Nigeria Magazine,* No. 74 (September, 1962) [Anm. im Text]
17. Elizabeth Pryse: 'Getting into Perspective', *Nigeria Magazine,* No. 74, (September, 1962) [Anm. im Text]
18. Anne Tibble, *African English Literature* (London, 1965), 100 [Anm. im Text]
19. Okogbule Wonodi, "The Role of Folk Tales in African Society", *Africa Report* (December 1965) [Anm. im Text]
20. Arthur Ravenscroft: *Chinua Achebe* (London, 1969), 8. See also: Miss A. G. Stock, "Yeats and Achebe", *The Journal of Commonwealth Literature,* No. 5 (1968) [Anm. im Text]
21. J. P. Clark, *op. cit.* [Anm. im Text]
22. Chinua Achebe, "Where Angels Fear to Tread", *Nigeria Magazine* 75 (December 1962) [Anm. im Text]. Repr. in: Chinua Achebe, *Morning Yet on Creation Day* (London, 1975), 46–48

²³ Adrian Roscoe, *Mother is Gold: a Study in West African Literature* (London, 1971), 73 [Anm. im Text]
²⁴ Solomon O. Iyasere, "Oral Tradition in the Criticism of African Literature", *The Journal of Modern African Studies*, XIII, I (March 1975), 107 [Anm. im Text]
²⁵ Yambo Ouologuem (geb. 1940) aus Mali veröffentlichte den Roman *Le Devoir de Violence* (Paris, 1968)
²⁶ Gerald Moore, *The Chosen Tongue: English writing in the tropical world* (London and New York, 1969), 163–6 [Anm. im Text]
²⁷ Ayi Kwei Armah (geb. 1939) aus Ghana; *The Beautyful Ones Are Not Yet Born* (London, 1969)
²⁸ A. Roscoe, *op. cit.*, 97 [Anm. im Text]
²⁹ A. K. Armah, *op. cit.*, 191–192 [Anm. im Text]
³⁰ E. N. Obiechina in: *Okike* (April 1971), 49 [Anm. im Text]
³¹ Ali Mazrui, *The Trial of Christopher Okigbo* (London, 1971)
³² S. O. Iyasere, *op. cit.*, 115–119 [Anm. im Text]
³³ Martin Owusu, *The Sudden Return and Other Plays*, (London, 1973)
³⁴ Obotunde Ijimere, *The Imprisonment of Obatala* (London, 1966)
³⁵ Laura Bohannan, "Hamlet and the Tiv", *Psychology Today* (New York, July 1975), 65–6. [Anm. im Text]
³⁶ Cf. Martin Tucker, *Africa in Modern Perspective* (New York, 1967), 262: "for the purpose of critical assessment of modern fiction about Africa, it is difficult to detect the presence of a specifically neo-African development or trend. The opposite seems to be the case. African writers have followed European models at the very moment they assail them." Tucker here seems unable to perceive the nuances of African literature, ironically those aspects that give it life and vitality – a commentary on the limitations of the Eurocentric approach. [Anm. im Text]
³⁷ Edwin Thumboo, "Kwesi Brew: the poetry of statement and situation", *African Literature Today*, 4 (1970), 35. [Anm. im Text] Kwesi Brew (geb. 1928) aus Ghana veröffentlichte eine Gedichtanthologie *Shadows of Laughter* (London, 1968)
³⁸ Janheinz Jahn, *A History of Neo-African Literature* (London, 1966), 63–4 [Anm. im Text]
³⁹ Cf. Christopher Heywood (ed.), *Perspectives on African Literature* (London and New York, 1971), 12. See also Solomon O. Iyasere, "African Critics on African Literature: a study of misplaced hostility", *African Literature Today*, 7 (1975), 20–27 [Anm. im Text]
⁴⁰ Charles Larson, *The Emergence of African Fiction* (Princeton U. P., 1973)
⁴¹ A. Agostinho Neto (1922–1979) aus Angola. Erster Präsident seines Landes 1975–1979. Veröffentlichte Gedichte
⁴² Cheikh Hamidou Kane (geb. 1928) aus Senegal veröffentlichte *L'aventure ambiguë* (Paris, 1961)
⁴³ Hans Zell and Helene Silver (1972: 102–111) list more than 30 major and minor learned journals entirely devoted to African literature and about 40 other journals and magazines on African studies which entertain articles on African literature and very often have special numbers on it. Almost all world journals on literature and criticism, as can be seen in the bibliography of critical materials on African literature in Zell and Silver (and also in other bibliographies and articles on African literature) welcome and publish articles on African literature. [Anm. im Text]
Cf. Hans Zell and Helene Silver (eds.), *A Reader's Guide to African Literature* (London, 1972)
⁴⁴ In many Universities in the United States and Europe African literature has now successfully extracted itself from the anthropology departments where it originally featured on courses on 'Area Studies' designed to help further a process of understanding and appreciating African anthropological features or African exotic ways of life. [Anm. im Text]
⁴⁵ Martin Tucker in *Africa in Modern Literature: A Survey of Contemporary Writing in English* (1967), gives a good account of the Eurocentric and racial prejudices which

colour the treatment given of the African by many non-African authors. [Anm. im Text]
⁴⁶ Bernth Lindfors, *Critical Perspectives on Amos Tutuola* (Washington, D. C., 1975)
⁴⁷ [H. Zell and H. Silver, *op. cit.,* listed] as many as 820 works by African authors South of the Sahara writing in English and French. Since 1972, many more works have been written [Anm. im Text]
⁴⁸ Among the many critical works written on individual authors and their works, one may cite, S. O. Mezu's *L. S. Senghor* (1968), Harold Collins's *Amos Tutuola* (1969), Michèle Dussutour-Hammer's *Amos Tutuola* (1976), G. D. Killam's *The Novels of Chinua Achebe* (1969), Arthur Ravenscroft's *Chinua Achebe* (1969), David Carroll's *Chinua Achebe* (1970), Gerald Moore's *Wole Soyinka* (1971), Eldred Jones's *The Writing of Wole Soyinka* (1973), Michael Wade's *Peter Abrahams* (1971), Thomas Melone's *The Novels of Mongo Beti* (1971), Mercier and Battestini's series on major francophone writers, Sunday Anozie's *Christopher Okigbo* (1971). [Anm. im Text]
⁴⁹ Gerald Moore (1965b: 95). Western critics have now come to share fully Moore's idea and to realise that oral tradition not only helps to cushion the content and form of African written literature and to contribute immensely to the social and linguistic atmosphere in the work but also influences such features as characterization, the didactic ending and the circular structures of most African works. See Bernth Lindfors, 'The Palm-Oil with which Achebe's words are eaten' (1968: 3–11) and Gareth Griffiths, 'Language and Action in the Novels of Chinua Achebe' (1971: 88–105) for an evaluation of Achebe's use of proverbs.
[Anm. in der Bibliographie: Gerald Moore, "Mots anglais, vies africaines", *Présence Africaine* 54 (1965), 116–126; Bernth Lindfors, "The Palm-Oil with which Achebe's words are eaten", Jones, E. D. (ed.), *African Literature Today* 1 (1968), 3–11; Gareth Griffiths, "Language and Action in the Novels of Chinua Achebe", Jones, E. D. (ed.), *African Literature Today* 5 (1968), 88–105]
⁵⁰ Malcolm Bradbury, The State of Criticism Today. *Contemporary Criticism* (London, 1970), 17
⁵¹ Emmanuel Obiechina, *Culture, Tradition and Society in the West African Novel* (London, 1975)
⁵² Bernth Lindfors, "New Trends in West and East African Fiction", *Review of National Literatures,* II, 2 (1975), 15–37

3. BIBLIOGRAPHIE

1 HINTERGRUND

Bibliographien

Catalogue of the Colonial Office Library, 15vols. (Boston, 1964); Suppl. 1 1963–67 (1967).

Duignan, Peter (ed.), *Guide to Research and Reference Works on Sub-Saharan Africa* (Stanford, 1971).

Bestermann, Theodore; Pearson, J. D. (eds.), *A World Bibliography of African Bibliographies* (Oxford, 1975).

Scheven, Yvette, *Bibliographies for African Studies 1970–75* (Waltham, Mass., 1972).

Halstead, John P. and Poreari, Serafino (eds.), *Modern European Imperialism. A Bibliography of Books and Articles 1815–1972*, 2 vols. (Boston, 1974).

Schmidt, Nancy J., *Children's Books on Africa and their Authors*, (New York, 1975).

Mzee, Said, *Printed and Published in Africa* (Frankfurt, 1980).

Nationalbibliographien

The Library, *Bibliography of Ghana* (Kumasi, 1957 ff.).

Research Library on African Affairs, *Ghana National Bibliography*, (Accra, 1965 ff.).

Sierra Leone Government, *Sierra Leone Publications* (Freetown, 1967–71).

National Archives of Zambia (comp.), *National Bibliography of Zambia* (Lusaka, 1970/71 ff.).

National Library of Nigeria (comp.), *The National Bibliography of Nigeria* (Lagos, 1973 ff.).

The Gambia National Library, *National Bibliography of the Gambia*, (Banjul, 1978 ff.).

Hilfsmittel

Foster, Philip John, *Africa South of the Sahara* (New York, 1968).

Paden, J. N. and Soja, E. W. (eds.), *The African Experience*, 3 vols. (Evanston, 1970).

Deutsches Institut für Afrika-Forschung, Afrikaverein, *Periodika-Verzeichnis* (Hamburg, 1970).

Pearson, James Douglas (ed.), *British Isles and their Cultures Today* (London, 1971).

Kane, Robert S., *Africa A to Z* (Garden City, N.Y., 1972).

Dokumentationsleitstelle im ADAF, *Dokumentationsdienst Afrika* (Hamburg, 1972 ff.).

Stadt- u. Universitätsbibliothek Frankfurt/Main, *Neuerwerbungen Afrika* (Frankfurt, 1972 ff.).
Morrison, Donald G., *Black Africa. A Comparative Handbook* (New York, 1972).
Library of Congress. *Africa South of the Sahara. Index to Periodical Literature 1900–1970*, 4 vols. (Boston, 1971; Suppl. 1, 1973).
Stadt- u. Universitätsbibliothek Frankfurt/Main, *Afrika Zeitschriften in der Stadt- u. Universitätsbibliothek Frankfurt* (Frankfurt, 1973; Suppl. 1, 1977).
Stadt- u. Universitätsbibliothek Frankfurt/Main, *Current Contents Africa* (Frankfurt, 1975 ff.; new series vol. 4 London, München, 1978 ff.).
Zell, Hans, *The African Book Publishing Record* (Oxford, 1975 ff.; München, 1980 ff.).
Travis, Carol and Alman, M. (eds.), *Periodicals from Africa. A Bibliography and Union List of Periodicals Published in Africa* (Boston, 1977).
Mansell Information Publ. *African Books in Print*, 2 vols. (London, 1975 and 1978).
Stadt- u. Universitätsbibliothek Frankfurt/Main, *Fachkatalog Afrika*
Band 1 *Geschichte* (Frankfurt, 1976)
Band 2 *Politik* (Frankfurt, 1977)
Band 3 *Literatur, Literaturwissenschaft* (Frankfurt, 1979)
Band 4 *Kulturanthropologie* (Frankfurt, 1980)
Knappert, Jan and Pearson, J. D. (eds.), *The Encyclopedia of Africa* (New York, 1976).
Dokumentationsleitstelle Afrika, *Verzeichnis afrikabezogener Zeitschriftenbestände* (Hamburg, 1976).
Darch, Colin and Mascarenhas, O. C. (eds.), *Africa Index to Continental Periodical Literature*, 2 vols. (Oxford, 1977 and 1980).
Zell, Hans, *The African Book World and Press: A Directory* (Oxford, 1977; 2nd ed. 1980).
Warwick, Ronald (comp. and ed.), *A Handbook of Library Holdings of Commonwealth Literature* (London, rev. ed. ²1977).
I C Magazine Ltd., *New Africa Year Book* (London, 1979 ff.).
Steinberg, Rolf (red.), *Africa. Texte, Dokumente, Bilder* (Berlin, 1979).
Crowder, Michael and Oliver, Roland (eds.), *The Cambridge Encyclopedia of Africa* (London, 1981).

Biographien

Surveys Ltd., *Who is Who in East Africa* (Nairobi, 1963/64).
Taylor, Sidney (ed.), *The New Africans* (London, 1967).
Melrose Press, *Dictionary of African Biography*, vol. 1 (London, 1970); vol. 2 (London, 1971).
Jahn, Janheinz u. a., *Who's Who in African Literature* (Tübingen, 1972)
Herdeck, Donald E. u. a., *African Authors: A Companion to Black African Writing*, vol. 1 *1900–1973* (Washington D.C., 1974).

Ikime, Obaro (ed.), *Leadership in Nineteenth Century* (London, 1974).
Ofosu-Appiah, L. H. (gen. ed.), *The Encyclopedia Africana. Dictionary of African Biography*, 22vols. (New York, 1977 ff.).
  vol.1 *Ethiopia – Ghana* (New York, 1977)
  vol.2 *Sierra Leone – Zaire* (New York, 1979)
Julien, Charles-André, Morsi, Magali u. a. (eds.), *Les Africains*, 12vols. (Paris, 1977–78).
Africa Journal Ltd., *Africa Year Book and Who's Who* (London, 1977 ff.)
Lipschutz, Mark and Rasmussen, R. Kent, *A Dictionary of Historical Biography* (London, 1978).

Landeskunde

Deutsche Afrika-Gesellschaft, *Die Länder Afrikas* (Bonn, 1958 ff.).
Suret-Canale, Jean, *Afrique noire occidentale et centrale* (Paris, 1964).
Kramer, Hans, Ernst, Klaus u. a. (eds.), *Die Länder Afrikas* (Berlin, 1969).
Europa Publ., *Africa South of the Sahara* (London, 1971 ff.).
Suggate, L. S., *Africa* (London, 1974).
Hance, William Adams, *The Geography of Modern Africa* (New York, 1975)
Knight, C. Gregory and Newman, James L. (eds.), *Contemporary Africa Geography and Change* (Englewood Cliffs, N.Y., 1976).
Udo, Reuben K., *A Comprehensive Geography of West Africa* (London, 1978).
Schiffers, Heinrich und Simons, Peter, *Die neuen Staaten dieser Erde* (Berlin, 1979).
Manshart, Walter, *Afrika – südlich der Sahara* (Frankfurt, 1980).

Geschichte

Allgemeine Darstellungen
Davidson, Basil, *Africa. History of a Continent* (London, 1966).
Ferkiss, Victor E., *Africa's Search for Identity* (New York, 1966).
Mazrui, Ali A., *On Heroes and Uhuru Worship* (London, 1967).
Omer-Cooper, John D. u. a., *The Making of Modern Africa*, 2vols. (London, 1968–72).
Meyer Fortes and Evans-Prichard, E. E. (eds.), *African Political Systems* (London, 1969).
Oliver, Roland and Fage, John D., *A Short History of Africa* (Harmondsworth, 1969).
Hallett, Robin, *Africa to 1875* (Ann Arbor, 1970).
Olu, Raphael, *A History of Africa Since 1800* (Ibadan, 1972).
Fage, John D. and Oliver, Roland (gen. eds.), *The Cambridge History of Africa*, 8vols. (Cambridge, 1975 ff.).
Büttner, Thea, *Afrika von den Anfängen bis zur territorialen Aufteilung Afrikas durch die imperialistischen Kolonialmächte* (Berlin-Ost, 1976; repr. 1979).
Davidson, Basil, *Africa in Modern History* (London, 1978).

Ayandele, E. A., *African Historical Studies* (London, 1979).
Ki-Zerbo, Joseph, *Die Geschichte Schwarzafrikas* (Wuppertal, 1979).
Ki-Zerbo, Joseph (ed.), *UNESCO General History of Africa*, vol.1 *Methodology and African Prehistory* (London, 1980).
Mokhtar, G. (ed.), *UNESCO General History of Africa*, vol.2 *Ancient Civilisations of Africa* (London, 1980).

Regionaldarstellungen
Fyfe, Christopher, *A History of Sierra Leone* (Oxford, 1962).
Davidson, Basil, *West Africa 1000–1800* (London, 1965).
Johnson, Samuel, *The History of the Yorubas* (London, 1921; repr. New York, 1969).
Ajayi, J. F. and Crowder, Michael (eds.), *History of West Africa*, 2vols. (London, 1971).
Buah, Francis K., *History Notes. West Africa Since A. D. 1000*, 2vols. (London, 1977).
Odhiambo, E. S. u. a., *A History of East Africa* (London, 1977).
Saul, John, *State and Revolution in Eastern Africa* (London, 1979).
Karugire, Sam R., *A Political History of Uganda* (London, 1980).

Kolonialgeschichte
Hall, Richard, *Zambia 1890–1964. The Colonial Period* (London, 1965).
Betts, Raymond F. (ed.), *The "Scramble" for Africa* (Boston, 1966).
Webster, James B., *The Revolutionary Years. West Africa Since 1800* (London, 1967).
Gann, L. H. and Duignan, Peter (eds.), *Colonialism in Africa 1870–1960*, 5vols. (Cambridge, 1969–75).
Clark, Leon E. (ed.), *The Colonial Experience* (New York, 1970).
Murray-Brown, Jeremy, *Faith and the Flag. The Opening of Africa* (London, 1971).
Rodney, Walter, *How Europe Underdeveloped Africa* (London, 1972).
Hallett, Robin, *Africa Since 1875* (Ann Arbor, 1974).
Pedler, Frederich J., *The Lion and the Unicorn in Africa. A History of the United Africa Company 1787–1931* (London, 1974).
Loth, Heinrich, *Afrika unter imperialistischer Kolonialherrschaft und die Formierung der antikolonialen Kräfte 1884–1945* (Berlin-Ost, 1976; repr. Köln, 1979).
Ikime, Obaro, *The Fall of Nigeria: The British Conquest* (London, 1977).
Isichei, Elisabeth, *History of West Africa Since 1800* (New York, 1977)
IMC / CBMS Archives / *Bestände der IMC und CBMS 1910–1945;* [1548 Positiv-Mikrofiches] (Zug, 1977).
Wilson, Henry S., *The Imperial Experience in Sub-Saharan Africa Since 1870* (Minneapolis, 1977).
Crowder, Michael, *Colonial West Africa* (London, 1978).
Garner, Joe, *The Commonwealth Office* (London, 1978).

Strayer, Robert W., *The Making of Mission Communities in East Africa* (London, 1978).
Fetter, Bruce (ed.), *Colonial Rule in Africa* (Wisconsin UP, 1979).

Unabhängigkeitsbewegung

Nkrumah, Kwame, *I Speak of Freedom* (London, 1961); *Towards Colonial Freedom* (London, 1962).
Fanon, Frantz, *Pour la Révolution africaine* (Paris, 1964).
Rotberg, Robert J. and Mazrui, Ali A. (eds.), *Protest and Power in Black Africa* (New York, 1970).
Crowder, Michael (ed.), *West African Resistance* (New York, 1972).
Kesteloot, Lilyan, *Intellectual Origins of the African Revolution* (Washington D. C., 1972).
Nkrumah, Kwame, *Revolutionary Path* (New York, 1973).
Smaldone, Joseph P. (comp.), *African Liberation Movements* (Waltham, Mass., 1974).
Ansprenger, Franz, *Die Befreiungspolitik der Organisation für Afrikanische Einheit 1963–1975* (München, 1975).
Asiwaju, A. J. and Crowder, Michael (eds.), *Protest Against Colonial Rule in West Africa* (London, 1977).
Freyhold, Michaelo von, *Ujamaa Villages in Tanzania* (London, 1979).
Falk, Rainer und Wahl, Peter (eds.), *Befreiungsbewegungen in Afrika. Politische Programme, Grundsätze und Ziele von 1945 bis zur Gegenwart* (Köln, 1980).

Nationalismus

Azikiwe, Nnamdi, *Renascent Africa* (London, 1938).
Padmore, George, *Pan-Africanism or Communism* (London, 1956).
Legum, Colin, *Pan-Africanism. A Short Political Guide* (London, 1963).
Mboya, Tom, *Conflict and Nationhood* (London, 1963); *Freedom and After* (Boston, 1963).
Friedland, William H. and Rosberg, Carl G. (eds.), *African Socialism* (Stanford, 1964).
Nkrumah, Kwame, *Africa Must Unite* (London, 1964); *Consciencism* (London, 1964).
Davidson, Basil, *Which Way Africa? The Search for a New Society* (Harmondsworth, 1967).
Geiss, Imanuel, *Panafrikanismus. Zur Geschichte der Dekolonialisation* (Frankfurt, 1968).
Davidson, Nicol (ed.), *Black Nationalism in Africa 1867. Extracts from the Political, Educational, Scientific and Medical Writings of Africanus Horton* (New York, 1969).
Sampson, Magnus J. (ed.), *West African Leadership. Speeches Delivered by J. E. Casely Heyford* (London, 1969).
Kedourie, Elie (ed.), *Nationalism in Asia and Africa* (London, 1970).
Kanza, Thomas R., *Evolution and Revolution in Africa* (London, 1971).

Ogot, Bethwell A. (ed.), *Politics and Nationalism in Colonial Kenya* (Nairobi, 1972).
Langley, J. Ayodele, *Pan-Africanism and Nationalism in West Africa, 1900–1945. A Study in Ideology and Social Classes* (Oxford, 1973)
Ajala, Adekunle, *Pan-Africanism. Evolution, Progress and Prospects* (London, 1974).
Nyerere, Julius K., *Ujamaa* (Dar-es-Salaam, 1974).
Touré, Sékou, *Révolution, culture, panafricanisme* (Conakry, ³1976).
Ogueri, Eze, *African Nationalism and Military Ascendancy* (Owerri, Nigeria, 1976).
Smock, David R. and Bentsi-Enchill, Kwamena (eds.), *The Search for National Integration in Africa* (New York, 1976).
Lynch, Hollis R. (ed.), *Edward W. Blyden. Selected Letters* (New York, 1978).
Langley, J. Ayo, *Ideologies of Liberation in Black Africa 1856–1970* (London, 1979).
Ziegler, Jean, *Afrika, die neue Kolonialisation* (Darmstadt, 1980).

Kultur- und Sozialgeschichte

Kenyatta, Jomo, *Facing Mount Kenya* (London, 1938).
Perham, Margery and Simmons, J., *African Discovery* (London, 1942).
Tempels, Placide, *Philosophie bantoue* (Paris, 1947).
Mannoni, Dominique O., *Prospero and Caliban. The Psychology of Colonialisation* (New York, 1956); urspr. Paris, 1950.
Jahn, Janheinz, *Muntu* (Düsseldorf/Köln, 1958).
Bascom, William R. and Herskovits, Melville J., *Continuity and Change in African Cultures* (Chicago, 1958).
Diop, Cheik Anta, *Les Fondements culturels, techniques et industriels d'un future Etat Fédéral d'Afrique Noire* (Paris, 1960).
Parrinder, E. G., *West African Religion* (London, 1961).
Abraham, William E., *The Mind of Africa* (London, 1962).
Idowu, E. B., *Oludumare: God in Yoruba Belief* (London, 1962).
Davidson, Nicol, *Africa. A Subjective View* (London, 1964).
Herskovits, Melville Jean, *L'Afrique et les Africains* (Paris, 1965).
Perham, Margery, *African Outline* (London, 1966).
Gabel, Creighton and Bennett, Norman R. (eds.), *Reconstructing African Cultural History* (Boston, 1967).
Maquet, Jacques, *Africanité traditionelle et moderne* (Paris, 1967).
Webster, Berlin and Boahen, H. Adu, *The Growth of African Civilisation, The Revolutionary Years. West Africa Since 1800* (London, 1967).
Barnes, Leonard, *African Renaissance* (London, 1969).
Clark, Leon E. (ed.), *Coming of Age in Africa: Continuity and Change* (New York, 1969).
Mbiti, John S., *African Religions and Philosophy* (London, 1969).
Cabral, Amilcar, *National Liberation and Culture* (Syracuse, 1970).

Lynch, Hollis R. (ed.), *Black Spokesman. Selected Published Writings of Edward W. Blyden* (London, 1971).
Kashamura, Anicet, *Culture et aliénation en Afrique* (Paris, 1977).
Onibonoje, G. O. u. a. (eds.), *The Indigenous for National Development* (Ibadan, 1976).
p'Bitek, Okot, *Africa's Cultural Revolution* (Nairobi, 1973).
Wilson, Bryan, *Magic and the Millenium* (London, 1973).
Skinner, Elliott P. (ed.), *Peoples and Cultures of Africa. An Anthropological Reader* (New York, 1973).
Wolfers, Michael, *Black Man's Burden Revisited* (London, 1974).
Ranger, T. O., *Dance and Society in Eastern Africa* (London, 1975).
Oluwasanmi, Edwina, McLean, Eva and Zell, Hans (eds.), *Publishing in Africa in the Seventies* (Ile-Ife, 1975).
Kaunda, Kenneth David, *A Humanist in Africa* (Lusaka, 1976).
Boulaga, F. Eboussi, *La Crise du Muntu* (Paris, 1977).
Gutkind, Peter C. W. and Waterman, Peter (eds.), *African Social Studies: A Radical Reader* (London, 1977).
Mazrui, Ali A., *Political Values and the Educated Class in Africa* (London, 1978).
Du Toit, Brian M. (ed.), *Ethnicity in Modern Africa* (Boulder, Col., 1978).
Ayisi, Eric C., *An Introduction to the Study of African Culture* (London, 1972; repr. 1979).

Bildungs- und Erziehungswesen

Jones, Thomas J. (ed.), *Education in Africa* (London, 1922).
Advisory Committee on Education of African Communities, Col. No. 103 (London, 1935); *Report on Higher Education in the Colonies*, Cmd. 6647 (London, 1945); *Education for Citizenship*, Col. No. 216 (London, 1948).
Secretary of State for the Colonies, *Report of the Commission on Higher Education in West Africa*, Cmd. 6655 (London, 1945).
Wise, C. G., *A History of Education in British West Africa* (London, 1956).
Foster, Philip J., *Education and Social Change in Ghana* (London, 1965)
Press, John (ed.), *The Teaching of English Literature Overseas* (London, 1963).
Sumner, D. L., *Education in Sierra Leone* (Freetown, 1963).
Ashby, Eric, *African Universities and Western Tradition* (London, 1964).
Scanlon, David G., *Church, State and Education in Africa* (New York, 1966).
UNESCO, *Educational Development in Africa* (New York, 1968).
Abernathy, David B., *The Political Dilemma of Popular Education. An African Case* (Stanford, 1969).
King, Kenneth James (ed.), *Pan-Africanism and Education* (Oxford, 1971)
Prewitt, Kenneth (ed.), *Education and Political Values. An East African Case Study* (Nairobi, 1971).
Raju, B. M., *Education in Kenya* (London, 1974).
Fafunwa, A. Babs, *History of Education in Nigeria* (London, 1974).
Lyons, Charles Henry, *To Wash an Aethiop White. British Ideas About African Educatability 1530–1960* (New York, 1975).

McWilliam, H. O. and Kwamena-Poh, M. A., *The Development of Education in Ghana* (London, ³1975).
Morrison, David R., *Education and Politics in Africa. The Tanzanian Case* (London, 1976).
Graham, C. K., *The History of Education in Ghana* (Tema, Ghana, 1976).
Ike, Chukwuemeka, *University Development in Africa: The Nigerian Experience* (London, 1976).
UNESCO, *Final Report: Conference of Ministers of Education of African Member States* (Paris, 1976).
Uchendu, Victor C. (ed.), "Education and Politics in Tropical Africa", *Conch Magazine* (New York, 1977–79).
Wandira, A., *The African University in Development* (London, 1977).
Furley, O. W. and Watson, T., *A History of Education in East Africa* (London, 1978).

Afrika und der Westen

Harris, John H., *Down in Darkest Africa* (London, 1912).
Fraser, Donald, *The New Africa* (London, 1927).
Westermann, Diedrich, *The African Today and Tomorrow* (London, 1939).
Gluckmann, Max, *Custom and Conflict in Africa* (Oxford, 1955).
Malinowski, Bronislaw, *The Dynamics of Culture Change* (New Haven, 1961).
Turnbull, Colin Macmillan, *The Lonely African* (New York, 1962).
Dumoga, John, *Africa Between East and West* (London, 1969).
Hill, Cromwell Adelaide and Kilson, Martin (eds.), *Apropos of Africa. Sentiments of Negro American Leaders on Africa from the 1800s to the 1950s* (London, 1969).
Hammond, Dorothy, *The Africa That Never Was. Four Centuries of British Writing about Africa* (New York, 1970).
Okoye, Felix N. C., *The American Image of Africa. Myth and Reality.* (Buffalo, N.Y., 1971).
Curtin, Philip D. (ed.), *Africa and the West. Intellectual Responses to European Culture* (Madison, 1972).
Irvine, S. H. and Sanders, J. T. (eds.), *Cultural Adaption within Modern Africa* (New York, 1972).
White, Jo Anne (ed.), *African Views of the West* (New York, 1972).
Paeffgen, Manfred, *Das Bild Schwarzafrikas in der öffentlichen Meinung der BRD 1949–1972* (München, 1976).
Diestel, Susanne, *Das Afrikabild in europäischen Schulbüchern* (Weinheim/Basel, 1978).
Lorimer, Douglas A., *Colour, Class and the Victorians. English Attitudes to the Negro in the Mid-nineteenth Century* (Leicester, 1978).
Hetherington, Penelope, *British Paternalism and Africa 1920–1940* (London, 1978).
Allen, C. (ed.), *Tales from the Dark Continent: Images of British Colonial Africa in the 20th Century* (London, 1979).

Sprache

Spenser, John (ed.), *Language in Africa* (London, 1963).

Okonkwo, Juliet, "African Language and its Language of Expression", *African Quarterly* XV (1977) 56–66.

Collins, Harold Reeves, *The New English of the Onitsha Chap Books* (Athens, Ohio, 1968).

Heine, Bernd, *Status and Use of African Lingua Francas* (München, 1970)

McGregor, C. M., *English in Africa* (London, 1971).

Alexandre, Pierre, *An Introduction to Languages and Language in Africa* (London, 1972).

Dwamina, Wingrove Charles, *English Literature and Language Planning in West Africa* (Buffalo, 1973).

Sey, K. A., *Ghanaian English* (London, 1973).

Mazrui, Ali A., *The Political Sociology of the English Language. An African Perspective* (The Hague, 1975).

2 LITERATUR

Bibliographien

Amosu, Margaret, *A Preliminary Bibliography of Creative African Writing in the European Languages* (Ibadan, ca. 1965).

Jahn, Janheinz, *Die neoafrikanische Literatur* (Düsseldorf/Köln, 1965).

Tibble, Anne (ed.), *African-English Literature. A Short Survey and Anthology of Prose and Poetry up to 1965* (London, 1965).

Ramsaran, John A., *New Approaches to African Literature* (Ibadan, 1965).

The Journal of Commonwealth Literature (London, 1965 ff.)

Abrash, Barbara, *Black African Literature in English Since 1952* (New York, 1967).

Zell, Hans, *Writings by West Africans* (Freetown, 1968).

Páricsy, Pál, *A New Bibliography of African Literature* (Budapest, 1969).

East, N. B., *African Theatre. A Checklist of Critical Materials* (New York, 1970).

Cordor, S. Henry, *The Bibliography of Liberian Literature* (Monrovia, 1971).

Harvard University Library, *African History and Literatures* (Cambridge, Mass., 1971).

Jahn, Janheinz, *Bibliography of Creative African Writing* (Nedeln, 1971).

Dickson Patten, Margaret, *Ghanaian Imaginative Writing in English 1950–1969* (Legon, 1971).

Zell, Hans and Silver, Helene, *A Reader's Guide to African Literature* (London, 1972).

Ganz David L., *A Critical Guide to Anthologies of African Literature* (Waltham, Mass., 1973).

Ghana Literary Board, *A Guide to Creative Writing by Africans in English* (Accra, 1973).

Chapman, Dorothy H., *Index to Black Poetry* (Boston, 1974).
Lindfors, Bernth, *A Bibliography of Literary Contributions to Nigerian Periodicals 1946–72* (Ibadan, 1975).
National Book League, *Black Writing from Africa, the Caribbean and the United States of America* (London, 1975).
Zell, Hans (ed.), *The African Book Publishing Record* (Oxford, 1975 ff.).
Pichenick, J., Rix, L. B. and Chennells, A. J. (comp.), *Rhodesian Literature in English. A Bibliography (1890–1974/75)* (Gwelo, 1977).
Stadt- u. Universitätsbibliothek Frankfurt/Main, *Fachkatalog Afrika*, Band 3 *Literatur, Literaturwissenschaft* (Frankfurt, 1979).
Saint André-Utudjian, Elaine, *A Bibliography of West African Life and Literature* (Waltham, Mass., 1977).
"Chinua Achebe: A Preliminary Checklist", *Nsukka Library Notes*, spec. issue, 3 (1978).
Lindfors, Bernth (ed.), *Black African Literature in English. A Guide to Information Sources* (Detroit, 1979).

Biographien

Cordor, S. Henry, *The Writers of the West African Republic of Liberia 1820 to 1971* (Monrovia, 1970).
Jahn, Janheinz, Schild Ulla und Nordmann, Almut, *Who's Who in African Literature?* (Tübingen, 1972).
Zell, Hans and Silver, Helene (eds.), *A Reader's Guide to African Literature* (London, 1972).
African and Afro-American Institute, *Palaver. Interviews with Five African Writers in Texas* (Achebe, Clark, Brutus, Mphahlele, Awoonor)(Austin, 1972).
Duerden, Dennis and Pieterse, Cosmo (eds.), *African Writers Talking* (London, 1972).
Herdeck, Donald E. (ed.), *African Authors. A Companion to Black African Writing*, vol. 1 *1300–1973* (Washington, D. C., 1973).
Agetua, John (ed.), *Interviews with Six African Writers* (Benin City, 1974).
Imfeld, Al, *Portraits of African Writers* (Deutsche Welle Transkriptionsdienst) (Köln, 1980).
Walsh, William (intr.), *Commonwealth Literature* (London, 1980).

Literaturgeschichte

Tibble, Anne, *African-English Literature* (London, 1965).
Jahn, Janheinz, *Geschichte der neoafrikanischen Literatur. Eine Einführung* (Düsseldorf, 1966).
Wauthier, Claude, *The Literature and Thought of Modern Africa* (London, 1966; repr. 1975).
Tucker, Martin, *Africa in Modern Literature* (New York, 1967).
Taiwo, Oladele, *An Introduction to West African Literature* (London, 1967).

Cartey, Wilfred, *Whispers from a Continent. The Literature of Contemporary Black Africa* (New York, 1969).
Moore, Gerald, *The Chosen Tongue* (London, 1969).
Ortová, Jarmila, *Modern Literatures of Sub-Saharan Africa* (Prague, 1971).
Dathorne, Oscar Ronald, *The Black Mind. A History of African Literature* (Minneapolis, 1974).
Awoonor, Kofi, *The Breast of the Earth. A Survey of the History, Culture and Literature of Africa South of the Sahara* (Garden City, N. Y., 1975).
Dathorne, Oscar Ronald, *African Literature in the Twentieth Century* (London, 1976).
Klima, Vladimir u. a. (eds.), *Black African Literature and Language* (Dortrecht, 1976).
Okam, Hilary H. (ed.), *Traditional and Contemporary African Literature* (New Haven, 1976).
Fiebach, Joachim, *Kunstprozesse in Afrika* (Berlin-Ost, 1979); repr. *Literaturen der Befreiung in Afrika* (München, 1979).
Riemenschneider, Dieter, „Die anglophone Literatur der siebziger Jahre", in: *Zeitschrift für Kulturaustausch* 29. Jg. 2(1979) 167–182; „West- und Ostafrika", in: Schäfer, Jürgen (ed.), *Commonwealth Literatur* (Düsseldorf, 1981) 147–173.

Regionale Überblicke
Taiwo, Oladele, *An Introduction to West African Literature* (London, 1967).
Laurence, Margaret, *Long Drums and Cannons. Nigerian Dramatists and Novelists 1952–1966* (London, 1968).
King, Bruce (ed.), *Introduction to Nigerian Literature* (London, 1971).
Roscoe, Adrian A., *Mother is Gold. A Study in West African Literature* (London, 1971).
Stewart, D., "Ghanaian Writing in Prose. A Critical Survey", in: *Présence Africaine 91* (1974) 73–105.
Lindfors, Bernth (ed.), *Critical Perspectives on Nigerian Literature* (Washington D. C., 1976).
Roscoe, Adrian A., *Uhuru's Fire. African Literature East to South* (Cambridge, 1977).
Priebe, R., "Popular Writing in Ghana: A Sociology and Rhetoric", in: *Research in African Literatures 9,3* (1978) 359–432.
Jestel, Rüdiger, *Literatur und Gesellschaft Nigerias* (Frankfurt, 1979).
Trenz, Günter, *Die Funktion englischsprachiger westafrikanischer Literatur* (Berlin, 1980).

Allgemeine Einführungen

McLeod, Alan L. (ed.), *The Commonwealth Pen: An Introduction to the Literature of the British Commonwealth* (Ithaca, N. Y., 1962).
Moore, Gerald (ed.), *African Literature and the Universities* (Ibadan, 1965).

Press, John (ed.), *Commonwealth Literature: Unity and Diversity in a Common Culture* (London, 1965).
Beier, Ulli (ed.), *Introduction to African Literature* (London, 1967; new ed. 1979).
Wästberg, Per (ed.), *The Writer in Modern Africa* (Uppsala, 1968).
Pieterse, Cosmo and Munro, Donald (eds.), *Protest and Conflict in African Literature* (London, 1969).
Third Press (ed.), *Algiers Festival 1969. The Role of Culture in African Society* (New York, 1970).
Okpaku, Joseph O. (ed.), *New African Literature and the Arts* 2 vols. (New York, 1970).
Goodwin, Kenneth L. (ed.), *National Identity* (London, 1970).
Heywood, Christopher (ed.), *Perspectives on African Literature* (London, 1971).
Cordor, S. Henry (ed.), *Towards the Study of Liberian Literature* (Monrovia, 1972).
Duerden, Dennis and Pieterse, Cosmo (eds.), *African Writers Talking* (London, 1972).
Ballard, W. L. (ed.), *Essays on African Literature* (Atlanta, Ga., 1973).
Gurr, Andrew and Zirimu, Pio (eds.), *Black Aesthetics* (Nairobi, 1973).
Killam, Gordon Douglas (ed.), *African Writers on African Writing* (London, 1973).
Wanjala, Chris (ed.) *Standpoints on African Literature* (Nairobi, 1973).
Gurr, Andrew and Calder, Angus (eds.), *Writers in East Africa* (Nairobi, 1974).
King, Bruce and Ogungbesan, Kolawole (eds.), *A Celebration of Black African Writing* (Oxford, 1975).
Maes-Jelinek, Hena (ed.), *Commonwealth Literature and the Modern World* (Brussels, 1975).
Heywood, Christopher (ed.), *Papers on African Literature* (Sheffield, 1976).
Lindfors, Bernth and Schild, Ulla (eds.), *Neo-African Literature and Culture* (Wiesbaden, 1976).
Niven, Alastair (ed.), *The Commonwealth Writer Overseas* (London, 1976).
Smith, Rowland (ed.), *Exile and Tradition: Studies in African and Caribbean Literature* (London, 1976).
Cook, David (ed.), *In Black and White: Writings from East Africa with Broadcast Discussions and Commentary* (Nairobi, 1976).
Schipper-de Leeuw, Mineke (ed.), *Text and Context. Methodological Explorations in the Field of African Literature* (Leiden, 1977).
Nwoga, Donatus J. (ed.), *Literature and Modern West African Culture* (Benin City, 1977).
Gachukia, Eddah and Akinaga, S. K. (eds.), *The Teaching of African Literatures in Schools* (Nairobi, 1978).
Breitinger, Eckhard (ed.), *Black Literature* (München, 1979).
Jones, Eldred D. (ed.), *African Literature Today 10: Retrospect and Prospect* (London, 1979).
Ogungbesan, Kolawole (ed.), *New West African Literatures* (London, 1979).

Tetsch, Ernst (Red.), *Afrikanische Literatur. Perspektiven und Probleme.* (Stuttgart, 1979); erschien zugleich in *Zeitschrift für Kulturaustausch* 2,3 (1979).

Madubuike, Chinweizu, Jemie, I. u. a. (eds.), *Toward the Decolonisation of African Literature*, 2 vols. (Enugu, 1980).

Literaturkritik

Allgemeine Darstellungen

Jahn, Janheinz and Ramsaran, John, *Approaches to African Literature* (Ibadan, 1959).

Mphalele, Ezekiel, *The African Image* (London, 1962).

Banham, M. J., "Beginnings of a Nigerian Literature in English", *Review of English Literature* 3,2 (1962) 88–97.

Hertlein, Siegfried, *Christentum und Mission im Urteil der neoafrikanischen Literatur* (Münsterschwarzach, 1962).

Anon., "A Language in Common", *Times Literary Supplement* (10. August 1962).

Wake, Clive, "African Literary Criticism", *Comparative Literature Studies* 1,3 (1964) 197–205.

Irele, Abiola, "Negritude or Black Cultural Nationalism", *Journal of Modern African Studies* III,3 (1965) 321–348; "Négritude – Literature and Ideology", *op.cit.* III,4 (1965) 499–526.

Kane, Mohamedan, "The African Writer and His Public", *Présence Africaine* XXX,58 (1966) 8–32.

Mphahlele, Ezekiel, "African Literature: What Traditions?", *University of Denver Quarterly* II,2 (1967) 36–68.

Povey, J. F., "Canons of Criticism for Neo-African Literature", *African Proceedings* 3 (1966) 73–91.

Cook, Mercer, *The Militant Black Writer in Africa and the United States* (Madison, 1969).

Markward, Edris, "Is There an African Approach to Literature?", *African Studies Centre UCLA* (Los Angeles, 1969).

Emenyonu Ernest, "African Literature: What does it take to be its Critic?", Jones, Eldred (ed.), *African Literature Today* 5 (1971) 1–11.

Obiechina, Emmanuel, *An African Popular Literature. A Study of Onitsha Market Pamphlets* (London, 1972); urspr. *Literature for the Masses* (Enugu, 1971).

Cook, David, *African Literature* (London, 1971).

Bishop, D. Rand, *African Critics and African Literature. A Study of Critical Standards 1947–1966*, unpubl. Ph. D. M. F. (Ann Arbor, 1971).

Nwoga, Donatus I., "The Limitations of Universal Critical Criteria", *Ufahamu* 4,1 (1972) 10–33.

Moore, Gerald, "The Debate on Existence in African Literature", *Présence Africaine* 81 (1972) 18–48.

Lindfors, Bernth, *Folklore in Nigerian Literature* (New York, 1973).

Nazareth, Peter, *Literature and Society in Modern Africa* (Nairobi, 1973).

Wright, Edgar, (ed.), *The Critical Evaluation of African Literature* (London, 1973).

Mutiso, G. C. M., *Socio-Political Thought in African Literature* (London, 1974).

Ogungbesan, Kolawole, "Nigerian Writers and Political Commitment", *Ufahamu* 5,2 (1974) 20–50.

Ebele, Ofoma Eko, *The Critical Reception of Amos Tutuola, Chinua Achebe and Wole Soyinka in England and America 1952–74* (Ann Arbor, 1975) [Positiv Mikrofilm]

Jones, Eldred D., *African Literature Today 7: Focus on Criticism* (London, 1975).

Izevbaye, Dan S., "The State of Criticism in African Literature", Jones, Eldred (ed.), *African Literature Today* 7 (1975) 1–19.

Bishop, D. Rand, "African Literature for Whom? The Janus-like function of African Literary Criticism", *Présence Africaine* 101/2 (1977) 57–80.

Cook, David, *African Literature. A Critical View* (London, 1977).

Egejuru, Phannel Akubueze, *Black Writers, White Audience* (Hicksville, N. Y., 1978).

Griffiths, Gareth, *A Double Exile* (London, 1978).

King, Bruce, *The New English Literatures – Cultural Nationalism in a Changing World* (London, 1980).

Bender, Wolfgang, *Kolonialismus, Bewußtsein und Literatur in Afrika* (Bremen, 1980).

Literaturkritik: Prosa

Gleason, Judith, *This Africa: Novels by West Africans in English and French* (Evanston, 1965).

Dathorne, Oscar Ronald, "The African Novel: Document to Experience", *Bulletin of the Association of African Literature in English* 3 (1965) 18–39.

Laurence, Margaret, *Long Drums and Cannons: Nigerian Dramatists and Novelists 1952–66* (London, 1968).

Lindfors, Bernth, *Nigerian Fiction in English 1952–67* (Ann Arbor, 1969) [Positiv Mikrofilm]

Klima, Vladimir, *Modern Nigerian Novels* (Prague, 1969).

Anozie, Sunday Ogbonna, *Sociologie du roman africain* (Paris, 1970).

Larson, Charles R., *The Emergence of African Fiction* (Bloomington, 1971).

Jones, Eldred (ed.), *African Literature Today 5: The Novel in Africa* (London, 1971).

Iyasere, Solomon Ogbede, *The Rhetoric of African Fiction* (Ann Arbor, 1972). [Positiv Mikrofilm]

Palmer, Eustace, *An Introduction to the African Novel* (London, 1972).

Ravenscroft, Arthur, "An Introduction to West African Novels in English", *The Literary Criterion* X,2 (1972) 38–56.

Buelow, George David, *The Ethnographic Novel in Africa* (Eugene & Portland, 1973).

Olney, James, *Tell Me Africa* (Princeton, 1973).

Boettcher, Karl-Heinz, *Tradition und Modernität bei Amos Tutuola und Chinua Achebe* (Bonn, 1974).
Stewart, Daniele, "Ghanaian Writing in Prose: A Critical Survey", *Présence Africaine* 91 (1974) 74–105.
Obiechina, Emmanuel, *Culture, Tradition and Society in the West African Novel* (Cambridge, 1975).
O'Flinn, J. P., "Towards a Sociology of the Nigerian Novel", Jones, Eldred (ed.), *African Literature Today 7: Focus on Criticism* (1975) 34–52.
Gakwandi, Shatto Arthur, *The Novel and Contemporary Experience in Africa* (New York, 1977).
Cham, Baboucai A. B., *Language and Style in the West African and West Indian Novel* (Ann Arbor, 1978) [Positiv Microfiches].
Githae-Mugo, Micere, *Visions of Africa. The Fiction of Chinua Achebe, Margaret Laurence, Elspeth Huxley and Ngugi wa Thiong'o* (Nairobi, 1978).
Wittmann, Ulrich, *Der Konflikt zweier Wertsysteme im Ibo-Roman* (Bonn, 1978).
Palmer, Eustace, *The Growth of the African Novel* (London, 1979).

Literaturkritik: Dichtung

Echeruo, Michael, "Traditional and Borrowed Elements in Nigerian Poetry", *Nigerian Magazine* 89 (1967) 142–155.
Jones. Eldred D. (ed.), *African Literature Today 6: Poetry in Africa* (London, 1973).
Egudu, Romanus N., *Modern African Poetry and the African Predicament* (London, 1978).
Nwoga, Donatus I., "Modern African Poetry: The Domestication of a Tradition", Jones, Eldred (ed.), *African Literature Today 10: Retrospect and Prospect* (1979) 32–56.
Burton, S. H. and Chacksfield, C. J. H., *African Poetry in English. An Introduction to Practical Criticism* (London, 1979).

Literaturkritik: Drama

Ogbuna, Oyin, "Theatre in Nigeria", *Présence Africaine* 30 (1966) 65–88.
Nwoko, D., "Search for a New African Theatre", *Présence Africaine* 75 (1970) 49–75.
Ogbuna, Oyin, "Modern Drama in West Africa", Heywood, Christopher (ed.), *Critical Perspectives on African Literature* (London, 1971) 81–105.
Adedeji, J., "Oral Tradition and the Contemporary Theatre in Nigeria", *Research in African Literatures* II,2 (1971) 134–149.
Traoré, Bakary, *The Black African Theatre and its Social Functions* (Paris, 1958; repr. Ibadan, 1972).
Graham-White, Anthony, *The Drama of Black Africa* (New York, 1974).
Jones, Eldred D. (ed.), *African Literature Today 8: Drama in Africa* (London, 1976).
"African Theatre", *Yale Theatre* 8,1 (1976) 6–71
de Graft, John, "Roots in African Drama and Theatre", Jones, Eldred (ed.), *African Literature Today 8: Drama* (1976) 1–25.

Banham, Martin and Wake, Clive, *African Theatre Today* (London, 1976).
Ogbuna, Oyin and Irele, Abiola (eds.), *Theatre in Africa* (Ibadan, 1978).
Etherton, M., "Trends in African Theatre", Jones, Eldred (ed.), *African Literature Today* 10: *Retrospect and Prospect* (1979) 57–85.

Monographien

Moore, Gerald, *Seven African Writers* (London, 1962); *Twelve African Writers* (London, 1980).
Killam, Gordon Douglas, *The Novels of Chinua Achebe* (London, 1969).
Ravenscroft, Arthur, *Chinua Achebe* (London, 1969).
Carroll, David, *Chinua Achebe* (New York, 1970; rev.ed. 1977).
Killam, Gordon Douglas, *The Writing of Chinua Achebe* (London, 1975).
Lindfors, Bernth and Innes, C. L. (eds.), *Critical Perspectives on Chinua Achebe* (London, 1979).
Wren, Robert M., *Achebe's World* (New York, 1980) [Microfiches]
Fraser, Robert, *The Novels of Ayi Kwei Armah* (London, 1980).
Emenyonu, Ernest, *Cyprian Ekwensi* (London, 1974).
Fyfe, Christopher, *Africanus Horton* 1835–1883 (New York, 1972).
Beard, Linda Susan, *Lessing's Africa* (Ann Arbor, 1979).
Robson, Clifford B., *Ngugi wa Thiong'o* (London, 1979).
Anozie, Sunday O., *Christopher Okigbo: Creative Rhetoric* (London, 1972).
Heron, George A., *The Poetry of Okot p'Bitek* (London, 1976).
Jones, Eldred D., *The Writing of Wole Soyinka* (London, 1973).
Moore, Gerald, *Wole Soyinka* (London, 1973; rev.ed. 1978).
Page, Malcolm, *Wole Soyinka* (London, 1979).
Ogbuna, Oyin, *The Movement of Transition. A Study of the Plays of Wole Soyinka* (Ibadan, 1975).
Boettcher-Woebcke, Rita, *Komik, Ironie und Satire im dramatischen Werk von Wole Soyinka* (Hamburg, 1976).
Lindfors, Bernth (ed.), *Critical Perspectives on Amos Tutuola* (Washington D. C., 1975).
Dussutour-Hammel, Michèle, *Amos Tutuola. Tradition orale et écriture du conte* (Paris, 1976).
Killam, Gordon Douglas, *An Introduction to the Writings of Ngugi* (London, 1980).

Studienreihen

Evans Brothers, *Modern African Writers* (London, 1971 ff.).
Heinemann Educational Books, *Studies in African Literature* (London, 1972 ff.); *Heinemann Students Guides* (London, 1973 ff.).
Frank Cass, *Africana Modern Library* (London)

Texte

Textreihen
Ein wesentlicher Teil der Literatur ist in Textreihen britischer und afrikanischer Verlage erschienen.
Heinemann Educational Books, *African Writers Series* (London, 1962 ff.) umfaßt bisher ca. 230 Titel.
Fontana/Collins, *Fontana African Novels* (Glasgow).
Evans Brothers, *African Readers Library* (London).
Heinemann Educational Books, *Spear Books,* Popular African Writing (Nairobi).
Onibonoje, *African Literature Series-Junior* (Ibadan).
Longman, *Drumbeat* (Harlow).
Hammer/Walter Verlag, *Dialog Afrika* (Wuppertal/Olten).

Anthologien (Kurzprosa, Romanauszüge)
Young, Cullen (ed.), *African New Writing: Short Stories by African Authors* (London, 1947).
Beier, Ulli (ed.), *Black Orpheus* (Ikeja, 1964).
Drachler, Jacob, (ed.), *African Heritage* (New York, 1964).
Edwards, Paul (ed.), *West African Narrative* (Edinburgh, 1964).
Komey, E. A. and Mphahlele, Ezekiel (eds.), *Modern African Stories* (London, 1964).
Rive, Richard (ed.), *Modern African Prose* (London, 1964).
Whiteley, Wilfred H., (ed.), *A Selection of African Prose* (Oxford, 1964).
Denny, Neville (ed.), *Pan African Short Stories* (London, 1965).
Tong, Raymond (sel.), *African Tales* (London, 1967).
Beier, Ulli (ed.), *Political Spider* (London, 1969).
Dathorne, Oscar Raymond and Feuser, Willfried (eds.), *Africa in Prose* (Harmondsworth, 1969).
Rutherford, Peggy (ed.), *African Voices* (New York, 1970).
Achebe, Chinua, Nwankwo, Arthur u. a. (eds.), *The Insider. Stories of War and Peace from Nigeria* (Ibadan, 1971).
Mezu, S. O. (comp.), *Igbo-Market-Literature* 5 vols. (Buffalo, 1972).
Obiechina, Emmanuel (ed.), *Onitsha Market Literature* (London, 1972).
Barcley, E. (ed.), *Anthology of Liberian Literature* (Monrovia, 1974).
Kwakwa, B. S. (sel.), *Ghanaian Writing Today* (Tema, Ghana, 1974).
Katz, Naomi and Milton, Nancy, (eds.), *Women of the Third World* (London, 1975).
Larson, Charles R. (ed.), *More Modern African Stories* (Glasgow, 1975).
Machin, N. P. F. (ed.), *Winds of Change* (London, 1977).
Cordor, Henry S. (ed.), *Modern West African Short Stories from Liberia* (Monrovia, 1977)
Manley, Deborah (ed.), *Growing Up* (Lagos, 1977).

Anthologien (Prosa und Lyrik)
Rutherford, Peggy (ed.), *Darkness and Light* (London, 1958).
Swanzy, Henry (ed.), *Voices of Ghana* (Accra, 1958).
Hughes, Langston (ed.), *An African Treasury* (New York, 1960; repr. 1977).
Ademola, Frances (ed.), *Reflections: Nigerian Prose and Verse* (Lagos, 1962).
Cook, David (ed.), *Origin East Africa* (London, 1965).
Tibble, Anne (ed.), *African-English Literature* (London, 1965).
Edwards, Paul (comp.), *Through African Eyes* 2 vols. (Cambridge, 1966).
Schrey, Kurt (sel.), *African Authors of English Expression* (Frankfurt, 1966).
Mphahlele, Ezekiel (ed.), *African Writing Today* (Harmondsworth, 1967).
Nolen, Barbara (ed.), *Africa is People* (New York, 1968).
Shelton, Austin J., (ed.), *The African Assertion* (New York, 1968).
Angoff, Charles and Povey, John (eds.), *African Writing Today* (New York, 1969).
Clark, Leon E. (ed.), *Coming of Age* (New York, 1969).
Cartey, Wilfred (ed.), *Palaver. Modern African Writing* (Camden, N. Y., 1970).
Green, Robert (ed.), *Just a Moment* (Nairobi, 1970).
Okpaku, Joseph (ed.), *New African Literature and the Arts* 2 vols. (New York, 1970).
Wells, David, Stevenson, M., King, N. (eds.), *From Black Africa* (New York, 1970).
Crane, Louise (ed.), *The Beauty of Being Black* (New York, 1971).
Wanjala, Chris, (ed.), *Faces At Crossroads* (Nairobi, 1971).
Nolen, Barbara (ed.), *Voices of Africa* (Glasgow, 1972).
Washington, William D., Beckhoff, S. u. a. (eds.), *Black Literature* (New York, 1972).
Bown, Lalage (ed.), *Two Centuries of African English* (London, 1973).
Huntsberger, Paul E. (comp.), *Highland Mosaic* (Athens, Ohio, 1973).
Sergeant, Howard (sel.), *African Voices* (New York, 1973).
Zabala, Pam and Rossell, Chris (eds.), *African Writing* (London, 1974).
Nolen, Barbara (ed.), *More Voices of Africa* (Glasgow, 1975).
MacLoughlin, T. O. (comp.), *New Writing in Rhodesia* (Gwelo, 1976).
Ekwensi, Cyprian (rd.), *Nigerian New Writing* (Lagos, 1977).

Anthologien (Lyrik)
Bassir, Olumbe (ed.), *An Anthology of West African Verse* (Ibadan, 1957).
Banham, Martin (ed.), *Nigerian Student Verse* (Ibadan, 1960).
Banks Henries, Doris (coll.), *Poems of Liberia 1836–1961* (London, 1963).
Moore, Gerald and Beier, Ulli (eds.), *Modern Poetry from Africa* (Harmondsworth, 1963).
Hughes, Langston (ed.), *Poems from Black Africa* (Bloomington, 1963).
Reed, John and Wake, Clive (eds.), *A Book of African Verse* (London, 1964).
Nwoga, Donatus Ibe (ed.), *West African Verse* (London, 1967).
Okola, Lennard (ed.), *Drum Beat. East African Poems* (Nairobi, 1967).
Sergeant, Howard (ed.), *Poetry from Africa* (Oxford, 1968).

Awoonor, Kofi and Adali-Mortty, G. (eds.), *Messages. Poems from Ghana* (London, 1971).
Cook, David and Rubadiri, David (eds.), *Poems from East Africa* (London, 1971).
Kemoli, Arthur, Pulsations. *An East African Anthology of Poetry* (Nairobi, 1971).
Azuonye, Chukwuma (ed.), *Nsukka Harvest. Poetry from Nsukka 1966–1972* (Nsukka, 1972).
Clark, Ebun and Manley, Deborah (eds.), *Poetry* (Lagos, 1972).
Allen, Samuel (ed.), *Poems from Africa* (New York, 1973).
Wanjala, Chris (ed.), *Singing with the Night* (Nairobi, 1974).
Fraser, Robert (ed.), *Reading African Poetry* (London, 1975).
Soyinka, Wole (ed.), *Poems of Black Africa* (London, 1975).
Kariara, Jonathan and Kitonga, Ellen (eds.), *An Introduction to East African Poetry* (Nairobi, 1976).
Senanu, Kojo E. and Vincent, Theo (sel.), *A Selection of African Poetry* (London, 1976).
Weaver, Roger and Bruchac, Joseph (eds.), *Aftermath. An Anthology of Poems in English from Africa, Asia, and the Caribbeans* (Greenfield Centre, New York, 1977).
Achebe, Chinua and Okafor, Dubem (eds.), *Don't Let Him Die* (Enugu, 1978).
Machin, Noel (ed.), *African Poetry for Schools* 2vols. (London, 1978).

Anthologien (Dramen)

Beier, Ulli (ed.), *Three Yoruba Plays* (Ibadan, 1964); repr. *Three Nigerian Plays* (London, 1967).
Cook, David and Lee, Miles (eds.), *Short East African Plays in English* (London, 1968).
Pieterse, Cosmo (ed.), *Ten One-act Plays* (London, 1968).
Litto, Frederic M. (ed.), *Plays from Black Africa* (New York, 1969).
Pieterse, Cosmo (ed.), *Short African Plays* (London, 1972).
Pieterse, Cosmo (ed.), *Five African Plays* (London, 1972).
Henderson, Gwyneth (ed.), *African Theatre* (London, 1973).
Henderson, Gwyneth (ed.), *Nine African Plays for Radio* (London, 1973)
Fiebach, Joachim (ed.), *Stücke Afrikas* (Berlin-Ost, 1974).
Harrison, Paul Carter (coll.), *Kuntu Drama* (New York, 1974).
Chirwa, C. H. (ed.), *Five Plays from Zambia* (Lusaka, 1975).
Etherton, Michael (ed.), *African Plays for Playing* 2vols. (London, 1975–76).
Wanjala, Chris (ed.), *The Debtors. A Collection of Plays* (Nairobi, 1977).
Gibbs, James (ed.), *Nine Malawian Plays* (Limbe, 1977).

Werkausgaben

Prosa
Abraham, J., *How to Make Friends with Girls* (Onitsha, ca. 1965).
Achebe, Chinua, *Things Fall Apart* (London, 1958).

No Longer at Ease (London, 1962).
The Sacrificial Egg and Other Stories (Onitsha, 1962) SS
Arrow of God (London, 1965).
A Man of the People (London, 1966).
Girls at War and Other Stories (London, 1972) SS
Abruquah, Joseph W., *The Torrent* (London, 1968).
The Catechist (Tema, Ghana, 1971).
Agunwa, Clement, *More Than Once* (London, 1967).
Ajoa, A., *On the Tiger's Back* (London, 1962).
Aidoo, Ama Ata, *No Sweetness Here* (London, 1970) SS
Our Sister Killjoy (London, 1977) SS
Aka, S. M. O., *The Midday Darkness* (Ibadan, 1973).
Akpabot, Anne, *Aduhe Makes Her Choice* (London, 1970).
Akpan, Ade, *The Wooden Gong* (London, 1965).
Aluko, T. M., *One Man, One Matchet* (London, 1964).
Kinsman and Foreman (London, 1966).
One Man, One Wife (London, 1972).
His Worshipful Majesty (London, 1973).
Chief, The Honourable Minister (London, 1975).
Amadi, Elechi, *The Concubine* (London, 1966).
The Great Ponds (London, 1969).
The Slave (London, 1978).
Aniebo, I.N.C., *The Anonymity of Sacrifice* (London, 1974).
The Journey Within (London, 1978).
Appiah, Peggy, *A Dirge too Soon* (Tema, Ghana, 1976).
Armah, Ayi Kwei, *The Beautyful Ones Are Not Yet Born* (Boston, 1968).
Fragments (Boston, 1970).
Why Are We So Blest? (New York, 1972).
Two Thousand Seasons (Nairobi, 1973).
The Healers (Nairobi, 1978).
Asalache, Khadambi, *A Calabash of Life* (London, 1967).
Awoonor, Kofi, *This Earth, My Brother* (London, 1972).
Bakaluba, Jane Jagers, *Honeymoon for Three* (Nairobi, 1975).
Balogun, Kolawole, *Village Boy* (Ibadan, 1969).
Bediako, Kwabena Asare, *Don't Leave Me Mercy* (Accra, 1966).
A Husband for Esi Ellua (Accra, 1967).
Rebel (London, 1969).
Blay, J. Benibengor, *Parted Lovers* (Accra, 1968).
Alomo (Accra, 1969).
Coconut Boy (Accra, 1970).
African Drums (Accra, 1972) SS
Boateng, Yaw M., *The Return* (London, 1977).
Bukenya, Austin, *The People's Bachelor* (Nairobi, 1972).
Casely Hayford, Joseph, *Ethiopia Unbound* (London, 1911)
Chahilu, Bernard P., *The Herdsman's Daughter* (Nairobi, 1974).

Chigbo, Thomas, *Odenigbo* (London, 1976).
Chiume, Murray W. K., *The African Deluge* (Nairobi, 1978).
Conton, William, *The African* (London, 1960).
Dembo, Samuel, *The Amber Eyes of the Lion* (London, 1963).
Desewo, P. M., *The Three Brothers and Other Ewe Stories* (London, 1951) SS
Djoleto, Amu, *The Strange Man* (London, 1967).
   Money Galore (London, 1975).
Dipoko, Mbella Sonne, *A Few Nights and Days* (London, 1966).
   Because of Women (London, 1968).
Duodu, Cameron, *The Gab Boys* (London, 1967).
Echewa, T. Obinkaram, *The Land's Lord* (London, 1976).
Egbuna, Obi B., *Daughters of the Sun and Other Stories* (London, 1970) SS
   Emperor of the Sea (Glasgow, 1974). SS
   The Madness of Didi (Glasgow, 1980).
Ekwensi, Cyprian, *Ikolo, the Wrestler* (London, 1947). SS
   Beautiful Feathers (London, 1963).
   An African Night's Entertainment (Lagos, 1964).
   Lokotown and Other Stories (London, 1966). SS
   People of the City (London, 1963).
   Burning Grass (London, 1968).
   Jagua Nana (London, 1961).
   Restless City and Christmas Gold (London, 1975). SS
   Survive the Peace (London, 1976).
   The Rainmaker and Other Stories (Lagos, 1977) SS
Emecheta, Buchi, *In the Ditch* (London, 1972).
   The Bride Price (New York, 1976).
   The Joys of Motherhood (London, 1980).
Enahoro, Peter, *You Gotta Cry to Laugh* (Köln, 1972).
Eric, Speedy, *Mabel, the Sweet Honey that Poured Away* (Onitsha, ca. 1960).
Etokahpan, E., *The Forces of Superstition* (Ibadan, 1972).
Farah, Nuruddin, *From a Crooked Rib* (London, 1970).
   A Naked Needle (London, 1976).
   Sweet and Sour Milk (London, 1979).
Gicheru, Mwangi, *Across the Bridge* (Nairobi, 1979).
Higiro, Joy, *Voice of Silence* (Nairobi, 1975).
Ibongia, John M., *The Magic Stone and Other Stories* (Nairobi, 1971). SS
Ibukun, Olu, *The Return* (Nairobi, 1970).
Ifejika, S. K., *The New Religion* (London, 1973).
Ike, Chukwuemeka, *Toads for Supper* (Glasgow, 1965).
   The Naked Gods (Glasgow, 1970).
   The Potter's Wheel (London, 1973).
   Sunset at Dawn (London, 1976).
   The Chicken Chasers (Glasgow, 1980).
   Expo 77 (Glasgow, 1980).

Juoli, F. M., *Stories of Life* (London, 1948). SS
  More Stories from Life (London, 1949). SS
Iroh, Eddie, *Forty-eight Guns for the General* (London, 1976).
  Toads of War (London, 1979).
Itayemi, Phebean, *The Torn Veil and Other Stories* (London, 1975). SS

Kachingwe, Aubrey, *No Easy Task* (London, 1966).
Kagiri, Samuel, *Leave Us Alone* (Nairobi, 1975).
Kahiga, Samuel, *The Girl from Abroad* (London, 1974).
  Lover in the Sky (Nairobi, 1975).
Kala, John, *The Valley of Flames* (Nairobi, 1975).
Kalimugago, Godfrey, *Dare to Die* (Nairobi, 1972).
  The Pulse of the Woods (Nairobi, 1974).
  The Department (Nairobi, 1975).
Karoki, John, *The Land is Ours* (Nairobi, 1970).
Katiyo, Wilson, *A Son of the Soil* (London, 1976).
  Going to Heaven (London, 1979).
Kayira, Legson, *The Looming Shadow* (Garden City, N. Y., 1967).
  Jingala (London, 1969).
  The Detainee (London, 1974).
Kibera, Leonard and Kahiga, S., *Potent Ash* (Nairobi, 1968). SS
Kibera, Leonard, *Voices in the Dark* (Nairobi, 1970).
Konadu, Samuel Asare, *A Woman in her Prime* (London, 1967).
  Shadow of Wealth (Accra, 1968).
  Ordained by Oracle (London, 1969).
Kwarteng, D. K., *My Sword is My Life* (Tema, Ghana, 1972).

LoLiyong, Taban, *Fixions and Other Stories* (London, 1969). SS
Lubega, Bonnie, *The Outcasts* (London, 1971).
  The Burning Bush (Nairobi, 1971).
  Cry Jungle Children (Nairobi, 1974).

Maddy, Yulisa Amadu, *No Past, No Present, No Future* (London, 1973).
Maillu, David G., *Unfit for Human Consumption* (Nairobi, 1973).
  Kadosa (Nairobi, 1975).
  No! (Nairobi, 1976).
  Dear Daughter (Nairobi, 1976).
Mangua, Charles, *Son of Woman* (Nairobi, 1971).
  A Tail in the Mouth (Nairobi, 1972).
Marechera, Dambudso, *The House of Hunger* (London, 1978). SS
  Black Sunlight (London, 1980).
Matata, Bingu, *Love for Sale* (o. O., 1975).
Mbise, Ismail R., *Blood on Our Land* (Dar-es-Salaam, 1974).
Mezu, S. O., *Behind the Rising Sun* (London, 1971).
Momodu, A. G. S., *The Course of Justice and Other Stories* (Ibadan, 1971)
Mude, M. D., *The Hills Are Falling* (Nairobi, 1979).
Mukasa, Ham, *Uganda's Katikiro in England* (London, 1904); repr. and ed. Lo

Liyong, Taban, *Ham Mukasa, Sir Apolo Kagwa Discovers Britain* (London, 1975).
Mulaisho, Dominic, *The Tongue of the Dumb* (London, 1971).
- *The Smoke that Thunders* (London, 1979).

Mulikita, F. M., *A Point of no Return* (Lusaka, 1968). SS
Mungoshi, Charles L., *Waiting for the Rain* (London, 1975).
Munonye, John, *The Only Son* (London, 1966).
- *Obi* (London, 1969).
- *Oil Man of Obange* (London, 1971).
- *A Wreath for the Maidens* (London, 1973).
- *A Danger of Fortune* (London, 1975).
- *Bridge to a Wedding* (London, 1978).

Mwangi, Meja, *Kill Me Quick* (London, 1973).
- *Carcase for Hounds* (London, 1974).
- *Taste of Death* (London, 1975).
- *Going Down River Road* (London, 1976).
- *The Bushtrackers* (Nairobi, 1979).

Mwaura, Mike, *The Renegade* (Nairobi, 1972).
Mwase, George Simeon, *Strike a Blow and Die* (Harvard, 1967).
Nakibimbisi, Omunjakko, *The Sobbing Sound* (Harvard, 1975).
Napal, Dayachand, *The Years of Tribulation* (Port Louis, Mauritius, ca. 1974).
Nazareth, Peter, *In a Brown Mantle* (Nairobi, 1972).
Ngutiah, Stephen N., *A Curse from God* (Nairobi, 1970).
Ngugi, James (wa Thiong'o), *Weep Not Child* (London, 1965).
- *The River Between* (London, 1965).
- *A Grain of Wheat* (London, 1967).
- *Secret Lives and Other Stories* (New York, 1975). SS
- *Petals of Blood* (London, 1977).

Nguyah, Lydiah Mumbi, *The First Seed* (Nairobi, 1975).
Ngwabe, Victor, *An Echo from the Past* (Nairobi, 1978).
Ng'weno, Hilary, *The Men from Pretoria* (London, 1975).
Njau, Rebeka, *Ripples in the Pool* (London, 1978).
Nicol, Davidson, *Two African Tales* (Cambridge, 1965). SS
- *The Truly Married Woman and Other Stories* (London, 1965). SS

Njoku, Charles, *The New Breed* (London, 1973).
Njoroge, James K., *The Greedy Host and Other Stories* (Nairobi, 1967). SS
Nwankwo, Nkem, *Danda* (London, 1964).
- *My Mercedes is Bigger than Yours* (New York, 1975).

Nwapa, Flora, *Efuru* (London, 1966).
- *Idu* (London, 1970).
- *Wives at War and Other Stories* (Enugu, 1980). SS

Nyabongo, Akiki N., *The Story of an African Chief* (New York, 1935).
- *Africa Answers Back* (London, 1936).

Nzekwu, Onuora, *Wand of Noble Wood* (London, 1961).
- *Blade Among the Boys* (London, 1962).

Obeng, E. E., *Eighteen Pence* (Ilfracombe, 1943).
   Highlife for Lizards (London, 1965).
Oculi, Okello, *Prostitute* (Nairobi, 1968).
Ogot, Grace, *The Promised Land* (Nairobi, 1966).
   Land Without Thunder (Nairobi, 1968).
   The Other Woman (Nairobi, 1976). SS
Onyeama, Dillibe, *Juju* (London, 1977).
   The Return (London, 1978).
Ogwu, Sulu, *The Gods are Silent* (Ibadan, 1978).
Okara, Gabriel, *The Voice* (London, 1964).
Okello, C., *The Prophet* (Nairobi, 1978).
Okoro, Anezi, *One Week, One Trouble* (Lagos, 1972).
   Dr. Amadi's Postings (Benin City, 1974).
Okpewho, Isidore, *The Victims* (London, 1970).
   The Last Duty (London, 1976).
Oludhe-Macgoye, Majorie, *Murder in Majengo* (Nairobi, 1972).
Omotoso, Kole, *The Edifice* (London, 1971).
   The Combat (London, 1972).
   Miracles and Other Stories (Ibadan, 1973). SS
   Fella's Choice (Benin City, 1974).
Onyango-Abuje, J. C., *Fire and Vengeance* (Nairobi, 1975).
Osahon, Naiwa, *The Climate of Darkness* (Lagos, 1971).
Osofisan, Femi, *Kolera Kolej* (Ibadan, 1975).
Owusu-Nimoh, Mercy, *The Walking Calabash and Other Stories* (Tema, Ghana, 1977). SS
p'Bitek, Okot, *Hare and Hornbill* (London, 1978). SS
Peters, Lenrie, *The Second Round* (London, 1965).
Rubadiri, David, *No Bride Price* (Nairobi, 1967).
Ruheni, Mwangi, *What a Life!* (Nairobi, 1972).
   The Future Leaders (Nairobi, 1973).
   What a Husband! (Nairobi, 1974).
   The Minister's Daughter (London, 1975).
Sellassie, B. M. Sahle, *Warrior King* (London, 1974).
Samkange, Stanlake J. T., *On Trial for My Country* (London, 1973).
   The Mourned One (London, 1975).
   The Year of the Uprising (London, 1978).
Sebukima, Davis, *Growing Up* (Nairobi, 1974).
   The Half-brothers (Nairobi, 1974).
Segun, Mabel, *My Father's Daughter* (Lagos, 1965).
Seruma, Eneriko, *The Experience* (Nairobi, 1970).
Serumaga, Robert, *Return to the Shadows* (London, 1969).
Soyinka, Wole, *The Interpreters* (London, 1965).
   Season of Anomy (London, 1973).
Taiwo, Oladele, *The Hunter and the Hen and Other Stories* (Lagos, 1965). SS
Tejani, Bahadur, *Day After Tomorrow* (Nairobi, 1971).

Tutuola, Amos, *The Palm-Wine Drinkard and His Dead Palm-Wine Tapster in the Deads' Town* (London, 1952).
My Life in the Bush of Ghosts (London, 1954).
Simbi and the Satyr of the Dark Jungle (London, 1955).
The Brave African Huntress (London, 1958).
Feather Woman of the Jungle (London, 1962).
Ajaiyi and His Inherited Poverty (London, 1967).
Ulasi, Adaora Lily, *Many Thing You No Understand* (London, 1970).
The Man from Sagamu (Glasgow, 1978).
Umobuaric, David, *Black Justice* (Ibadan, 1976).
Uzodiuma, E. C. C., *Our Dead Speak* (London, 1967).
Vambe, Lawrence, *An Ill-fated People* (London, 1967).
Wachira, Godwin, *Ordeal in the Forest* (Nairobi, 1968).
Watene, Kenneth, *Sunset on the Manyatta* (Nairobi, 1974).
Were, Miriam K., *The Eighth Wife* (Nairobi, 1972).
Worku, Daniachew, *The Thirteenth Sun* (London, 1973).
Yusuf, Ahmed B., *The Reckless Climber* (Ibadan, 1978).

Lyrik.

Achebe, Chinua, *Beware, Soul Brother* (Ibadan, 1971; London, 1972).
Christmas in Biafra and Other Poems (Garden City, N. Y., 1974).
Angira, Jared, *Juices* (Nairobi, 1970).
Silent Voices (London, 1972).
Soft Corals (Nairobi, 1973).
Cascades (London, 1979).
Armattoe, R. E. G., *Between the Forest and the Sea* (Londonderry, 1950).
Deep Down the Black Man's Mind (Ilfracombe, 1953).
Awoonor, Kofi, *Night of My Blood* (Garden City, N. Y., 1971).
Ride Me, Memory (Greenfield, N. Y., 1973).
Blay, J. Benibengor, *Ghana Sings* (Accra, 1965).
Earlier Poems (Accra, 1971).
Brathwaite, E., *Black and Blues* (Benin City, 1977).
Brew, Kwesi, *The Shadows of Laughter* (London, 1968).
Buruga, Joseph, *The Abandoned Hut* (Nairobi, 1969).
Cheyney-Coker, Syl, *Concerto for an Exile* (London, 1973).
The Graveyard also has Teeth (London, 1980).
Chima, Richard, *The Loneliness of a Drunkard* (Lusaka, 1973).
Clark, J. P., *Poems* (Ibadan, 1962).
A Reed in the Tide (London, 1965).
Casualities (New York, 1970).
de Graft, Joe C., *Beneath the Jazz and the Brass* (London, 1975).
Dei-Anang, Michael, *Wayward Lines from Africa* (Cape Coast, 1949).
Africa Speaks (Accra, 1959).
Ghana Semi-tones (Accra, 1962).
Dempter, Roland F., *A Song Out of Midnight* (Monrovia, 1960).

Dipoko, M. S., *Black and White in Love* (London, 1972).
Echeruo, Michael, *Mortality* (London, 1968).
Fowowe, Oyelehe, *Who Has Blood?* (Ife, 1972).
Githae-Mugo, Micere M., *Daughter of my People, Sing!* (Nairobi, 1976).
Higiro, Joy, *Voice of Silence* (Kampala, 1975).
Jemie, Ohwuchekwa, *Requiem for the Dead in War* (Port Moresby, 1970).
Kayoya, Michel, *My Father's Footprints* (Nairobi, 1973).
Kayper-Mensah, A. W., *The Dark Wanderer* (Tübingen, 1970).
 The Drummer in Our Time (London, 1975).
 Akwaaba (Tema, Ghana, 1976).
Kithinji, Gerald, *Whispers at Dawn* (Nairobi, 1976).
Konadu, Samuel Asare, *Nightwatchers of Korlebu* (Accra, 1968).
Kyei, Kojo Ghinaye, *The Lone Voice* (Accra, 1969).
LoLiyong, Taban, *Frantz Fanon's Uneven Ribs* (London, 1971).
 Another Nigger Dead (London, 1972).
 Ballads of Underdevelopment (Kampala, 1976).
Maillu, D. G., *My Dear Bottle* (Nairobi, 1974).
Macgoye, Marjorie Ohudhe, *Song of Nyarloka and Other Poems* (Nairobi, 1977).
Mancham, James R., *Reflections and Echoes from Seychelles* (Victoria, Mahe, Seychelles, 1972).
Mbiti, John S., *Poems of Nature and Faith* (Nairobi, 1969).
Mezu, S. O., *The Tropical Dawn* (Buffalo, N. Y., 1970).
Moore, Bai Tamia, *Ebony Dust* (Monrovia, 1965).
Mustapha, Mukhtarr, *Thorns and Thistles* (London, 1971).
Mutiso, Muli, *Sugar Babies* (Nairobi, 1975).
Ndu, Pol, *Golgotha* (Ife, 1971)
 Songs for Seers (New York, 1974).
Njoroge, James Kingangi, *Spectrum* (Nairobi, 1970).
Ntiru, Richard C., *Tensions* (Nairobi, 1971).
Nwanodi, Okogbule Glory, *Icheke and Other Poems* (Ibadan, 1964).
Obasa, G., *Sleepless Nights* (Kampala, 1975).
Obiechina, Emmanuel, *Locusts* (Greenfield Centre N. Y., 1976).
Okuli, O., *Malak* (Nairobi, 1977).
Odeku, Emmanuel Latunde, *Whispers from the Night* (Ibadan, 1976).
Ojaide, Moses Tanure, *Children of Iroho and Other Poems* (Grennfield Centre, N. Y., 1973).
Okai, John, *The Oath of the Fontomfrom and Other Poems* (New York, 71).
Okara, Gabriel, *The Fisherman's Invocation* (London, 1978).
Okigbo, Christopher, *Limits* (Ibadan, 1964).
 Labyrinths. With: Path of Thunder (London, 1971).
Osadebaye, D. C., *Africa Sings* (Ilfracombe, 1952).
Ojienda, Fred, *The Native* (Nairobi, 1975).
Peters, Lenrie, *Poems* (Ibadan, 1964).

Satellites (London, 1967).
Katchikali (London, 1971).
Samuel, J. M., *I Remember!* (Lusaka, 1973).
Simoko, Patu, *Africa is Made of Clay* (Lusaka, 1975).
Soyinka, Wole, *Idanre and Other Poems* (London, 1967).
A Shuttle in the Crypt (London, 1972).
Ogun Abibiman (London, 1976).
Uka, Kalu, *Earth to Earth* (Greenfield Centre, N. Y., 1972).
Wonodi, Okogbule, *Dusts of Exile* (Ife, 1971).
Yambo, Mauri, *Flame Hands* (Nairobi, 1975).
Man Without Blood (Nairobi, 1975).

Songs
Maillu, David, *After 4.30* (Nairobi, 1975).
Mote, Jasintha, *The Flesh* (Nairobi, 1975).
Oculi, Okello, *Malak* (Nairobi, 1976)
p'Bitek, Okot, *Song of Lawino* (Nairobi, 1966).
Song of Ocol (Nairobi, 1972)
Two Songs (Song of Prisoner, Song of Malaya) (Nairobi, 1971).

Drama
Aidoo, Ama Ata, *The Dilemma of a Ghost* (Accra, 1965).
Anowa (London, 1970).
Akar, John, *The Valley of Echo* (perf. London, 1954).
Amadi, Elechi, *The Dancer of Johannesburg* (Ibadan, 1978).
Amali, S. O. O., *The Downfall of Ogbun* (Ibadan, 1968).
The Leaders (Ibadan, 1972).
Aririguzo, C. N., *The Work of Love* (Onithsha, ca. 1960).
Ayodele, S. O., *The Church is the Problem* (Ibadan, 1973).
Bediaho, Kwabena Asare, *The Stubborn* (Nairobi, 1976).
Brathwaite, Edward, *Odale's Choice* (London, 1971).
Brown, Nigel, *The Last Laugh* (Nairobi, 1970).
The Play of the Shepherds (Nairobi, 1971).
Cantey, R. A., *The Mystery of a Cockrow* (Accra, 1971).
Clark, John Pepper, *Song of a Goat* (Ibadan, 1961).
Three Plays (London, 1964).
Ozidi (London, 1966).
Danquah, J. B., *The Third Woman* (London, 1943) [erstes in englischer Sprache veröffentlichtes Stück eines Westafrikaners]
de Graft, John C., *Sons and Daughters* (London, 1964).
Through a Film Darkly (London, 1970).
Muntu, (Nairobi, 1977).
Dei-Anang, Michael, *Cocoa Comes to Mampong* (Cape Coast, 1949; repr. Nendeln, 1970).
Okomfo Anokye's Golden Stool (Ilfracombe, 1959; repr. Accra, 1963).

Easmon, R. S., *Dear Parent and Ogre* (London, 1964).
  The New Patriots (London, 1965).
Egbuna, O. B., *The Anthill* (London, 1965).
Eze, Ezenta E., *The Cassava Ghost* (Benin City, 1974).
Fiawoo, F., *The Fifth Landing-Stage* (London, 1943).
Gabre-Medhin, Tsegaye, *Oda-oak Oracle* (London, 1965).
Gachago, David, *The Scapegoat* (Nairobi, 1971).
Gbadamosi, Rasheed, *Echoes from the Lagoon* (Ibadan, 1973).
Githae-Mugo, Micere M., *The Long Illness of Ex-chief Kiti* (Nairobi, 1976).
Henshaw, James E., *This is Our Chance: Three Plays from West Africa* (London, 1957).
  Children of the Goddess (London, 1964).
  Medicine for Love (London, 1966).
  Dinner for Promotion, (London, 1967).
Hutchinson, Alfred, *The Rain-killers* (London, 1964).
Ijimere, O., *The Imprisonment of Obatala and Other Plays* (London, 1966)
Imbuga, Francis Davis, *The Fourth Trial* (Nairobi, 1972).
  The Married Bachelor (Nairobi, 1973).
  Betrayal in the City (Nairobi, 1976).
  Game of Silence (Nairobi, 1976).
Kasoma, Kabwe, The Fools Many (Lusaka, 1976).
Kibwana, John Mike, *Utisi* (Nairobi, 1974).
Kinteh, Ramatoulie, *Rebellion* (New York, 1968).
Ladipo, Duro, *Three Yoruba Plays* (Ibadan, 1964)
  Edá (Ibadan, 1970)
  Moremi (London, 1970).
Leshoai, Benjamin B., *Wrath of the Ancestors and Other Plays* (Nairobi, 1972).
Maddy, Pat Amadu, *Obasai and Other Plays* (London, 1971).
Marshall, Bill, *Stranger to Innocence and Shadow of an Eagle* (Accra, 1969).
  The Son of Umbele (Tema, Ghana, 1973).
Masiye, Andreya S., *The Lands of Kazembe* (Lusaka, 1973).
Maxwell, Highbred, *Public Opinion of Lovers* (Onitsha, ca. 1960).
Mwiwawi, Andrew M., *The Act* (Nairobi, 1976).
Nazareth, Peter, *Two Radio Plays* (Kampala, 1976).
Ngugi (wa Thiong'o), James and Githae-Mugo, Micere, *The Trial of Dedan Kimathi* (London, 1976).
Ngui, James, *The Black Hermit* (Nairobi, 1969).
  This Time Tomorrow (Nairobi, 1970).
Njau, Rebecca, *The Scar* (Moshi, Tanzania, 1965).
Ogali, Ogali Agu, *Veronica, My Daughter* (Onitsha, ca. 1960).
Ogunmola, K., *The Palm-Wine Drinkard* (Ibadan, 1968).
Ogunyemi, Wale, *Business Headache* (London, 1966; repr. Nendeln, 1973)
  Obaluaye (Ibadan, 1972).
Omotoso, Kole, *The Curse* (Ibadan, 1976).
  Shadows in the Horizon (Ibadan, 1977).

Owusu, Martin, *The Sudden Return and Other Plays* (London, 1973).
Oyono-Mbia, Guillaume, *Three Suitors: One Husband* (London, 1968).
Parker, Lester, *Pioneers and Providence* (Monrovia, 1974).
Rotimi, Ola, *The Gods are Not to Blame* (London, 1971).
    Kurunmi (Ibadan, 1971).
    Ovonramwen Nogbaisi (Ibadan, 1974).
    Our Husband has Gone Mad Again (Ibadan, 1977).
Ruganda, John, *The Burdens* (Nairobi, 1972).
    Black Mamba (Nairobi, 1973).
Rugyendo, Mukotani, *The Barbed Wire and Other Plays* (London, 1977).
Sekye, Kobina, *The Blinkards* (London, 1974); written in 1915
Serumaga, Robert, *A Play* (Kampala, 1967).
    The Elephants (Nairobi, 1971).
    Majangwa (Nairobi, 1974).
Sofola, S. A., *When a Philosopher Falls in Love* (New York, 1956).
Sofola, Zulu, *The Disturbed Peace of Christmas* (Ibadan, 1971).
    The Wedlock of the Gods (Ibadan/London, 1972).
    King Emene (London, 1974).
Sondhi, Kuldip, *Undesignated and Other Plays* (New Delhi, 1973).
Soyinka, Wole, *Three Plays (The Swamp Dwellers, The Trials of Brother Jero, The Strong Breed)* (Ibadan, 1963);
    The Lion and the Jewel (London, Ibadan, 1963);
    Five Plays (A Dance of the Forests, The Swamp Dwellers, The Trials of Brother Jero, The Strong Breed) (London, Ibadan, 1964).
    The Road (London, 1967);
    Madmen and Specialists (London, 1973).
    The Jero Plays (London, 1973).
    Collected Plays vol. 1 (London, 1973).
    Collected Plays vol. 2 (London 1975).
    Death and the King's Horseman (London, 1975).
Sutherland, Efua, *Foriwa* (Accra, 1967).
    Edufa (London, 1967).
    Vulture! Vulture! (Accra, 1968).
    The Marriage of Anansewa (London, 1975).
Watene, Kenneth, *My Son for My Freedom and Other Plays* (Nairobi, 1973).
    Dedan Kimathi (Nairobi, 1974).
Were, Gideon S., *The Survivors* (Nairobi, 1968).
Zirimu, Elvania N., *When the Hunchback Made Rain* (Nairobi, 1975).

Autobiographien
Abruquah, Joseph W., *The Catechist* (Tema, Ghana, 1971).
Amadi, Elechi, *Sunset in Biafra* (London, 1973)
Awokwo, Obafemi, *Awo: The Autobiography of Chief Obafemi Awokwo* (London, 1960).
Azikiwe, Nnamdi, *My Odyssey* (London, 1971)

Bello, Ahmadu, *My Life* (London, 1962).
Clark, John Pepper, *America, Their America* (London, 1964).
Egbuna, Obi B., *Diary of a Homeless Prodigal* (Enugu, 1976).
Equiano, Olaudah, *The Interesting Narrative of the Life of Olaudah Equiano or Gustavus Vassa the African* (London, 1789); abr. ed. Paul Edwards, *Equiano's Travels* (London, 1967).
Kaunda, K. D., *Zambia Shall Be Free* (London, 1962).
Mboya, Tom, *Freedom and After* (London, 1963).
Odinga, Oginga A., *Not Yet Uhuru* (London, 1967).
Soyinka, Wole, *The Man Died* (London, 1972).

Essays
Achebe, Chinua, *Literature and Society: An African View* (Enugu, 1978)
  Morning Yet on Creation Day (London, 1975).
Clark, John Pepper, *The Example of Shakespeare* (London, 1970).
Duerden, Dennis, *African Art and Literature: The Invisible Present* (London, 1975).
Gordimer, Nadine, *The Black Interpreters* (Johannesburg, 1973).
Lessing, Doris, *Going Home* (London, 1957).
Liyong, Taban Lo, *The Last Word. Cultural Synthesism* (Nairobi, 1969).
  The Uniformed Man (Nairobi, 1971).
  Meditations (London, 1978).
Mphahlele, Ezekiel, *Voices in the Whirlwind and Other Essays* (London, 1973).
Nazareth, Peter, *An African View of Literature* (Evanston, 1974).
  The Third World Writer. His Social Responsibility (Nairobi, 1978).
Ngugi, James, *Homecoming* (London, 1972).
Soyinka, Wole, *Myth, Literature and the African World* (Cambridge, 1976).

3 EINRICHTUNGEN ZUR PFLEGE UND FORSCHUNG DER ENGLISCHEN LITERATUR AFRIKAS

Zeitschriften, die sich besonders oder regelmäßig der afrikanischen Literatur widmen, sind:
African Literature Today (London, 1968 ff.).
African Perspectives (Leiden, 1976 ff.).
Asemka (Cape Coast, 1974 ff.).
Ba Shiru (University of Wisconsin, 1970 ff.).
Black Orpheus (Ibadan, 1957–67; new series Lagos/Ife, 1968 ff.).
Busara (Nairobi, 1968 ff.).
Ch'indaba (Accra, 1975/76 ff.; contd. *Transition*).
The Conch (Austin, Texas/New York, 1969 ff.).
Dhana (EALB Kampala/Nairobi, 1971 ff.).
Journal of Commonwealth Literature (London, 1965 ff.; Oxford, 1979 ff.).
Journal of Modern African Studies (London, 1963 ff.).

Kunapipi (Aarhus, 1979 ff.).
Nigeria Magazine (Lagos, 1933 ff.).
Odu (Ile-Ife, 1968 ff.).
Okeyama (Accra, 1961 ff.).
Okike (Amherst, Mass., 1971 ff.).
Penpoint (Kampala, 1964–69)
Présence Africaine (Paris, 1947ff.).
Research in African Literatures (Austin, Texas, 1970 ff.).
Transition (Kampala, 1961–75/76)
Ufahamu (Log Angeles, 1970 ff.).
Umma (Dar-es-Salaam/Nairobi, 1971 ff.).
World Literature Written in English (Arlington, Texas, 1962 ff.).

Literatursammlungen gibt es in Universitäts- und Institutsbibliotheken in Bremen, Frankfurt, Göttingen, Hamburg, Köln, Marburg, Mainz und Saarbrükken. Bayreuth befindet sich im Aufbau. Mainz verfügt über die Sammlung Janheinz Jahns (Institut für Ethnologie- und Afrika Studien). Über sehr gute Buchbestände verfügt Library and Resource Centre des Commonwealth Institute, London, die Bibliothek der Royal Commonwealth Society, London (insbesondere Theaterliteratur) und School of Oriental and African Studies, London.

Foreign and Commonwealth Office and Overseas Development Administration, London, archiviert vor allem Literatur aus der Kolonialzeit (Colonial Office Archives und Foreign Office Archives). Über Spezialbibliotheken verfügt Church Missionary Society Archives, London, und Institute of Education, University of London.

Über *Forschungsinstitutionen* in der Bundesrepublik berichten der Arbeitskreis der Deutschen Afrika-Forschungs- und Dokumentationsleitstelle (ADAK) in: *Institutionen der Afrika Arbeit in der Bundesrepublik und Berlin* (West) (Hamburg, 1971) und A. Nordmann-Seiler, *Afrikanische Literatur an deutschen Universitäten* (Wiesbaden, 1972). Beide Publikationen sind überholt. Eine neuere Veröffentlichung ist: Brigitte Benzing und Reinhardt Bolz (eds.), *Methoden der afrikanischen Forschung und Lehre der BRD* (Hamburg, 1976). Zentren der Afrikaforschung neben den genannten Institutionen sind in Deutschland das Deutsche Institut für Afrikaforschung, Hamburg, in Großbritannien das International Africa Institute und das Africa Centre (mit regelmäßigen Kulturprogrammen) in London sowie das Institute of Commonwealth Studies in Oxford.

Die einzige *wissenschaftliche Organisation* in Deutschland, die sich besonders mit afrikanischer Literatur beschäftigt, ist die Gesellschaft zur Förderung der Literatur in Afrika, Asien und Lateinamerika, Frankfurt. Die Association for Commonwealth Literature and Language Studies (ACLALS) mit wechselndem Sitz führt Konferenzen in dreijährigem Turnus durch; ihre europäische Unterorganisation EACLALS, Aarhus, veranstaltet ebenfalls regelmäßig Konferenzen. Vorwiegend tätig in den USA ist die African Literature Association (ALA) mit wechselndem Sitz und jährlichen Konferenzen.

Deutschsprachige Veröffentlichungen afrikanischer Literatur erschienen in den letzten Jahren vor allem im Erdmann Verlag, Tübingen, Peter Hammer Verlag, Wuppertal, Walter Verlag, Olten, Otto Lembeck und Suhrkamp Verlag, Frankfurt, sowie im Athenäum Verlag, Königstein.

REGISTER

Das Register besteht aus Personen- und Titelindex sowie Sachindex. Es erfaßt Einleitung, Texte und Anmerkungen. Im Personen- und Titelindex wird mit kursiv gesetzter Seitenzahl auf die Seiten verwiesen, wo sich ausgiebigere Information findet. Im Sachindex wird auf literatur- und sprachwissenschaftliche Begriffe, Institutionen, Periodika, Titel ohne Autorenangabe, kulturelle, politische und geographische Begriffe bzw. Ereignisse und Namen verwiesen.

1. Personen und Titel

Abasiekong, Daniel, 62
Abrahams, Peter, 115, 193, *211*
– *A Wreath for Udomo*, 211
– *Mine Boy*, 211
– *Tell Freedom*, 211
Abrahams, Willie, 38
– *The Mind of Africa*, 38
Achebe, Chinua, 15, 16, 17, 18, 36, 37, 41, 46, 47, 51, 54, 59, 115, *118*, 123, 125, 138, 143, 145, 147, 148, 152, 154, 163, 176, 182, 183, 184, 193, 194, 208, 209, 213, 217
– *A Man of the People*, 21, 22, 118, 147, 190, 212
– *Arrow of God*, 17, 141, 191, 213
– "The English Language and the African Writer", 145
– *Morning Yet on Creation Day*, 118, 138, 213, 215
– *No Longer at Ease*, 17, 18, 182, 190, 191, 201, 202, 208
– ed., *Nsukka-scope*, 209
– ed., *Okike*, 118
– *Things Fall Apart*, 16, 17, 18, 24, 116, 118, 136, 147, 182, 189, 193, 195, 196, 201, 202, 204, 205, 208, 211, 213
– "Where Angels Fear to Tread", 215
Adejumo, 177
Adelugba, Dapo, 62
Ademola, Francis
– ed., *Reflections*, 116, 211
Adepoju, Olanrewaju, 177
Aidoo, Ama Ata, 24
Aig-Imokhuede, Frank, 62, *210*
Ainsworth, J. B., 80
Akar, John, 40
Akiga, Benjamin, 115, *211*
– *Akiga's Story: the Tiv Tribe as Seen by One of its Members*, 211
Akintola, Chief S., 212
Akpan, Eton (Akpan, Ntieyong Udo), 143, *213*

– *The Wooden Gong*, 213
Álvares, Alfonso, 44, *208*
Aluko, T. M., 54, 182, 183, *209*, 212
– *His Worshipful Majesty*, 209
– *One Man, One Matchet*, 209
– *One Man, One Wife*, 182, 215
Amadi, Elechi, 20, 23
– *The Concubine*, 20
– *The Great Ponds*, 20, 202
– *Sunset in Biafra*, 23
Amin, Idi, 26
Anand, Mulk Raj, 33, 170, 172, *208*, 214
– "By mouth or by book", 214
– *Coolie*, 208
– *Untouchable*, 208
Angira, Jared, 175, 176, *214*
– *Juices*, 173, 214
Aniebo, I. H. C., 25
– *The Journey Within*, 25
Anozie, Sunday
– *Christopher Okigbo*, 217
Aristotle, 131, 196
– *The Poetics*, 196
Armah, Ayi Kwei, 21, 22, 24, 25, 163, 171, 195, *216*
– *The Beautyful Ones Are Not Yet Born*, 21, 22, 25, 195, 206, 216
– *Two Thousand Seasons*, 24, 26
Armattoe, R. E. G., 19
– *Between the Forest and the Sea*, 19
Armstrong, L. and I. Ward
– *A Handbook of English Intonation*, 105
Ashby, Sir Eric, 103, 104
– *Universities: British, Indian and African*, 211
Atieno-Odhiambo, E. S., *165*
Austen, Jane, 51
Awolowo, Chief Obafemi, 13
– *Path to Nigerian Freedom*, 13
Awoonor, Kofi, 25, 139, *213*
– *The Breast of the Earth*, 207
– *This Earth, My Brother*, 25, 196

Axworthy, Geoffrey, 62
Azikiwe, Nnamdi, 16, *89*, 118, 212
- *Renascent Africa*, 12, 89

Bablola [Babalola], Adebaye, 122, *148*, 212
- *The Content and Form of Yoruba Ijala*, 148
Baldwin, James, 193
Banham, Martin, 62
Banham, Martin and Clive Wake
- *African Theatre Today*, 210
Barnes, Leonard, 84
- *Empire or Democracy?*, 210
Battestini, 217
Beaubru, Theodore [called Languichatte]
- *Anna*, 211
Beaumont, Francis and John Fletcher
- *The Knight of the Burning Pestle*, 106
Behan, Brendan
- *The Quare Fellow*, 188
Beier, Ulli, 131, *213*
- "Contemporary African Poetry in English, Conference of African Writers Report", 213
- ed., *Introduction to African Literature*, 213
- ed., *Three Nigerian Plays*, 207
Beti, Mongo, 139, *213*
- *Le pauvre Christ de Bomba*, 213
- *Perpétue et l'habitude du malheur*, 213
Blake, William, 171
Blyden, Edward Wilmot, 10, 11, 12, 55, 76, 89
- *African Life and Customs*, 11
- *A Voice from Bleeding Africa on Behalf of Her Exiled Children*, 10
- *Christianity, Islam and the Negro Race*, 76
- "Inaugural Address as President of Liberia College", 207
Boateng, Yaw M., 24
- *The Return*, 24
Bodurin, A., 146
Bohannan, Laura
- "Hamlet and the Tiv", 216
Bown, Lalage, *53*
- ed., *Two Centuries of African English*, 53
Bradbury, Malcolm, 205
- *Contemporary Criticism*, 217
Braine, John
- *Room at the Top*, 117
Brew, Kwesi, *216*
- *Shadows of Laughter*, 216
- "The Vulture", 197

Bukenya, Austin, 175, *215*
- *The People's Bachelor*, 215
Bunyan, John
- *The Pilgrim's Progress*, 106

Calder, Angus, *173*
Caliban (Shakespeare, *The Tempest*), 145, 147
Carroll, David
- *Chinua Achebe*, 217
Cartey, Wilfred and Martin Kilson
- eds., *The African Reader. Independent Africa*, 207
Cary, Joyce, 40, 46, 116, *208*, 211
- *The African Witch*, 208
- *Aissa Saved*, 208, 211
- *Mister Johnson*, 208, 211
Casely Hayford, Joseph E., 12, 36, 55, 89, *107*
- *Ethiopia Unbound*, 12, 13, 55, 107, 201
- *Gold Coast Native Institutions*, 12
Castro, Fidel, 100
Césaire, Aimé, 155
Chase, James Hadley, 173
Chaucer, Geoffrey
- "The Squire's Tale", 106
Chesterfield, Lord (Chesterfield, Earl of), 54
Christ, Roland, 205
Churchill, Sir Winston
- *History of the Second World War*, 173
Clark, John Pepper, 16, 24, 47, 51, 59, 62, 115, 131, 135, 139, *145*, 193, 194, 195, 209, 215
- *America, Their America*, 185, 215
- *The Example of Shakespeare*, 145
- "For Granny (Written at Hospital)", 62
- "Ivbie", 62
- "Our Literary Critics", 215
- *Ozidi*, 145, 196, 198
- *Song of a Goat*, 130, 213
- *Three Plays*, 196
Clay, Bertha
- *Beyond Pardon*, 171
Clemen, Wolfgang, 147
Coleman, James, 58
Coleridge, S. T., 106
Collins, Harold
- *Amos Tutuola*, 217
Conrad, Joseph, 33, 115, 141, 176, 181, 185, 186, *215*
- *Heart of Darkness*, 25, 215
- *Lord Jim*, 105

Conton, William, 115, 123, 125, 183, *211*
- *The African*, 182, 183, 211
Corelli, Marie, 170, 171, *214*
- *The Sorrows of Satan*, 214
Cowley, Malcolm, 131
Creighton, T. R. M., 26, 40, 41
Crowther, Samuel Adjai, 83, *210*
- *Experiences with Heathens and Mohammedans in West Africa*, 53, 209
Cuguano, Ottobah, 8, *9*, 10, 11
- *Thoughts and Sentiments of the Evil and Wicked Traffic of Slavery and Commerce of the Human Species*, 9

dan Fodio, Usman, 140
Danquah, J. B., 12
- *Gold Coast: Akan Laws and Customs*, 12
Darwin, Charles, 133
Dathorne, O. R.
- *African Literature in the Twentieth Century*, 207
Defoe, Daniel, 58
de Graft, Joe, 24
- *Muntu*, 24
Dei Anang, Michael, 122, *212*
- *Africa Speaks*, 212
- *Wayward Lines from Africa*, 212
Demoke (W. Soyinka, *A Dance of the Forests*), 190
Dickens, Charles, 52
Diop, Birago, 115, 170, *211*
- *Les Contes d'Amadou Koumba*, 214
- *Stories of Amadou Koumba*, 171
Diop, Cheikh Anta, *214*
- *Nations Nègres et Culture*, 171, 224
Diop, David, 114, 115, 119, 122, 170, *211*
- *Coups de pilon*, 211
- *Hammer Blows*, 212
- "The Time of Martyrdom", 212
Diop, Ousmane Socé [Socé, Ousmane], *214*
- *Karim*, 171, 214
Donne, John, 132
Dostoevsky, Fedor M., 176
Dunn, Thomas, 41
Dussutour-Hammer, Michèle
- *Amos Tutuola*, 217

Easmon, Sarif, 139, *213*, 215
- *Dear Parent and Ogre*, 213
- *The New Patriots*, 190, 213
Ebiere (J. P. Clark, *Song of a Goat*), 131
Echeruo, Michael, *209*

- ed., *The African Writer*, 209
- ed., spec. issue *The Conch*, 209
- *Mortality*, 209
Edwards, Paul
- ed., *Equiano's Travels*, 209
Egbuna, Obi, *215*
- *The Anthill*, 185, 215
Ekpenyong, J. O., *142*
Ekwensi, Cyprian, 16, 25, 34, 36, 37, *38*, 41, 58, 115, 120, 143, 182, 183, 202, 212
- *Ikolo the Wrestler and other Ibo Tales*, 58
- *Jagua Nana*, 117, 182, 208, 212
- *People of the City*, 25, 38, 51, 58, 182, 208
- *When Love Whispers*, 58
Ekwere, John, 116, *212*
Eliot, T. S., 131, 133, 176, 193
- *Murder in the Cathedral*, 105
Emenyonu, Ernest, *191*
Enahoro, Chief Anthony, 120
Equiano, Olaudah, 8, *9*, 10, 11, 36
- *The Interesting Narrative of the Life of Olaudah Equiano or Gustavus Vassa, the African*, 9, 36, 53, 209

Fafunwa, A. Babs, *103*
- *A History of Nigerian Higher Education*, 103
Fagunwa, D. O., 36, 45, 115, 142, 171, 188, *213*
- *The Forest of a Thousand Demons*, 211
- *Igbo Oludumare*, 208
- *Ogboju-ode-ninu igbo Irunmale*, 208
Fagg, William
- *Nigerian Images*, 139, 157, 213
Fanon, Frantz, 97, 157, *210*
- *Les damnés de la terre*, 210
- *Peau noire, masques blancs*, 210
- *Pour une Révolution Africaine*, 210
Fiebach, Joachim
- *Kunstprozesse in Afrika*, 207
- *Literaturen der Befreiung in Afrika*, 207
Fishman, J. A., C. A. Ferguson and J. Das Gupta, 149
- eds., *Language Problems of Developing Nations*, 213
Flaubert, Gustave, 34
Fleming, Ian, 173
Fonlon, B.
- "African Writers Meet in Uganda", 215
Forster, E. M.
- *Passage to India*, 116
Fraser, Alexander Campbell, 133
Freud, Sigmund, 133

Galsworthy, John, 34
Gide, André, 186
Gilliatt, Penelope, 188, 189
Gobineau, Count, 93, 210
- *Essai sur l'égalité des races humaines*, 210
Goodwin, K. L.
- ed., *National Identity*, 125
Goody, Jack, 48
- ed., *Literacy in Traditional Society*, 209
Greene, Graham
- *The Heart of the Matter*, 39, 208
Grey, Earl, 71
Griffiths, Gareth
- "Language and Action in the Novels of Chinua Achebe", 217
Gronniosaw, James Albert Ukawsaw, 8
Gurr, Andrew and Angus Calder
- eds., *Writers in East Africa*, 173
Gurr, Andrew and Pio Zirimu
- eds., *Black Aesthetics*, 165

Haggard, Henry Rider, 181, *215*
- *Ayesha, or the Return of She*, 215
- *King Solomon's Mines*, 215
Hammon, Briton, 8
Hammon, Jupiter, 8
Hardy, Thomas
- *Far from the Madding Crowd*, 105
Harmann, H. A.
- *The Sounds of English for African Students*, 105
Hay, Ian
- *Pip*, 117
Hazlitt, William, 106
Herskovits, Melville J., 58
Heywood, Christopher,
- (ed.), *Perspectives on African Literature*, 49, 53, 216
Higo, Aig, 62, *210*
Hopkins, Gerald Manley, 131
Horton, James Africanus Beale, 11, *74*
- *West African Countries and People*, 74
Howe, Arthur, 91
Howells, Bishop, 83
Hussein, Ebrahim
- *Kinjeketile*, 176, 215

Ijimere, Obotunde
- *The Imprisonment of Obatala*, 216
Ike, V. C., 120, *212*
- *The Chicken Chasers*, 212
- *The Naked Gods*, 212
- *Toads for Supper*, 212
Irele, Abiola, 62, *210*

Iroh, Eddie, 23
- *Forty-eight Guns for the General*, 23
- *Toads of War*, 23
Iyatemi, Phebean, 34
Iyatemi, Phebean and P. Gurrey
- eds., *Folk Tales and Fables*, 208
Iwara, A. U. and E. Mveng
- eds., *Second World Black and African Festival of Arts and Culture: Colloquium on Black Civilization and Education. Colloquium Proceedings*, vol. I, 63

Jahn, Janheinz, *43*, 130, 199, 214
- *A History of Neo-African Literature: Writing in Two Continents*, 43, 207, 216
- *Bibliography of African and Neo-African Literature*, 185
- *Geschichte der neoafrikanischen Literatur: Eine Einführung*, 43, 207
- *Muntu: Umrisse der neoafrikanischen Kultur*, 43, 44, 208, 211
- *Schwarzer Orpheus*, 212
Jahn, Janheinz and Claus Peter Dressler
- *Bibliography of Creative Writing*, 215
- *Die neo-afrikanische Literatur: Gesamtbibliographie*, 215
Jahn, Janheinz and J. Ramsaran
- *Approaches to African Literature*, 208
Jahoda, Gustav, 171
Jegede, John
- "School Magazines", 210
Johnson, Dr. Samuel, 124
Johnson, Samuel, 12
Jones, Eldred Durosimi, 41, 42, *114*, 188
- ed., *African Literature Today*, 114, 120, 191, 207, 217
- *Othello's Countrymen: The African in English Renaissance Drama*, 114
- *The Writing of Wole Soyinka*, 114, 217

Kane, Cheikh Hamidou, *216*
- *L'aventure ambiguë*, 216
Kane, M.
- "The African writer and his public", 214
Kanti, C. G.
- ed., *Modern Poetry from Zambia*, 207
Kariuki, Joseph E., 42, 140, *208*
- "Come Away My Love", 140
Kariuki, Joseph M., *213*
- *Mau Mau Detainee*, 213
Kayira, Legson, 20
- *The Looming Shadow*, 20
Keats, John, 50, 106, 116
- "Odes", 105
Kennedy, John, 61

Kenyatta, Jomo, 12, 93
- *Facing Mount Kenya,* 13, 165, 214
Kibera, Leonard, 21, 163, 175
- *Voices in the Dark,* 21
Kibera, Leonard and Samuel Kahiga
- *Potent Ash,* 215
Kidd, Benjamin, 92
- *Social Evolution,* 210
Kilham, Hannah, *68*
Killam, G. D.
- ed., *African Writers on African Writing,* 154
- *The Novels of Chinua Achebe,* 217
Kimble, H.
- "A reading survey in Africa", 214
King, Bruce, *198*
- ed., *Literatures of the World in English,* 198
Koinange, Peter, 93
Koomsoon (A. K. Armah, *Die Beautyful Ones Are not yet Born*), 195
Kotei, S. I. A., *169*

Ladipo, Duro, 20
- "Oba Koso", 207
- "Oba Moro", 207
- "Oba Waja", 207
- *Three Yoruba Plays,* 196, 207
Lakunle (W. Soyinka, *The Lion and the Jewel*), 18
Larson, Charles, 199
- *The Emergence of African Fiction,* 216
Laurence, Margaret, *211*
- *Long Drums and Cannons: Nigerian Dramatists and Novelists 1952–1966,* 211
- *This Side Jordan,* 116, 211
- *The Tomorrow Tamers,* 116, 211
Lawino (O. p'Bitek, *Song of Lawino*), 18, 127, 167
Lawrence, D. H., 52
Laye, Camara, 115, 171, 202, *211,* 213, 215
- *The Dark Child,* 155
- *Dramouss,* 190, 211
- *L'enfant noir,* 211
- *Le regard du roi,* 211
Leslie, Omolara, 62, *210*
Lessing, Doris, 41, *208*
- *The Grass is Singing,* 208
Lewis, L. J.
- "Some principles of writing for new literatures in Africa", 214
Lindfors, Bernth, 59, 203, 205, 207
- ed., *Critical Perspectives on Amos Tutuola,* 59

- "New Trends in West and East African Fiction", 217
- "The Palm-Oil with which Achebe's words are eaten", 217
- ed., *Research in African Literatures,* 59
Liyong, Taban Lo, 157, 162, 167, 169, 175, 176, *214*
- *The Last Word, Cultural Synthesism,* 168, 214
Lobengula, 55
Lumwama, F., 63
Lynch, Hollis R.
- ed., *Black Spokesman,* 76

Macaulay, Lord, 54
MacCarthy, P. A. D.
- *English Pronunciation,* 105
Maclean, Una, 130, 131, 135
- "Song of a Goat", 213
Mahood, Molly, 46, 62
Makward, Edris, 191
- "African Approach to African Literature", 215
Mallarmé, Stephane
- *L'Après-midi d'un Faune,* 131
Mangua, Charles, 175, 215
- *A Tail in the Mouth,* 215
- *Son of Woman,* 215
Manley, James, 81
Marvant, John, 8
Mata Kharibu (W. Soyinka, *A Dance of the Forests*), 190
Marx, Karl, 123
Maxwell, D. E. S., 209
Mazrui, Ali
- *The Trial of Christopher Okigbo,* 196, 216
Mboya, Tom, 168, *214*
- *The Challenge of Nationhood,* 214
- "Kenya Intellectuals and the KANU Government", 214
Melone, Thomas
- *The Novels of Mongo Beti,* 217
Mercier, 217
Mezu, S. O.
- comp., *Igbo Market Literature,* 5 vols., 207
- *L. S. Senghor,* 217
Mill, John Stuart
- *On Liberty,* 105
Milton, John, 106, 132, 134
- "Shorter Poems", 106
Miranda (Shakespeare, *The Tempest*), 147
Mofolo, Thomas, 115, *211*
- *Chaka: an Historical Romance,* 211

Moore, Gerald, 8, 38, 40, 41, 42, 45, 51, 195, 205, *208*, 217
- ed., *African Literature and the Universities*, 38, 213
- *The Chosen Tongue*, 207, 216
- "Mots anglais, vies africaines", 217
- *Seven African Writers*, 157, 208
- *Wole Soyinka*, 217
Moore, Gerald and Ulli Beier
- eds., *Modern Poetry from Africa*, 212
Morgue, Efua [vgl. Sutherland, Efua], 122, *212*
Mpashi, Stephen, 37
Mphahlele, Ezekiel, 40, 41, 115, 130, *134*, 208, 213
- *Down Second Avenue*, 134
- "*Press Record*, Conference of African Writers of English Expression", 213
Mungeam, G. H.
- comp., *Kenya Select Historical Documents 1884–1923*, 80
Munonye, John, 23, 120, *212*
- *A Wreath for the Maidens*, 23, 212
- *Bridge to a Wedding*, 212
- *The Only Son*, 212
Mutiga, Joe, 167, *214*
- "In the City", 214
Mwangi, Meja, 25
- *Going Down River Road*, 25
- *Kill Me Quick*, 25

Naipaul, V. S., 116, *211*
- *Mr. Stone and the Knight's Companion*, 116, 211
Nehru, Jawaharlal, 145
Neto, Agostinho, 200, *216*
Ngubiah, Stephen, 175
Ngugi wa Thiong'o [Ngugi, James], 17, 22, 49, 115, *151*, 157, 162, 173, 175, 176, 212
- *A Grain of Wheat*, 17, 21, 218, 173, 212
- *The Black Hermit*, 17
- *Devil on the Cross*, 151
- *Homecoming*, 157, 162
- *Ngaahika Ndeenda*, 151
- *Petals of Blood*, 17, 26
- *The River Between*, 128, 212
- *Weep Not, Child*, 17, 128, 175, 212
Ngweno, Hilary [N'gweno, Hilary], 174, *215*
- *The Men from Pretoria*, 215
Nicol, Davidson, *33*, 115, 122
- "On Not Being a West African", 34
Nketia, Kwabena, 123, *212*

- *African Music in Ghana*, 212
- *Folk Songs of Ghana*, 212
Nkosi, Lewis, 186, *215*
- *Home and Exile*, 215
Nkrumah, Kwame, 13, 22, 28, *92*, 100, 118, 122, 173, 183
- *Africa Must Unite*, 92
- *Consciencism*, 168, 214
- *Towards Colonial Freedom*, 13
Nkwoh, Marius
- *Talking About Love*, 213
Ntiru, Richard 175, *215*
- *Tensions*, 215
Nwankwo, Nkem, 16, 25, 120, 212
- *My Mercedes is Bigger than Yours*, 29, 212
- *Danda*, 212
Nwanodi, Glory O. [Okogbule], 60, 62, *210*
- *Icheke and Other Poems*, 210
Nwapa, Flora, 20, 120, *212*
- *Efuru*, 20, 212
- *Idu*, 20, 212
Nwoga, Donatus I., 39, *208*
Nyabongo, Akiki, 13
- *Africa Answers Back*, 13, 55, 209
Nzekwu, Onuora, 16, 120, 139, 182, 183, *212*
- *Highlife for Lizards*, 212
- *Wand of Noble Wood*, 184, 212

Obi (C. Achebe, *No Longer at Ease*), 17, 18, 182
Obiechina, Emmanuel N., 46, 56, 62, 120, 193, 195, 205, 216
- *Culture, Tradition and Society in the West African Novel*, 217
- *Literature for the Masses: An Analytical Study of Popular Pamphleteering in Nigeria*, 56
- *Onitsha Market Literature*, 207
Obierka (C. Achebe, *Things Fall Apart*), 147
Ocol (O. p'Bitek, *Song of Lawino*), 18
Oculi, Okello, 18, 175
- *Orphan*, 18, 52, 128
O'Flinn, J. P.
- "Towards a Sociology of the Nigerian Novel", 207
Ofori, E.
- "Traditionalism in African Literature", 207
Ogali, O. A., 14
- *Veronica My Daughter*, 14

Ogot, B. A.
- "Reintroducing the African Man into the World", 214
Ogot, Grace, 52, 175, *209*, 212
- *Land without Thunder*, 209
- *The Promised Land*, 128, 209
Ogunde, Hubert, 118, *212*
- *Yoruba Ronu*, 212
Ogundipe, Omolara, 62
Ojo-Ade, Femi, *203*
Okara, Gabriel, 16, 22, 120, 122, *136*
- *The Voice*, 21, 22, 136, 189, 196
Okigbo, Christopher, 16, 17, 22, 47, 62, 115, 119, 120, 130, 131, 139, 176, 185, 204, 215
- *Heavensgate*, 19
- *Labyrinths with Path of Thunder*, 207
- *Limits*, 19
- "Path of Thunder, Poems prophesying War", 22
- *Silences*, 131, 213
Okola, Lennard
- ed., *Drum Beat*, 214
Okonkwo (C. Achebe, *Things Fall Apart*), 147, 182
Okpaku, Joseph Ohiomogben, *183*
- ed., *Journal of the New African Literature and the Arts*, 183
Okpure, Obuke O.
- "Characterization in Zambian Literature", 207
Olorunyomi, T. I.
- *The Andrian*, 209
Oluwasanmi, E., E. McLean and H. Zell
- eds., *Publishing in Africa in the Seventies*, 168
Oluwole, Bishop, 83, *210*
Omotoso, Kole, 23, *177*
- *The Combat*, 23
Onibonoje, G. O., Kole Omotoso, O. A. Lawal
- eds., *The Indigenous for National Development*, 177
Opubor, Alfred, 62
Ord, Colonel, 75, 210
Orr, J. R., *80*
- *The System of Education in the East African Protectorate*, 80
Osadebaye, Denis, 19
- *Africa Sings*, 19
Ottenberg, Simon, 58
Ouologuem, Yambo, 195, *216*
Ousmane, Sembène, 174, 200, 202, *214*
- *Le docker noir*, 214
- *Le mandat*, 214

Owomoyela, Oyekan, 62
Owuor-Anyumba, Henry, 157, 162
Owusu, Martin
- *The Sudden Return and Other Plays*, 196, 216

Palangyo, Peter, 175, 176
- *Dying in the Sun*, 215
Palmer, H. E.,
- *English Intonation with Systematic Exercise*, 105
Parkes, Francis, [Parkes, Frank K.], 122, *212*
- *Songs from the Wilderness*, 212
Pasteur, Louis, 84
p'Bitek, Okot, *18*, 52, 163, 167, 175, 176, 201
- *Lak Tar*, 209
- *Song of Lawino*, 18, 49, 51, 52, 126 ff., 173, 175
- *Song of Malaya*, 18
- *Song of Ocol*, 18
Pepys, Samuel, 54
Phelps-Stokes Commission
- *Education in Africa*, 84, 88
- *Education in East Africa*, 84
Pound, Ezra, 131, 133
Press, John
- ed., *Commonwealth Literature: Unity and Diversity in a Common Culture*, 114, 142
Prospero (Shakespeare, *The Tempest*), 147
Pryse, Elizabeth
- "Getting into Perspective", 215

Quaison-Sackey, Alex
- *Africa Unbound: Reflections of an African Statesman*, 53, 209

Racine, Jean, 100
Ramsaran, John, 47, 208
- "African Twilight: Folktale and Myth in Nigerian Literature", 208
- "Nigerian School Journals: Key to Nationhood", 209
Ratnam, Raja
- *At Eight-fifteen*, 131
Ravenscroft, Arthur, 41, *208*, 215
- "African Literature V: ‚Novels of Disillusionment'", 207
- *Chinua Achebe*, 215, 217
Redfield, Robert, 101
Reed, J. and C. Wake
- eds., *A Book of African Verse*, 214

Reindorf, Carl Christian, 12, 36
- *The History of the Gold Coast and Asante*, 36
Rhodes, Cecil, 55
Richardson, Samuel, 58
Riemenschneider, Dieter
- "Die anglophone Literatur der siebziger Jahre", 207
Rive, Richard, 38, *208*
- ed., *Modern African Prose*, 208
Robbins, Harold, 173
Robert, Shabaan, 139, 140, *213*
Robertson, Stuart and Frederic A. Cassidy
- *The Development of Modern English*, 213
Roscoe, Adrian, 194, 195, 216
- *Mother is Gold: A Study in West African Literature*, 216
Rotimi, Ola, 24
- *Kurunmi*, 24
- *Ovonramwen Nogbaisi*, 24
Ruark, Robert, 39
Rubadiri, David, 21, 22, *49*, 125, 175, 176
- *No Bride Price*, 21, 49, 128, 162
- "Stanley Meets Mutesa", 162, 214
Ruganda, John, 24
Ruheni, Mwangi, 25
- *The Future Leaders*, 25

Samkange, Stanley
- *On Trial For My Country*, 55, 209
Sampson, Magnus
- (ed.), *West African Leadership*, 36, 207
Sancho, Ignatius, 8, 9, 10
- *Letters of the Late Ignatius Sancho*, 9
Sarbah, John Mensa, 12
- *The Fanti National Institution*, 12
Schreiner, Olive, 181, *215*
- *God's Stepchildren*, 215
- *The Story of an African Farm*, 215
Scott, Sir Walter, 106
Selormey, Francis
- *The Narrow Path*, 184, 215
Senghor, Leopold Sedar, 115, 122, 157, 170, 185, 188, 202, *211*
- ed., *Anthologie de la nouvelle poésie nègre et malgache*, 211
- *Chants d'Ombre*, 211
- *Ethiopiques*, 211
- *Nocturnes*, 211
Seruma, Eneriko, 175
- *The Experience*, 215
Serumaga, Robert, 21, 22, 24, 175, 176
- *The Return to the Shadows*, 21
Seton, Anya, 173

Shakespeare, William, 60, 100, 105, 106, 132, 134, 147, 185, 196
- *Antony and Cleopatra*, 106
- *Hamlet*, 196
- *Julius Caesar*, 62
- *Macbeth*, 105
- *The Tempest*, 105, 106
Shepherd, Lord, 120
Simon, Neil, 193
Snow, P. C.
- *The Masters*, 117
Soyinka, Wole, 15, 16, 17, 18, 19, 22, 23, 24, 25, 27, 39, 40, 47, 59, 62, 115, 119, 122, 130, 136, 143, 163, 176, 187, 188, 189, 193, 195, 204, *207*, 209, 212
- *A Dance of the Forests*, 17, 131, 133, 155, 190
- *Before the Blackout*, 118, 212
- "From a Common Backcloth", 207
- *Idanre and Other Poems*, 19
- "The Immigrant", 116
- *The Interpreters*, 21, 25, 190, 196, 215
- *Kongi's Harvest*, 21
- *The Lion and the Jewel*, 18, 133
- *The Man Died*, 23, 207
- "The Other Immigrant", 116, 212
- ed., *Poems of Black Africa*, 19
- "Salutations to the Gut", 116
- *Season of Anomy*, 23, 24, 30
- *The Strong Breed*, 196
- "Telephone Conversation", 116, 212
- "The Writer in an African State", 207
Speedy, Eric, 14
- *Mabel the Sweet Honey that Poured Away*, 14
Spencer, Herbert, 78
Spenser, Edmund, 106, 132, 139
- *The Faerie Queene*, 106
Stock, A. G., 193
- "Yeats and Achebe", 215
Stoddard, Lothrop, 92
- *The Rising Tide of Color Against White World Supremacy*, 210
Stuart, 41
Sutherland, Efua, 24, 122, *212*
- *Edufa*, 212
- *Foriwa*, 212
- *The Marriage of Aanansewa*, 212

Tagore, Rabindranath
- *Stray Birds*, 131
Tennyson, Lord Alfred
- "Selected Poems", 105
Theroux, Paul
- "Hating the Asians", 210

Thumboo, Edwin
- "Kwesi Brew: the poetry of statement and situation", 216
Tibble, Anne
- *African English Literature,* 192, 193, 215
Tucker, Martin, *181*
- *Africa in Modern Literature: A Survey of Contemporary Writing in English,* 181, 216
- *Africa in Modern Perspective,* 216
Tutuola, Amos, *13,* 19, 20, 33, 34, 36, 45, 47, 51, 59, 123, 130, 141, 143, 157, 171, 195, 199, 203
- *The Brave African Huntress,* 208
- *The Feather Woman of the Jungle,* 141, 213
- *My Life in the Bush of Ghosts,* 144, 208, 213
- *The Palm-Wine Drinkard,* 13, 19, 20, 36, 45, 47, 145, 191, 193, 196, 208

Udezue, Juliet, 62
Uka, Kalu, 62, *210*

van den Berghe, Pierre, *96*
Venn, Reverend Henry, 76
Verwoerd, Hendrik Frensch, 155
Vilakazi, Benedict Wallet, *211*
- "In the Gold Mines", 114, 115, 211
von Schmid, Christoph, *214*
- *Basket of Flowers,* 171, 214

Wade, Michael
- *Peter Abrahams,* 217
Wästberg, P.
- "Themes in African Literature Today", 207
- ed., *The Writer in Modern Africa,* 188

Wali, Obiajunwan, *130,* 134, 135, 136
Warner, Allen
- "A New English in Africa", 143
Washington, Booker T., 210
Waugh, Evelyn
- *The Loved One,* 116
Webster, Noah, 144
Wheatley, Phyllis, 8
Whiteley, Wilfried Howell, *34*
- *Swahili: The Rise of a National Language,* 34
Williams, Raymond, 48
- *The Long Revolution,* 209
Williams, Tennessee, 130, 131
Wilson, Harold, 119
Willspeare
- "Julius Caesar in Cinemascope", 210
Woddis, Jack
- *Africa, the Roots of Revolt,* 210
Wonodi, Okogbule, 192, 193
- "The Role of Folktales in African Society", 215
Woodson, Carter G., 90
Wordsworth, William, 50
- *Lyrical Ballads,* 105
Wyatt, Alfred John
- *Anglo-Saxon Reader,* 106

Yeats, W. B., 193
- "The Second Coming", 16
Young, Michael, 98
- *The Rise of the Meritocracy,* 210
Yu Tang, Lin, 33, 208
- *The Red Peony,* 208

Zell, Hans and Helene Silver
- eds., *A Reader's Guide to African Literature,* 216, 217

2. Sachen

Abolitionisten, 10
abolitionistische Bewegung, 9
Abyssinia, 91
Accra, 39, 171
acculturation, 149, 150
Achimota, 95, 108, 109, 211
Achimota College, 11, 92, 93
Acoli, 52, 175, 209
Advisory Committee on Native Education in British Tropical African Dependencies, 84
Africa Report, 215

African
- aesthetic, 199
- art, 183–185
- audience, 115
- civilization, 122
- Cultural Research Centres, 113
- culture, 90, 101, 120, 121, 131, 134, 162, 166, 170–171, 178, 183, 185, 186, 187, 193, 200
- educators, 90
- experience, 135, 141
- *Forum,* 189

- historical consciousness, 101
- history, 103, 189–190
- independence, 116, 118, 120, 123, 143, 166, 198–199
- language(s), 68–70, 101, 102, 133, 136, 143, 145, 146
- language policy, 33, 64, 115, 149–151
- literary criticism, 65–66, 132–133, 135, 183–188, 191, 216, 217
- literature in African languages, 133, 134, 135, 136, 148, 151–153, 158–160, 162, 163–164, 175, 177
- literature in English
  Abgrenzung, 33–67, 109–114, 151–153, 191
  Allegorie, 23, 24
  audience, 169–173, 173–174, 177–178, 184
  Autobiographie, autobiographisch, 9, 10, 13, 23
  Biafra war, 26–27, 118–120, 165
  Briefliteratur, 9, 10
  course of studies, 161
  definition, 38, 39–43, 43–46, 63–65, 132, 138–139, 141, 185
  development, 43, 44, 45, 53–56, 58–59, 63, 191–192, 198–199, 205
  Dichtung, 8, 15, 18–19
  didacticism, 55, 124, 125, 181
  discursive writing, 36, 50, 53–55
  Drama, 15, 17–18, 24–25, 112–113, 130–131, 161, 175, 187, 196, 199, 210, 213
  and English language, 130–153, 167, 174, 188, 204
  and English literature, 40–41, 56, 58, 158–159
  fiction, 36–37, 48, 54, 58–59, 125, 128, 147–148, 167, 170, 176, 199
  function, 41–42, 43, 57, 64, 111, 117, 120, 124, 125, 166–169, 202
  history in East Africa, 50–52, 126, 166–169, 175
  journalism, 10, 12–13
  literary quality, 15, 26, 56–57, 59, 161, 167, 181–183, 204
  Literaturgeschichte, 7, 26
  Literaturgeschichtsschreibung, 8, 26
  mass media, 16, 57–58
  as national literature, 139
  and oral tradition, 46–49, 54, 64, 110, 191, 192–193, 194, 195–198, 199, 204–205, 209, 217
  pamphlet literature, 13–15, 56–59, 60–63, 144
  period of disillusionment, 21–22, 163, 199, 200
  poetry, 60–61, 62, 122, 131, 167, 176, 197, 199
  "private voice", 19, 50, 194
  and publishing, 50, 52, 66–67, 110, 136, 174, 175–176, 177–180
  Reisebericht, 10
  Roman, 13, 15, 16–17, 20, 21–24, 25, 46
  school and university journals, 59–63, 209
  short story, 13, 15, 50, 60, 133
  "song", 18, 52, 167
  specific genres, 13, 19–20, 55–56
  themes, 12, 34, 52, 57, 60, 114, 116, 123, 126, 129, 147, 154–156, 162, 165–166, 170, 181–182, 189, 191, 199, 200, 203–204
  and traditional forms, 19–20, 24, 111–112, 123, 125
  urbane Literatur, 25
- *Literature Today*, 216
- nationalism, 114, 121, 125, 126
- nationality, 108
- Personality, 64, 77, 93, 96, 121, 122, 123, 130, 148, 149, 170
- Perspectives, 203
- publishing, 177–180
- Schools of Dramatic Art, 113
- sensibility, 48, 133
- sensitivity, 64, 65
- Socialism, 201
- socialists, 100
- *Statesman*, 146, 213
- Studies Association, 215
- traditions and beliefs, 45, 79, 82, 85, 90, 96, 104, 110, 125, 171, 178, 182, 196
- university, 74–75, 87, 100, 107, 131, 133, 135, 159, 163, 203, 205, 211
- *Writer*, 209
Africanism, 45
Africanity, 64
afrikanisch
- Emanzipation, 11, 16, 20, 26
- Erbe, 9, 11
- "expatriates", 12
- Geschichte, 19, 20, 23
- Geschichtlichkeit, 18, 20, 26
- Gesellschaftssystem, 11
- Identität, 12
- Kultur, 17
- künstlerische Tradition, 17
- Literaturkritik, 19, 26
- Theatergruppen, 25
- Unabhängigkeit, 8, 12, 21

– Universität, 11
The Afro-American, 90
Afro-American literature(s), 158–161
Afro-Arab, 44
Afro-European literature, 151
Aggrey Memorial College, 60
Aiyetoro, 23, 207
Akamba, 159
Akan, 123, 212
Alawada Theatre, 177
alienation, 52, 126, 200, 205
Ambiguous Adventure (Cheikh Hamidou Kane), 200
America, 10, 90, 143, 172, 203
American literature, 8, 64
American Scholar, 207
Anansi (Brer Spider), 117
"Ancestors and Gods" (W. Soyinka (ed.), *Poems of Black Africa*), 19
ancestral spirits, 18, 166
"Animistic Phases", (W. Soyinka (ed.), *Poems of Black Africa*), 19
Anglophone African writers, 203
Anglophones, 189
Angola, 216
Antilles, 112
Arabic, 135, 159
Aro, 59
Asaba, 144
Ashanti, 36
Ashby Commission, 104, 211
Ashquith colleges, 104
australische Literatur, 8
authors
– elite background, 34, 199
– intellectuals, 56–59
– "mushroom" authors, 61, 63
– Negro-African, 66–67, 111
– pamphleteers, 56–59
– social role, 15, 19, 21, 25, 117, 124, 125, 154–157, 162, 166–169, 172, 174, 184, 189–190, 201
avatar(s), 112, 211

"Babu" English, 46
B. A. General Examination, 105
Bantu languages, 135
– poetry, 135
Basel Mission, 94
Bassa, 70
The Beacon, 59, 61, 62, 210
Bemba, 37
Beware of Women, 14
Bible, 60
Biafra, 22, 23, 118, 120, 212

Biafran-Nigerian conflict, 165
Black Orpheus, 16, 22, 208, 209, 213
Board of Study for the Preparation of Missionaries, 87
Botswana, 98
"Brave New World", 129
Brazil, 112
British and Foreign Bible Society, 69, 86f.
British East Africa, 80
British West African University, 107, 108
Brussels, 91
Bryn Mawr College, 92
Bubi, 89
Bürgerkriegsliteratur, 22
Bulletins of the United States Department of Aqriculture, 84
Burundi, 98
Busara, 207
"bush stories", 19

Cambridge, 103
Cameroun, 139
Cape Coast, 95
Cape Town, 87
Caribbean, 43, 121, 122, 158, 161
Catholic Undergraduate, 59
"celebration of the past", 17
"Celtic Twilight", 125
Chad, 171
Chi, 156, 213
China, 98, 99, 208
Church Missionary Society (C.M.S.), 45, 74, 82, 83, 210
College of Arts, Science and Technology Kumasi, 96
colonial experience, 50
colonialism, 121, 134, 140, 142, 166, 191, 198, 200
Colonial Office Library, 71
colonial situation, 51, 64, 113–114, 163, 164
colonization, 66, 109, 189, 190
Columbia, 89
commitment, 21, 111, 166, 174
Committee of Council on Education, 71
Commonwealth, 158
Commonwealth-Literatur, 7, 158
Conch, 118, 209
Conference on African Literature and the University Curriculum, 38
Conference on Writing in English in the Commonwealth, 125
Congo, 65, 98
Convention People's Party, 92
Cowries, 193

Creole, 33, 112, 139
Cultural Events in Africa, 209
"cultural formalism", 194, 196, 198
cultural identity, 65, 66, 149, 150, 199, 205
– nativism, 121
– revival, 177
– revivalism, 102

Daedalus, 207
Dakar, 187
Dakers, 208
Dar-es-Salaam, 209, 214
Department of African Literature and Languages, 159, 162
Development of Public Libraries in Africa: the Ibadan Seminar, 214
Diaspora, 7, 65
Diogenes, 34
documentary, 36

The Eagle, 59
East African Community, 209
East African Cultural Heritage (Conference), 51
East African Journal, 214
East African Literature Bureau, 51, 176, 209, 215
East African Protectorate (E.A.P.), 210
East African Publishing House, 52, 176, 209, 215
Edo, 139
education
– and B.N. Azikiwe, 89–92
– and E. W. Blyden, 11–12, 76–79
– and J. E. Casely Hayford, 107
– and colonial policy, 11, 27, 71–74, 76, 80–82, 83, 84–88, 93, 108, 126, 136, 164
– Committee of the Privy Council, 71
– and J.A.B. Horton, 74–76
– "industrial education", 71, 81, 90, 91, 107, 108
– and languages, 35–36, 68–70, 72, 81, 83, 85–88, 97–98, 101–103, 109
– and mass education, 92
– and missionaries, 82–83
– in post-colonial Africa, 94–96, 115, 133
– and schools, 13–14, 68, 75–76, 80–82, 91–92, 93–96, 103, 149–150, 175, 208, 210
Efik, 89, 139
Egypt, 172
elite, 15, 21, 22, 35, 59, 60, 97, 98, 99, 100, 101, 104, 151, 163, 164, 165, 166, 177, 178, 179, 198, 199, 200, 201

Engagement-letters and How to Know a Girl to Marry, 14
England, 8, 9, 10, 11, 69, 76, 77, 92, 115, 116, 137, 143, 185, 208, 209
English language
– in Africa, 33, 35, 56, 68–70, 115–116, 134, 139–141, 156–157
– in Nigeria, 142–145
– varieties, 138
Ethiopia, 98, 120
Europe, 9, 11, 12, 19, 21, 23, 85, 115, 118, 120, 146, 154, 156, 172, 177, 196, 199, 201, 203
European
– economy, 90–91
– education, 77
– influence on African literature, 19, 20, 58, 131, 135, 192–193, 199, 203, 204, 216
– languages, 146, 151, 171, 177, 188
– literature(s), 10, 64, 132, 146, 159, 160–161, 162
Europeanised African(s), 11, 92
Exilliteratur, 7

Faber, 208
Fanti, 89
Fate, 171
FESTAC 1977, 63
Financial Times, 120
First Congress of Negro Writers and Artists, 109
folk literature, 186
– -lore, 83, 101, 104, 137, 171, 204
– material, 37
– narratives, 170
– opera, 212
– tale(s), 34, 38, 46, 47, 48, 50, 117, 123, 143, 160, 171, 191 f., 192, 193, 195, 208, 209
Fourah Bay College, 11, 38, 74, 75, 93, 108, 109, 114, 122, 172
France, 97, 137, 210
Francophones, 189
frankophone Literatur, 120
Freetown, 10, 38, 39, 76, 157
French Equatorial Africa, 93
Freretown, 80, 210
Fresh Buds, 59
From Fear to Confidence, 14
Fulani Empire, 140

Ga, 89
Gambia, 69, 211
Garri, 180

Ghana, 9, 16, 21, 22, 24, 65, 93, 109, 113, 116, 118, 122, 123, 190, 197, 210, 211, 212, 213, 216
Ghana Association of Writers, 211
Ghana Drama Studio, 212
Giriama, 80
Githunguri, 93
Golah, 79
Gold Coast, 94, 108
Gold Coast Aborigines Rights Protection Society, 12
Gold Coast Leader, 12
Goldküste, 93
Gordon College, 94, 210
Government College Gold Coast, 108
Government College Ibadan, 60
griot, 35
Grub Street Pamphleteering, 58

Haiti, 109, 112
Hampton, 90
Hampton Institute, 91
Hampton Leaflets, 84
Hampton Normal and Agricultural Institute, 210
Haussa, 89, 101, 114, 133, 135, 136, 139, 153
Heinemann, 173, 176, 208, 310
Heinemann Educational Books, 176
Heinemann's *African Writers Series*, 209
Helen of Troy, 190
Higher College in Yaba, 11
Hindi, 145
Hindustani, 159
Hope Waddell Training College, 60
The Horn, 59, 62
How to Write and Reply Letters for Marriage, 18
Hutchinson, 208

Ibadan, 11, 16, 25, 59, 61, 62, 93, 103, 104, 118, 119, 145, 177, 209
Ibadan, 208, 213
Ibadan, University College Press, 34
Ibo, Igbo, 58, 89, 119, 123, 125, 136, 137, 138, 139, 152, 153, 154, 156, 212
Ibo-Gesellschaft, 16, 17
Iboland, 156
Iboness, 152
Ibovolk, 23
Identitätsproblematik, 9, 12, 13, 17, 125
identity, 52, 63, 64, 123, 126, 127, 148, 174, 201, 203
Ife, 25, 49, 103
Ijala, 148

Ijaw, 39, 89, 137, 139, 145
Ilesha Grammar School, 60
illiteracy, 47, 66, 91, 113, 172
The Imprisonment of Obatala, 196
India/Indien, 116, 145, 208
indigenous languages, 150
individualism, 57, 200, 202
Industrial Schools, 71
Inostrannoi Literatury, 173
Institute of African Studies, 212
intellectual(s), 57, 58, 59, 168, 187, 189, 201, 202
Intellektuelle, 12
Intermediate Examination, 105
The Interpreter, 60
Isiolo, 168
Islam, 11
Islamic Cultures, 44

Japan, 154
Jekri, 89
Johannesburg, 87, 93
John the Baptist, 118
Jolof(f), 69, 70, 89
Journal of the African Society, 89
The Journal of Commonwealth Literature, 207, 208, 215
The Journal of Modern African Studies, 59, 194, 216

Kakamega, 168
Kalenyin, 164
Kamerun, 213
Karibik, 76
Kenia/Kenya, 13, 17, 18, 21, 22, 24, 93, 98, 128, 134, 140, 153, 159, 163, 164, 168, 174, 175, 208, 209, 210, 213, 214
Kenya Teacher's College, Khartoum, 11, 93
Kikamba, 81
Kikuyu, 93, 151, 152, 153, 159, 175
Kikuyu Independent Schools Association, 93
King's College Lagos, 60, 108, 109, 211
Kinjeketile, (Ebrahim Hussain), 176
Kiriyaga, 168
Kisii, 168
Ki-Swahili, 81
Kitui, 80, 81, 82
Kolonialismus, 7, 8, 11, 13, 14, 20, 24
Kongo, 14
Kroomen, 79
Kru, 89
Kulturkonflikt, 17, 20

Kumasi, 96
Kwame Nkrumah University, 96

Lagos, 63, 102, 182
Lagos Grammar School, 210
Laibou, 164
Latin, 132, 134, 146
Lawrence and Wishart, 173
Legon, 25, 214
Leopoldville, 94
Lesoto, 98, 211
Liberia, 10, 76, 91, 98
Liberia College, 76, 77, 207
lingua franca, 36, 88, 101, 102, 144, 149, 151, 174
literacy campaigns, 179
Literature and Publication Bureaux, 35, 37
Literature Bureaux, 135
Literature Department, University of Nairobi, 16, 157
littérature des noirs, 43 f.
littérature noire, 43
literature of disillusionment, 200
London, 90, 91, 115, 174, 192, 209
Lovanium, 94
Lusaka, 37
Luo, 18, 152, 153, 159

Machakos, 81, 82
Macmillan, 173
Macumba, 112
Makarere, 11, 49, 133, 136, 214
Makarere College, 93
Makarere University, 118, 151, 163
Malawi, 20, 21, 30, 49, 207
Mali, 190, 216
Malindi, 168
Man Know Thyself, 14
Mandingo, 70, 79, 89
market literature, 14
Mau Mau, 17, 93, 214
Mauritius, 76
Mbari Club, 16
Mbari Publications, 16
Mbotela, 168
Mende, 89
"meritocracy", 98, 99
The Mermaid, 60
Miscellaneous Pamphlets, 71
missionary, 10, 16, 55, 86, 87, 88, 90, 143, 182
mission bookshops, 94
– presses/missionary presses, 35, 136
– schools, 10, 43, 60, 68

Mombasa, 210
The Murder of Adesua, 196

national bourgeoisies, 98, 99
National Congress of British West Africa, 12, 107
national identity, 126, 127
nationalism, 126
native language, 86, 87, 88
– speech, 85
– tongue, 85, 88
"nativism", 121
Naturalists, 147
"negative capability", 116
Negritude, 7, 44, 45, 64, 117, 120, 121, 122, 123, 125, 130, 161, 208, 211
Negritudists, 199
Negro, 77, 78, 79, 122
-Africa, 109
-African Civilization, 112
-African cultures, 109, 123
-African intellectuals, 122
-African writers, 113
– education, 77–79
– literature(s), 43, 110
– writer, 111
Nelson, 173, 208
Neo-African development, 216
Neo-African literature, 44, 45–46, 171, 203, 205
neo-classicists, 124
neo-colonialism, 97, 100, 152, 168, 200
Neuguinea, 214
New Guinea, 213
New Testament, 84, 85
New York, 91
Niger, 144
Nigeria, 9, 11, 16, 17, 20–22, 24, 26, 36, 37, 46, 47, 53, 56, 59–63, 65, 82, 89, 93, 97, 98, 103–105, 116–120, 134, 136, 139, 140, 143, 145, 148, 149, 169, 172, 177–180, 191, 196, 202, 203, 207–213
Nigeria Magazine, 38, 154, 207, 215
Nigerian Periodicals and Newspapers 1950–1970, 209
Nigeria's National Magazine, 213
"Nigerrimandering", 118
Northern Rhodesia, 37, 93
novels of disillusionment, 199
nsaasia, 196
Nsukka, 46
Nupe, 89

OAU (Organisation of African Unity), 119

The Observer, 188
Occultist, 171
Ogoga of Ikerre, 197
Okike, 210, 216
Old Testament, 84, 85
Onitsha, 13, 14, 56, 58, 144
- chap books, 199
- Market, 144, 170
- Market Literature, 13, 15
- Pamphlet Literature, 58, 59, 202
oracy, 66
oral heritage, 196
- literature(s), 10, 35, 44, 45, 48, 63, 64, 66, 109, 110, 148, 150, 161, 170, 177, 191, 193, 194, 197, 199, 204, 208
- past, 194
- poetry, 204
- tradition(s), 20, 34, 36, 37, 45, 46, 47, 48, 50, 64, 103, 159, 160, 170, 187, 194, 195, 198, 201, 205, 209, 217
oriki, 197
Outlook, 207
Oxford, 89, 90, 174
Oxford University Press, 172, 176
The Oyemekun, 210

palavers, 204
Pamphletliteratur, 13, 14, 38
Panaf Publications, 173
Pan-Africanism, 64
pan-Negroism, 122
Paris, 91, 125
People's Union, 12
"perceptivism", 196
Pergamon, 176
period of disillusionment, 21, 22, 23, 25
Pessah, 79
Phelps-Stokes Commission, 83, *84*
pidgin English, 143, 144, 147, 192, 204
Popo, 89
popular literature, 60
Portugal, 97
Portuguese Africa, 94
Prediction, 171
Présence Africaine, 33, 46, 109, 148, 193, 208, 214, 217
Pretoria, 87
Prince of Wales' College, 108, 211
Psychology, 171
Psychology Today, 216

race consciousness, 107
Reader's Digest, 213
reading population, 35

Report of the Conference on the Development of Higher Education in Africa, 211
A Review of English Literature, 211, 213
Review of National Literatures, 217
Rhodesia, 55, 119
Rift Valley, 210
ritual drama, 204
Roman Catholic University, 94
Rousseauist, 125
Rwanda, 98, 102

Sacred Songs and Solos, 118
Sahara, 94, 98, 217
Sambia, 26
Sandhurst, 101
School of Oriental Studies London, 87, 114
secondary schools, 11
secondary school magazine, 59, 60 ff.
Second Congress of Negro Writers and Artists, 109, 113
Senegal, 171, 210, 211, 214, 216
Sesuto, 211
shamba, 80, 163, 210
Shangana-Tsonga, 135
Sierra Leone, 9, 10, 16, 38, 68, 69, 70, 74, 75, 76, 82, 93, 108, 114, 122, 123, 139, 210, 213
Simbabwe, 26, 108
Sklaverei, 7, 8, 9, 11, 26
slave, 68, 121, 210
Society of African Culture, 113
Society of Friends, 68
Somalia, 64, 98, 102
"song", 18
Songhai, 190
Sotho, 135
South Africa, 35, 38, 40, 43, 98, 102, 135, 155, 172
South America, 135
Southern Rhodesia, 93
S.P.C.K., 35, 208
St. Cyr, 101
St. Thomas, 76
Stage sixty, 188
State Publishing Corporation, 173
Stratford East, 188
Suaheli, 213
Sudan, 94, 172, 214
Südafrika, 208, 211, 215
Südrhodesien, 208
Suffers of Africans: A Complete History of White Imperialism Towards African Nationalism, 14
Swahili, 37, 50, 80, 101, 102, 114, 135,

140, 146, 158, 159, 160, 161, 167, 174, 175, 176, 184
Swaziland, 98
"synthesism", 168

Tanganyika, 140
Tansania/Tanzania, 26, 102, 129, 175, 213
Theatre in Malawi, 207
The Third Press, 183
Time Magazine, 144
The Times Educational Supplement, 209
The Times Literary Supplement, 214
Timny, 89
Tiv(s), 196, 211, 212
Tracts, 68
traditional African theatre, 112
– culture, 123
– literature, 110, 171
– verbal art, 195
Transition, 96, 130, 136, 207, 210, 213
tribalism, 100, 119, 205
Trinidad, 211
Trobrianders, 101
Tupi, 101
Turu, 196
Tuskegee, 90
Tuskegee Normal and Industrial Institute, 210

Uganda PH, 176
uhuru, 164, 165, 214
Umofia, 193
Umuahia Government College, 59
Umuahian, 59
UNESCO, *Books in the Promotion of Development in Africa, Unesco Meeting of Experts on Book Development in Africa, Accra, 13–19 February,* 1968, 214
UNESCO Conference Tananarive, 104, 211
Union of South Africa, 87
United Gold Coast Convention, 92
United Kingdom, 97, 103, 104, 145
Universitas, 214
University College Ibadan, 103, 211
University College Salisbury, 93
University for Western Africa, 75
The University Herald, 59
university magazine, 59
University of Calabar, 191

Universtiy of Ghana, 169, 212, 214
University of Ibadan, 130, 209, 210
University of Ife, 169, 207
University of Lagos, 145, 148
University of Malawi, 207
University of Nairobi, 151, 157, 165, 173
University of Nigeria in Nsukka, 208, 209
University of Sierra Leone, 114
university publications, 61 ff.
USA, 10, 77, 85, 92, 97, 137, 145, 208
Utopia, 201

Vai, 89
vernacular, 37, 46, 126, 143, 146
– expressions, 137
– language(s), 136, 199
– literature(s), 87, 109, 142
Veys, 79
Virgin Islands, 76
voodoo, 112, 211

Wa-kamba, 81
Wangala, 89
waragi, 127, 211
Wa-zungu, 80
West Africa, 181
West African English, 138
West African Examination Council, 144, 213
West African Journal of Modern Languages, 198
West African School Certificate, 149
West African School Certificate Examinations, 145
West Indian Colonies, 71, 72
– personality, 65
– literature, 41
West Indies, 41, 77, 161

Xhosa, 135

Yoruba, 20, 36, 45, 50, 89, 101, 114, 123, 133, 136, 139, 148, 152, 153, 177, 193, 197, 212
Yorubasage, 211
Young Kikuyu Association, 214

Zaire, 65
Zeitschrift für Kulturaustausch, 207
Zulu, 89, 101, 114, 135

UTB Fink

Text und Geschichte
Modellanalysen zur englischen und amerikanischen Literatur

Hrsg. von Rüdiger Hillgärtner, Edgar Kamphausen und Malte C. Krugmann

Band 1
1158 Bernd Peter Lange
George Orwell: „1984"
1982. 105 Seiten.

Nach einer Rekonstruktion des zeitgeschichtlichen und biographischen Entstehungszusammenhangs von „1984" wird das Verhältnis von antiutopischem Schreckbild zur historischen Wirklichkeit analysiert und verdeutlicht, wie Orwell mit der zugleich inhaltlichen wie perspektivischen Figuration des Blicks den Roman organisiert. Ein kritischer Literaturbericht faßt abschließend den Stand der Diskussion um „1984" zusammen.

Band 2
1154 Dieter Petzold
Daniel Defoe: „Robinson Crusoe"
1982. 106 Seiten.

Das Phänomen „Robinson Crusoe" ist weder durch eine werkimmanente Interpretation des Textes noch allein durch eine Erklärung des Textes vor seinem historischen Hintergrund adäquat zu erfassen. Die Analyse konzentriert sich deshalb neben der Entstehungsgeschichte auf die wechselvolle Rezeptionsgeschichte und erschließt so das jeweils aktualisierte Sinnpotential des Romans.

Band 3
1157 Ulrich Schneider
James Joyce: „Dubliners"
1982. 106 Seiten.

Die Analyse erhellt Aspekte des irischen Kontextes, die zum Verständnis des Kurzgeschichtenzyklus „Dubliners" wesentlich beitragen können, und verdeutlicht die Vielschichtigkeit von historischem Zusammenhang der Erzählungen und Joyceschen Symbolen, Leitmotiven und thematischen Querverbindungen.

Band 4
1155 Thomas M. Stein
Patrick White: „Voss"
1983. Ca. 110 Seiten.

Der 1957 erschienene historische Roman „Voss" des australischen Literaturnobelpreisträgers Patrick White zählt im englischsprachigen Raum zu den modernen Klassikern. Die Analyse geht auf den soziokulturellen Hintergrund des Werks ein und hebt auf dieser Folie Whites Kritik an der australischen Nachkriegsgesellschaft hervor.

Band 5
1228 Klaus Ensslen
„The Autobiography of Malcolm X"
Schwarzes Bewußtsein in Amerika
1983. Ca. 110 Seiten.

Die Werkanalyse stellt die kulturspezifischen Prämissen der Rezeption der 1965 erschienenen „Autobiogprahy" heraus und erläutert die Entstehung des Buches in einer der politisch bewegtesten Perioden der jüngeren Geschichte der USA.

Band 6
Eberhard Kreutzer
Lewis Carroll: „Alice in Wonderland", „Through the Looking-Glass"

Band 7
Ingrid von Rosenberg
Alan Sillitoe: „Saturday Night and Sunday Morning"

Uni-Taschenbücher
wissenschaftliche Taschenbücher für alle Fachbereiche.
Das UTB-Gesamtverzeichnis erhalten Sie bei Ihrem Buchhändler oder direkt von
UTB, 7 Stuttgart 80, Breitwiesenstraße 9, Postfach 80 11 24.

UTB Fink

1194/1195 Gerhard Hoffmann (Hrsg.)
Der zeitgenössische amerikanische Roman 1/2
Zwischen Realismus und postmodernem Experiment.
1983. Je ca. 270 Seiten.

Seit den 50er Jahren hat sich der zeitgenössische Roman in den USA immer stärker in Richtung auf die Überwindung traditioneller fiktionaler Modelle durch das literarische Experiment entwickelt. Der erste Band beschreibt die Entstehungsgeschichte einer neuen Ästhetik. Sie wird systematisch analysiert und in ihren Elementen und Perspektiven untersucht.
Der zweite Band stellt die Tendenzen und Gruppierungen im zeitgenössischen amerikanischen Roman in Einzeldarstellungen und Werkanalysen vor.

1111 Rüdiger Ahrens (Hrsg.)
William Shakespeare: Didaktisches Handbuch 1
1982. 344 Seiten.

1112 Rüdiger Ahrens (Hrsg.)
William Shakespeare: Didaktisches Handbuch 2
1982. 426 Seiten.

1113 Rüdiger Ahrens (Hrsg.)
William Shakespeare: Didaktisches Handbuch 3
1982. 354 Seiten.

Das dreibändige Handbuch enthält didaktische Modellanalysen zu Shakespeares Werken, die im engen Zusammenhang mit der Diskussion um die Funktion und Methodik des Literaturunterrichts und der Shakespeare-Lektüre stehen.

1116 Heinrich F. Plett (Hrsg.)
Englisches Drama von Beckett bis Bond
1982. 438 Seiten.

In einer Reihe von Einzelinterpretationen behandelt das Werk repräsentative Stücke der bedeutendsten Autoren des britischen Dramas der Gegenwart. Gattungs-, sozial- und theatergeschichtliche Aspekte sind in die Interpretation mit einbezogen. Ein Essay gibt einen Überblick über die Entwicklung des englischen Dramas seit Mitte der fünfziger Jahre.

Reihe: Literaturstudium

Hrsg. von Herbert Mainusch

1071 Willi Erzgräber
Utopie und Anti-Utopie
(Literaturstudium 1). Morus, Morris, Wells, Huxley, Orwell.
1981. 216 Seiten.

Das Buch behandelt Thomas Morus' „Utopia", William Morris' „News from Nowhere", H. G. Wells' „A Modern Utopia", A. Huxleys „Brave New World" und G. Orwells „1984".

1073 Armin Paul Frank
Das englische und amerikanische Hörspiel
(Literaturstudium 4).
1981. 178 Seiten.

Eine Einführung in eine medienorientierte Literaturwissenschaft. Frank entwickelt eine Typologie des Hörspiels und analysiert paradigmatisch die gattungsspezifischen Merkmale einiger englischer und amerikanischer Hörspiele.

Uni-Taschenbücher
wissenschaftliche Taschenbücher für alle Fachbereiche.
Das UTB-Gesamtverzeichnis erhalten Sie bei Ihrem Buchhändler oder direkt von
UTB, 7 Stuttgart 80, Breitwiesenstraße 9, Postfach 80 11 24.